The Sceptical Idealist

British Idealist Studies Series 1: Oakeshott

www.imprint-academic.com/idealists

The Sceptical Idealist

Michael Oakeshott
as a
Critic of the Enlightenment

Roy Tseng

ia

IMPRINT ACADEMIC

Published in the UK by Imprint Academic
PO Box 1, Thorverton EX5 5YX, UK

Published in the USA by Imprint Academic
Philosophy Documentation Center
PO Box 7147, Charlottesville, VA 22906-7147, USA

ISBN 0 907845 22 3

A CIP catalogue record for this book is available from the
British Library and US Library of Congress

Contents

Acknowledgements

Some parts of the book were presented to the Political Theory Workshop at the London School of Economics and Political Science. I am thankful to the participants, especially Professor Brian Barry, Professor John Charvet, Dr. Paul Kelly, Dr. Cillian McBride and Dr. Jeff Rabin for their comments which helped me to develop my argument and to eradicate absurdities in the drafts. I also would like to thank Professor Genesis Chen of National Taiwan University for introducing me to the enterprise of political philosophy in general and the thought of Michael Oakeshott in particular. My special thanks, nevertheless, must go to Professor Janet Coleman. I could not have written the thesis without her careful supervision. This study owes a great deal to her inspiration and encouragement.

I am grateful to Dr. Maureen Taylor, who checked the draft and improved my English. I wish to thank Miss I-Fen Huang and Miss Nai-Yua Yeh for their editorial assistance. I am, as well, pleased to have the opportunity to acknowledge the financial support of the Ministry of Education in Taiwan. Many thanks are due to Keith Sutherland of Imprint Academic for his help in preparing this book for publication.

I would like to express my gratitude to Michael Huang and Andy Hsu for their sincere friendship lasting so many years. For the intellectual stimulus that has inspired me to continue thinking about politics philosophically, I truly appreciate my students at National Sun Yat-Sen University and my fellow political theorists in Taiwan. I am particularly indebted to Professor Ying-Wen Tsai of Academia Sinica, from whom I have learnt so much. Finally, I would like to acknowledge the great debt I owe to my parents, my sisters and, especially my wife, Nadia Lin, who have always supported me in every respect. This book is dedicated to my son and daughter, Eli and Kelly.

Abbreviations

Works by Oakeshott

Chapter I

Introduction:
A Unique Voice

I.1. Oakeshott on Politics, History and Philosophy

The purpose of this book is to interpret the works of Michael J. Oakeshott (1901-1990, the Professor of Political Science at the LSE, 1951-1969) as a substantial critic of the Enlightenment project by concentrating on his philosophy of politics and history. In this context, my ambition is to clarify some debated issues in Oakeshott studies by a fresh approach to understanding the philosopher's unique voice in the "conversation of mankind".

Oakeshott is, of course, best known today for his political philosophy, for which he has been acclaimed "the greatest political philosopher in the Anglo-Saxon tradition since John Stuart Mill — or even Burke", and "the most original academic political philosopher of this century".[1] Oakeshott's philosophical position on politics and morality, however, continues to be in dispute. Whilst the initial reception of *Rationalism in Politics* (1962) has been coloured by some scholars with a progressive attitude and labelled loosely as "pessimistic", "traditionalist" or "conservative" in a somewhat negative sense,[2] more recent scholarship, by contrast, has tried to show that with *On Human Conduct* (1975) Oakeshott's political philosophy can be treated as a comprehensive restatement of liberalism.[3]

---

[1] *Daily Telegraph*, December 21, 1990, *The Guardian*, December 22, 1990; quoted by J. L. Auspitz, 1993: 1. See also J. Casey, 1993: 58; J. Hart, 1993: 82; R. Grant, 1990: 9.

[2] Cf. T. Fuller, 1991: xiv-xv. For the detailed charge of Oakeshott being a conservative, see, for example, N. Wood, 1959: 645-62; B. Crick, 1963: 65-74; H. Pitkin, 1973: 496-525.

[3] For the interpretation of Oakeshott as a liberal, see P. Franco, 1990a, and 1990b; J. Gray, 1989: 199-217, and 1993: 40-7; W. J. Coats, Jr., 1985: 773-87. Cf. D. Thomas, 1977: 454; N. O'Sullivan, 1993: 106; D. Manning, 1997.

It is my view that Oakeshott is not a doctrinal liberal any more than a dogmatic conservative,[4] but a sceptical philosopher who is the *"victim of thought"*.[5] Political philosophy, as Oakeshott understands it, is nothing if not philosophy, inasmuch as it is the application of a doctrine about the nature of philosophy to the study of the nature of politics.[6] Philosophical thinking, as established in *Experience and It Modes* (1933), is the persistent re-establishment of completeness, which aims to transcend the abstractness of modes of understanding such as history, science, poetry and practice (mainly including morality and politics) for its own sake, but does not take the place of the modes. Hence, Oakeshott's political philosophy is self-limited in the sense that it aims to *explain* rather than *suggest*, and it is self-critical in the sense that the explanation on which it embarks is a tireless consideration of the conditionality of the conditions of political practice.

In the course of this philosophical adventure, liberal ethics has been unveiled as an incomplete form of understanding politics that Oakeshott's traditionalist, conservative or sceptical politics intends to transcend; and a notable concern of this book is to provide a platform for looking at Oakeshott's criticisms of liberalism. For the moment, however, it is only significant to note that in addition to self-limitation and self-criticism, Oakeshott's notion of philosophy also entails a Montaignean scepticism which contends that human understanding is "an engagement to abate mystery rather than to achieve definitive understanding",[7] because it always involves a world of ideas, a tradition of behaviour which is too comprehensive to be totally grasped. It is without doubt that Oakeshott's traditionalist politics, maintaining that politics is a way of living in which the participants are learning how to recognise plausible statements for given contingent circumstances through the "pursuit of the intimations" of a political tradition, is likewise a consequence of this philosophical scepticism. Moreover, as I hope to show, this non-foundationalist practical reasoning deeply embedded in Oakeshott's thought is actually a re-establishment (which is some-

---

[4] For the differences between the conservative disposition in Oakeshott's thought and conservatism as a political ideology, see, for example, J. Ryaner, 1985: 313, 316, 334-8. Cf. B. Barber, 1976: 446-50.

[5] *EM*: 321; *RP*: 150. Insofar as I agree with T. Nardin's remark that "to read Oakeshott narrowly as a conservative critic of the welfare state or liberal defender of individualism and pluralism", is "to misunderstand, and seriously to underrate, his contribution to philosophy" (2001: 235; cf. 225-6).

[6] See esp. *RP*: 236.

[7] *HC*: 2ff.

what uncritical, though) of Aristotelian rhetoric in association with *phronesis*. Thus, in any event, it is intellectually arbitrary to depreciate Oakeshott's political philosophy simply because of his conservative identification, nor is it practically sound to regard his theory of *civitas* as one which "came down earth" in the practice of Thatcherism.[8]

In addition to politics, Oakeshott has also "done as much as anyone in the modern world to establish [history] as an independent manner of thinking".[9] "For anyone interested in the contribution of English idealism to the philosophy of history, Oakeshott's writings are an indispensable source".[10] Even though one may not agree that Oakeshott's theory of history "ranks with Vico's in its originality and scope",[11] it has been widely accepted that it "represents the high-water mark of English thought upon history".[12] It is more than clear that the current of historical thought against which Oakeshott argues constantly is positivist historiography. But I believe it would be a misconception to decipher Oakeshott as an historicist.

To transcend the positivist–historicist debate in favour of Oakeshott's historiography, it is advantageous if where appropriate we distinguish a number of different references related to the ambiguous term "history". To put it briefly, they are: (1) **history** as a mode of understanding, i.e. an enquiry; (2) **History** as "what really happened" in the Past, i.e. the Past in itself as a whole; (3) *history* as a habit of the human mind, i.e. the *historicity* or *historical consciousness* of human understanding, meaning that human knowledge involves a hermeneutic-self, a tradition of ideas, rather than a Cartesian-self, a set of principles; and (4) *the* **history** of a certain subject-matter which refers to the recorded evidence, *res gestae*, about such subject-matter that is surviving in the present and available to the interpreters.

Before examining these references in more detail, there are accordingly three types of historiography that can be concisely expressed in this way: First, positivist historiography is the view that history as an enquiry is the causal representation of the course of

---

[8]   J. Hart, 1993: 83. As T. Fuller puts it, Oakeshott "never really became the guru of Thatcherism as some who lack subtlety have alleged" (1993a: 68).

[9]   W. H. Greenleaf, 1966: 29.

[10]   W. Dray, 1968: 19.

[11]   A. Sullivan, *The New Republic*; quoted by T. W. Smith, 1996: 598.

[12]   R. G. Collingwood, 1946: 158-9. Cf. J. L. Auspitz, 1993: 22. where he writes that "if R. G. Collingwood was correct in calling that earlier 'the high water mark of English thought upon history', the essays published fifty years later [i.e. *On History and Other Essays*] must be the flood tide".

"what really happened" in History. Secondly, historicist historiography is the doctrine that since the human mind must be *historically* conditioned, only through the lens of the historical mode may we comprehend the genuine meaning of things; insofar as all knowledge proper is historical. Thirdly, compared to positivism, Oakeshottian historiography is the belief that the Past in itself is out of our reach in the present, instead there are several forms of reading past in terms of *res gestae*, corresponding to several modes of experience in the present (e.g. the historical past, the practical past, the scientific past etc.); on this view, not everything concerning the past is historical,[13] but rather, history as an enquiry is a *specific* way of narrating *res gestae*; in short, history exists only in the work of the historian. And, although Oakeshott would not deny that human understanding must be *historically* or traditionally conditioned, as we shall see, unlike historicists such as Collingwood, he does not intend to identify our *historicity* or traditional knowledge with historical knowledge without modifications.[14]

That is to say, regarding the map of human knowledge, it is Oakeshott's major point that reasoning appropriate to a mode of understanding or a tradition of activity (which may contain *a* certain type of *historicity*) cannot be applied to any others without being self-deconstructed.[15] As a result of this, we are approaching Oakeshott's objection to philosophical modernity, i.e. the conception of philosophy par excellence, which suggests that philosophy should be a master discipline that lays foundations for the natural sciences and authorises the validity of any other knowledge in terms of an objective scientific-criterion. In other words, philosophical modernity expresses the view that human reasons can be united in the form of Universal Philosophical Reason elucidated by science.[16]

At this point, nonetheless, Oakeshott's anti-foundationalist position likewise calls for a debate. For, inspired by the work of Rorty

---

[13]   Cf. D. Boucher, 1991: 721.

[14]   Cf. T. Nardin, 2001: 172-5.

[15]   Indeed, a significant aspect of Oakeshott's enterprise is to reconcile the sharp contrast between Reason and Tradition (rationality and *historicity*) led by the Enlightenment thinkers.

[16]   T. Nardin also accentuates the anti-foundationalist character of Oakeshott's philosophy (2001: 10, 18, 24, 49). And although modern foundationalism is often related to scientism (or positivism), Nardin follows Oakeshott to contend that it can be equally expressed in the forms of pragmatism, some sort of hermeneutics, and historicism (2001: 5, 14, 81, 96, 111, 174, 192-3, 208). By interpreting Oakeshott as a critic of Enlightenment positions, the author shares with Nardin his major concern that what unites Oakeshott's ideas is "the idea of difference", not the idea of universality (2001: 230-1).

and other post-modern writers, many believe that the only way out of philosophical foundationalism is to put an end to the enterprise of philosophy in terms of epistemology. Oakeshott's idealistic connection, however, has led him to believe in the possibility of a self-independent epistemological discourse. Additionally, it thus seems liable for some interpreters to maintain that there, in fact, exists a "shift in Oakeshott's philosophy from idealism to scepticism",[17] namely, from *Experience and Its Modes* where Oakeshott establishes his idealist epistemology to the latter purely sceptical works such as *The Voice of Poetry in the Conversation of Mankind* (1959).

Be that as it may, I believe that though Oakeshott takes traditional philosophical issues seriously in *Experience and Its Modes*, that does not necessarily make him into an advocate of foundationalism. For, influenced by Bradley, in that very work Oakeshott has viewed the absolute idealism of Hegel through a sceptical lens that may be hereafter referred to as "sceptical idealism". As a result, I shall argue instead that no *fundamental* change in spirit has ever occurred in Oakeshott's idea of philosophy in terms of a sceptical character.[18]

Moreover, precisely because Oakeshott's sceptical idealism leaves his reflection upon the despotism of philosophical modernism at a philosophical level, it actually offers us an alternative answer to the self-image of philosophy without claiming "the end to philosophy". And so, I think, the clearer we become about Oakeshott's *philosophical* rejection of foundationalism, the less we should worry about Rorty's insistence on the necessary connection between epistemology and foundationalism. Consequently, if my interpretation of Oakeshott's philosophical thought is plausible, we may reach the understanding that Oakeshott may have successfully resolved Rorty's problematic proposal in a way which is safe from the charge of "total scepticism", a charge that scholars often make against Rorty's case.

---

[17] S. A. Gerencser, 2000: 7. Cf. T. Modood, 1980: 315-22; B. Parekh, 1979: 487-8; J. Gray, 1989: 202.

[18] This, of course, does not mean that there are no discernable changes at all in Oakeshott's later works. To take a few examples, in *RP* Oakeshott redefines "practice" from the world of values to be as a tradition of action or an idiom of performance, and in *HC* he actually comes to see the exhibitions of intelligence or non-intelligence as the different "orders" of research by means of which human sciences and natural sciences can be distinguished, and thus he opens a wider possibility for the idioms of enquiry within the same order to converse more essentially with each other. Since my purpose here is to examine the sceptical character that penetrates throughout Oakeshott's life-long critique of the Enlightenment, I shall not bring these changes into *special* consideration in the course of this study, although relative references will be stated where appropriate.

I.2. The Structure of Chapters

Now, it is of little wonder to say that philosophical modernity, liberal ethics and positivist historiography, the three main targets to which Oakeshott's critique of Western intellectual fashion points, are exactly the elements that underlie the so-called Enlightenment project. By re-placing Oakeshott into this very context, it would then become possible for us to arrive at a new level of assessing Oakeshott's thought as a whole where his profound philosophical reflection upon politics and history could be better understood. And this, as already indicated, is presumably the major contribution to Oakeshott studies that this book wishes to make.

To achieve this goal, I therefore begin Chapter II with an examination of philosophical modernism, by means of which I shall unveil the Enlightenment project in terms of three positions: (1) foundationalism in philosophy, (2) formalism in ethics and (3) naturalism in historiography. The crisis of the Enlightenment project has indeed achieved serious attention from contemporary thinkers such as Foucault, Habermas, Derrida, Rorty and MacIntyre, to name only a few. Among these major figures, however, it is MacIntyre's position that I take to be closest to Oakeshott's, even though there are still significant differences between them.

Put briefly, in Oakeshott's case the Enlightenment ethical position in terms of formalism results in an *empty* concept of rationality, and the scientific attempt to generalise history has exactly obscured the possible route of returning us to traditions to which the concrete moral and political exemplifications belong. And further, since the Enlightenment positions constitute a whole package in favour of philosophy par excellence, to untie the bond that is required in the first place is therefore a non-foundationalist conception of philosophy itself.[19]

Here we thus come to Chapter III which takes Oakeshott's notion of philosophy into full consideration. The approach I am adopting to re-interpret *Experience and Its Modes*, the key text of Oakeshott's philosophy, is basically to see it as a response to the crisis of *philosophisme*, inasmuch as it contains a very clear sense of renouncing ideas from philosophical modernity that scholars used to follow. Although, with regard to his idealistic background, Oakeshott retains Hegel's understanding of philosophy as the perpetual

---

[19]   Whilst in *VP* Oakeshott concedes that "to rescue the conversation from the bog into which it has fallen and to restore to it some of its lost freedom of movement would require a philosophy more profound than anything I have to offer" (*VP*: 15), it seems to me that earlier in *EM* Oakeshott has attempted to seek this philosophy.

re-establishment of coherence, yet at the same time he subscribes to Bradley's revised idealism which argues that "hence no total truth, only more or less of validity",[20] i.e. human thought (which can have a number of spheres or worlds) must be conditional: every idea refers to reality from a *limited* standpoint and has its own *degree* of truth. That is, Oakeshott has actually merged Hegel's notion of completeness and Bradley's idea of "degrees of truth and reality" into a form of sceptical idealism, which purports to maintain the following:

Even though philosophy is the self-critical thought which is concerned with the conditionality of human understanding for its own sake, i.e. to be complete, this pure thinking is so self-limited and sceptical that it contributes nothing to the fact that ordinarily we live in an abstract world, and that we have at our disposal a number of self-consistent but incomplete ways of understanding. In short, Oakeshott creates two themes in *Experience and Its Modes* which he has ever since retained throughout his whole academic career: a non-foundationalist philosophy characterised in terms of self-independence (or self-criticism), self-limitation and scepticism, and the self-consistency of modes of experience.

Having examined Oakeshott's philosophical idea per se, Chapter IV comes to terms with his philosophical understanding of morality and politics. In summing up, the central problem which concerns this chapter is this: Oakeshott's attack on Rationalism can be well understood as an extension of his criticism of the Enlightenment project, not merely because the quality Oakeshott gives to Rationalism fits perfectly with the assumptions of formalism in ethics that we shall disclose, but also because the philosophical foundations Oakeshott traces to Rationalism are nothing but the assumptions of foundationalism in philosophy that we shall unveil. It is on the interpretation of *Rationalism in Politics* that Oakeshott's endeavour to ponder the crisis of Enlightenment positions becomes most evident.

Moreover, given Oakeshott's position on formalism in ethics, a contradiction would at once become evident if Oakeshott is interpreted as a liberal.[21] For, formalism in ethics or rationalism in politics, as we shall see, is that which portrays Lockean natural law theory, the Kantian categorical imperative and Millian utilitarianism, the three main traditions of justifying liberalism. And yet, in contrast to the characteristics of liberalism in terms of (1) a set of

---

[20] Bradley, 1969: chap. xxiv.

[21] Here I am not denying that Oakeshott's rationalism in politics mainly embraces both socialism and liberalism. A qualified consideration about this matter will be provided when I come to examine Oakeshott's political philosophy in more detail.

principles, (2) radical individualism and (3) formalistic argumentation, Oakeshott basically follows Aristotle in comprehending conservatism in politics as (1) a "way of living" in which (2) the
traditionalist-individual is engaged, (3) a "rhetorical form of reasoning" which deals with plausible statements in given circumstances
through the "pursuit of intimations" of a political tradition. And if
questioned thus: isn't it true that Oakeshott has "a love of freedom"?[22] my reply is that his love of freedom does not have the same
quality as the liberal's.

But further, all this does not simply suggest that Oakeshott has
tried to purge liberalism of whatever defects it may contain, in order
to restate it in terms of a theory of civil association in *On Human Conduct*. In the first place, the conditions that Oakeshott employs to classify civil association consist in philosophical scepticism and the
devotion to freedom, and these two elements are categorically inseparable. In this respect, civil association is a more sophisticated reconstruction of conservatism in politics, by bringing a Hobbesian
legalistic character of civil authority into consideration. More crucially, although in *On Human Conduct* Oakeshott keeps liberalism
out of the most remarkable fountain of enterprise association or
universitas,[23] he does not embrace it in civil association or *societas*,
either.[24] The absence of liberalism in the work is because part of
Oakeshott's interests there is to show a *societas cum universitate* as the
"unsolved tension" limiting the identification of modern European
political character and consciousness.[25] To interpret Oakeshott as a
liberal, it seems to me, is simply to impose on him a practical anxiety
that his philosophy tries so hard to avoid.

The aim of Chapter V is to give a detailed analysis of Oakeshottian
historiography. There are basically three main issues concerning
contemporary historiographical debate that will be put forward
here: first, the epistemological problem of historical knowledge; second, the autonomous problem of history; and third the problem of
historicism. Oakeshott indeed battles with positivist historiography
over the first two issues; but here, once again, Oakeshott's contribution to this field can be more profitably perceived while understanding him as a critic of the Enlightenment historiographical position.

Epistemologically, it is my understanding that there are two intricate impasses inherent in scientific historical thought from the *philo-*

---

[22]   N. O'Sullivan, 1993: 101. Cf. M. Cranston, 1967: 82.

[23]   See *HC*: 136-313.

[24]   See esp. *HC*: 245, n2.

[25]   See esp. *HC*: 200-1, 320. Cf. *PFPS*.

sophes to neo-positivism. In the first place, it produces a "temporal dilemma in history". That is, to say that historical study is the causal representation of "what really happened" in the Past, i.e. the course of successive events, is to identify history with a naturalised conception of History which shows the historical to be unrepeatable and past. And yet this identification must at the same time conflict with the modern epistemological conditions that neo-positivism adopts, namely, the view that genuine knowledge should be repeatable and present. In the second place, positivist historiography is unable to deal with the "epistemic tension in history" that bothered philosophers such as Descartes and Locke: the nature of history is particular and concrete whereas that of science is general and abstract. By way of contrast, in Oakeshott's historical theory, as we shall see, there is a theory of time and a hermeneutic-like view of historical narration, both of which are capable of removing the naturalistic traps in historiography under consideration.

Again, if one of the main arguments that Oakeshott takes to impugn foundationalism is that the monopoly of the scientific voice will make our conversation "boring and insidious",[26] it would appear that the meaning of rescuing the autonomous voice of history (and that of poetry) in the conversation of mankind is no less than to dissolve Enlightenment Universal Rationality. That is, the significance of history in Oakeshott's thought lies in the important role of the historian in bringing out concrete knowledge to nourish our ability to converse. But, the theme of the autonomy of history is frequently related to the theoretical context of historicism, a school of historical thought to which Oakeshott objects. Consequently, to interpret the uniqueness of Oakeshott as a non-historicist critic of positivist historiography, part of my concern in this chapter will be directed to making a comparison between Oakeshott's and Collingwood's philosophies of history.

---

[26] See esp. *VP*: 12-4.

Chapter II

The
Enlightenment
Positions

II.1. Introduction: Philosophy Par Excellence

The purpose of this chapter is to unveil the Enlightenment positions:
(1) foundationalism in philosophy, (2) formalism in ethics and (3)
naturalism in historiography, by way of an enquiry into philosophical modernism. It aims to deal with a most powerful modern paradigm of understanding the function of philosophy in relation to
"science"[1] and its influences upon ethical and historical thought,
ranging from Descartes through Kant, and stretching into liberalism
and positivism. Time and again in the course of examining
Oakeshott's work I must return to this establishing context, as it is
my plan to interpret Oakeshott as one of the most substantial critics
of the Enlightenment project in the twentieth century.

Although historians of ideas used to restrict the age of the Enlightenment to the eighteenth century, in this study I am basically tracing
the emergence of Enlightenment positions back to Descartes and
Locke, amongst other thinkers. This is because the intellectual landmark of the eighteenth century was the search for "one king, one
law, one faith" over all spheres of human life. The eighteenth century, to quote D'Alembert, was "the century of philosophy par excel-

---

[1] The term "science", as it was understood within a much older tradition of
Western thought, was taken to mean *episteme*, *scientia* or *Wissen*, i.e. ways to
knowledge or forms of knowing. Such knowledge could be of God and Nature,
of the good and the cosmos, of the *polis* and the *psyche* etc. With this meaning,
"science" was certainly not merely referring to our modern natural science
alone. Be that as it may, in this study I take it to mean the natural sciences all the
time.

lence",[2] and this version of *philosophisme* was of course largely rooted in the seventeenth century.

Following Oakeshott and some other scholars,[3] I do not take the Enlightenment to be a "closed historic episode" either; rather, I believe the Enlightenment positions have surely become a part of the Western tradition in the present day. That is to say, whether or not one likes or dislikes the notion of rationality it carries, the fact is that a true understanding of the conditions of Western cultural milieux must demand a diagnosis of Enlightenment positions. And if this is the case, according to Oakeshott, what we really need in order to transcend the intellectual crisis of our times is to revitalise those which have been destroyed by the Enlightenment project: the importance of traditional knowledge in human activity (Chapter IV) and the multiplicity of non-scientific voices (such as history or poetry) in the conversation of mankind (Chapter V). But in each case, we must appeal to a non-foundationalist conception of philosophy in the first place (Chapter III).

Moreover, my understanding is that an overall look at modern philosophy reveals a certain tradition about the self-identification of philosophy. And this tendency in principle is that philosophy is a master discipline that lays foundations to science and authorises the validity of any other knowledge in terms of an objective scientific criterion rooted in a specific kind of rationality. It is a tendency which at once implies the notion of an "integral philosophical system", in that the proper subject of a philosophical study is no less and no more than the entire universe — Nature, Man and History. In short, within that tradition philosophy is understood as the yardstick against which everything can be measured, and the role of the *philosophe*, is identified as nothing but a "cultural arbitrator".[4]

To illuminate: the key to the Enlightenment project is the notion of rationality, understood as objective thinking, indifferent to traditions and institutions, and elucidated by science. On the one hand modern philosophy is indeed inspired by modern science and the property of rationality it wears; on the other the philosopher at the same time intends to objectify scientific knowledge and to spread that very rationality over entire human engagements. That is, modern natural philosophy is not only concerned with the basis of science itself, i.e. the possibility of knowing the external world with certainty; it also works as the link between the diverse areas of

---

[2]   Quoted by E. Cassirer, 1979: 3.

[3]   See, for example, M. Foucault, 1984; J. Habermas, 1989.

[4]   Cf. R. Rorty, 1980: esp. 139.

human understanding. It is accordingly with this meaning that I come to the term "foundationalism in philosophy" below.

Among the diverse areas of human intelligence, two are central to this book: ethics and historiography. First of all, Nature, the very subject matter of science, has been described by many Enlightenment thinkers as an "ethical norm" on the basis that what is "natural" must be "good".[5] It follows that the Enlightenment ethical position is nothing but the hope for "human affairs to be guided by rationality rather than by faith, superstition, or revelation; a belief in the power of human reason to change society and liberate the individual from the restraints of custom or arbitrary authority; all backed up by a world view increasingly validated by science rather than by religion or tradition".[6] This points to the belief that for them morality can be objectified in the same way as the scientist deals with Nature, that the business of moral philosophy must consist in "a systematic attempt to discover a rational justification for morality".[7] In what follows I take this position to be "formalism in ethics"; and it is not unlikely that the representative of such a moral position is liberal ethics, appearing in the moral and political thought of Locke, Kant, Mill and so forth.

Additionally, a brief description of what I mean by "naturalism in historiography" is this. Although seventeenth-century thinkers such as Descartes and Locke demonstrate a lack of interest in history, many of the *philosophes* in the next century unite in the belief that "an analogy of Newtonian science, a reduction of facts to laws, should also be possible in history",[8] and that the development of Human History should be seen as man's capacity for "progress". As a result of this, there emerges the conception of Universal History, which is *actually* based on an identification of the historical (a mode of understanding) with a naturalised conception of History (the occurrence of events, "what really happened" in the Past), in accordance with the modern philosophical discussions of the structure of Natural Time as successiveness. Despite the fact that the notion of Universal History later animates the reaction of German classic historicism, by posing a Romantic reflection upon the inadequacy of the Enlightenment idea of Universal Rationality, the assumption of a naturalised conception of History penetrates into traditional positivist historiography where it is claimed that the purpose of the historical study

[5]   D. Outram, 1997: 48.

[6]   *Ibid.*: 3.

[7]   A. MacIntyre, 1985: 39.

[8]   E. Cassirer, 1979: 216.

is to represent "what really happened" in the Past in terms of causal explanation, and as such, as J. B. Bury says, "history is a science; no less, and no more".[9] At this point, I presume, neo-positivism should be brought into consideration on two counts. In one, it reconstructs the project of philosophy par excellence in the name of the "fusion of sciences"; in another, as I hope to show, it is exactly the Enlightenment historiographical position, i.e. an identification of the historical with a naturalised conception of History, that neo-positivists such as K. Popper and C. Hempel take for granted in establishing their "covering law model"[10] in historiography.

In short, the ideal form of Enlightenment civilisation is that of "argumentation" as exemplified in the natural sciences; what we are directed to live by in terms of the *philosophes* is a goal-orientated life aiming to "solve problems" by discovering the most advanced scientific answers. "At bottom, the mistake of the Enlightenment project is the failure to see that rationality is as such an abstract capacity".[11] But more critically, it produces an intricate paradox. That is, while its incapability of recognising the emptiness of the concept of rationality is partly due to its neglecting the importance of history in constructing some more concrete knowledge to be received in the conversation of mankind, the historiography that is in compliance with it requires the historian to abide by abstract scientific methods and thus gives over the autonomy of history to the natural sciences.

In the main body of this chapter, I shall strive to examine further the metaphysical and epistemological grounds on which the notion of philosophy par excellence rests ([II.2.]), and the character and crisis of modern ethics and historiography it has brought out ([II.3.] & [II.4.]). And, in giving a brief and necessarily inadequate sketch of the development of modern philosophy this way, I think it will be sufficient to draw attention only to the basic doctrines of great philosophers.[12]

---

[9]   J. B. Bury, 1956.

[10]   The name "covering law model" was first coined in W. Dray, 1957.

[11]   C. Larmore, 1996: 49.

[12]   This means that in what follows I am not adopting the historical mode to examine the *history* of modern philosophy, but rather, it is the quasi-philosophical past, implicit in Oakeshott's modal theory of the past, that I am following.

II.2. Philosophical Modernity

Let me now begin with the proposal of foundationalism in philosophy which, to use Locke's language, is eager "to enquire into the original, certainty, and extent of human knowledge".[13]

II.2.1. Science and Knowledge Proper

Modern Western philosophy, it has been said, arose out of the reflection on the progress made by mathematics and physics in the late sixteenth and early seventeenth centuries. Being stimulated by Renaissance science and the work of Galileo, many modern philosophers were apt to draw a determinable structure of the natural world and its process in quantitative and geometrical terms. This inclination to understand the universe was summed up in Galileo's proclamation, in 1623, that "the great book of the universe cannot be understood unless one can read the language in which it is written — the language of mathematics".[14]

It was under the influence of the new science of mathematical physics that Descartes came to systematise our knowledge, though he did not completely exclude the spiritual substance from his philosophy. "The whole philosophy", Descartes once argued, "is a tree whose roots are metaphysics, whose trunk is physics, and whose branches are the other sciences".[15] This clearly implies that all truths (of practical sciences, natural philosophy and metaphysics) should be proved in an orderly way by proceeding from an indubitable metaphysical basis, namely, *cogito ergo sum* (that I think therefore I am), to derived propositions. In other words, the logic Descartes took to formulate his ultimate context of thought was mathematical deduction in the conviction that by inspecting the one absolute objective truth, a criterion can be discovered about all other truths.

Those who followed Descartes in principle and are called rationalists today are Spinoza and Leibniz. There are two reasons for the basis of this assertion. First, that which Descartes supposed philosophy to be, namely: the formulation of an orderly system of objective knowledge by means of mathematical deduction, and this can also be said of Spinoza and Leibniz. That which constituted the central part of Spinoza's philosophy was the idea that all genuine explanation is deduction in nature and everything is explicable from an absolutely infinite being which he called "God". In Spinoza's own

---

[13] Locke, 1975: 1.

[14] Quoted by J. Cottingham, 1988: 5.

[15] Quoted by A. Flew ed., 1983: 92.

words, "everything is determined by the necessity of the divine nature".[16] In his *Ethics*, the subject that concerned him most, Spinoza presented his views on what "good" should be in the form of geometry, and he derived it from the more fundamental truths about the nature of God and its relation to matter. Leibniz also conceived the notion of a universal logical method, by means of which we can not only systematise all existing knowledge but also deduce hitherto unknown truths. And, like Spinoza, Leibniz regarded everything as explicable in a mathematical sense. "There cannot", he wrote, "be any true or existent fact, or any true proposition, without there being a sufficient reason why it should be so and not otherwise".[17] This is his famous Principle of Sufficient of Reason which was originally found in mathematics.

Second, none of the three thinkers would deny that, in our knowing, reason is the only genuine source from which our true knowledge can be gained. They assumed that true knowledge is already with us, it is self-evident. Truths do not depend on experience; rather, there are *a priori* truths which are true in themselves. Descartes, for example, saw reason as an inborn "natural light" that would enable us to understand things clearly and distinctly. For Spinoza, likewise, reason alone can perceive things "truly, as they are in themselves". Leibniz, too, believed that we have "innate principles" of reasoning, such as the Principle of Sufficient Reason and the Principle of Contradiction, which are self-evident and through which we can attain "the universal and necessary truths of the sciences". For all of them, as a result, all my knowledge of the world, if it is true, is not just knowledge of my own point of view but of all humankind's shared points of view. In other words, objective knowledge is and only can be derived from the operation of reason, and it purports to draw an objective description of the world, indifferent to the particular experience of any observer. Truth, in short, is knowable only to, or through, reason.

If scientific progress provided continental rationalists with the notion of mathematical certainty and method of deduction for their philosophical systems, there was considered to be another aspect of the new science besides its use in mathematics. That is, "scientific progress was also felt to depend very largely on the attention to empirical data and on the use of controlled experiment".[18] Here we come to the central doctrine of empiricism, rationalism's traditional

[16] Spinoza, 1989: part 1, prop, 29.

[17] Leibniz, 1991: par. 32.

[18] F. Copleston, 1958: 24.

opposite, that the source through which our knowledge comes to us is sense experience. As Locke put it, "Whence has it all the materials of reason and knowledge? To this I answer, in one word, from *experience*. In that all our knowledge is founded, and from that it ultimately derives itself".[19] For Locke as for other empiricists, we then have no "innate ideas" in knowing. Although mathematical deduction at its best will give us the certain logical relation of things, yet it can not give us the factual information about the natural world. If we wish for the latter, empiricists would argue, we must content ourselves with probabilities, which is all that induction-based generalisation can give us.

Like the mathematical method for rationalists, empiricists believed that the experimental and inductive methods which have been applied with such success in accounting for the coherence of astronomy, physics and biology should also be applied in the study of man, which is entitled to be called a "science of man". In other words, as empiricists assigned to philosophy the task of studying the nature of knowledge which is to be given in the form of experience of the mind (ideas or perceptions), in their investigations of the human mind, they were, in fact, using the same experimental methods that natural scientists applied in their study of Nature. In the case of Locke, such a "science of man" was developed from the belief that "an analogue of Newton's particle mechanics for 'inner space' would somehow be 'of great advantage in directing our Thoughts in the search of other Things'".[20] That is, Locke's discussion of the causal theory of perception can be seen as working out the philosophical implications of Newtonian mechanics. Hume, to take another example, believed that he was dealing with human nature by using the scientific method in his *Treatises* and other works. "The science of man", he wrote, "which is the only solid foundation we can give to this science itself must be laid on experience and observation".[21] "In pretending, therefore, to explain the principles of human nature", he continued, "we in effect propose a complete system of the sciences, built on a foundation almost entirely new, and the only one upon which they can stand with any security".[22]

Accordingly, it seems from this that neither Descartes nor Locke nor Hume identified their task *qua* philosophers to be fundamentally different from that of those involved in the pursuit of science

[19] Locke, 1975: II. 1. 2.

[20] R. Rorty, 1980: 137.

[21] Hume, 1978: xx.

[22] *Ibid.*: xx.

which we today refer to as the natural sciences. In fact, an identification of knowledge proper with knowledge acquired by scientific methods has been made by almost every important modern philosopher.

II.2.2. The Invention of the Mind[23]

So far we have seen that modern philosophy arose from the reflection on scientific development. However, it does not necessarily follow that modern philosophy has since become "the charwoman of the natural sciences". On the contrary, although it received its input from the natural sciences, it proclaimed its own autonomy in the sense that it took up an independent task to understand the meaning of the entire universe and thus laid foundations to the natural sciences. Descartes was obviously inspired by the work of Galileo, but the Cartesian mechanism and its supporters, in denying the purposeful tendency in the physical world, at the same time provided a metaphysical basis for Galileo's physical theory which soon became the orthodox approach in scientific research. It "allowed scientists to pursue their enquiries without paying more than passing attention to theology and metaphysics", and therefore "provided the conceptual framework for a spectacular advance in the sciences".[24]

In order to understand the whole universe with scientific certainty or reliability, a rigorous access to all truths or a firm basis of knowledge is required for modern philosophers. Aristotle had already told us that "all men by nature desire to know". But in the search for the scientific criteria of knowledge modern philosophy is likely to know the world as a whole especially in terms of the mind-body relation, the notion of objective knowledge and the condition of subjectivity. Like many others, I believe it was Descartes whose motivating mind was behind this philosophical fashion and ever since compelled a lot of philosophers to investigate the so-called problem of "the foundation of knowledge".

It has been indicated that for Descartes all knowledge should be derived from an absolute objective truth, which must be so "certain" that "all the most extravagant suppositions brought forward by sceptics would be incapable of shaking it".[25] And, those being interested in philosophy must know that it is through his famous "method of doubt" that Descartes reached such "a firm and abiding

---

[23]   R. Rorty, 1980: chap. 1.

[24]   F. L. Baumer, 1977: 51.

[25]   Descartes, 1990: 119.

superstructure in the sciences".[26] Through a striking excursion of casting some possible doubts about our sense experience, mathematical knowledge and Deity, Descartes took the proposition *cogito ergo sum* to be indubitable: For, no matter how deceivable my understanding of the world could be, Descartes insisted, there must exist an "I" who is deceived; any doubts after all only confirm the existence of a subject, an "I" who is doubting. If I am in error, it must be an "I" who is in error; if I am mistaken, it must be an "I" who is mistaken. I must be, I exist, then, I can be positive whether I am deceived or not. "So that it must, *in fine*, be maintained, all things being maturely and carefully considered, that this proposition (*pronunciatum*) I am, I exist, is necessarily true each time it is expressed by me, or conceived in my mind".[27]

Furthermore, according to Descartes, the reason why I am so certain that "I think therefore I am" is true is that I see or understand "clearly and distinctly" what is being said. Many of my ideas about the world, coming from my sense experience or imagination, are either unclear or indistinct; only "innate ideas" from my inborn "natural light of reason" would enable me to grasp clarity and distinctness, which are certainly the mark of truth. Descartes thus reaches the conclusion that we can have objective knowledge about the fact that "I exist" and this fact is a universal "innate idea" about the world not just about someone's perception. For everyone by the use of his own "natural light of reason" will see *cogito ergo sum* as "clearly and distinctly" as Descartes himself saw in *Meditations*.

But, what precisely do I affirm as existing? This interrogative brings us to the Cartesian problem of *sum res cogitans*. As Descartes puts it, "I am a being whose whole essence or nature is to think, and whose being requires no place and depends on no material thing".[28] That is, for Descartes, when I am certain that "I think therefore I am", I am affirming the existence of myself as something which "thinks". Given that we not only exist as a thinking thing but we are able to apprehend "things" clearly and distinctly which can be created by God, Descartes now proceeds to prove the existence of the body, of the material world, though he deals rather briefly with it. His general argument is that in understanding the world we must receive impressions and ideas and that as God, who is no deceiver, has implanted in us "a very great inclination to believe that they (impressions and ideas) are conveyed to me by corporeal objects, I

[26] *Ibid.*: 112.

[27] *Ibid.*: 119.

[28] *Ibid.*: 119.

do not see that He could be defended from the accusation of deceit if these ideas were produced by causes other than corporeal objects. Hence we must allow that corporeal objects exist".[29] In short, Descartes affirmed two incompatible kinds of *substances*: the unextended and indivisible mind (*res cogitans*) and the extended and divisible matter (*res extensa*), which in some ways depend on God, who is what creates the unity between the two substances, and what makes knowledge possible.

It follows that Descartes made the task of understanding the whole world possible by affirming *cogito ergo sum* as our rigorous access, which contains two main elements: the assertion of an ontological category of subjectivity which can think and the validity of "innate ideas" as objectivity. But Descartes himself failed to answer sufficiently the problem of how knowledge is possible. There are consequently some answers to this question Descartes left by concentrating on the tension between the Cartesian notion of objective knowledge and "innate ideas" developed in rationalism and the Cartesian condition of subjectivity developed in empiricism.

That is to say, in formulating an entire structure of knowledge about the world in terms of scientific method, post-Cartesian modern philosophers basically accepted that to know is to "realise" or "represent" *what is there* in the natural world in terms of our natural faculties, namely, experiencing or reasoning. And here, the term "to realise" denotes to become self-conscious about the created objective world by the use of reason or "innate ideas" in the context of rationalism ("how the world itself appears to *me*?"), while the term "to represent" refers to experiencing things in the world in one's mind (subjectivity) in the context of empiricism ("how can *I* come to represent the world?"). Instead of elucidating the doctrines of modern rationalism and empiricism in more detail, however, my purpose here allows me only to take on a review of Kant's philosophy, attempting to reconstruct the two streams of philosophical thought at stake by virtue of a synthesis of subjectivity and objectivity.

II.2.3. A Synthesis of Subjectivity and Objectivity

In some respects the cardinal problem with which Kant was concerned was not so different from that of Descartes: man and the physical world. Kant himself declared that what he wondered most about were two main things, "the starry heavens above me and the

---

[29]   F. Copleston, 1958: 117.

moral law within me".[30] This expression re-emphasises two of the most important aspects of the thought of the seventeenth and the eighteenth centuries: One is the scientific conception of the world which modern physics — more especially, Newton — has given us; the other is the rational creature who can understand the physical world, as mind to body or as subject to object, and who is at the same time conscious of moral sense and freedom.

Both the main groups of modern philosophy, rationalism and empiricism, were accused by Kant of underestimating either the subjectivity of human agents or the objectivity of the physical world. Rationalism's general presupposition that there is a given world created by God would be inclined to determinism. Although rationalists tried to make metaphysics as firm as the natural sciences, the struggle amongst competing rationalist theories rasises the questions of the validilty of their plan to extend our knowledge to one that transcends our sense experience. One of the main tasks of Kant's *Critique of Pure Reason* was thus to pose a critique "of the faculty of reason in general, in respect of all knowledge after which it may strive independently of all experience".[31] That is, he wanted to decide the extent of pure reason so that he might make sure whether metaphysics is possible and, if so, in what sense it is possible. On the other hand, by asserting that thought must be constrained by sense experience, empiricism is incapable of justifying Newtonian physics. For Newtonian physics does not completely rely on observation. In Kant's view, Newtonian physical science presupposed the "uniformity of Nature" to which empiricists cannot reply sufficiently. Furthermore, empiricism cannot account for what Kant calls "*a priori* synthetic judgements"[32] which, he claims, are the basis for Newtonian physics. Moreover, according to Hume's analysis of ideas and perceptions, we can be certain of very little. It is not surprising then

---

[30] Kant, 1993c: 169.

[31] Kant, 1993a: 9.

[32] Kant believed that a science is a systematic complex of judgements; knowledge occurs in judgements. Judgement is either analytic or synthetic. The former is one whose predicate is contained in the notion of the subject. For example, "All bachelors are unmarried". The latter is one whose predicate is not included in the notion of the subject. For example, "All bachelors are unhappy". At first glance it seems that analytic judgements are *a priori* judgements and synthetic judgements are *a posteriori* judgements. But, there are some *a priori* synthetic judgements which are of value to science, because whatever *a priori* is universal and necessary and whatever synthetic will augment our knowledge. We find *a priori* synthetic judgements in mathematics: "2+2=4"; and in metaphysics: "man is free", "God exists". Thus, the question of how Newtonian physics is possible is reduced to the question: How are *a priori* synthetic judgements possible in it?

that, Kant was, as he says, aroused by Hume from his "dogmatic slumbers".[33]

In epistemological terms, the difficulties in rationalism and empiricism can be expressed in two ways. According to rationalism, knowledge is knowledge of things, and its objectivity transcends me. Whilst, according to empiricist theory, knowledge is knowledge of my ideas and impressions which are in me but there is no absolute guarantor of objectivity. As a result, the modern pre-Kantian philosophical debate can be restated as follows: Knowledge can be either *a priori* or *a posteriori*. The former is knowledge whose objectivity is based on forms or concepts (logic), and this is all that rationalism believes knowledge to be. The latter approach encompasses knowledge whose reliability depends on the contents of experience and reflects the empiricist belief about knowledge. All this encouraged Kant to propose a synthesis of forms and contents for human understanding.

Kant believes that every item of knowledge must at the same time bear the marks of reason (forms or objectivity) and of experience (contents or subjectivity) together. "Without sensibility", to quote Kant himself, "no object would be given to us, without understanding no object would be thought. Thoughts without content are empty, intuitions without concepts are blind".[34] For Kant, then, our experience contains two elements: what is given (content) and what is posited by the thinking subject who carries the "objective reference" (concepts). This is not to say that we have innate ideas, nor that objective reference, such as space, time and causality, are antecedent to experience. But it implies that the thinking subject has a natural ability to synthesise or constitute the given data in a certain way. It may be said that, by claiming such constituting activity of "the transcendent ego", Kant raises "the science of man" from a Lockean empirical level to an *a priori* one.[35] But, in contrast to Locke, Kant asserts that such knowledge is genuine and objective. Although knowledge must be constituted by man, none the less it transcends one's particular point of view, and it is therefore possible for him to make legitimate claims about an independent world. Objects do not depend for their existence on being perceived as the empiricist claims; rather their nature is only determined by the fact that they can be perceived. And, objectivity is not knowable to reason alone as rationalists claim, because objective reference is within experience

---

[33]   Kant, 1997: 9.

[34]   Kant, 1993a: 91.

[35]   Cf. R. Rorty, 1980: 137-9.

itself. Hence all that Kant is suggesting is that in describing my experience I am in the act of referring to an ordered perspective on an independent world. The world of experience is not simply my construction; it is also the result of an application of *a priori* forms and categories (objective reference) to what is given. *A priori* knowledge provides the physical world with necessary support, but it also derives its content from the physical world. The principle question of Kant's philosophy, as a result, becomes how *a priori* knowledge is possible.

Kant accepts that there are three basic kinds of *a priori* knowledge: mathematics, physics and metaphysics, and he thus tries to formulate a complete philosophical system in terms of three major questions: How is mathematics possible? How is pure physics possible? Is metaphysics possible? Real knowledge, it may seem from the above, is possible only when my experience is added to *a priori* objective reference; man sorts out the manifold of sensations, first in "time and space", and then according to categories. By the analysis of the *a priori* elements in human experience, Kant proves the first two questions and the uniformity of Nature. However, traditional metaphysics is an attempt to acquire knowledge of God, the soul and the world, which are beyond our sense experience. It is therefore a vain attempt, because all the things known with the aid of *a priori* formal principles are phenomena that manifest themselves via time and space. God, the soul and the world are neither spatial nor temporal, but no one can conceive anything that is outside of time and space. They are thus merely *things-in-themselves* which are inaccessible to my subjectivity. Put another way, traditional metaphysics is exactly the case of "thoughts without content" which therefore must be empty. It is thus useless to employ a subjective category of the understanding to transcend experience, e.g. employ causality to prove the existence of God. This is the reason why Kant tries to show that traditional metaphysics leads to insoluble "antinomies" which makes no progress comparable to that of physical science.

Although the themes of traditional metaphysics have nothing to do with real science, for Kant they remain as matters of faith: "I had therefore to remove *knowledge* in order to make way for *belief*".[36] That is, Kant endeavoured to set up a different basis from that of the realm of theoretical and scientific knowledge for the study of man and God. This is not the place to look at Kant's moral philosophy. The point to be made here is merely that by claiming this Kant leaves us with a bifurcated world: the physical world and the world of free-

---

[36]   Kant, 1993a: Preface.

dom (or in later versions, Nature and History). On the one hand, there is the world of Newtonian physics: an objective world governed by causal laws and which contains *a priori* formal principles which make "understanding" possible. On the other hand, there is the world of freedom and of God. We cannot ascertain the world of freedom by Scientific Reason, but at the same time our Scientific Reason does not, as rationalism and empiricism suppose, prove that the physical world is the only possible world. And if the understanding of the physical world depends on Scientific Reason, i.e. depends on the operation of objective reference to experience, the moral life, the consciousness of obligation, depends on Practical Reason and opens to a sphere of reality which man affirms by faith as a demand of the moral law. The division of Nature and History, as we know, plays a central part in the historical ideas of neo-Kantianism.

II.2.4. The Superiority of Universal Reason

Closely connected with what we have said so far is the idea of the superiority of Universal Reason recognised in philosophy. Although some empiricist thinkers may maintain that there are aspects of reality outside of human experience and therefore unknowable, this opinion does not alter the basic belief that for the most part the human natural faculty of Reason is effective for the accomplishment of a complete philosophical system in which all human problems can be considered. In this respect, it should be noted that even empiricists like Locke, Berkeley and Hume would claim that they relied on Universal Reason in their philosophical reflection. The distinction between rationalism and empiricism, as we have seen, can only be fundamentally drawn by their differing views on the sources of knowledge.

The notion of an integral philosophical system must depend on the superiority of Philosophical Reason. And, given the belief that all knowledge proper is knowledge acquired by scientific methods, pre-Kantian philosophers tended to identify Philosophical Reason with Scientific Reason, by means of which the most genuine form of knowledge (i.e. a scientific criterion of knowledge) can be established. In other words, the united Reason in the form of the natural sciences makes it possible for the notion of the unity and interconnectedness of all knowledge. Thus, Descartes proclaimed that "all the items of knowledge that lie within the reach of human mind are linked together with a marvellous bond".[37] Whilst Spinoza studied

[37]   J. Cottingham, 1988: 7.

ethics following a method incorporating a geometrical pattern, Hume argued that all the sciences, such as logic, aesthetics, politics, mathematics and natural philosophy, have some relation to human nature which is "the capital of the sciences". That is, the "science of man" aims to consider all the fields of human life in terms of scientific observation.

At first sight, the unification of Human Reason seems to undergo modification in Kant's philosophy. For Kant, we not only have Scientific Reason which refers to "the starry heavens above", a pure knowledge of things; but also Practical Reason which refers to "the moral law within", a rational conduct of life. However, I think in Kant's system Scientific Reason acquired by philosophy is still superior to any other areas of human life. The reasons are twofold, each of which will be re-emphasised in the discussions that follow.

First of all, even though Kant distinguishes Scientific Reason from Practical Reason, it must be remembered that Kant claims a theory of morality must come after an *a priori* theory of knowledge. In philosophical terms, the existence of the physical world must be confirmed in the first place, then we may come to consider the possibility of moral consciousness. As Rorty argues, Kant's epistemology steps into a traditional metaphysics' role of "guarantor of the presupposition of morality".[38]

Secondly, what Kant refers to as Practical Reason is not simply our *actual practical reasoning* in the Aristotelian sense of dealing with plausible statements in given situations, but, more crucially, it is a different kind of Theoretical Reason, in accordance with the law of Nature, that governs our moral activity. Put clearly, although Kant concedes that the capability of "judgment" (that man learns from experience so as to link "theory and practice" properly within certain contexts) cannot be reduced to principles,[39] one should never be content with this experiential world of life without appealing to the supreme Reason. Indeed, Kant's ethics consists of an attempt to mark out the formality of our moral discourse, on the deontological premise that every individual, when well enlightened, must be presumed as having the same kind of Practical Reason to follow the moral laws that impose obligations on his free will *in the first place*.

[38]   R. Rorty, 1980: 138.

[39]   See esp. Kant, 1991: 61-3.

II.2.5. Foundationalism in Philosophy

To sum up, for the development of modern natural philosophy the influential relation between philosophy and science is in actuality reciprocal. On the one hand, philosophy received its input from science by assuming the belief that there is only one genuine form of knowledge which is knowledge acquired by means of scientific methods, i.e. the notion of identifying knowledge proper with scientifically certain and objective knowledge alone. On the other hand, however, philosophy proclaimed its own superior function by taking up the fundamental task to understand the meaning of the entire world and thus laid *external foundations* to science. That is to say, with scientific methods philosophy is not anxious about particular things but about the nature of the world as a whole, thus "to know is to realise or represent the natural world as it is" in terms of our natural faculties, namely, reasoning and experiencing. In other words, men, at least philosophers among them, are capable of making a complete description of public reality; and for this reason, any incomplete description of reality must fall short of being *real*. This, therefore, resulted in the modern mainstream philosophers' zealous attempt to justify the existence of an objective external world independently of us. Accordingly, with such an attitude to reality, there thus came up the belief that the aim of philosophy is to establish a universal *ab extra* criterion of truth, which corresponds to the order of Nature, and by which everything claimed to be true should abide. In summary,

(1) **foundationalism in philosophy** is the philosophical project searching for

    (1.1) **scientific certainty** as the criterion of all knowledge claims by establishing

    (1.2) **a foundationalist theory of knowing** which is concerned with the relationship between subjectivity (a concept of mind) and objectivity (a complete description of public reality); and this project is supported by

    (1.3) **the superiority of Universal Reason** which demands that Philosophical Reason identified as Scientific Reason is superior or prior to the non-scientific reasonings of art, politics, morality and of history in the sense that it is the guarantor of their validity and the guidance to their practices.

These are what I take to be the assumptions underlying modern natural philosophy as an integral philosophical system. What remains to be considered, as a result, are their applications to the spheres of ethics and historiography. And here, let me first turn to consider the Enlightenment ethical position by taking liberalism as the moral and political theory of modernity.[40]

II.3. Liberal Ethics

In discussing liberalism, it is not my intention to provide the reader with an analysis of its "conceptual system"[41] or "conceptual constellation"[42] in terms of equality, freedom, authority, rights, citizenship, property, the market economy and *laissez-faire* etc., but rather to deal with its philosophical commitment in a brief outline. In other words, I am here far more concerned with the *philosophical foundation* of liberalism or liberal ethics than with the *historical establishment* of liberal values.

II.3.1. Liberal Elements

That the term "liberalism" is an "essentially contested concept"[43] lacking an exclusive definition seems plain to me and to many other scholars. Historically, some say that liberalism is a notoriously ambiguous concept which more than anything else "has led to persistent historical contests for the idea";[44] whereas theoretically others say that "liberalism has never been a closely integrated or firmly fixed doctrine".[45]

However, according to J. Gray, liberalism is "no older than the seventeenth century" and it can be characterised as a recognisable identity by reference to four features:[46] *individualism* in that it alleges the moral primacy of the person against the demands of any social collectivity; *egalitarianism* inasmuch as it confers on all men the same moral status and denies the relevance of legal or political order to differences in moral worth among human beings; *universalism* on the account that it asserts the moral unity of the human species and accords a secondary importance to specific historic associations and

---

[40]   See, for example, J. Gray, 1995b; A. MacIntyre, 1985; J. Appleby eds., 1996; J.S. McClelland, 1996: 427-49.

[41]   Cf. W. Connolly, 1993: 13-5.

[42]   Cf. R. E. Flathman, 1972: xiv.

[43]   W. B. Gallie, 1964: chap. 8. See also W. Connolly, 1993: chap. 1.

[44]   K. Haakonssen ed., 1988: xi.

[45]   R. E. Flathman, 1989: 2.

[46]   J. Gray, 1995b: Introduction. For a history of the appearance of liberalism, see H. J. Laski, 1997. in which the view that "liberalism is no older than the seventeenth century" is affirmed.

cultural forms; and finally, *meliorism* because of its affirmation of the corrigibility and improvability of all social institutions and political arrangements.

Of the four liberal elements, the last two are of most importance to Gray, because they seem to be definitive of liberalism as a political philosophy.[47] But anyhow, for my concern, it is equally significant to note that according to Gray's understanding of the first two liberal features, egalitarian individualism can be seen as a different expression of the so-called "radical individualism"; that is the view that "the individual is ontologically and morally independent of the social groups and institutions to which they belong, and the cognate idea that social institutions are ontological fictions".[48] By way of contrast, there is also another form of "individualism" which I shall refer to as "traditionalist individualism" in the discussions that follow, and it argues that the value of the individual is not unimportant but it is meaningful only if the individual acts on a tradition of meanings, that morality is to pursue the ethical exemplification embodied in tradition rather than to follow the universalistic, formalistic or abstract moral rules alone.

At this point, Gray's interpretation of Oakeshott as a liberal thinker[49] seems to have been at odds with Oakeshott's own theoretical system. For an understanding of liberalism as the heir of the Enlightenment as such, it appears to me, is equal to Oakeshott's apprehension of rationalist politics. Oakeshott could not be regarded as a liberal philosopher, if one accepts Gray's attributing universalism and meliorism as "centrally constitutive of a liberal outlook".[50] Also, Oakeshott was never an advocate of radical individualism but only of traditionalist individualism.[51]

Indeed, in my discussion of Oakeshottian Rationalism, we shall have a chance to examine the problems of liberalism as those of rationalist politics and Oakeshott's rehabilitation of sceptical politics as a balance against it. Leaving Oakeshott for now, however, my business here is, first, to show liberal ethics as an Enlightenment plan to discover a rational justification for morality, by choosing Locke's natural right theory, Kant's categorical imperative and Mill's utili-

---

[47]   Cf. J. Gray, 1995b: 86-7.

[48]   This is a dense examination of what A. MacIntyre takes radical individualism to be, provided by D. MacNiven, 1996: 352.

[49]   For Gray's interpretation of Oakeshott as a liberal, see 1989: 199-217; 1993: 40-7.

[50]   J. Gray, 1995b: 86.

[51]   For a detailed analysis of Oakeshott's idea of freedom, the self or individuality in terms of the spirit of traditionalism or conservatism, see A. Farr, 1998: chaps. 6-9.

tarian principle as test cases, each of which, as we shall see, has been impugned by Oakeshott; and second, to demonstrate the moral crisis it produces.

II.3.2. Locke: The Natural Right Theory

Let me begin with Locke's natural right theory which appears in the *Second Treatise of Government*. I am aware that an interest in the study of past political theory has for the last few decades been associated with the "historical approach", casting doubt upon Locke's "intention" in writing the *Second Treatise* as a defence of the revolution of 1688.[52] My concern, nonetheless, permits me not to take sides in the debate, but simply to accept that the central problem of Locke's political philosophy was that of political obligation,[53] a problem that is most urgent when the state is sick. And, by political obligation, following J. Dunn, I take it to be "the duty incumbent on any person or set of persons legitimately subject to a legitimate political authority to obey the legitimate commands of that authority".[54]

That the problem of political obligation played a central part in the history of modern political thought has been granted by many scholars.[55] Moreover, on the account that obligation means to be "voluntarily incurred or created", i.e. to make "a moral commitment that is freely entered into by individuals, and freely taken upon themselves through their own actions",[56] some have argued further that the appearance of political obligation has replaced the ground of pre-modern moral and political philosophy with a new basis of its own. For example, J. Chapman says that:

> If we apply the plain historical method to Western experience, there has been one big shift in the moral foundations of political obligation, and that may be described as a movement from moral functionalism to moral individualism . . . Moral functionalism transforms into moral individualism as the concept of natural law inverts into that of natural rights, conceived initially as metaphysical attributes of men who recognise, in Locke's word, a "law of reason" as their moral and political guide. With this fundamental change in orientation the modern theory of political

[52]   See esp. P. Laslett, 1997: 3-133; J. Dunn, 1969; R. Ashcraft, 1986.

[53]   See, for example, J. P. Plamenatz, 1968: 164-65, 1992: 336-7; S. I. Benn and R. S. Peters, 1958: 299-300.

[54]   J. Dunn, 1991: 23.

[55]   See, for example, J. Dunn, 1991: 24; J. R. Pennock and J. W. Chapman, eds. 1970: xiv; P. Harris ed., 1990: 151.

[56]   H. L. A. Hart, 1973: 187-201; C. Pateman, 1979: 2. See also A. Gewirth, 1970: 55-89, esp. 88.

obligation begins to develop and to elaborate as Western thinkers have
had to cope with a succession of intellectual and situational concerns.[57]

What Chapman says here represents the character of radical individualism we have mentioned above. And it is no wonder that to justify
political obligation on such an individualistic ground, the approach
Locke adopted was contractarian.

According to Locke, there existed a "state of nature" in which men
were supposed to possess certain natural rights which are inalien-
able and independent of "political society", as there was no political
society existing in the primitive situation.[58] Locke wrote that:

> The *State of Nature* has a Law of Nature to govern it, which obliges every-
> one: And Reason, which is that Law, teaches all Mankind who will but
> consult it that, being all equal and independent, no one ought to harm
> another in his Life, Health, Liberty or Possession.[59]

It follows from this that "men are naturally free"[60] by virtue of the
natural laws which govern them in their relations with each other.
But the natural right that Locke had drawn most attention to was
"property". Locke's usage of the term, however, seems ambiguous.[61] On the one hand, Locke seemed to believe that man cannot be
free unless he is possessive of his property in the usual sense of lands
and goods.[62] On the other hand, by contrast, he also took it to
embrace all natural rights: "man . . . hath by Nature a Power . . . to
preserve his Property, that is, his Life, Liberty and Estate"; ". . . for
the mutual *Preservation* of their Lives, Liberties and Estates, which I
call by the general name, Property".[63] Here, we need only notice that
for Locke the natural rights are universal, because the natural law,
i.e. the law of "reason" is applied to every man.

Although men, considered in the state of nature, are independent
of one another, they find it inconvenient to coerce every member to
obey the law of nature and reason. For in the state of nature men are
bound only in conscience to obey this law, which does not mean that
they actually obey this law or respect the rights of others. So it is in
men's own interest to bind themselves together by contract in order
to establish an authority for the better security of the majority. "The

---

[57] J. W. Chapman, 1970: 149.

[58] For the characteristics of natural rights used here, see J. P. Plamenatz, 1968: 84-9.

[59] Locke, 1997: II. 6.

[60] *Ibid.*: II. 5.

[61] See, for example, C. B. Macpherson, 1962: 198, 220, 247ff.

[62] For a Marxist attack on this assumption, see *ibid.*

[63] Locke, 1997: VII. 87, IX. 123.

great and *chief end* therefore, of Mens uniting into commonwealths and putting themselves under Government", Locke insisted, "is the *Preservation of their Property*".[64]

To sign a contract is to consent explicitly to the setting-up of political authority; and in so doing men thus show their promise to fulfil the obligation to obey that authority and the laws it issues.[65] But if we are already living in a certain arranged political society, Locke believed that:

> every Man, that hath any Possession, or Enjoyment, of any part of the Dominions of any Government, doth hereby give his tacit Consent, and is as far forth obliged to Obedience to the Laws of that Government, during such Enjoyment, as any one under it, whether his Possession be of Land, to him and his Heirs forever, or a lodging for only a Week; or whether it be barely travelling freely on the Highway; and in Effect, it reaches as far as the very being of anyone within the Territories of that Government.[66]

The debates arising around the consent theory are beyond my concern here. It is only important to stress once again some crucial points. First, the contract theory is generally understood to be a political theory which is nothing if not based on moral individualism: consent is "voluntarily incurred". And if the hallmark of authority is unquestioning recognition by those who are asked to obey, what is required in political philosophy is neither coercion nor persuasion but "individual judgement" to prove the legitimacy of authority. And second, for writers like Locke, we should maintain a number of natural rights in political participation because this is why we entered into political community in the first place. "According to this theory", thus,

> it is a fundamental moral truth that human beings may make valid and weighty claims in justice against each other, society and government. Human beings possess the moral rights in virtue of which they may make these claims of justice not as members of any specific moral community or as subjects of any positive legal order, but simply in virtue of their nature as the sort of creatures they are. The natural rights ascribed to human beings in this theory are natural, accordingly, in the sense that they are pre-conventional, morally prior to any social institution or contractual arrangement, and they are natural in the related sense, also, of being grounded in the natures of the creatures that possess them.[67]

---

[64] *Ibid.*: IX. 124.

[65] For a linguistic approach to show the connection between consent-promise and obligation, see R. B. Brandt, 1964: 374-93.

[66] Locke, 1997: VIII. 119.

[67] J. Gray, 1995b: 45-6.

Consequently, the natural rights that we have in our political practice are simply a set of abstract moral claims.

Indeed, one might conjecture here whether the principle of natural rights validated by a law of "reason" would contradict Locke's
empiricist position: that all knowledge comes from sense-experience. Within the system of *An Essay Concerning Human Understanding* itself, however, it seems that Locke himself would not have
thought of this as a problem. For even though all simple moral ideas
are from experience, once they are obtained, Locke argues, we have
the ability to examine, relate or abstract them in order to gain some
complex moral ideas. And if, in so doing, they express necessary
relations of agreement or disagreement, we may then claim certain
moral rules subsist in their relations. That is, in Locke's system of
ethics, the ideas of a moral law must come from experience, but the
truth of a moral rule is independent of its observance.[68]

Locke identifies three kinds of moral law: the divine law, the civil
law and the law of opinion or reputation, of which the first is ultimate and exactly understood as "that law which God has set to the
actions of men, whether promulgated to them by the light of nature,
or the voice of revelation".[69] According to F. Copleston, "Locke's
distinction between the light of nature and revelation recalls Aqui-
nas's distinction between the natural law, known by reason, and the
divine positive law; and this distinction was doubtless inspired
largely by Hooker, who had taken over a good deal from mediaeval
philosophy". "The influence of Hooker", Copleston continues, "and
of mediaeval philosophy through Hooker, on Locke's thought can
be seen in the latter's notion of natural rights".[70] It is thus reaffirmed
here that the distinction between empiricism and rationalism is only
a matter regarding the source of knowledge; and that Locke has been
promoting the Enlightenment ethical position in terms of a rational
justification of morality.

II.3.3. Kant: The Categorical Imperative

We may now turn to Kant's moral philosophy by concentrating on
Grounding for the Metaphysics of Morals, the philosopher's ethical
propaedeutic.

The major objective in our moral life, for Kant as for many ethical
thinkers, is to be "good". But Kant's key point is that "there is no pos-

---

[68] See F. Copleston, 1959: 123.

[69] Locke, 1975: II. 28. 8.

[70] F. Copleston, 1959: 127.

sibility of thinking of anything at all in the world, or even out of it, which can be regarded as good without qualification, except a good *will*".[71] Intelligence or courage may be good only if they are not put to ill use; happiness or pleasure cannot be good unless a will thinks it to be so. A "good will", then, points to the fact that we, fully rational beings, are in essence free agents who can autonomously judge our own moral status by the use of reason. The theme of Kant's ethics thus exists in the following form: "Morality makes sense only if men are free; freedom is just the ability to act from reason; thus morality will make sense only if it is grounded on rationality".[72] For this reason, Kant simply regarded his whole ethical theory as an attempt to discover "a supreme law of freedom",[73] that is, rational principles for the intelligent direction of the activities of free agents. In other words, for Kant, morality is a system of laws of freedom, indicating what ends the fully rational beings ought to choose for themselves and how they ought to act with regard to these ends. And as already mentioned, this *transcendental freedom* in Kant's system of critical philosophy is beyond the realm of cognitive knowledge; it is a rational guide for action in the light of which a person can be sure *that he is free*.[74]

It follows from this that Kant's methodology in ethics, as in epistemology, is transcendental. As J. G. Murphy comments,

> A transcendental argument or deduction, it will be recalled, proceeds from experience to a discovery of those conditions making this experience possible. It discovers presuppositions or necessary conditions for intelligibility ... Similarly in morality. We do not discover that freedom is a value by inductive argument. We do not note that people say things like "Freedom is a good thing" with great frequency. Rather, we see that unless freedom is *presupposed* as a basic value, much of our ordinary moral talk — that which it is the business of the moral philosopher to analyse — would not make sense, would not be intelligible.[75]

This means that the aim of Kant's moral philosophy is not to discover a new morality, nor to deny our moral discourse, but to ascertain the possibility of moral certainty by discovering *a priori* principles underlying the whole body of discourse and rendering

---

[71] Kant, 1993b: 7.

[72] J. G. Murphy, 1994: 26-7.

[73] Kant, 1993b: 62.

[74] *Ibid.*: 62-3.

[75] J. G. Murphy, 1994: 32.

this discourse intelligible, and hence to put our moral life on a purely rational basis.[76]

All this re-affirms that although Kant distinguishes Practical Reason from Scientific Reason, each for him has a reality of its own: the world of the Will and the world of Nature. By the former he does not simply mean our *actual* moral judgement but a kind of Universal Practical Philosophy[77] aiming to provide it with a rational criterion, an end-in-itself.[78] Hence, Kant would not deny that Practical Reason understood as man's free will to follow moral rules must be prior to his *practical reasoning*, developed from substantial moral conversations, and expressed in various contingent situations.[79] For, as indicated, whereas the latter falls into the world of varying experience, the former alone belongs to the universal category of morality. So, Kantian Practical Reason as a specific form of Theoretical Reason, in point of fact, retains the "supremacy of theory over practice" held by the Enlightenment thinkers; indeed Kant is a writer of a normative ethical theory.[80]

In Kant's ethics the laws of freedom or morality set forth by reason, as we know, are identified in favour of various formulations of "categorical imperative" which culminate in the "kingdom of ends". In *Grounding*, before moving to an examination of the categorical imperative, Kant first set out to clarify the nature of morality, i.e. goodness in terms of three propositions:

Firstly, Kant believed that moral conduct is to act "from duty" by the guidance of "reason" irrespective of any desire or inclination,[81] that is, to act by understanding the action as our own duty. As D. Ross points out, for Kant to maintain that "it is my duty to do act *A*" is to maintain that "it is my duty to do act *A* from the sense that it

[76] Cf. J. W. Ellington, 1993: vi.

[77] Cf. Kant, 1993b: 3-4.

[78] To apply the categorical imperative, mainly the Formula of the End in Itself, to test maxims in concrete moral cases is a task that Kant later came to take up in *Metaphysics of Morals*.

[79] Cf. G. Schrader, 1975: 65-90.

[80] Note that many interpreters would refer to *Grounding for the Metaphysics of Morals* and *Critique of Practical Reason* as Kant's "meta-ethical" work which deals with the formations and methods of moral philosophy, whereas *Metaphysics of Morals* as his "normative ethics" which copes with concrete moral cases in the light of the categorical imperative. But, here as elsewhere in this study, what I mean by a normative ethics is the attempt to seek a universal theoretical principle as a guide in our practical reasoning. Kant's whole ethical project, which is contained in the three works mentioned, is perhaps the most outstanding case which concerns me here, i.e. it is the biggest target of Oakeshott's critique of morality as abstract moral laws.

[81] Kant, 1993b: 9-12.

is my duty to do act *A*".[82] That is to say, neither desire nor self-interest bestows moral implication; they are just non-moral.[83] Moral worth is always accomplished on the condition that we behave ourselves without reference to any reward.

As a result, "the second proposition is this: An action done from duty has its moral worth, not in the purpose that is to be attained by it, but in the maxim according to which the action is determined. The moral worth depends, therefore, not on the realisation of the object of the action, but merely on the principle of volition according to which, without regard to any objects of desire, the action has been done".[84] This means that moral activity is to act not only from duty but also on the principle of the moral law. On this basis, Kant is surely a rigourist in that the claims of duty are always against inclinations and there can be no expectations from any basic moral rules.[85] It is thus not difficult for the reader to realise that the moral self in Kant's moral thought is a "principled self" and morality consists in a set of abstract rules. They are abstract because it is the *form* of the principle not the *content* of the principle that instructs moral action: moral life, for Kant, is governed by the categorical imperative rather than by concrete moral exemplification by which it is driven.

"The third proposition, which follows from the other two, can be expressed thus: Duty is the necessity of an action done out of respect for the law".[86] What concerned Kant regarding the principle of morality, it says, was its character as a command. When we act from duty and on principle we must be acting because the law demands it; and as such we are paying our respect to the law.

> Therefore, the pre-eminent good which is called moral can consist in nothing but the representation of the law in itself, and such a representation can admittedly be found only in a rational being insofar as this representation, and not some expected effect, is the determining ground of the will.[87]

It is no surprise then that, for Kant, when we act from duty, on maxim and out of the respect for the law we are acting according to the moral law, namely, the categorical imperative. Kant grants that conceptually all imperatives, which must contain an "ought", can be in two forms: the hypothetical or the categorical. Morality can never

---

[82]   D. Ross, 1930: 5.

[83]   Cf. W. K. Frankena, 1973: 4.

[84]   Kant, 1993b: 12-3.

[85]   H. B. Acton, 1970: 64.

[86]   Kant, 1993b: 13.

[87]   *Ibid.*: 13-4.

be truly conducted by the former, because it represents "the practical necessity of a possible action as a means for attaining something else that one wants (or may possibly want)".[88] That is, the hypothetical imperative indicates that: "If you want x, you ought to do y"; and so it must be associated with a certain utilitarian principle. By way of contrast, "the categorical imperative would be one which represented an action as objectively necessary in itself, without reference to another".[89] It is thus by definition the only criterion in accordance with the nature of goodness to be revealed.

There are a number of versions of the categorical imperative which, in fact, all amount to the same thing. The best-known is the Formula of Universal Law: "Act only according to the maxim whereby you can at the same time will that it should become a universal law".[90] Or alternatively, since the universality of law according to which effects constitute what is properly called "nature", the categorical imperative also can be rephrased thus: "Act as if the maxim of your action were to become through your will a universal law of nature".[91] This is often called the Formula of the Law of Nature. However, each of these directives means equally that

> an action has moral worth only if it is done from duty, in a sense there is only one categorical imperative, the one that demands of us that we act on maxims or principles we can universalise and that we act on them *because* they can be universalised, i.e., that we act from respect for law.[92]

For example, one who believes in the maxim of promising falsely could not "will it as a universal law".

> For the universality of a law which says that anyone believing himself to be in difficulty could promise whatever he pleases with the intention of not keeping it would make promising itself and the end to be attained thereby quite impossible, inasmuch as no one would believe what was promised him but would merely laugh at all such utterances as being vain pretenses.[93]

In short, to will a maxim as a universal law is to will it as a ubiquitous moral institution, a general system of values.

---

[88] *Ibid.*: 25.

[89] *Ibid.*: 25.

[90] *Ibid.*: 30. The formula of universal law first appeared as "I should never act except in such a way that I can also will that my maxim should become a universal law" (*ibid.*: 14).

[91] *Ibid.*: 30.

[92] R. L. Arrington, 1998: 275.

[93] Kant, 1993b: 31.

There are three other closely intertwined principles that can be derived from the above. The first of these is the Formula of the End in Itself: "Act in such in way that you treat humanity, whether in your own person or in the person of another, always at the same time as an end and never simply as a means".[94] That the result of the test of this formula is equivalent to that of the previous ones should not be questioned. To use the same example again, if one is to make a false promise one is using others as a means to achieve one's own ends and thus one breaks the principle of the end in itself. Conversely, when someone is treated as a means, his humanity is defaced; when the principle of such treatment is universalised, the agent of such treatment must in turn be willing to be similarly treated. But every one wants to be treated as a human and not as a thing. Thus, any violation of the Formula of the End in Itself must be morally wrong according the Formula of Universal Law.[95]

What is more, there is also the Formula of Autonomy which commands that "everything be done from the maxim of such a will could at the same time have as its object only itself regarded as legislating universal law".[96] This suggests that the notion of autonomy is the very idea running through all of those formulations of the categorical imperative, because it ensures once again that we, fully rational beings, are not merely the subject of the moral law, but its legislators; that we must be free agents conceived as an end in itself and able to make universal law. "Hence autonomy is the ground of the dignity of human nature and of every rational nature"; "freedom must be presupposed as a property of the will of all rational beings". [97]

And finally, all that has been said gives rise to the concluding Formula of the Kingdom of Ends, to which a rational being belongs as a member "when he legislates in it universal laws while also being himself subject to these laws".[98] Thus where the Kingdom of Ends is an ideal moral community in which every rational member is freely and equally co-operating with each other according the same universal laws, what is eventually confirmed is a bifurcated reality that Kant has already set forth in the *Critique of Pure Reason*:

> Therefore he [a rational being] has two standpoints from which he can regard himself and know laws of the use of his powers and hence of all his actions: first, insofar as he belongs to the world of sense subject to

[94] *Ibid.*: 36.

[95] J. W. Ellington, 1993: 12.

[96] Kant, 1993b: 39.

[97] *Ibid.*: 41, 50.

[98] *Ibid.*: 40.

laws of nature (heteronomy); secondly, insofar as he belongs to the intelligible world subject to laws which, independent of nature, are not empirical but are founded only on reason. As a rational being and hence belonging to the intelligible world, man can never think of the causality of his own will except under the idea of freedom; for independence from the determining causes of the world of sense (an independence which reason must always attribute to itself) is freedom.[99]

This, of course, does not mean that for Kant human beings can be indifferent to nature and live in the Kingdom of Ends alone. In fairness to him, as already indicated, it only says that although Scientific Reason cannot penetrate into Practical Reason, logically the existence of the physical world must be established in the first place, then we may come to consider the possibility of moral consciousness. As Kant puts it,

> The former view of a countless multitude of worlds annihilates, as it were, my importance as an animal creature, which must give back to the planet (a mere speck in the universe) the matter from which it came, the matter which is for a little time provided with vital force, we know not how. The latter, on the contrary, infinitely raises my worth as that of an intelligence by my personality, in which the moral law reveals a life independent of all animality and even of the whole world of sense.[100]

To conclude, it has been shown that, for Kant, morality derives neither from traditions and communities, nor from the natural law, nor from the inclination of the nature of men, but from "pure reason" alone. "Kant's ethics", as O. O'Neill comments, thus "remains the paradigmatic and most influential attempt to vindicate universal moral principles without reference to preferences or to a theoretical framework".[101] And it is true that the possibility of these principles is based on a form of radical individualism: "Everything in nature works according to laws. Only a rational being has the power to act according to his conception of laws, i.e. according to principles, and thereby has he a will".[102] According to Kant's renowned claim in "What Is Enlightenment?", the motto of enlightenment is: "Have courage to use your own reason", and for this enlightenment, "nothing is required but freedom".[103] As a result, the nature of Kant's ethics is both formalist and abstract.

---

[99]   *Ibid.*: 53-4.

[100] *Ibid.*: 169.

[101] O. O'Neill, 1994: 184.

[102] Kant, 1993b: 23.

[103] Kant, 1991: 54, 55.

II.3.4. Mill: The Utilitarian Principle

The third and last module of liberal ethics on which I shall comment here is utilitarianism. In its standard form, utilitarianism presents the ethical thought teaching that "happiness is desirable, and the only thing desirable, as an end"[104] in human actions — i.e. a sum of pleasures, and that moral activity is the promotion of "the greatest happiness of the greatest number": "the rightness of an action is determined by its contribution to the happiness of everyone affected by it".[105] Thus, the two features which are of particular significance in classic utilitarianism are *hedonism* and *consequentialism*,[106] and both of these can be found in J. S. Mill's *Utilitarianism* subsumed under his definition of the utilitarian principle:

> The creed which accepts as the foundation of morals, Utility or the Greatest Happiness Principle, holds that actions are right in proportion as they tend to promote happiness, wrong as they tend to produce the reverse of happiness. By happiness is intended pleasure, and the absence of pain; by unhappiness, pain, and the privation of pleasure.[107]

First, utilitarianism involves a form of hedonism because neither Jeremy Bentham nor Mill would deny that "end", "utility", "happiness", "interest", "good", "benefit" etc., are all different expressions of the same thing, that is, the enjoyment of "pleasures" or the relief of "pains". But, in many cases, the utilitarian is also an egoist in the sense that the individual is believed to desire pleasures or interests in actual fact by ways of which his actions are motivated. A most obvious implication of egoism, indeed, is expressed in the first three sentences of Bentham's *Principle of Morals and Legislation*:

> Nature has placed mankind under the governance of two sovereign masters, *pain* and *pleasure*. It is for them alone to point out what we ought to do, as well as to determine what we shall do. On the one hand the standard of right and wrong, on the other the chain of causes and effects, are fastened to their throne.[108]

Whether or not Mill was an egoist is debatable, as he did have a subtler position about the "development of person excellence"[109] and he put much more stress on the importance of the consensus and

---

[104] Mill, 1991a: 168.

[105] A. Quinton, 1989: 1.

[106] For the general characteristics of utilitarianism, see A. Quinton, 1989: 1-10; G. Scarre, 1996: 1-26; J. P. Plamenatz, 1949: 1-10.

[107] Mill, 1991a: 137.

[108] Quoted by A. Quinton, 1989: 6.

[109] G. Scarre, 1996: 5. Cf. A. Ryan, 1974: 105, 125, 131-3.

stability of common good than either Bentham or James Mill.[110] But in each case, it still seems that egoism plays a major role in the premise of Mill's "proof" of the Greatest Happiness Principle mentioned:

> The only proof capable of being given that an object is visible, is that people actually see it. The only proof that a sound is audible, is that people here it: and so of the other sources of our experience. In like manner, I apprehend, the sole evidence it is possible to produce that anything is desirable, is that people do actually desire it. If the end which the utilitarian doctrine proposes to itself were not, in theory and in practice, acknowledged to be an end, nothing could ever convince any person that it was so.[111]

That is to say, Mill's proof of the utilitarian principle somehow rests on "a psychological theory according to which the only promoting which moves a man to action is the pleasure of so acting or the pain of acting otherwise".[112] If it is so, it demands that the ground of the Greatest Happiness Principle should be originally based on an account of human nature: all men often seek pleasure and avoid pain; all men are utilitarian in practice; it is common human experience to increase the best and decrease the worst. And thus, it may not be going too far to say that the egoistic hedonism of utilitarianism, even in Millian terms, contains a psychological transformation of radical individualism. The individual is dependent on the determination of human nature in order to make his responses to situations. Besides, the fact that men's endless capacity to aggregate and maximise happiness implied in any form of utilitarianism must have reinforced the strength of radical individualism in its theoretical context.[113]

Secondly, as indicated, that which is closely related to Mill's Greatest Happiness Principle is its consequentialist implication, in that it maintains that the rightness of an action is judged by the goodness of its outcome.[114] In its later version, consequentialism has been developed into "act consequentialism" and "rule consequentialism",[115] but, what is important here is that any form of consequentialism is appropriate in a universal theory of moral justifica-

[110] Cf. A. Ryan, 1974: 127.

[111] Mill, 1991a: 168.

[112] A. Ryan, 1974: 118.

[113] Cf. G. Scarre, 1996: 14-25.

[114] Some writers, indeed, thus intend to make no difference between utilitarianism and consequentialism. See, for example, P. Kelly, 1994: 127-45.

[115] For act utilitarianism and rule utilitarianism, see G. Scarre, 1996: 122-32.

tion.[116] For, to judge the rightness of an action in favour of the goodness of its result must have logically implied that a criterion of moral
judgement is prior to the performance of human activity. At this
point, it means that consequentialism or teleology and deontology
are fundamentally different only if the moral worth of actions
should be determined according to their consequences for the promotion of a set of moral values, or on the basis of their agreement
with *a priori* moral laws. Both of these, to be sure, make an attempt to
establish some one ultimate principle of morality.[117] It is thus no
wonder that the two major approaches in modern ethics generally
lead to similar moral conclusions in practice. For example, breaking
promises is morally wrong because it is breaking the moral law from
a deontologist point of view, or because it produces negative impact
on common human interest from a utilitarian point of view.[118]

The view that a rational system of ethics must contain the first
principle of utility is certainly relevant to Mill's case. Mill's *Utilitarianism* not only revises his predecessors' teachings, for example, by
putting emphasis upon the qualities of happiness,[119] but it also
addresses those of his enemies, especially, in criticism of
W. Whewill's intuitionism which tried to replace the criterion of
morality with our common "moral sense".[120] In *A System of Logic*,
Mill had tried to surmount intuitionism by establishing a *philosophia
prima* of "the Art of Life" which would allow us to justify and rank
the ends of life:

> I shall content myself with saying that the doctrine of intuitive moral
> principles, if true, would only provide for that portion of the field of con-
> duct which is properly called moral. For the remainder of the practice of
> life, some general principle, or standard, must still be sought; and if that
> principle be rightly chosen, it will be found, I apprehend, to serve quite
> as well for the ultimate principle of Morality, as for that of Policy or
> Taste.[121]

And by the same token, in *Utilitarianism* Mill attempts to define the
first principle of utility as follows:

> The truths which are ultimately accepted as the first principles of a sci-
> ence, are really the last results of metaphysical analysis, practised on the

---

[116] For this foundationalist or Rationalist character of utilitarianism in terms of
    Bentham's ethical thought, see also *RP*: 132-50.

[117] Cf. Mill, 1991a: 134-5.

[118] G. Scarre, 1996: 11-3.

[119] See Mill, 1991a: 139-43.

[120] Cf. A. Ryan, 1974: 99-101; J. Skorupski, 1993: 51-4.

[121] Quoted by A. Ryan, 1974: 104.

elementary notions with which the science is conversant; and their relation to the science is not that of foundations to an edifice, but of roots of a
tree, which may perform their office equally well though they be never
dug down to and exposed to light.[122]

Utilitarianism understood in terms of consequentialism, then, is a
rational programme whose ambition is to order our moral life into a
whole system. The first principle of utilitarianism, the Greatest Happiness Principle, is regarded as the rational guide in practice — "the
test of right and wrong", [123] as Mill used to call it — but, like any
moral principle, it must suffer from being abstract and formalist.

Aside from the combination of egoistic hedonism and
consequentialism, however, classic utilitarianism produces a
self-contradiction. In the case of Bentham or James Mill, the difficulty is this: If egoistic hedonism means that the individual is always
motivated by his own pleasure, there can be no sense in saying that
the "greatest happiness of the greatest number" is desirable to him at
the same time.[124] But this perhaps was more important to the critics
of utilitarianism than Bentham or James Mill had actually thought it
to be. Because the resolution for reconciling the two factors was to
maintain the harmony of self-interests. That is, as long as a society
makes every effort to create a harmony of the interests of individuals, the Greatest Happiness Principle can be desirable to its numbers.
And here, we can not see any reason for John S. Mill to deny this in
principle.

But, Mill's whole situation is far more complicated. Because what
he had to conciliate was not merely self-interest and common good,
but, more importantly, liberty and the utilitarian principle; the two
matters that now give him a distinguishable place in *the* history of
political thought. And in which case, the principle paradox of
Millian utilitarian liberalism is: "the Principle of Liberty actually dis-
qualifies utility-promotion as a reason for the restraint of liberty".[125]

Although, in the first chapter of *On Liberty*, Mill told us that his
object was to defend the principle that:

> the sole end for which mankind are warranted, individually or collec-
> tively, in interfering with the liberty of action of any of their number, is
> self-protection. That the only purpose for which power can be rightly
> exercised over any member of a civilised community, against his will, is

---

[122] Mill, 1991a: 132.

[123] *Ibid.*: 132ff.

[124] J. Plamenatz, 1949: 9-10; A. Quinton, 1989: 6.

[125] J. Gary, 1991: xix.

to prevent harm to others. His own good, either physical or moral, is not a sufficient warrant.[126]

And he seemed to believe that it is not a theory of natural rights but the very principle of utility on which the justification of liberty rests: "It is proper to state that I forego any advantage which could be derived to my argument from the idea of abstract right, as a thing independent of utility".[127] However, it does seem that it is not quite this direct position that Mill really took to defend liberty for the remainder of his prestigious essay. As J. Plamenatz states, "what he [Mill] is himself concerned to do is not to show that there are good utilitarian grounds for the non-interference he advocates, but to determine the limits of the interference which he regards as permissible"; that is, "he leaves undone all those things that a utilitarian ought to do, but what he does is as well worth doing as anything he ever attempted".[128] Some contemporary liberals, thus, would like to interpret Mill more as a liberal than as an utilitarian.[129]

Recent revisionist scholarship, however, has tried to connect Mill's utilitarianism with his liberalism by linking *Utilitarianism* with *On Liberty*.[130] And two major pieces of evidence have been provided in support. Firstly, the two works were almost written contemporaneously. And second, perhaps more importantly, the liberal principle can best be seen as a "secondary principle", which can be driven by the first principle of utility and allowed in the whole system of *Utilitarianism*, to govern society's political and moral treatment of the individual. Thus, as R. Crisp argues, the principles Mill recommends in *On Liberty*, "even though they make no explicit reference to the utility principle, derive their plausibility from that principle":

> The liberty principle states that such interference [with the lives of individuals] is justified only to prevent harm to others, and this principle not only rules out paternalistic justifications for interference, but provides the underpinning for a protected self-regarding sphere. The liberty principle rests upon individuality, which has welfare value in itself when instantiated in people's lives, as well as being of great instrumental value as humanity progresses. The same sorts of justification underlie Mill's defence of freedom of speech: the value of understanding, and the importance of vivid belief, both of which can *be productive of welfare for*

---

[126] Mill, 1991b: 14.

[127] *Ibid.*: 15.

[128] J. Plamenatz, 1947: 126.

[129] See, for example, I. Berlin, 1991; C. L. Ten, 1980.

[130] See, for example, J. Gray, 1983 and 1991: vii-xxx; R. Crisp, 1997: viii.

society as a whole [emphasis mine].[131]

And yet, if it is so, the universal and formalist features of utilitarianism must be reflecting an ultimate utilitarian principle of liberty.

II.3.5. Formalism in Ethics

By formalism in ethics, then, I mean the attempt to produce a normative moral and political theory, maintaining that the task of moral philosophy is to establish a set of self-evident and universal principles which can govern our practical life as a whole. And thus, there are three points of "family resemblance"[132] being of particular importance to this ethical position, which can be restated as follows:

(2) **formalism in ethics** means the hope to establish

   (2.1) **a set of moral principles** which would ensure our moral certainty; and this hope is based upon a form of

   (2.2) **radical individualism**, which contains an anti-traditional or anti-institutional attitude towards our moral life; and thus this treatment of morality has the character of a

   (2.3) **formalism** in order to be applied universally.

Now, it would not be surprising to say that foundationalism in philosophy and formalism in ethics are theoretically allied. Locke, Kant and Mill basically accept the premise that the rationality discovered by science and applied to objectify the external world, at least in philosophical terms, can be likewise used to order our moral life in terms of a set of rules. And just as the ideal form of Enlightenment civilisation is a mode of "argumentation" in which the philosopher is engaged in the pursuit of some ultimate values rather than in "an unrehearsed intellectual adventure" recognised as "conversation",[133] the liberal thinkers have tried to establish, so to speak, the "technique or rule of morality", the "morality of faith" or a set of "demonstrative moral truths".[134]

More precisely, as we shall see in greater detail in terms of Oakeshott's understanding of Rationalism, a set of moral and political (liberal) principles are made for the sake of Cartesian certainty. Furthermore, radical individualism is closely related to the notion of the instrumental mind, or to use contemporary communitarian

---

[131] R. Crisp, 1997: 199.

[132] Wittgenstein, 1968.

[133] *RP*: 490.

[134] These, as we shall see, are the Oakeshottian terms.

terminology, the "unencumbered self",[135] the "disengaged subject",[136] or the "emotivist self",[137] which hovers over modern philosophy in order to establish an absolute system of things and values. And finally, the inclination to formalism indicates that the rational authority of moral principles is possible only if the superiority of Human Reason is presupposed. In short, formalism in ethics or rationalism in politics is the belief that our abstract Theoretical Reasoning can be and must be used as a guide in our complicated practical reasoning.

We may thus reach the point that liberalism and foundationalism mutually entail one another; they constitute the whole package of Enlightenment positions. This, of course, does not mean that every important antecedent of modern natural philosophy we have mentioned must be a liberal thinker: Descartes, for example, made no claim to the concept of liberal thought. But it does say of liberalism and foundationalism that if one is repudiated the other must also be repudiated. And thus, if "the moral crisis of our day is a 'crisis of Enlightenment thought'",[138] it predicts a crisis for liberal ethics, viz. rationalist politics, too. [139]

II.3.6. The Crisis of the Enlightenment Ethical Position

The mistake of the Enlightenment project, as indicated, largely lies in the abstract concept of rationality it carries. And recently, for those who are concerned with the crisis of Enlightenment ethics in terms of this view, the name Alasdair MacIntyre has become something of an institution. A short review of this thinker's scholarship will help to shed light on my concern here.

---

[135] See M. Sandel, 1982.

[136] See C. Taylor, 1989.

[137] See A. MacIntyre, 1985.

[138] D. Harvey, 1989: 4.

[139] It must be reiterated that what I mean by liberalism here is more the philosophical commitment to classical liberal ethics than to the established institutions of to-day's liberal values such as freedom of the individual, the rule of law, constitutionalism and so forth. And thus, I do not intend to deny that it may be possible for writers like Richard Rorty to free liberal values from Enlightenment foundationalism. For Rorty's liberal project, see J. Gray, 1995a: chap. 10; S. Mulhall and A. Swift, 1997: chap. 8. For the separation of liberal values from liberal philosophy, see D. MacNiven, 1996: 353, in which he argues that "it may be possible to reject foundationalism, radical individualism, and the fact/value dichotomy, yet retain the principle of individual liberty, equality and defended democracy". But, as we shall see, I do not think the same case can be applied to Oakeshott's theory of civil association.

It is MacIntyre's observation that contemporary moral and political culture is in a state of disarray in the sense that we are no longer able to resolve the actual moral debates concerning nuclear war, abortion, freedom, justice and so forth. He begins in *After Virtue* by noting that:

> The most striking feature of contemporary moral utterance is that so much of it is used to express disagreements; and the most striking feature of the debate in which those disagreements are expressed is their interminable character. I do not mean by this just that such debates go on and on — although they do — but also that they can find no terminus. There seems to be no rational way of securing moral agreement in our culture.[140]

And he concludes that book with the claim that:

> on the one hand we still, in spite of the efforts of three centuries of moral philosophy and one of sociology, lack any coherent rationally defensible statement of a liberal individualist point of view; [and] on the other hand, the Aristotelian tradition can be restated in a way that restores intelligibility and rationality to our moral and social attitudes and commitments.[141]

The main reason why the present moral position has become so bewildering, according to MacIntyre, has mostly to do with the Enlightenment project of providing a vindication of morality, in terms of which Western people have now become accustomed, by classifying judgements, arguments and deeds in everyday moral discourse.[142] On the one hand, that which is closely related to the ideal of a rational justification of morality is the Enlightenment's premise of radical individualism — teaching that morality is really about the individual's capacity to act — which is independent of historic and social context. On the other hand, ironically, those moral arguments, which are put forth by the individuals as the best solutions derived from the universal principles fortified by the rational ethical theories, are so diverse that they actually conflict with one another in a way which is logically "incommensurate":[143]

> Every one of the arguments is logically valid or can be easily expanded so as to be made so; the conclusions do indeed follow from the premise. But the rival premises are such that we possess no rational way of weighing the claims of one as against another. For each premise employs some

---

[140] A. MacIntyre, 1985: 6.

[141] *Ibid.*: 259. See also, 1988: ix.

[142] A. MacIntyre, 1985: chap. 4.

[143] *Ibid.*: 6-10.

quite different normative or evaluative concept from the others, so that the claims made upon us are of quite different kinds.[144]

The appearance of emotivism in the twentieth century, MacIntyre declares, precisely symbolises this chaos of moral reasoning and the breakdown of the very tradition of ethics. For, by claiming that moral judgements embrace an emotional aspect which is allowed by different moral theories and can hardly be reasonably denied,[145] emotivism stands for an extreme form of moral relativism giving up the possibility of any rational reflection upon morality and politics.[146] Moreover, in view of the fact that "a moral philosophy . . . characteristically presupposes a sociology",[147] it can be noted that emotivism is actually in accordance with the character of the modern world. That is, the social content of emotivism "entails the obliteration of any genuine distinction between manipulative and non-manipulative social relationships"[148] which characterises our time; emotivist ethical thought simply regards all moral discourse as an expression of a "manipulative interpersonal relationship".[149]

In an emotivist society, then, morality is treated as the selfish desire for power in terms of the bureaucratic rationality of "matching means to ends economically and efficiently".[150] And consequently, the "emotivist self" thus conceived, "utterly distinct on the one hand from its social embodiments and lacking on the other any rational history of its own, may seem to have a certain abstract and ghostly character":

> The appearance of an abstract and ghostly quality arises not from any lingering Cartesian dualism, but from the degree of contrast, indeed the degree of loss, that comes into view if we compare the emotivist self with its historical predecessors . . . The self is now thought of as lacking any necessary social identity, because the kind of social identity that it once enjoyed is no longer available; the self is now thought of as criterionless, because the kind of *telos* in terms of which it once judged and acted is no longer thought to be credible.[151]

---

[144] *Ibid.*: 8.

[145] T. Honderich ed., 1995: 225.

[146] A. MacIntyre, 1985: 11-22.

[147] *Ibid.*: 22.

[148] *Ibid.*: 23.

[149] S. Mulhall and A. Swift, 1997: 75.

[150] A. MacIntyre, 1985: 25.

[151] *Ibid.*: 33.

In short, the crisis of modern ethics does not simply lie in its substituting one morality for another but lies in its substituting morality for "power politics".[152]

In order to rescue the malaise of ethical modernity that the Enlightenment project has brought about, as mentioned, MacIntyre suggests that we should revert to an Aristotelian tradition. The three elements that MacIntyre learns from Aristotle and takes as opposed to the Enlightenment ethical assumptions are: practice, the narrative self and tradition[153] (in contrast to a set of moral rules, radical individualism or the emotivist self, and formalism respectively). It is in his discussion of the implications of these conceptions, especially that of Aristotelian *phronesis*, as we shall see, that MacIntyre expresses his affinity with Oakeshott's critique of Rationalism.

II.4. Positivist Historiography

The next topic that I am going to explore here is the Enlightenment historiographical position, i.e. the notion of scientific history backed up by an identification of the historical with a naturalised conception of History, which I believe empowers the philosophical commitment of pro-positivist historiography. Before we go any further, however, I intend to clarify the meanings of history, History or the Past and historiography used in the book from the outset.

II.4.1. History, the Past and Historiography

In English the locution of "history" is ambiguous; and I have tried to gather together some of its distinguishable meanings in the previous chapter. Yet, two of these concepts, to which the word "history" most frequently refers, must be particularly discriminated here, namely, history as an enquiry and History as the Past.[154]

History, as we commonly conceive it, may stand for all the events or occurrences that have ever happened in the lives of human beings, especially where the events are seen as a long process which leads up to the present. In other words, the word "History" may be taken to mean the Past, the Human Past, which precisely signifies all the other events that have really happened "in" it before any now-points that can be arbitrarily determined by men. To cite one

---

[152] D. MacNiven, 1996: 351.

[153] J. Horton and S. Mendus, 1994: 8-14; S. Mulhall and A. Swift, 1997: 82-92.

[154] *OH*: 1-2. For the discussions of this two-fold meaning of the word "history", see also F. H. Bradley, 1993: 3-4; W. H. Walsh, 1967: 16-7; K. Jenkins, 1991:3-26; Nardin, 2001: 141.

simple example, it is possible in standard English to say either "Parliamentary government is a product of the Past" or "Parliamentary government is a product of History". Furthermore, in academic writings, one finds reference to the concept "historical context" or "historical situation" which is commonly used in the social sciences to mean "the social, political, economic and cultural circumstances prevailing in the particular society being studied".[155] The adjective "historical" used here, without doubt, does not refer to the historian's understanding of past ideas at all; but rather, refers to people, situations, etc. that used to exist there and then, in respect of this identity, whether or not we know anything whatever about them. In what follows, to avoid confusion, I shall substitute the adjective "historic" for "historical" in this context of usage.

In another meaning, however, history stands for a certain sort of enquiry into some such passage of events in a particular subject; the engagement and the conclusions of an historian. That is to say, in respect of this sense, the word "history", just as the Greek word from which the English word "history" is derived, indicates a kind of human enquiry; it is used to mean an individual manner of interpreting, understanding past ideas, or an organised body of knowledge about something past, which is produced by no one but the historian alone. Here, the adjective "historical" denotes an enquiry that, whatever we may think about the truth of its conclusions, is recognised in terms of certain characteristics to be an historical enquiry; and it denotes the kind of understanding reached in the course of such enquiry.

It has now become clear that the locution of "history" as such refers to two different levels of human activity. In one it reflects our activity of "making history". It was in this sense that, for example, Karl Marx made his famous comment: "Men make their own history, but not of their own free will".[156] In another, however, it reflects the historian's activity of "writing history": "it is made by nobody save the historian, to write history is the only way of making it".[157] It is undoubted that all of us all the time are participants in "Human History", but only a few of us at the same time have ever engaged in writing "a history", one among many other "histories", about that "History".

These two meanings of the word "history" are certainly different but they are not unrelated. For, history as interpretation is a human

[155] Cf. A. Marwick, 1989: 10.

[156] Marx, 1973: 146.

[157] *EM*: 99.

way of understanding the Past recognised in terms of certain characteristics to be the historical (and this is what I mean by historiography). Nevertheless, here and everywhere else, we need to get
clear in our minds this very distinction, because the word "history"
used by many unreflective historians and in pro-positivist theories
of history where it is thought that "it refers both to what actually
happened in the past and to the representation of that past in the
work of historians",[158] has unquestionably given rise to the belief
that the Past existed objectively in itself and is now understandable,
and that the historian's principle business is to discover those
"objective facts", to represent the occurrence of "what really
happened" in The Past in terms of causal explanation. It is mainly
this premise of an identification of history with History that I shall
call into question in this study.

By the term "historiography", on the other hand, I mean the theory of the writing of history. However, following M. Stanford, there
are three basic aspects of writing history that must be distinguished
here:[159] Firstly, there is "the descriptive theory of history" that simply describes the historian's practices and points to their methods
and procedures. Secondly, we also have what is often called "a history of history" that looks at the different ways in which people have
written history from the time of the ancient Greek, Herodotus. And
finally, there is "the philosophy of history" which, as we know it
today, embraces the so-called "analytical philosophy of history" (in
relation to logical positivism) as well as the "critical philosophy of
history" (in relation to writers such as Dilthey, Collingwood and so
forth), both of which attempt to discuss some of the concepts and
philosophical problems that arise from the writing of history.

Also, it should be observed that, like the word "history" itself, the
term "philosophy of history" has been used in two basic senses.[160] In
addition to analytical and critical historiography, this term has long
been indiscriminately applied to all speculative schemes of the
Human Past. This is what may be called the "speculative philosophy
of history", (or the capitalised term Philosophy of History), which
has been undertaken with the aim of providing us with some general
laws or patterns that underlie the whole process of the Human Past,
a general review of the whole course of human life, or the plan of
History considered as a whole.[161] We may find the idea of a

[158] J. Tosh, 1991: vi.

[159] See M. Standford, 1994: 5-7.

[160] Cf. W. H. Walsh, 1967: 19.

[161] *EM*: 154-5.

Philosophy of History in the work of nineteenth-century thinkers such as Hegel, Ranke,[162] Comte, Marx, Tolstoy or Spengler, for example.

In this book, by the Enlightenment historiographical position I am referring to a certain tradition of philosophy of history that adopts a naturalistic view of historical knowledge, but I am leaving aside the case of the Philosophy of History. For the latter is actually concerned with a metaphysical reading of History rather than with the characteristics of the writing of history. To make an obvious distinction: it is one thing to suppose that the Human Past has a meaning in the sense that all that has happened has been dominated by some "hidden hand": for example, the hand of Hegel's "cunning of reason"; whilst it is quite another to think about the human way of understanding and enquiring *about* that Past.[163] That is, to Hegel, the historian's understanding of History must be "in his own spirit which is different from the spirit of the object itself"; only the philosopher who aims to discover "absolute knowledge" is eligible to realise how God's wisdom has expressed itself in World History.[164]

More precisely, I take the Enlightenment historiographical position to be a scientific attempt to study history by identifying the historical with a naturalised conception of History; it is a position, although having been encouraged by the eighteenth-century *philosophes*, which becomes most unambiguous when represented in pro-positivist historiography. I said most unambigious because Western people, without doubt, have had experience in writing history as far back in time as the ancient Greeks. Yet, if by now in Western culture "history" means "academic history", it is less than two centuries old.[165] And given the view that to write history is separable from thinking about the nature of historical writing, it is not until the nineteenth century that the largest number of discussions about historiography have been made by pro-positivism and its theoretical competitors.

Moreover, it is true that "the first stage in the development of modern historical thought came when the historians of the Enlight-

[162] Note that there seems to have been two different faces of Ranke in terms of philosophy in Germany and in terms of historiography in Anglo-America. In German philosophical circles, Ranke is often taken to be a theological-historicist who believed that Universal History was organised according to providential design. In historiography, however, he was seen by Anglo-American scholars as a historical objectivist who claimed it was possible to uncover the past and speak about it — "*wie es eigentlich gewessen*" (G. Iggers, 1973).

[163] Cf. P. Gardiner, 1959: 7.

[164] Hegel, 1993: 16, 25.

[165] See, for example, A. MacIntyre, 1985: 4.

enment, inspired by seventeenth-century science, launched a large-scale exploration of the past".[166] But, it is also those *philosophes* who, by applying the notions of universal human nature, totality and progress to surmount the Past, created the idea of Universal History and developed insights that pointed in the direction of the Philosophy of History in the following century.

To adopt the rational standard in understanding History, Voltaire, for example, wrote that:

> it is clear that everything which belongs intimately to human nature is the same from one end of the universe to the other; that everything depends on custom is different, and it is accidental if it remains the same. The empire of custom is much more vast than that of nature; it extends over manners and all usages, it sheds variety on the scene of the universe; nature sheds unity there, she establishes everywhere a small number of invariable principles. Thus the basis is everywhere the same, and culture produces diverse fruits.[167]

And, from the notion of totality one learnt that: If one reads "history" from a particular point of view, Human History breaks apart into "fragments" (historical particulars); it was therefore urgent to insist on its wholeness by means of "a kind of secularised theology of cause and effect which presumed the coherence of all events".[168] In addition, as Lord Acton pointed out, the view of Universal History relied on the Enlightenment notion of human progress, too:

> By Universal History I understand that which is distinct from the combined history of all countries, which is not a rope of sand, but a continuous development, and is not a burden on the memory, but an illumination of the soul. It moves in a succession to which the nations are subsidiary. Their story will be told, not for their own sake, but in reference and subordination to a higher series, according to the time and the degree in which they contribute to the common fortunes of mankind.[169]

In sum, the *philosophes* played a paradoxical role in the development of historical thought: In respect of Universal History they were unhistorical in the sense of distorting the concrete and particular characteristics of historical knowledge, whilst in respect of providing a new conceptual instrument for scientific history they contrived a modern mode of treating history.[170] And here, it is the latter that will be further discussed.

---

[166] T. R. Tholfsen, 1967: 14.

[167] Quoted by E. Cassirer, 1979: 219.

[168] Cf. C. R. Bambach, 1990: 6.

[169] Quoted by E. Breisach, 1994: 321.

[170] Cf. T. R. Tholfsen, 1967: 93-4.

On the whole, then, it is my view that the philosophical commitment of positivist historiography, both traditional and contemporary, is predicated on an Enlightenment position which makes no distinction between history as a mode of understanding and History as a naturalised entity. For the rest of this section, as a result, I intend to examine first the characteristics of that naturalised conception of History; second, and most importantly, the grounds of neo-positivist historiography; and finally some philosophical problems arising from the notion of scientific history in general. In the course of discussing neo-positivist historiography, nonetheless, I shall pay some attention to its foundationalist character. In so doing, my argument is that neo-positivism is incapable of solving the pitfalls embodied in Enlightenment historical thought, as it remains within the Cartesian-Kantian tradition of philosophy in terms of scientism, dualism-representationism and universalism upon which the notion of scientific history is based. And thus, bringing neo-positivism into consideration will enable a more complete examination of the development of modern foundationalist philosophy to be extended on the one hand, and provide an opportunity for further study of the contemporary debate over historiography with regard to a certain Enlightenment position on the other.

II.4.2. The Naturalised Conception of History

To begin with, by a naturalised conception of History, I mean the attempt to impose a law of Nature upon History. Since History is literally related to the Past, the law of Nature at stake can be understood as a "temporal rhythm given in Nature",[171] namely, successiveness. In this sense the naturalised conception of History is a "Historical Perspective" in association with a certain notion of Time; its typical definition can hereby be understood as a series of "what happened", the course of successive events.[172] It follows that this notion of History does not necessarily amount to a Philosophy of History, (although it may be regarded as the presupposition: It seems harder to believe in the progressive process of Human History if past events are not believed to be successive in the first instance). And thus, even though one of the main features which characterises logical positivism is its striving to reject the traditional metaphysical system and the Philosophy of History, in claiming his-

---

[171] R. Koselleck, 1985: 95.

[172] Bosanquet, for example has negatively used the phrases: a "tissue of mere conjunction" or the "doubtful story of succesive events" (quoted by P. Franco, 1990a: 33).

tory as the representation of what really happened in the occurrence of events in terms of general laws, its historiography must be dependent on this naturalised conception of History, which clearly assumes: (1) the existence of History as the only legitimate object of historical study, (2) the conception of Time as successiveness and a definition of History as a series of successive events, and (3) the application of scientific methods to the study of history. Let me now illuminate these characteristics in relation to the Enlightenment philosophical and historical thoughts of the moment.[173]

First of all, we have seen that, for Descartes, to understand things credibly one has to seek out a rigorous access to the absolute certain truth; and this implies that there are always objective answers about the natural world waiting to be disclosed by the self-conscious *cogito*. This belief was so influential in the modern world that, when "history" was taken into account, many scholars were concerned to assume that there is only one genuine answer corresponding to any historical question we may ask. That is, they maintained history to be an account of "what really happened" by postulating the existence of History in a singular form (note that the plural expression of "histories" is a more recent phenomenon).

For example, E. Chambers in his famous and seminal *Cyclopaedia*, the English forerunner of the French *Encyclopedie*, offered a standard definition of history as "a recital or description of things as they are, or have been; in a continued, orderly narration of the principle facts, and circumstances thereof".[174] Voltaire, in his prestigious article "Histoire" which appeared in the French *Encyclopedie*, defined history as "the account of things represented as true, as contrasted with fable, which is the account of things represented as false".[175] And Gibbon once claimed that history is "the knowledge of the events that have happened on the soil which we inhabit".[176]

The notion of the singularity of History indeed would make it possible for the *philosophes* to order History in a way that corresponds to the "uniformity of Nature" as Newton had postulated in physics. It thus requires that History, "what really happened" in the Past, must

---

[173] Indeed, I am not suggesting that the great philosophers, especially those of the seventeenth century, anticipated the basic issues of modern and contemporary historiography; on the contrary, most of them demonstrated a lack of historical interest. Rather, I only suggest that there are some deep philosophical difficulties in our historical thinking whose roots should be traced back to the Cartesian-Kantian philosophical tradition.

[174] E. Chambers, 1991: 440.

[175] Voltaire, 1991: 442.

[176] E. Gibbon, 1991: 461.

be governed by the law of Nature, especially the law of Natural Time, so that a linear temporal sequence of the cause and effect of historical events can be regarded as objectively as Nature. In other words, when History is seen to be the temporal development of past events, its objectivity demands a notion of Time as a constituent of reality on a par with absolute Space. The indispensable element of such a naturalised conception of History, i.e. the notion of Natural Time, I think, had eventually been recognised in Kant's philosophical system, when he came to justify the existence of a common-sense world of science in order to correspond exactly to Newtonian natural science.[177] Although, in physics, Newton's paradigm of Time might have been revised by Einstein's paradigm of relative time, it remains as an orthodox human understanding of time and change (successiveness), even up to the present day, not to mention the time of positivism.

On this interpretation, however, one might argue that Kant seemed to have claimed that the world of Will should be separated from the world of Nature. But, it should be recalled that for Kant, Scientific Reason must be prior to Historical Reason. Furthermore, when "history" came into discussion, in his "Idea of a Universal History from a Cosmopolitan Point of View", Kant in fact accepted the view that Nature has implanted certain capacities in human beings in order that they may develop and be progressive, and that Human History exhibits the mechanisms by which Nature ensures the development and progress of these.[178] Thus, Kant's conception of History cannot be said to be non-naturalistic.

In Western philosophical theories, the concept of "time" has always occupied an important place; we are usually told that "[o]ne cannot read metaphysics, either of this age or of any other, without finding frequent reference to the problem of time".[179] And, many thinkers have remarked that time in itself is nothing; it is man himself who makes time measurable and meaningful. That time is in itself meaningless and indescribable is actually a traditional notion that can also be found in Greek philosophy. In *Timaeus*, for example, Plato says that "time" is a process of becoming and perishing and never really is. In *Physics*, again, Aristotle claims that since time itself is not movement, it must somehow have to do with movement. Following this viewpoint of time, Kant in his *Critique of Pure Reason*, takes time to be "the form of inner sense", the "objective reference"

[177] R. Scruton, 1982: 31.

[178] Cf. P. Gardiner, 1959: 22.

[179] M. F. Cleugh, 1937: 1.

within experience, but does not exist of itself: "Time is not something which exists of itself, or which inheres in things as an objective determination, and it does not, therefore, remain when abstraction is made of all subjective conditions of its intuition". "(I)f we abstract from the subjective conditions of sensible intuition, time is nothing, and cannot be ascribed to the objects in themselves (apart from their relation to our intuition) in the way either of subsistence or of inherence".[180]

Even though time is in itself nothing, it seems undeniable that change is in time. We usually speak of what has changed, what happens and what will occur "in time", to realise changes around us. And, because time itself cannot be "removed", all we can do is to ascribe the change of things in it. Kant thus says that "the concept of alteration, and with it the concept of motion, as alteration of place, is possible only through and in the representation of time"; "(o)nly in time can two contradictorily opposed predicates meet in one and the same object, namely, *one after the other*".[181] That is to say, time as "the context of changing" does not exist of itself, but by the human way of understanding things in it, then, the temporal notions of coexistence or succession, before or after, continuity or discontinuity . . . and so on, would be able to come into our perception.

So far I agree with Kant's viewpoint which is acknowledged by many other contemporary philosophers as well. Heidegger, for example, indicates that "time is initially encountered with regard to those entities which are changeable; change is *in* time"; and that time is "the context of the fundamental kind of Being pertaining to natural beings: change, change of place, locomotion".[182] However, given the view that time is a thing of our own creation, it seems to me that we can possibly have several ways of speaking of time and change which exactly correspond to our different modes of experience. But this is not the case for Kant. He argues that "time has only one dimensionality; different times are not simultaneous but successive". "We represent the time-sequence", he continues, "by a line progressing to infinity, in which the manifold constitutes a series of one dimensionality only; and we reason from the properties of this line to all the properties of time, with this one exception, that while the parts of the line are simultaneous the parts of time are always successive".[183] In short, for Kant, there is one dimensionality of time,

[180] Kant, 1993a: 76, 78.

[181] *Ibid.*: 74.

[182] Heidegger, 1992: 3E.

[183] Kant, 1993a: 75, 77.

i.e. the "temporal rhythm given in Nature", and the only principle of time and change is successiveness.

That time has only one dimensionality and must be successive is an opinion that can be found in the work of almost every modern mainstream natural philosopher that has been discussed above. Leibniz, for example, remarked that "time is nothing but the order of succession of creatures".[184] For Locke, time can be understood through the conception of duration which like extension is derived from "the fleeting and perpetually perishing parts of succession".[185] And, this reading of time remains acceptable to many contemporary thinkers. For example, "with regard to time", Russell seems to believe that "our feeling of duration or of the lapse of time is . . . [according] to the time that has elapsed by the clock", ". . . time is constituted by duration", it "consists in an order of before and after".[186]

Yet, if an appeal to the formulation of Natural Time is made in this way, Kant's view would be that:

> These principles cannot be derived from experience, for experience would give neither strict universality nor apodeictic certainty. We should only be able to say that common experience teaches us that it is so; not that it must be so. These principles are valid as rules under which alone experiences are possible; and they instruct us in regard to the experiences, not by means of them.[187]

That is, just as the aim of Kant's philosophy is to justify the existence of a common-sense world of science corresponding to Newtonian natural science, for him Natural Time has only one dimensionality and the course of that time must be successive because our "natural experience" teaches and instructs us so.

How and in what ways, does our natural common experience teach us about Time? This, I presume, can be understood as the way in which we learn from a clock. It is true that, at first and for the most part, as Heidegger indicates, we are really concerned with "time" from a physicist's viewpoint: Our "grasping and determining of time have the character of measuring". "Measuring indicates the how-long and the when, the from- when-till-when", between two different temporal points.[188] The possibility of Natural Time that our natural experience has taught us is, thus, only the Astronomical

[184] Quoted by W. H. Newton-Smith, 1980: 6.

[185] Quoted by S. Priest, 1990: 91.

[186] Russell, 1991: 16.

[187] Kant, 1993a: 75.

[188] Heidegger, 1992: 4E.

Time by which we standardise our calendars and clocks. There are, consequently, three relative characteristics about Natural Time which a clock teaches us that correspond to Kant's notion of Time: Firstly, successiveness. It is without doubt that to measure time different peoples have used different methods to standardise their calendars and clocks. But, clearly, in doing so, they must have accepted a common proposition prior to all calendars and clocks, that is, the proposition of the existence of a temporal sequence, a conception of successiveness. Through our common sense (that is to say, natural experience), we do commonly believe that 1998 must be successive to 1997; 4:01 must be successive to 4:00. Secondly, irreversibility. Simply learning from a calendar and a clock, we also often believe that a past hour will never return. We cannot reverse Human History. Thirdly, absoluteness. It follows from above that any span between any two different temporal points must be absolute in the sense that, with the same clock and calendar, the quantitative measure of that span can be attained by men with certainty. It is at this point that S. W. Hawking simply calls the traditional paradigm of reading Time as that of "Absolute Time".[189]

What follows from the existence of unique History and the notion of successiveness is the definition of History as the course of successive events. But what is more, the Enlightenment thinkers were also likely to apply scientific methods to the study of history. "Perhaps", Voltaire wrote, "the same change which has lately happened in physics may soon take place in the manner of writing history". Later, he reiterated that "history is in the same situation as mathematics and physics: its scope has increased tremendously".[190]

With scientific belief and the notions of universal human nature and progress, as already mentioned, the eighteenth-century Rationalists tried to write history *en philosophe*, the result of which was an unhistorical study of Universal History. Irrespective of its metaphysical approach to reading History, however, the ambition to assimilate history into the scientific category of genuine knowledge was later to be rehabilitated in pro-positivist historiography by keeping the identification of the historical with a discovery of the course of successive events. To this I must now turn.

---

[189] S. W. Hawking, 1988: chap. 2.
[190] Quoted by T. R. Tholfsen, 1967: 106.

II.4.3. Neo-Positivism and The Turning Point of Modern Philosophy

In considering positivist historiography, I think it is proper to focus mainly on the notion of scientific history refined by neo-positivism appearing at the beginning of the century. And here, I would like to start with the character of neo-positivism in general in relation to the turning point of modern philosophy. As we shall see, it was exactly within this context that Oakeshott's *Experience and Its Modes* worked as well.

The whole of Western thinking, Heidegger once argued, is metaphysical thinking. Modern philosophy, as we have reviewed it, is linked to a general theory of reality and a universal system of knowledge. From Descartes to Kant philosophical thought as a whole was pursued under the name of metaphysics; and in the early nineteenth century there finally developed "the most remarkable flowerings of metaphysical speculation" with the Subjective Idealism of Fichte and Schelling, the Absolute Idealism of Hegel, Schopenhauer's philosophy of the world as presentation and will, Nietzsche's philosophy of the will to power and so forth.[191] Therefore, it is arguable that since the turn of the century modern metaphysics has disintegrated. Kant once regarded the battles between earlier metaphysical systems as a "scandal" and tried to overcome this. His own "universal solution", however, has failed to win "universal acceptance". For post-Kantian German philosophers, Kant's metaphysical judgement was closely related to his own system. But no one escaped Kant's dilemma. When Fichte declared that philosophy is the fundamental science, he was referring to his own theory, to his *Wissenschaftslehre*, as did Schelling, Hegel and Nietzsche. In short, they all claimed their metaphysical systems to be universal, but it is questionable that their philosophies are mutually compatible.

Moreover, the demise of metaphysics was also due to the growth of separate disciplines in the human and natural sciences which posed a serious challenge to the unity of Reason. In the nineteenth century the Hegelian notion of philosophy as the only genuine "scientific knowledge of truth" in realising the Absolute was fundamentally resisted not only by scientists trained in laboratory methods of every specific scientific field but by professional historians attempting to write a history rather than to seize on the whole meaning of History. All this implies historical and scientific provocation for traditional metaphysics. One German scholar thus argues, "(n)ineteenth-century consciousness as a whole achieved its eman-

[191] F. Copleston, 1960: 1.

cipation from idealism [Hegelian metaphysics] in the name of science and history".[192] Consequently, philosophers were confronted by "the crisis of philosophical-identity"; they had to rethink the nature and purpose of their own task. And in so doing, the question of "What is the real task of philosophy" was identified and linked to that of "What is the principal relationship of philosophy to science and history as a model and to the human and natural sciences as specific forms of research?"; and most of them went further by asking "What is the relationship of science to history?".

The dispute, like its origins, took place primarily within a specific philosophical context: that of German philosophy in the late nineteenth century; but by the beginning of the twentieth century it had spread to the whole of the Western world. Insofar as the currents of thought worth mentioning were logical positivism's attempts to re-construct a philosophical synthesis of different sciences, and neo-Kantianism's attempts to reduce philosophy to the *scientia scientiarum*, i.e. the science of all sciences. And, it is their shared belief that even though philosophy might no longer serve a metaphysical system, it could, under the name of epistemology, still function as the "methodological foundation of all scientific knowledge". The notions such as "the synthesis of the sciences" (positivism), and *scientia scientiarum* (neo-Kantianism) are thus no more than an attempt to re-formulate an integral philosophical system which is associated with an "extraneous" interest of the natural sciences. Here, for the purpose of this study, we need to talk about the case of positivism in more detail.

Neo-positivism or logical positivism was originally launched by an intellectual group known as the "Vienna Circle" whose participants included M. Schlick, R. Carnap and O. Neurath, among other thinkers. Broadly speaking, however, it may also include those non-Circle philosophers such as A. J. Ayer, Karl Popper[193] and C. Hempel. In many respects, logical positivism fell within the movement of "analytical philosophy" as a whole, one of the most substantial contemporary philosophical movements which was initiated by G. E. More and B. Russell; more particularly, the "Vienna

[192] Quoted by C. R. Bambach, 1990: 42.

[193] Popper disliked to be identified as a positivist for two main reasons: firstly, he has a different view concerning the demarcation of science and non-science, namely, the idea of falsifiability, and secondly he emphasises the importance of "critical reason" or "theoretical conjecture" in promoting the progress of scientific research. However, insofar as the naturalistic assumptions in historiography are concerned, it is undeniable that Popper has influenced the work of neo-positivists, especially the covering-law model developed by C. Hempel.

Circle" also used to be regarded as having been "influenced" by the early Wittgenstein's *Tractatus Logico-Philosophicus*.[194] In this study I merely intend to highlight three central doctrines of logical positivism by comparing each of them with the foundationalist assumptions in philosophy referred to above.

First of all, scientism. Just as modern natural philosophy was influenced by the work of Galileo and Newton, logical positivism adopted the benefits of the recent developments in logic and mathematics to enhance its analysis of language. In other words, for logical positivists all knowledge proper comprises logical and mathematical truths, i.e. scientific knowledge, and the common belief is that logic and the principles of mathematics can be taken as a new instrument for solving many meaningless traditional philosophical problems. One might even remark that logical positivists were "science-intoxicated" in the sense that "it was almost as if philosophy were synonymous with the philosophy of science, which in turn was synonymous with the study of logic (language) of science".[195]

Secondly, a foundationalist analysis of knowledge. It is suggested above that with the tool of logical analysis, positivism aimed to provide new and more reliable foundations for science.[196] Before the Vienna Circle, Russell in his *Principia Mathematica* had already envisaged the so-called mathematical logic or symbolic logic which, unlike traditional logic dealing with the categories of things, makes an investigation into propositions or sentences presenting the linguistic structure of the world. According to Russell, any native language has a basic structure corresponding to that of the world and by putting the sentences of language into their proper symbolic logical forms all information about the world may be acquired. On the other hand, following the Russellian method of symbolism, Wittgenstein in his *Tractatus* also tried to set out a new theory of representation, i.e. "the picture theory of representation" in which a perfect language is thought to be a map capable of mirroring the world.

In a like manner, logical positivism takes a realist position towards the world and uses language as a method for analysis. And it was to round off their ideal of constructing the world within a framework of language: sentences, statements or propositions, that

[194] Note that the influential relation between logical positivism and early Wittgenstein has sometimes been called into question. See, for example, A. C. Grayling, 1988: 55-62.

[195] N. Fotion, 1995: 508.

[196] This tendency, indeed, can be found in the title of Vienna Circle's Manifesto itself: "The Scientific Conception of the World: The Vienna Circle".

Schlick, Carnap and their fellow positivists arrived at what is today believed to be the most central issue in logical positivism, i.e. verificationism, or the motto that "the sense of a proposition is the method of its verification".[197] In other words, for them, the meaning of a proposition relies on some sort of actual step we take to decide on its truth or falsity: "The principle of verification", as Ayer puts it, "is supposed to furnish a criterion by which it can be determined whether or not a sentence is literally meaningful".[198] Although many discussions have arisen around the principle of verifiability or the theory of meaning in the work of logical positivists, in one way or another they all contain an attempt to clarify the truth-value of scientific statements as the only genuine description of the world.

In the case of Ayer, for example, meaningful statements are divided into two categories: analytical propositions which are true by definition or by an appeal to the grammatical structure that constitutes them, and part of synthetic propositions which can be verified by sense-experience. For Ayer, as for many logical positivists, the former category is a tautology which has no factual implications and thus tells us nothing important about the world itself; while it is the latter category that contains the possibility for us to determine the truth-value of all *sciences* and to exclude those meaningless statements as pseudo-questions. That is, since the language of the *sciences* such as natural sciences (except mathematics), metaphysics, ethics, aesthetics, history and so forth, can all be transformed into synthetic statements: "water is composed of H_2O", "God exists", "rape is wrong", "this picture is beautiful" or "Ayer was born in 1910", their meaningfulness may be established by putting them to a verifiability test. And it is not surprising that for Ayer metaphysics, aesthetics and ethics are the three subjects which would fail to meet the criterion of verifiability. For the sentences like "water is composed of H_2O" may be verified as true or false by empirical experiment, and so it is scientific. The other three things at issue, however, are said to be neither true nor false as they are beyond the realm of our sense-experience; and as such they are synthetically *meaningless*. Here we arrive at one of the most distinguished features of the positivist movement, i.e. anti-metaphysics.

Thirdly, universalism. The notion of superiority, reunification and universality of Scientific Reason was also fully re-located in the neo-positivist project of the synthesis of sciences. As one scholar comments, for logical positivists "only those statements about the

[197] J. Skorupski, 1993: 201.

[198] A. J. Ayer, 1987: 7.

world whose content can be controlled by means accessible to all are entitled to the name of knowledge", and that "there are no legitimate ways of attaining knowledge of the world other than those used by natural science and mathematics".[199]

II.4.4. Popper and Hempel: Scientific History

The claim that all meaningful statements are scientific statements in the sense of being observable and verifiable would have given logical positivism the ability to fuse the *sciences* by maintaining that the language of any other *sciences* should be transformed into scientific statements in order to be true. And this foundationalist proposal was eventually confirmed in the Popperian-Hempelian covering law model.

Popper conceded that "history is characterised by its interest in actual, singular, or specific events, rather than in laws or generalisation";[200] and those whose interests are in laws, Popper argued, should concentrate on the generalising sciences such as sociology.[201] However, historical particularity does not alter the fact that the study is a genuine science because historical explanation still conforms in its essential structure to scientific explanation, based on the premise that "while the theoretical sciences are mainly interested in finding and testing universal laws, the historical sciences take all kinds of universal laws for granted and are mainly interested in finding and testing singular statements".[202] This is to say that "a singular event is the cause of another singular event — which is its effect — only relative to some universal laws. But these laws may be so trivial, so much part of our common knowledge, that we need not mention them and rarely notice them".[203] In other words, Popper claims that while the historian is describing a particular event he is involved in a "disentanglement of causal threads"[204] which are interwoven and supplement each other. Therefore, from the standpoint of its causality, explanations of historical events are always typical and scientific; although from the standpoint of the historian's mentality, they are peculiar and unique.

---

[199] L. Kolakowski, 1972: 207.

[200] K. Popper, 1957: 143.

[201] Cf. K. Popper, 1962: 264.

[202] K. Popper, 1957: 143-4.

[203] *Ibid.*: 145.

[204] *Ibid.*: 147.

Hempel, on the other hand, provides us with a similar but more comprehensive consideration on the subject at issue. In his classical work, "The Function of General Laws in History", he attempts to emphasise three premises: First, general laws or universal hypotheses have quite "analogous functions" in history and in the natural sciences; second, they offer an "indispensable instrument" for historical study; and third, they even constitute the "common basis of various procedures" which have often been taken to separate the social and historical from the scientific.[205]

On the first topic, Hempel first asks us to look at the logical structure of a physical explanation. Suppose that a set of events $C1, C2, \ldots Cn$ have occurred within which the situation E is to be explained. According to Hempel, the explanation of the occurrence of E must consist of:

(1) a set of statements asserting the occurrence of certain events $C1, C2, \ldots Cn$ at certain times and places, [i.e. the "determining conditions" for the event to be explained]

(2) a set of universal hypotheses, such that

    (a) the statements of both groups are reasonably well confirmed by empirical evidence,

    (b) from the two groups of statements the sentence asserting the occurrence of event E can be logically deduced.[206]

The second point that Hempel reminds us of is that even when the logical structure of a scientific "prediction" parallels the structure of a scientific explanation, the difference is a pragmatic one: while in a scientific explanation the event to be explained is known to have happened and its determining conditions have to be sought, in a scientific prediction the initial conditions are given and their "effect" has to be determined. Ideally, a complete scientific explanation may well exhibit predictive character at the same time, but this rarely happens as the determining conditions are frequently incomplete.

Based on these views, Hempel moved to prove that historical explanation in nature makes no different to scientific explanation:

> Historical explanation, too, aims at showing that the event in question was not "a matter of chance", but was to be expected in view of certain antecedent or simultaneous conditions. The expectation referred to is not prophecy or divination, but rational scientific anticipation which rests on the assumption of general laws.[207]

[205] C. Hempel, 1965: 231.

[206] *Ibid.*: 232.

[207] *Ibid.*: 235.

And like Popper, Hempel upholds two possible replies to the rejection of resorting to general laws in history: First, in history general laws are often "tacitly taken for granted" as they are familiar to everybody through everyday experience; and secondly, frequently hidden behind the terms such as "hence", "therefore", "consequently, "because", "naturally", "obviously" etc., is "the tacit presupposition of some general law".[208]

Hempel does not deny that in most cases historical explanations are based on the assumption of probability hypotheses rather than on general "deterministic" laws in the form of universal conditions. But since this situation also exists in many empirical sciences it remains true that the logical form of historical explanation corresponds to that of the empirical sciences. Similarly, the contention that the content of the Human Past is too infinite to be generalised also seems irrelevant to Hempel. Even though this may be the case, Hempel argues, historical explanation may be understood as something like an "explanation sketch" which "consists of a more or less vague indication of the laws and initial conditions considered as relevant, and it needs 'filling out' in order to turn into a full-fledged explanation".[209] In this case, history no less than science is a progressive process in which hypotheses could gain empirical import while evidence could well be confirmed. And consequently, although the function of historical prediction may be very limited, it is not impossible. In short, what really excludes historical explanation from being scientific is not its probability and sketchy explanation but the attempt to mistake any metaphysical theory of History as an explanation plan, for Hempel's fellow positivists have already ruled out the testability of such a plan.

For Hempel, then, general laws are indispensable to historical study. In developing this idea, Hempel takes the historicist method of "empathic understanding" as his target further and refers to it as nothing more than a "heuristic device" whose function is to provide "psychological hypotheses" which serve as the explanatory principles we are considering. Also, Hempel argues, these explanatory principles stand behind the other research procedures that scholars take to distinguish the social and historical from the scientific, the procedures such as the "interpretation of historical phenomena", the "meaning of given historical events", the "analysis of the development of the institution", and the "notions of determination and of dependence" and the like. In the case of the "meaning of given his-

---

[208] *Ibid.*: 236.
[209] *Ibid.*: 238.

torical events", for example, Hempel argues that its scientific import lies in it aiming to determine the causal and effective relation of other events to the event concerned; and as such the statement of the relevant connections must involve the form of explanations or explanation sketches which contain universal hypotheses.

By claiming this, Hempel's point is not really about the plausibility of "empathic understanding" or the workability of the procedures in question; but rather it is to reaffirm the positivist general belief that our logical reasoning is so penetrating that it could help us discover a *universal* logical structure about the entire world, a structure which, no matter how willing we are to recognise it or not, we can never set our language free from it. The consequences for historiography arising from Hempel's viewpoints are two: First, the historian cannot confine his research to a description of the Past without applying "hypothetical generalisation and theory-construction" to his research; and second, it is groundless to claim the autonomy of history from the united scientific world.[210]

II.4.5. Naturalism in Historiography

Although A. J. Ayer once doubted "whether we have sufficient ground for accepting any statement at all about the past, whether we are even justified in our belief that there has been a past",[211] the Popperian-Hempelian covering law model has clearly assumed otherwise. For them, the events in History are in no fundamental way different from those in Nature. They are "what really happened" in the Past — existing objectively and independently of the historian and waiting to be discovered by him.

That is to say, when Popper remarked that "a singular [historical] event is the cause of another singular event", and Hempel maintained that historical statements like the scientific statements which assert "the occurrence of certain events C_1, C_2, ... C_n at certain times and places", they are saying History is a temporal series of successive events in accordance with the notion of Time as successiveness. Put differently, that the historian always takes general laws for granted can be true only if the temporal structure that underlies causal explanation has been identified as successive such that the causality of events may be pre-determined as an existing fact without recognition by the historian.

---

[210] *Ibid.*: 243.
[211] A. J. Ayer, 1954: 168.

At this point, it may be inferred that the roots of this conception of explanation lie in Hume's theory of causation,[212] according to which all we can ever observe is the "constant conjunction" of events, but which does not deny the existence of the natural world. That is, the covering law model is based on the belief that History exists in the same way as Nature does, and thus the temporal rhythm given in Nature must be likewise given to History: they are both the occurrence of successive events.

It follows that the theory of history in question presupposes at the same time the view, shared by traditional positivism, that the task of the historian is simply to discover the course of events as it really was. In other words, according to pro-positivism, in view of the fact that History exists as objectively as Nature, the business of an historian is only to make a "historical picture" which exactly corresponds with that objective Past World. As Ranke remarked in the 1830s, it is "simply to show how it really was (*wie es eigentlich gewesen*)",[213] but not to think, judge or criticise historical evidence in his mind. What Popper and Hempel tried to do, as a result, was to make the most sense of Bury's motto: "history is a science; no less, and no more".

Thus far, then, we have reviewed modern naturalised historical thought from the *philosophes* to neo-positivists. To conclude, we may revise the Enlightenment historiographical position with the following propositions:

(3) **naturalism in historiography** stands for the ideal of scientific history by identifying the historical with a naturalised conception of History which suggests

    (3.1) **the existence of History as the only legitimate object of historical study**, that is, the Cartesian belief that there exists only one genuine answer corresponding to any historical question that may be asked, and defines

    (3.2) **History as the course of successive events**, governed by Time in Nature, i.e. the notion of Absolute Time as successiveness; as a result, (following Lockean representation in the case of pro-positivism), historical study is understood as the representation of what really happened by

    (3.3) **applying scientific methods (such as general laws) to historical explanation and analysis**, insofar as the scientific objectivity of historical knowledge can be secured as it abides by the epistemological conditions which have been successfully used to explain the relation of mind to Nature.

[212] Cf. W. Outhwaite, 1987: 7-9.

[213] Quoted by E. H. Carr, 1961: 9.

Like formalism in ethics, the above discussions show that natural-ism in historiography is a theoretical extension of modern foundationalism. Before leaving this section, let us revisit some philosophical problems which have emerged from the Enlighten-ment historical position as such.

II.4.6. *The Problems of the Enlightenment Historical Position*

In the first place, it appears to me that naturalism in historiography produces a self-contradiction about the temporal character of his-tory. For while the first and second statements above hold the histor-ical to be unrepeatable, particular and past, ironically the third statement must come to discard history as genuine knowledge since modern epistemological conditions suggest that knowledge must be repeatable, general and present. Or alternatively, in the specific case of pro-positivist historiography, the pastness of history must be in conflict with its own motto that "the real is the observable in the present".[214] Hence, the three assumptions together within the juris-diction of the Cartesian-Kantian tradition of philosophy demon-strate an intricate "temporal dilemma in history".

Secondly, the application of scientific method (such as general laws) to history is doubtful; it provides too easy an escape from the tension between scientific generalisation and historical particular-ity. As a matter of fact, it is exactly due to this "epistemic tension in history" that seventeenth-century thought *basically* "concentrated itself on the problems of natural science and left those of history on one side";[215] that "it has always tended to look to the natural sciences for material for its studies, and has formed its criteria of what to accept as known by reference to scientific models".[216] Descartes, for example, expelled history from the body of genuine knowledge at the beginning of his *Discourse on the Method*.[217] For, it is evident that the scientific method aims to formulate generalisations; but history in essence is something particular. Hence, in *The Idea of History*, Collingwood refers to Schopenhauer to demonstrate this anti-historical epistemological situation:

---

[214] Cf. H. Kragh, 1987: 41-2.

[215] R. G. Collingwood, 1946: 59.

[216] W. H. Walsh, 1967: 12.

[217] It may be argued that Leibniz was once an historian, and Hume wrote his *History of England*, for instance. Be that as it may, it seems to me that they basically treated history as a way of moral education, a discipline of morality rather than as a genuine way to understand the world, a legitimate mode of knowledge.

[History] lacks the fundamental characteristic of science, namely the subordination of the objects of consciousness; all it can do is to present a simple co-ordination of the facts it has registered. Hence there is no system in history as there is in the other sciences . . . The sciences, being systems of cognition, speak always of kinds; history always of the individual, which implies a self-contradiction.[218]

Indeed, the eighteenth-century *philosophes*, as we have seen, had expressed an ambition to undergo "the conquest of the historical world".[219] But, the obstacle presented to them was thus: If history remains defined in terms of its essence of particularity and pastness, agreement would lie with the thinkers such as Descartes and Locke to place history in a secondary position beneath philosophy and science; however, if the legitimacy of history is claimed in terms of the epistemological condition of generalisation and presentness, it could only be done at the price of destroying the essence of historical thinking. With the notions of Universal Reason and progress, the *philosophes* seem to have taken the second alternative, by assimilating history into science.

Given the growth of historical interest since the nineteenth century, positivism has thus tried to establish the nature of the historical by rejecting any metaphysical reading of Human History. However, the notion of scientific history still calls for the application of general laws to historical study. Both Popper and Hempel aim to adjust the tension between the scientific general and the historical particular by assuming that the scientific structure of the world (including History) is a necessary premise of existence that the historian cannot escape and that it does not conflict with the historian's interest in particularity. However, their philosophy eventually penetrates into their historiography to recommend that history can be a progressive scientific-like discipline if the historian is conscious of the general laws embodied in explanation and establishes a framework for their inquiry. But, as Oakeshott puts it, "the moment historical facts are regarded as instances of general laws, history is dismissed".[220]

It appears to me that these pitfalls remain unsolved within the theoretical framework of neo-positivism. For the foundation of positivism, as it has been shown, is established within modern natural philosophy in terms of scientism, dualism-representationism and universalism upon which its claim of historical study as a representation of "what really happened" in the Past is based. Instead,

[218] R. G. Collingwood, 1946: 167.

[219] E. Cassirer, 1979: chap. v.

[220] *EM*: 154; also quoted by W. Dray, 1957: 49-50.

neo-positivists are new *philosophes* with a *more* confident belief in harnessing the Enlightenment technocratic premises by overcoming its main adversary, i.e. "history". The *characteristica universalis* Leibniz favours predicts exactly the project of the fusion of sciences. Like the *philosophes*, then, neo-positivists maintain the scientific objectivity of historical knowledge at the price of dismissing genuine historicity in what today may be termed the debate over "the autonomy of history".

But possibly, the lesson that the assimilationists (as opposed to autonomists)[221] have to learn is that if all human utterance is in one mode, our civilisation will be tedious and humdrum. And, if the interest of history as a narrative of traditional and historical teachings is to be replaced by that of a set of rules, it would deepen the moral and political crisis that the Enlightenment project carries. For, as already indicated, what is required to fill in the "emptiness" of the Enlightenment's conception of rationality may be a kind of historical study which aims to offer us the *concrete* moral and political exemplifications that have been placed in a vacuum by a scientific attempt to discover the *abstract* justification for ethics.

In short, scholars have for a long time been incapable of setting history free from the naturalistic traps. And, this inability to act is not simply because a philosopher may not also be a good historian; but, more importantly, it is because the naturalistic forms of pseudo-historical ideas arise from a great tradition within which many philosophers still work, i.e. the Cartesian-Kantian tradition of natural philosophy. Consequently, it is my view — a view which penetrates throughout my examination of Oakeshott's historiography — that a search for genuine historicity not only needs a historiography reflecting the conditions of historical thinking; but it needs a non-Cartesian-Kantian, i.e. a non-naturalistic or non-scientific meaning of philosophy itself.

---

[221] E. Breisach, 1994: 327.

Chapter III

Philosophy and Modes of Experience

III.1. Introduction: Some Interpretative Problems

Having investigated the Enlightenment positions in the last chapter, we now turn to examine Oakeshott's reflection upon philosophical modernity, liberal ethics and positivist historiography respectively. Here, let us first start with an analysis of Oakeshott's non-foundationalist notion of philosophy, on which his sceptical politics and his idealistic historiography rest.

This chapter, more specifically, is a study of *Experience and Its Modes* (1933; hereafter *EM*), which is Oakeshott's major philosophical work. However, it appears to me that there are some difficulties in attempting to interpret Oakeshott's philosophical work in general and *EM* in particular. First of all, as Oakeshott believes that "there are no 'authorities' in philosophy", that "there is no book which is indispensable for the study of philosophy", he has often omitted to acknowledge the authors against whom his theory of experience argues, and he has merely remarked in passing that he is conscious of having learnt most from Hegel's *Phenomenology of Spirit* and Bradley's *Appearance and Reality*.[1] Being an interpreter whose concern is to make the writer more understandable, in this study I not only intend to decipher *EM* by reference to rationalism, empiricism and the Kantian "thing-in-itself", i.e. the aspects of philosophical thought to which Oakeshott mainly objects, but I also wish to clarify

---

[1]   *EM*: 8, 6. For the influence on Oakeshott of idealism in general and of British idealism in particular, see D. Boucher, 1984: 194-202.

especially the extent to which his writings are influenced by Bradley's work.

Another interpretative problem in the study of Oakeshott is that one of the main tasks which Oakeshott has constantly taken on during his academic life is to categorise the modes of human activity for the interest of philosophy itself. His undertaking however is too unique to be fitted neatly into any of the main categories. As M. Cranston, Oakeshott's former colleague at the LSE, put it:

> [Oakeshott] is a traditionalist with few traditional beliefs, an "idealist" who is more sceptical than many positivists, a lover of liberty who repudiates liberalism, an individualist who prefers Hegel to Locke, a philosopher who disapproves of *philosophisme*, a romantic perhaps (if Hume could also be called one), and a marvellous stylist. Oakeshott's voice is unique.[2]

Here, with *EM* alone we cannot yet gain a complete understanding of Oakeshott's political ideas, although it is where the thinker's conception of a "philosophy of practical experience"[3] is envisaged. But, to make Oakeshott's philosophical position clearer, in what follows I shall pay careful attention to his qualified statements on idealism, scepticism and non-foundationalism (non-*philosophisme*), and to his rejections of historicism, logical positivism and pragmatism.

From the standpoint I have been taking, the non-foundationalist character of Oakeshott's philosophical thought in *EM* is the most crucial point to which this chapter points. All through the examination below there will appear several perspectives leading to the idiosyncrasies of *EM*, and a comprehensive synthesis will be set out in [III.4.]. Also, it is my view that Oakeshott's unique philosophical voice has in fact provided an exception to Rorty's concern about the necessary connection between epistemology and foundationalism; what he offers us is a non-post-modernist critique of philosophical modernity.

Perhaps, not wishing to assimilate Oakeshott's metaphysical feature in *EM* to his "conversational" feature in *Rationalism in Politics* (1962; hereafter *RP*), previous research has sometimes interpreted Oakeshott as having changed his mind on the conception of philosophy from *EM* to *RP*.[4] And, with the recent publication of S. A. Gerencser's book-length study of Oakeshott's political

---

[2]   M. Cranston, 1967: 82.

[3]   *EM*: 249.

[4]   See, for example, T. Modood, 1980: 315-22; B. Parekh, 1979: 487-8; J. Gray, 1989: 202.

thought, this interpretation seems to have become more and more prominent.[5]

My view, however, is that *EM* can be basically taken as "propaedeutic" or as a "research programme" which sets out the initial steps leading to the consequent development of Oakeshott's ideas of history, politics, education, aesthetics and indeed philosophy in his later work.[6] As T. Nardin correctly remarks, in *On Human Conduct* (1975; hereafter *HC*), "as in most of his later writings, Oakeshott is pursuing the intimations of ideas articulated in *Experience and Its Modes*".[7] In other words, I believe that Oakeshott's "general philosophical position has remained constant throughout",[8] and what seems to have changed from one stage to another is just a matter of terminology. From one standpoint, I shall argue that Oakeshott's "sceptical idealism" in *EM* (a combination which, for me, differs from the way in which Cranston observes it) may have embraced the attempt to revive Montaignean traditionalist elements to balance against the emptiness of Rationalism in *RP*. And, from another standpoint, that which may be considered as linking together all of Oakeshott's philosophical texts is his repeated insistence on (1) the non-foundationalist notion of philosophy in terms of three characteristics: self-independence, self-limitation and scepticism, and (2) the self-consistency of modes of experience.

In interpreting *EM*, my approach will be arranged as follows: First and foremost, I shall account for Oakeshott's theory of experience and modality ([III.3.]), such that we may be in the best position to grasp his concept of philosophy in terms of the three non-foundationalist characteristics at stake ([III.4.]). And then I shall turn to take the mode of practice as a test case to show further the categorical distinction amongst philosophy and modes of experience illustrated by Oakeshott ([III.5.]). Before we move on to the main body of *EM* itself, nonetheless, it would be advantageous to make some preliminary remarks on the setting of the work from the outset ([III.2.]).

---

[5]   See S. A. Gerencser, 2000: chaps.1-2.

[6]   See, for example, R. Grant, 1990: 37; K. Minogue, 1993a: 44; T. Fuller, 1991: xiii; P. Franco, 1990a: 66.

[7]   T. Nardin, 2001: 17.

[8]   W. H. Greenleaf, 1966: 5.

III.2. The Aim and Background of the Work

Regarding the context of *EM*, there are a number of issues that must be *initially* marked out in this section, and each will be developed in the discussions that follow. For the sake of clarity, I shall put these issues into two categories: the aim of *EM*, and the idealistic background of Oakeshott's thought.

III.2.1. The Aim of the Work

It seems unquestionable that the intellectual environment within which *EM* establishes itself concerns the debate over the nature of philosophy in terms of the question "What is the relation of philosophy to science and to history?", launched by neo-positivism, neo-Kantism and historicism at the turn of the century.[9] Oakeshott's persistent rejection of any form of scientism is well-known today. The scientific voices embroiled in the dispute, as mentioned in the previous chapter, include logical positivism trying to re-construct a philosophical synthesis of different sciences, and neo-Kantians trying to reduce philosophy to the *scientia scientiarum* (i.e. the science of all sciences). In the introduction to *EM*, Oakeshott exactly cites the names "the fusion of sciences" and *scientia scientiarum* by questioning them thus:

> Yet, what are the sciences that they must be accepted as datum, and as a datum not to be changed, of valid knowledge? And if we begin with sciences, can our conclusion be other or more than merely scientific? These and other questions like them are what anyone must consider who, in search of a complete and satisfactory world of experience, is tempted by science.[10]

For Oakeshott, the only complete and satisfactory world of experience is philosophy itself; and "when philosophy is sought, it must be sought for its own sake".[11] That is, according to Oakeshott, what appears to be fundamentally wrong with the logical positivist's attempt to appeal to the authority of science in philosophy, among other things, is the commitment to a categorical mistake of identifying philosophy with the scientific, which would at once destroy both the self-independence of philosophy and the self-consistency of science.[12]

Thus, in the positivist–historicist debate Oakeshott is equally against positivism and historicism. The latter claims that since

[9]   Cf. P. Franco, 1990a: 3-4, 13-5.

[10]   *EM*: 2.

[11]   *EM*: 3.

[12]   Cf. *RPML*: 142.

human understanding must be "a 'captive' of the *historical* condition",[13] all knowledge proper is historical; as a result, a similar sort of categorical confusion is made over philosophy and history. On this reading, it may be indicated here that Oakeshott's scepticism is never absorbed into an extreme form of relativism which dissolves the value of philosophy, but rather the point pervading throughout his thought is that philosophy is a self-independent universe of discourse having interests of its own, and it is self-limited and sceptical only in the sense that, in the process of philosophising, it does not interfere with the autonomous logic of modes of experience such as history and science. What Oakeshott rejects, in other words, is the despotism of positivism (which has earlier been disclosed as a form of foundationalism) and the pessimism of historicism rather than the importance of our scientific and historical knowledge or the legitimacy of philosophical thinking itself.

Oakeshott's bid to transcend both scientism and historicism is, of course, important to this book. But there is a third type of thought which constitutes Oakeshott's life-long target and thus needs to be emphasised where appropriate, that is, pragmatism.[14] Generally speaking, as W. James puts it, pragmatism suggests that "the whole function of philosophy ought to be to find out what definite difference it will make to you and me, at definite instants of our life, if this world-formula or that world-formula be the true one".[15] In other words, pragmatism maintains that the value of knowledge is determined by its contribution to the practical world, and so it comes under attack in *EM* for its lack of a categorical distinction between theory (philosophy) and practice.

In short, *EM* can be regarded as Oakeshott's response to the turning point of modern philosophy and he tries to find an alternative answer to the problem of the nature of philosophy rather than pursuing those solutions which have been offered by positivism, historicism and pragmatism. This is, accordingly, the main reason

---

[13]   R. D'Amico, 1989: x.

[14]   In discussing pragmatism Oakeshott cites the name of W. James alone (see *EM*: 318-9). But, in contemporary philosophy there are numerous forms of "pragmatism". For example, Habermas also takes the view that "all knowledge is practical knowledge because it is a tool for making sense of the world in relation to human concerns", and in the hermeneutic tradition of Heidegger and Gadamer it is argued that "all knowledge must reflect the interests of the interpreter" (T. Nardin, 2001: 9, 8; cf. 81-2, 94, 108). Following Oakeshott, however, I shall limit the meaning of pragmatism to its American connections.

[15]   W. James, 1995: 20. For a general discussion about the development of pragmatism in the States, see J. P. Murphy, 1990.

why in this pure philosophical work Oakeshott attests history, science and practice to be three abstract modes of experience in his act of clarifying the meaning of philosophy.[16] For, if philosophy is to be self-independent, according to Oakeshott it must be self-critical thought which does not rely for its authority on science, history or practice as positivism, historicism and pragmatism have respectively argued.

The attempt to categorise the diversified reasons for philosophy and modes of experience has given us a hint about Oakeshott's aversion to an integral philosophical system, i.e. *philosophisme*. At the beginning of *EM* Oakeshott thus writes that "there is little or nothing in common between the philosopher and the *philosophe*".[17] And throughout the work, Oakeshott's intention is to offer his readers a possible view of philosophy rather than an institution of *philosophie*. To elaborate on this anti-*philosophisme* aim of *EM*, I think, we may further refer to "The New Bentham", an article published one year before *EM*.[18]

In understanding Bentham as a typical *philosophe*, Oakeshott singles out the three prime elements in this type of mind. Firstly, according to Oakeshott, "an age of *philosophisme* implies a peculiar confidence in knowledge, indiscriminate knowledge; it implies an hydropic thirst for information about the present world, its composition and its laws, and about human nature, its needs and desires".[19] That is, *philosophisme* is the belief in the pursuit of encyclopaedic knowledge; indeed, *philosophisme* is foundationalism. "At all events in these days when we are more conscious of the futility of knowl-

---

[16]   In addition to history, science, and practice, a study of aesthetics or artistic experience is supplemented in *VP*. Moreover, it is noticeable that Oakeshott's posthumous book, *RPML*, embraces a series of essays on religion written in the late 1920s. He records in a letter to P. Riley that: "… I would like, more than anything else, to extend those brief pages in *On Human Conduct* into an essay … on religion, and particularly on Christian religion" (quoted by G. Worthington, 2000: 377). Yet, Oakeshott's reflections on religion seem to have much more to do with "an understanding of religion and the place of God in his political philosophy" than with the philosophical features of religion as a mode of understanding (R. Devigne, 1999: 132). That is, for Oakeshott "religion is practical activity" and "it is different from other forms of practice only by degree"; "religious experience may require a poetic dimension, but it does so without shedding its practical character" (T. Nardin: 66, 67; cf. 60-9). For an overall investigation into the religious and aesthetical aspects of Oakeshott's political philosophy, see G. Worthington, 2000, 2002.

[17]   *EM*: 1.

[18]   "The New Bentham" has now been collected in the new and expanded edition of *RP*: 132-50.

[19]   *RP*: 138.

edge than its blessing", Oakeshott thus restates in *EM*, "it is not to be expected that an encyclopaedia will attract him who is looking for a philosophy".[20]

Secondly, "for the *philosophe* the world is divided between those who agree with him and 'fools'; 'science' is contrasted with superstition, and superstition is identified with whatever is established, generally believed or merely felt".[21] In saying this, Oakeshott is saying that for the *philosophe* if there were only one indiscriminate voice to be heard in human conversation, it would be that of science. Indeed, the most central grounding of *philosophisme* is scientism to which Oakeshott objects.

And finally, for Oakeshott, *philosophisme* or foundationalism is, without doubt, apt to Rationalism. "The genius of the *philosophe* is a genius for rationalisation, for making life and the business of life rational rather than for *seeing* the reason for it, for inculcating precise order, no matter at what expense, rather than for apprehending the existence of a subtle order in what appears to be chaotic".[22] In other words, it is the intention of the *philosophe* to establish a rational programme for conducting human practice, and to deny the traditions of the past. As a result, the ambitions of the *philosophe* such as Bentham are "to create a science of politics, to apply the scientific method to the field of law, to unite law and science, to discover some means for measuring accurately political satisfactions".[23] And yet, as Oakeshott points out, "it is not the philosopher, the victim of thought, who influences our practical conduct of life, but the philosophaster, the *philosophe*".[24] Even later in *OH*, Oakeshott retains the distinction between the philosopher and the pejorative view of the *philosophe* as the *theoretician*.[25]

Oakeshott's serious attack on Rationalism in *RP* will be individually dealt with in the next chapter. But now, it has become clear that there does exist a strong connection between the purpose of *EM* and that of *RP*; they are both concerned with the defects of *philosophisme*, foundationalism and Rationalism, i.e. the Enlightenment positions.

---

[20]   *EM*: 2.

[21]   *RP*: 139.

[22]   *RP*: 139.

[23]   *RP*: 140-1.

[24]   *RP*: 150. See also *EM*: 2.

[25]   *HC*: 26, 30.

III.2.2. Bradley (I): Appearance and Reality

What has been said so far highlights the aim of *EM*. But it should be remembered that there are two influences behind the thought of Oakeshott in *EM*, namely, Hegel and Bradley. Oakeshott's connection with Bradley, at least so far as *EM* is concerned, is much more *direct* than with Hegel. I shall merely introduce Bradley's philosophy to a point where those of his ideas, with only minor modifications and changes of emphasis, are revealed in *EM*: first, the notion of the concrete universal as the given in understanding; second, the features of truth in the light of coherence, colligibility and degrees; and third, the assumptions of reality in the light of monism, idealism and degrees.

Bradley's philosophical system was first established in his *Principles of Logic*,[26] aiming to reject the empiricist theory of the mind and its working. According to empiricism, all knowledge comes from the Lockean ideas or the Humean impressions which represent discrete facts or events making up the external world. Since each one of those facts is independent of all others, for the empiricists, the world is a *pluralist* world and reality is *the sum* of particular objects. And thus, human knowledge is made up of knowledge of separate facts, and the criterion of truth is the correspondence between experience and reality, thought and object, i.e. the mind and the external world.

For Bradley, however, empiricist representationism simply neglects the importance of "artificiality" and "generality" inherent in all "symbolism" upon which any meaningful expression of thoughts must rely. In the first place, the meaning of an idea is not dependent on the observable property that it bears, but on the use to which it is artificially put by the knower. In the second place, no meaning is in isolation, because every meaning is possessed by the general unity to which the idea being understood belongs. Or alternatively it may be said that for Bradley the meaning of an idea does not lie in its external relation to the object it represents, but in its "internal relations" to some other idea than itself. That which is given in every understanding is not the external world outside the mind but the "concrete universal" indicating a system of meanings within the mind. That is, Bradley would not deny Hegel's proverb that "the true is the whole".[27] And consequently, all facts are not separate but united in one, and truth demands the conception of coher-

[26] For the brief discussions on this work provided below see R. Wollheim, 1969: chaps. 1, 2 & 3.

[27] Hegel, 1977: 11.

ence rather than that of correspondence. Later in *Appearance and Reality*, Bradley restates this "doctrine of internal relations" conceived in his study of logic as such:

> (a) A merely external relation has no meaning or existence, for a relation must (at least to some extent) qualify its terms. (b) Relations imply a unity in which they subsist, and apart from which they have no meaning or existence. (c) Every kind of diversity, both terms and relations alike are adjectives of one reality, which exists in them and without which they are nothing.[28]

To comprehend Bradley's notions of truth and reality in more exact terms, interpreters turn to *Appearance and Reality* and *Essays On Truth and Reality*. Here, let me begin with Bradley's theory of knowledge and truth in the first instance.

Bradley believes that the development of the mind involves the elaboration of knowledge which contains three levels: (1) feeling, (2) internal relational thinking, i.e. thought, and (3) the Absolute. To start with, feeling is the undivided non-relational unity of immediate experience, that provides the foundations on which all higher forms of knowledge are constructed. Feeling has a finite content. However,

> this content is not consistent within itself, and such a discrepancy tends to destroy and to break up the stage of feeling. The matter may be briefly put thus — the finite content is irreconcilable with the immediacy of its existence. For the finite content is necessarily determined from the outside; its external relations (however negative they may desire to remain) penetrate its essence, and so carry that beyond its own being.[29]

As a result, there appears a higher form of intellectual consciousness in which an attempt is made to rectify this grossest error, that is the thought of "internal relations".

At the second stage of relational thinking, Bradley believes, the mind is concerned with negation, contradiction, identity, inference and judgement regarding ideas; as such it is about what thought is *for*, namely, truth. However, as already indicated, for Bradley truth is not the copy of Nature or the representation of objects; rather he insists that all judgements are ideal and relational. In other words, Bradley's theory of truth is necessarily in conflict with the correspondence theory of truth precisely on the account that for him

---

[28]   Bradley, 1969: 559.

[29]   *Ibid.*: 407.

thought is ideal but Nature, natural; relations are general but objects particular.[30]

Thirdly, it follows that Bradley's concept of truth is an attribute that a judgement enjoys by being the member of a unity of judgements, i.e. a system of ideas; it is not a *fixed* category outside thoughts, but a *corrigible* quality within judgements. Ideally, then, there must exist the Absolute Truth — reality as a concrete and coherent whole in which all relations are internalised — by means of which the truth value of every judgement can be tested. However, thought, i.e. internal relational thinking, by its very nature is inadequate in being able to reach such a total truth, the final stage in knowledge. On this limitation of thought, Bradley writes that:

> It [thought] aims at an all inclusive whole, not in conflict with its elements, and at elements subordinate to a self-dependent whole . . . [But such a completion], would prove destructive; such an end would emphatically make an end of mere thought. It would bring the ideal content into a form which would *be* reality itself, and where mere truth and mere thought would certainly perish . . . Thought can form the idea of an apprehension, something like feeling in directness, which contains all the character sought by its relational efforts. Thought can understand that, to reach its goal, it must get beyond relations. Yet in its nature it can find no other working means of progress. Hence it perceives that somehow this relational side of its nature must be merged and must include some other side. Such a fusion would compel thought to lose and to transcend its proper self. And the nature of this fusion thought can apprehend in vague generality, but not in detail; and it can see the reason why a detailed apprehension is impossible. Such anticipated self-transcendence *is* an Other; but to assert Other is *not* a self-contradiction.[31]

Put simply, there is a paradox inherent to all thought, that is, it "is relational and discursive, and if it ceases to be this, it commits suicide",[32] therefore what is absolutely true requires more than itself: It is only at the stage of supra-relational thought, the fusion of thoughts, that the Absolute Truth may be arrived at, and thus the apprehension of the Absolute *becomes* reality. On each occasion, it is beyond the ability of our mind, even at its most acute level of perception, to know the *detail* of the Absolute, and all that can be apprehended is nothing more than its *generality*, namely, the fact that the Absolute exists:

> Our complete inability to understand this concrete unity in detail is no good ground for our declining to entertain it. Such a ground would be

---

[30]   Cf. R. Wollheim, 1969: 168.

[31]   Bradley, 1969: 160.

[32]   *Ibid.*: 150.

irrational, and its principle could hardly everywhere be adhered to. But if we can realise at all the general features of the Absolute, if we can see that somehow they come together in a way known vaguely and in the abstract, our result is certain.[33]

Closely related to this aspect of Bradley's coherence theory of truth is, therefore, the notion of the degrees of truth. That is to say, since it is the case that our common thinking and judgement "must in the end be called conditional", we are obliged to concede that human understanding in general "can never reach as far as perfect truth, and must be content merely to enjoy more or less of *Validity*".[34] Or put another way, although logically the Absolute Truth is necessary and possible, it cannot be denied "that truth has to satisfy the intellect"[35] whereas "Absolute Truth is corrected only by passing outside the intellect".[36] And consequently, "it must be admitted that":

> in the end, no possible truth is quite true. It is a partial and inadequate translation of that which it professes to give bodily. And this internal discrepancy belongs irremovably to truth's proper character. Still the difference drawn between absolute and finite truth must none the less be upheld. For the former, in a word, is not *intellectually* corrigible. There is no intellectual alternation which could possibly, as general truth, bring it nearer to ultimate Reality.[37]

In a nutshell, then, Bradley's notion of the degrees of truth can be understood in terms of this motto: "Hence no total truth or error, only more or less of Validity".[38] R. Wollheim has given this view in four propositions which are so instructive that they can be cited as follows:[39] (1) no judgement is wholly true; (2) no judgement is entirely false; (3) no judgement is neither true nor false; (4) all judgements are partly true, partly false.

Having examined Bradley's idea of truth and knowledge, we may now turn to the issue of reality. For Bradley, whatever is self-contradicted, in the sense of being irreconcilable with its contents and existence, is phenomenal, that is, "appearance";[40] by way

---

[33] *Ibid.*: 140-1.

[34] *Ibid.*: 320, 321.

[35] *Ibid.*: 509.

[36] Quoted by R. Wollheim, 1969: 179.

[37] Bradley, 1969: 482-3.

[38] *Ibid.*: chap. xxiv.

[39] R. Wollheim, 1969: 177.

[40] As Wollheim points out, "for to him (Bradley), denying that something is real is equivalent not to saying that it is unreal but to saying that it is appearance" (*ibid.*: 208).

of contrast, "ultimate reality is such that it does not contradict itself; here is an absolute criterion".[41] On this account Bradley believes not only that feelings and thoughts, but also things, space, time, causation, activity, the self and even things-in-themselves are all phenomena.[42] In the above discussions we have already seen in brief how feelings and thoughts must be committed to self-contradiction. Here let me take just one example from those other spheres of phenomena, i.e. things. According to Bradley, the self-contradiction of a thing lies in this fact: on the one side, a thing must have an identity which persists as itself throughout time, change and motion; on the other side, however, to introduce an identified character into a thing is to enter the sphere of ideality which does not belong to existence but to relational thinking. As a result, a thing is not real in the ultimate sense, as "a thing may be identical or different according as you look at it".[43]

To Bradley, however, no matter how incomplete phenomena may appear to be, it does not follow that reality is absent in them. Far from it, Bradley states that:

> Reality is one in this sense that it has a positive nature exclusive of discord, a nature which holds throughout everything that is to be real. Its diversity can be diverse only so far as not to clash, and what seems otherwise anywhere cannot be real. And, from the other side, everything which appears must be real. Appearance must belong to reality, and it must therefore be concordant and other than it seems. The bewildering mass of phenomenal diversity must hence somehow be at unity and self-consistent; for it cannot be elsewhere than in reality, and reality excludes discord. Or again we may put it so: the real is the individual. It is one in the sense that its positive character embraces all differences in an inclusive harmony. And this knowledge, poor as it may be, is certainly more than bare negation or simple ignorance. So far as it goes, it gives us positive news about absolute reality.[44]

There are accordingly some crucial insights concerning Bradley's idea of reality that may be derived from this quotation. First of all, it implies that reality is One not Many; the world is a concrete universe not a collection of discrete facts. "Plurality and separateness without a relation of separation", says Bradley, "seems really to have no meaning".[45] Indeed, Bradley is a monist rather than a pluralist, and

---

[41]   Bradley, 1969: 120.

[42]   *Ibid.*: Book I.

[43]   *Ibid.*: 69.

[44]   *Ibid.*: 123-4.

[45]   *Ibid.*: 101.

"there is nothing which, to speak properly, is individual or perfect, except only the Absolute".[46]

Furthermore, it follows that to say that an object is phenomenal is not equal to saying that it does not exist, but that it exists as parts, aspects, i.e. appearances of the Absolute: "everything phenomenal is somehow real"; "reality without appearance would be nothing".[47] Thus, what Bradley's phenomenalist account of the Absolute really intends to show us is that the phenomena do exist but not all exist to the same extent, that is, corresponding to there being the degrees of truth, there are also degrees of reality. And yet, instead of deciding the *exact* degree of truth and reality that an idea may enjoy, it is only in fairness to the philosopher to compromise that the Absolute is so comprehensive that within it everything has a relative home for itself: "to hold a thought is, more or less vaguely, to refer it to reality".[48] Consequently, whilst Bradley's famous quote says that "the world is the best of all possible worlds, and *everything* in it is a necessary evil",[49] he is making room for Oakeshott, surely one of his best descendants, to develop the notion of degrees of truth and reality into a more sophisticated form of scepticism by adding traditionalist elements to it.

And finally, in rejecting empiricist-realism, Bradley is of course expressing a preference for idealism. For Bradley the possibility of considering further the concrete nature of the Absolute exists in the very conception of experience:

> When we ask as to the matter which fills up the empty outline, we can reply in one word, that this matter is experience. And experience means something much the same as given and present fact. We perceive, on reflection, that to be real, or even barely to exist, must be to fall within sentience. Sentient experience, in short, is reality, and what is not this is not real.[50]

That is, for Bradley as for other idealists, because no thinking can be possible outside the mind, everything understandable must be found combined with ideas, i.e. experience. And because reality is indivisible from experience, it must be nothing but experience itself.

Turning now to *EM*, one sees that its Bradleyian influence is evident and significant. First of all, Oakeshott keeps Bradley's notion of

---

[46] *Ibid.*: 217.

[47] *Ibid.*: 127, 432.

[48] *Ibid.*: 350.

[49] *Ibid.*: Preface. Also quoted in *RP*: 66.

[50] *Ibid.*: 127.

concrete universal as the given in understanding, by virtue of which he defines experience as a "single concrete whole".[51] Again, Oakeshott believes in the Bradleyian sense that truth is "what is finally satisfactory and coherent in experience"[52] (coherence), "even if truth is difficult to come at, nothing can be dismissed as mere error"[53] (degrees), and "where error is impossible, truth is inconceivable"[54] (corrigibility). What is more, Oakeshott also follows Bradley to accept that "reality is one, a single system, and it is real only as a whole"[55] (monism), that "reality is experience"[56] (idealism), and that "experience is a single whole within which modifications may be distinguished"[57] (degrees).

Many of those ideas that Oakeshott shares with Bradley are, of course, indebted to Hegel. But, due to the revised notion of the degrees of reality and truth, there are two related points that I think both Bradley and Oakeshott do not accredit to Hegel: the "absolute" and the "hierarchy of knowledge". In Oakeshott's case, this revision has occurred in his philosophy with the consequences of self-limitation and scepticism which concede the self-consistency of modes of experience. Let me now try to expand on this matter.

III.2.3. The Absolute and the Hierarchy

The major purpose of Hegel's *Phenomenology of Spirit*, as we know, is to describe the "coming-to-be of *Science as such* or of *Knowledge*",[58] by way of an analysis of how the Spirit will undergo a series of phases, stages or moments in order to achieve its final position, i.e. the Absolute, where "it is Spirit that knows itself in the shape of Spirit, or a *comprehensive knowing* [in terms of the Notion]".[59] According to Hegel, "the necessary progression and interconnection of the forms of the unreal consciousness will by itself bring to pass the *completion*

---

[51]   *EM*: 9ff.

[52]   *EM*: esp. 27-48.

[53]   *EM*: 2.

[54]   *EM*: 112.

[55]   *EM*: 58.

[56]   *EM*: 49ff.

[57]   *EM*: 10ff.

[58]   Hegel, 1977: 15; cf. 486.

[59]   *Ibid.*: 485.

of the series".[60] For the process in question is a *negative* one.[61] This means, as J. N. Findlay points out, that "its successive phases bring out what is logically implicit in its earlier phrase, in the Hegelian sense of representing throughout an insightful, higher-order *comment on* (emphasis mine) previous contents".[62] In other words, the Hegelian Spirit, in the search for its own goal, must involve a procedure of self-refusal until it comes to the end of the spiritual adventure. Although Hegel did not think that the sequence of thought-phases described in *Phenomenology* is the only possible sequence that may be taken,[63] he surely assumed that this process must have a final state "where knowledge no longer needs to go beyond itself, where knowledge finds itself, where Notion corresponds to object and object to Notion".[64]

It follows that for Hegel the development of human mind results in a hierarchy of knowledge in which the existence of a certain form of thought is dependent on the realisation of that which logically supersedes it; and philosophy, the Absolute, is at the apex of the hierarchy as it is the sole self-autonomous thinking which "has won the pure element of its existence, Notion".[65] And thus, it is only in philosophy that the Spirit realises that it is "the phases of content in which it externalises itself and the process of leading these phases back to a full consciousness of self".[66]

Here, it may also be significant to note that the attempt to consider the successive moments of the Spirit, with specific regard to "provinces" of experience, has been rephrased in Collingwood's *Speculum Mentis*, and *Outlines of A Philosophy of Art*. According to Collingwood, there are five stages developing through the life of the Spirit in a way that the higher form of experience "presupposes and includes within itself those that logically precede it":[67] Art is the pure act of imagination whose indifference to the distinction between real and unreal is to be superseded by religion as a quest after truth, whose errors of superstition and idolatry are to be destroyed by science as the apprehension of a self-sufficient intelligent world, whose

[60] *Ibid.*: 50.

[61] *Ibid.*: 50 ff.

[62] J. N. Findley, 1977: vii.

[63] *Ibid.*: v-vi.

[64] Hegel, 1977: 51.

[65] *Ibid.*: 490.

[66] *Ibid.*: 591.

[67] R. G. Collingwood, 1994: 94.

inclination to abstract facts is to be abolished by history as a concrete study, whose shortcoming of reaching a unity of the mind is only to be overcome in philosophy by the Absolute.[68]

By way of contrast, it may be surmised from our earlier discussions that, the first and foremost concept running through Bradley's philosophical work is the Hegelian Absolute which is identified with "ultimate reality" in ontological terms, and with "total truth" in the epistemological sense. Unlike Hegel, nevertheless, Bradley believes that the Absolute might be beyond the grasp of thought which has its own degrees of truth and refers to reality from a limited point of view. And although Bradley understands the development of human mind in the order of feeling–thought–the Absolute, he does not really concur with Hegel's notion of the "hierarchy of knowledge". Instead, Bradley seems to accept that "hence no total truth or error, only more or less of validity", such that there exist "self-independent" *spheres* of thought making their own contribution to reality and truth. And in the context of *Appearance and Reality*, these spheres of thought actually include "the worlds of duty and religious truth", "hope, desire and dream", "the various worlds of politics, commerce, invention, trade and manufacture", "the intellectual province of truth and science, and more or less apart from this, the whole realm of the higher imagination" and so forth.[69]

Here again, it appears to me that Oakeshott's particular position on the relation of philosophy to modes of understanding is in spirit closer to Bradley than to Hegel or Collingwood.[70] At first glance, it seems true that Oakeshott does not follow Bradley to take the Absolute as what is beyond our thinking. According to Oakeshott:

> what is absolute means here that which is absolved or emancipated from the necessity of finding its significance in relations with what is outside itself. It means that which is self-complete, whole, individual, and removed from change. What is absolute, in this sense, is no *inscrutable Absolute* (emphasis mine), beyond conception and outside the world of experience, it is the world of experience as a coherent unity, for that alone *is* absolute.[71]

Consequently, as Greenleaf points out, Oakeshott takes philosophy to be the "perpetual re-establishment of coherence", which "is suspi-

[68]   *Ibid.*: 88-94.

[69]   Cf. W. H. Greenleaf, 1966: 9-11; R. Grant, 1990: 29.

[70]   Cf. D. Boucher, 1984: 197, 1993: 699-702; T. Nardin, 2001: 41.

[71]   *EM*: 47.

cious of any stopping-place or any attempt to limit the enquiry";[72] or alternatively, it may be said that for Oakeshott "philosophy is the engagement of continuous re-examining"[73] whatever is conditional and partial. And this understanding of philosophy, indeed, is where Oakeshott stands closest to Hegel.[74] Later in *HC*, Oakeshott continues to interpret Hegel as a philosopher who "engaged in a tireless exploration of the conditions of conditions",[75] an interpretation which reflects perfectly his own definition of philosophising.

But, for Oakeshott, philosophy is certainly not a system of knowledge on which all other knowledge depends; this, as already indicated, is a form of *philosophie* not philosophy. Rather, it is in Oakeshott's unique voice that, although philosophy is absolute as such, it does not necessarily mean that it should supersede or include modes of experience, as the task of philosophy is "not to anticipate or suggest arrests in experience, but to consider the character of those which *actually* exist [emphasis mine]".[76] In other words, as we shall see, in *EM* Oakeshott somehow combines Hegel's notion of philosophy as an endless enquiry and Bradley's idea of the degrees of reality and truth into a sort of "sceptical idealism" which means that: although philosophy is a self-critical thought which aims to transcend abstractness in order to achieve completeness, it is also a "mood",[77] an "escape",[78] a "parasitic activity",[79] i.e. a self-limited pure thinking which does not intend to alter *what already exists in experience*. Thus, whilst Hegel's phases of knowledge can never be self-independent because only the Absolute has such a privilege, and whilst Bradley's worlds of experience can be self-consistent because the Absolute is out of our reach, for Oakeshott they *must be* so because this is the way that they really are in the present situation.

As a result, Oakeshott plainly rejects the notion of the "hierarchy of knowledge", because modes of experience do not constitute "a mere series of what is successive, but a world of what is

[72] W. H. Greenleaf, 1966: 12-3.

[73] T. Fuller, 1993b: 24.

[74] As Oakeshott puts it elsewhere, this understanding of philosophy, in some sense, is also in favour of the Socratic dialogues, with which he sees no specific reason to quarrel (*RPML*: 130).

[75] *HC*: 257.

[76] *EM*: 331.

[77] *EM*: 2.

[78] *EM*: 3, 296-7.

[79] *RP*: 491.

co-existent".[80] And if what he has tried to explain in *EM* is plausible, Oakeshott thus believes, "experience is no longer seen as a hierarchy of abstract worlds of ideas, but as a single concrete whole in which every modification represents an arrest, and every arrest a failure".[81]

But, if it be the case that modes of experience are abstract and co-existing and that philosophy has no right to put their failure right, there must at the same time remain a sceptical note in Oakeshott's thought. As Oakeshott states it elsewhere, "the denial of a hierarchical order among the voices is not only a departure from one of the most notable traditions of European thought (in which all activity was judged in relation to the *vita contemplativa*), but will seem also to reinforce the scepticism".[82] The character of such a form of scepticism will be one of the main topics that this study aims to clarify.

To conclude: In *EM*, on the one hand, Oakeshott intends to maintain the self-independence of philosophy by rejecting positivism, historicism and pragmatism; on the other hand, in receiving inspiration from Bradley, especially in connection with the notion of the degrees of truth and reality, he tries to develop a self-limited and sceptical notion of philosophy that points in the direction of setting history, science and practice free from philosophy. Oakeshott's suggestion in *EM*, as in his other works, is the anti-foundationalist belief that reason appropriate to a world of discourse cannot be applied to any others without committing the mistake of *ignoratio elenchi*,[83] that is "categorically absurd".[84] This "most insidious and crippling of all forms of error — irrelevance",[85] Oakeshott has never tired of reminding us, should be prevented from relating philosophy to modes of experience and from that of one mode to another.

III.3. Experience and Modality

So much, then, for a contextual background to *EM*. Let us now proceed to the main argument of the work under consideration. Since

[80] *EM*: 91; cf. 72-3.

[81] *EM*: 326.

[82] *VP*: 14.

[83] *EM*: 5ff. In logic, the fallacy of *ignoratio elenchi* simply means "irrelevant conclusion", that is, "an argument in which one starts out to prove that something is the case, but instead proves something else ... What happens in an *ignoratio elenchi* is that the disputant thinks he is proving *p* when in reality he is proving *r*. Thus, he arrives at a conclusion which is irrelevant to the conclusion he was trying to prove" (R. H. Popkin & A. Stroll, 1993: 315).

[84] *HC*: 15.

[85] *EM*: 5.

Oakeshott's philosophy is ultimately connected with a certain view on the nature of experience, in this section I shall first attempt to discuss four related topics in his theory of experience: the general character of experience, truth, reality and modality.

III.3.1. Experience: A Single Whole

We have indicated that for Oakeshott "experience is a single whole, within which modification may be distinguished, but which admits of no final or absolute division".[86] This, as I understand it, signifies the core meaning of experience which Oakeshott aims to discover throughout the whole book. In the first place, it suggests that the distinguishable modes of experience such as history, science and practice are not separate kinds of experience corresponding to the separate parts of experience which the empiricist might think of, but rather they are the single whole of experience modified by the conditions that characterise each of them. That is to say, in the spirit of Oakeshott there is only one reality, a single system of experience; the modes of experience are not the "sum-totals" of our knowledge, but different ways for us to approach the world as a whole through certain standpoints.

Applying the problem of modality to what follows, we only need to notice that, by expressing "experience as a single whole knowing no final division", Oakeshott's major point is to employ an objection to some of the divisions built into experience upon which modern natural philosophy depends for its discussions of knowing: first, dualism, i.e. the division between experiencing and what is experienced, between experience and reality, between subjectivity and objectivity and the like; second, the empiricist division as to the different forms of experience — immediate and mediate experience; and third, the rationalist division of experience and intuition. Here, for expository purposes, it is convenient to look at the non-empiricist and non-rationalist character of Oakeshott's idea of experience by remarking on his objection to the last two divisions, and leave the problem of dualism unexplored until we come to understand his attitude to reality.

According to Oakeshott, every experiencing must be a way of thinking; everything experienced must be a form of thought. Experience and thought are inseparable; experience always and everywhere involves thought or judgement, that is, a single homogeneous world of ideas. The view that experience is a self-governing whole

[86] *EM*: 10, 27.

which needs no outside authority, since no such thing exists, to vindicate it, is indeed a view that Oakeshott takes from idealism in general. And, it accordingly follows that everything understandable can be neither falling short of nor passing beyond the condition of thought, i.e. experience. At this point, Oakeshott, with his fellow idealists, is at odds with traditional empiricism and rationalism.

Empiricism holds that since the raw material of knowledge is sensation (immediate experience), there is a "pre-thinking stage of experience" distinguishable from our reflection (mediate experience). In other words, for empiricists, there exists a final division between experience as sensation and experience as thought; and sensation is thus an independent form of experience which is *less than* thinking and reflection. And, among those who have made this point, I think, it is particularly Locke that Oakeshott takes as his target for attack on the origin of such a form of division in experience.

It is Locke's view that man at birth is like "white paper, void of all characters, without any ideas", that "all ideas come from sensation and reflection".[87] Through the former our minds are provoked by physical objects to receive *passively* all the ideas that we have of the world. Once the mind has hoarded its sensed ideas, i.e. sense-data, we have a faculty — "the operations of our own minds within us"[88] to reflect upon those ideas or data. Rather as the ideas of sensation are caused by physical objects, the ideas of reflection, which include perception, thinking, doubting, believing, reasoning, knowing, willing and all the different actings of our minds are caused by the ideas of sensation.

According to Oakeshott, what lies behind the Lockean separation of sensation from reflection or judgement is nothing but a misconception purporting to presume that the given sensation must be isolated, simple and even inexpressible. All we have in sensation, it is said, is therefore no more than a bare "this" or "that", "here" or "there", "now" or "then" without involving thinking. To argue against this, Oakeshott makes two points, which I think exactly correspond to Bradley's notions of "generality" and "artificiality" that we have mentioned above: First, Oakeshott argues that nothing in experience is ever isolated, unrelated, unmodified by previous experience; that any general concept, in terms of being a concept itself, is not inexpressible without a name. To take a simple example, "yellow, as it is in actual experience, is characterised by connection with

[87]   Locke, 1975: II. 1. 2.

[88]   *Ibid.:* II. 1. 4.

previous experience recognised as different or similar either in kind or in degree".[89] If I do not recognise the concept of yellow in the first place, then, no matter whether other people see it or not, I have no idea of referring yellow to the thing I am seeing at all. But if I see something as yellow, I must at the same time see it as not blue or red. For without such *relevance* built into my previous experience, in which the concept of yellow can be connected to a more complex unity (i.e. generality), say, of colour, to experience something as yellow is not possible. Second, as Oakeshott goes on to say, there is no reliable distinction that can be made between the concept of yellow and the judgement that "this is yellow". Experiencing, at least, implies *consciousness* (i.e. artificiality); a bare "this" is nothing but nonentity. Consequently, the statement "this is yellow" in fact means that "I recognise that this is yellow". Since recognition and consciousness must involve us at once "in judgement, in inference, in reflection, in thought";[90] experience, Oakeshott concludes, is always and everywhere significant.

It is vital to note that Oakeshott here is clearly aware of the reason why it is so important for empiricism to suppose that there is immediate experience outside thought. In the first place, this is a consequence of the empiricists' obsession with dualism, an issue to which I shall return shortly. But further, the division between immediate and mediate experience is made in the service of a certain epistemological premise regarding knowledge as a mental process which needs some sort of raw material to begin with. Oakeshott characterises this theory of knowledge as follows:

> Experience, it is said, must begin somewhere, and if thought involves mediation, it cannot begin with thought. It is as if one should say that in building a wall every brick must be laid on the top of another brick and none directly on the ground.[91]

But does thought require raw material to accomplish itself? Is there anything in thought analogous to the builder's brick? Oakeshott has doubts on this, because he argues that there is no "out-there" raw material needed in thinking. Instead, to take an analogy from Plato's *Theaetetus*, Oakeshott creates his own metaphor in the following way: thinking "is a process of catching not wild birds, not what is outside experience (such as objects in mere sensation), but tame

[89]   *EM*: 13.
[90]   *EM*: 14.
[91]   *EM*: 18.

birds already within the cage of the mind".[92] That is to say, thinking begins neither from sense-data, nor from given feelings or perceptions, but begins with a world of ideas within our mind. According to Oakeshott,

> What is at first given in experience is single and significant, a One not a many. The given in thought is the complex situation in which we find ourselves in the first moments of consciousness. There is nothing immediate or "natural" in contrast to what is mediate or sophisticated; there are only degrees of sophistication.[93]

In short, simply following Bradley, the view Oakeshott wishes to recommend is that the given in experience is always a world, not a series nor a collection, of ideas. It is from this viewpoint, as we shall see, that Oakeshott's notion of truth develops.

In contrast to empiricism, on the other hand, rationalism upholds that since the only genuine source of knowledge is reason or intuition, there exists a "supra-thinking stage" through which our experience can become *truer* than what it seems to be. Intuition, it is claimed, is independent of experience for it is *more than* thought. In other words, truths do not depend on experience; rather, there are *a priori* truths which are true in themselves and which can be realised through reason alone. Accordingly, as Oakeshott assumes, it is the rationalists' general creed that there is "a direct knowledge of the whole, freed from the distortion of analysis and the artificial distinctions of judgement", that "intuition is, therefore, a fuller experience; it is a form of experience from which the defeats of judgement have been banished".[94]

Oakeshott's comment on rationalism is considerably brief in comparison to his views on empiricism and he imputes the impossibility of the division between intuition and experience to the fact that, although there are forms of thought that may fall below the full character of thought, no thought can be foreign to itself, i.e. to recognise reality to a certain extent. That is to say, according to rationalism, the distinction implies a "strong" version of dualism or realism[95] which alleges that reality exists independently of our experience and our apprehension of it is necessarily different from what it really appears to our innate reason. "This view implies, among much else, an absolute distinction between what is called "knowledge *of*" and

---

[92]   *EM*: 19.

[93]   *EM*: 20.

[94]   *EM*: 23.

[95]   Cf. R. Grant, 1990: 25.

"knowledge *about*", it implies that the object in thought is never reality but a mere being-for-thought, it implies that the so-called categories of thought stand between the subject and reality, and it implies that a direct and immediate experience, because it is direct and immediate, is a complete experience".[96] But, rationalism with its "passwords of 'Either — Or'"[97] neglects that "understanding is not such that we either enjoy it or lack it altogether";[98] truth is not such that it is either absolute or nothing. There are, instead, degrees of truth and reality to accompany every understanding; and thinking is not the qualification of reality by another idea, it is a qualification of reality by itself.

III.3.2. Truth: A Condition of Thought

I have indicated that Oakeshott claims experience begins with ideas, and ideas can never be isolated; the given in experience is always a world of ideas. And, a world means "a complex integral whole or system; whenever there is a world there is unity".[99] On this basis, Oakeshott argues that truth is not *an external standard* outside experience; but it is *an internal condition* within experience, the condition of the world of experience in which the world is satisfactory to itself. In other words, truth is not itself an independent category outside thinking, but a relative degree of satisfaction that experience enjoys. Nothing save the world of experience itself is the arbiter of truth; there are no external means by which truth can be established. It is consequently senseless to ask where truth can be known — without truth there can be no thinking; without thinking there can be no truth.

In order to explain this point, Oakeshott goes on to explore the process of understanding by maintaining that in thinking the given, the unity is given in order to be *transformed*. That is to say, thinking must involve itself in a process of self-criticism, or using a Hegelian concept, dialectic in which our mind never merely acquiesces in the presented condition of what appears to be partial; but rather our mind is so positive and critical that it always embarks on an establishment of a concrete whole. That said, in thinking, we start with the *negation* of the presented unity wherever that is seen to be false or inadequate in order to recognise a given world of ideas into a closer

[96]   *EM*: 23-4.

[97]   This is a Hegelian phrase, quoted in *EM*: 25.

[98]   *HC*: 1.

[99]   *EM*: 28.

unity. That which is eventually achieved in experience is "first, a world which differs from the given world only by being more of a world; the given and the achieved are both worlds, but not equally worlds; and second, it is a world of ideas".[100] Hence, following Bradley, Oakeshott also argues that the only criterion of truth is "coherence": "knowledge is always a coherent system of ideas, knowledge consists in whatever in experience we are obliged to accept, whatever in experience we are led to and find satisfaction in".[101]

Furthermore, Bradley's "doctrine of internal relations" applies to Oakeshott's proposition. Since the given in experience is always a world of ideas, every single constituent of the unity has no meaning of its own in isolation from the concrete whole. Each single idea's character rests not upon a given causal relation as empiricism and positivist historiography argue, but upon the whole system to which it belongs. There is no fixed meaning for a single idea; its meaning is its place in the whole system. Thus, to enhance an idea is to enhance the integral whole; to interpret the meaning of an idea is to undertake a "pursuit of implications"[102] of its unity. And consequently, the process of understanding is never a process of mere "accretion". To speak of "adding to knowledge" is to speak of a misconception. This returns us at once to dualism, to the *ab extra* theory of truth. We can extend nothing to a given series or collection of ideas outside ourselves, because no such world exists. Instead, "each advance affects retrospectively the entire whole, and is the creation of a new word".[103] "To modify the system as a whole is to cause every constituent to take on a new character; to modify any of the constituents is to alter the system as a whole".[104] But in each case, it follows that for Oakeshott as for Bradley, every truth is corrigible, that "where error is impossible, truth is inconceivable". And consequently, Oakeshott does not intend to deny that truth may not be fully achieved in experience, although, since it is a necessary condition of experience, it can never be wholly absent in thinking. Hence, he takes once again Bradley's notion of the degrees of truth by saying that "even if truth is difficult to come at, nothing can be dismissed as mere error"; that truth is not a matter of "take-it-or-leave-it", on the contrary, what

---

[100] *EM*: 29.

[101] *EM*: 40.

[102] *EM*: 41.

[103] *EM*: 41.

[104] *EM*: 30.

really concerns the philosopher is a problem of how to discover "the half-truth in the error, and the error in the half-truth".[105] This and other related points, it seems to me, have prevented Oakeshott from an extreme form of scepticism in the sense of eliminating any possibility of truth. But how far and in what sense Oakeshott in *EM* can be regarded as a sceptic is a question that I do not intend to pursue in detail here.

In view of his insistence on the lack of separation of truth from thinking, Oakeshott's premise repudiates the Cartesian belief that truth "is an Absolute not inherent in the character of experience but dictated *ab extra*, a prize, extraneous to the race itself, and (when the race is finished) more frequently withheld than awarded".[106] Since this correspondence theory of truth is associated with dualism, to understand better Oakeshott's repudiation of it, we must turn to examine his attitude to reality.

III.3.3. Reality: The Given in Experience

In connection with the relation of experience to reality, Oakeshott argues that no separation is possible between them:

> Knowledge, if we are to avoid contradiction, must be seen to have its place in the universe of the real; and reality must lie within the universe of knowledge. For, if experience be not, in some sense, real, then, nothing can be real, and consequently nothing unreal. And if reality be separated from knowledge, it must resign itself to the condition of nonentity, an empty concept, an idea without meaning or significance.[107]

Oakeshott's observation here is, of course, a re-statement of the central doctrine of idealism: mind (experiencing) can never be independent of its objects (what is experienced), which implies that: to be real is to be in thinking; to be in thinking is to be real; in experience, thinking and reality are elements given in connection.

In order to illuminate this point, Oakeshott identifies and objects to two forms of dualism: The first is the form purporting to suppose that reality is independent of experience and it is real because it is unknowable. And the second is the form suggesting that reality is the object of experiencing, but, due to the limitation of our natural faculty, we cannot claim to be able to comprehend reality itself.

With regard to the first observation, it is, I think, the Kantian unknowableness of the thing-in-itself that Oakeshott takes to be the

---

[105] *EM*: 2, 4.
[106] *EM*: 28.
[107] *EM*: 50.

case. In his *Critique of Pure Reason*, Kant set out to consider the demarcation of our reason by asking what it can and what it cannot achieve in the way of knowledge. It was Kant's conclusion that knowledge is possible only if our experience is added to *a priori* objective reference through the function of our mind, i.e. we arrange our experience, first in time and space, and then according to categories. That is to say, in order to get real knowledge our mind must play a dynamic role in organising what we experience, insofar as space, time and categories are merely *creations* in our mind without which we could not get to understand the world. But this does not mean that these realities do not exist; it only means that they belong to, as Kant called it, a world of the "thing-in-itself", which *should* exist and whose nature is completely unknowable to us.

Here Oakeshott makes a twofold objection to this view. First, it contains an attempt to define reality "as not something else". But, "reality, whatever else it is, cannot be a thing among things; it must be everything, and has not even the alternative of being nothing". And second, "to assert the impossibility of knowledge is always to assert a piece of knowledge, and is therefore self-contradictory".[108] The unknowableness of reality, in the end, only contradicts itself as there being nothing to know.

The second form of dualism is perhaps found, again, in Locke's theory of reality. We have shown that for Locke ideas are capable of representing physical objects in the external world, yet we are never directly acquainted with physical objects themselves (and the mind as substance). For the physical world is only postulated by Locke as the cause of our ideas; and, for this reason, it must exist independently. It provides us with the objects of thought, but does not give us knowledge in any given form. The Lockean representationism is thus not to see the realities of mind and body, but to see "what Objects and our Understandings were, or were not fitted to deal with".[109]

To this view, Oakeshott's critique is that if reality (Objects) is independent of experience (Understanding), any move to relate one to the other, "to get acquainted with it must be stupid rather than presumptuous, and to restrain a man from the undertaking would be not less foolish than to prohibit his drinking the sea".[110] Since the view Oakeshott is recommending is that reality is knowable because

---

[108] *EM*: 50-1.

[109] Quoted by R. Rorty, 1980: 137.

[110] *EM*: 53-4.

of its lack of separation from experience, it seems nonsense for him to speak of reality as beyond the limits of human knowledge. Again, as Oakeshott argues, how could we be aware of the limits of our thought and where they should lie, if we do not know anything beyond these limits? It is thus difficult to hold such a view without being abstract and arbitrary.

Empiricism since Locke has formulated a more and more sceptical view on metaphysics raising doubt on any attempt to penetrate reality. Hume and positivism, the latest form of empiricism, for example, are significant cases. By questioning such a sceptical attitude to metaphysics, it has become clear that Oakeshott's idealism has led him to be positive about the hope for metaphysics, at least so far as *EM* is concerned, and thus his scepticism seems to have nothing to do with the Humean tradition of empiricism. We should therefore be careful about Cranston's remark that "[Oakeshott] is an idealist who is more sceptical than many positivists".

If reality is, in effect, a world of ideas, it follows that reality is nothing but that which is given in every experience. At this point, Oakeshott continues, reality is what is achieved and satisfactory in experience. And, in view of the fact that what is satisfactory in experience is always a coherent world of ideas; reality is thus a coherent world of ideas, i.e. of things. It is one, a single system, and it is real only as a whole. Reality "is what we are obliged to think; and since to think is to experience, and to experience is to experience meaning, the real is always what has meaning, or is rational".[111] Accordingly, as with the nature of reality, Oakeshott makes his own motto as follows: "we have, and all we have, is a world of 'meanings'" — "Whatever has a meaning, if we give it its full meaning, is real; and whatever is real has a meaning",[112] a motto which at once reminds us of that of Hegel: the rational is the real and the real the rational. In short, for Oakeshott, what is real is what is "objective".

While seeing the real world as an objective world in this way, however, there appears a need to distinguish the notion of *objectivity* from what dualism, or so-called realism presumes. For, on this issue, it has been said that *objectivity* must signify independence: whatever is objective must be uninterfered with by experience and indifferent to our understanding of it. Consequently, related to the correspondence theory of truth, it is now suggested that knowing is concerned solely with *subjectivity* and *objectivity*. And following from this, the

[111] *EM*: 58.
[112] *EM*: 61; 58.

most fundamental question that should be asked in philosophy is: "How can we get outside our purely personal experience to a world of objective, real existence"?[113]

For Oakeshott, an object is always an object of consciousness, and reality which is untouched by experiencing is the unknowable and thus a contradiction. Following Hegel and Bradley, Oakeshott believes that the Cartesian-Kantian problematic of what we can know of the external world, of how objects are related to subjects is not merely misleading but nonsensical. If reality is given always and everywhere in experience, the real problem concerning *objectivity* in philosophy should be replaced by "Where is the experience in which reality is given fully?".[114] And, just as in experience what is satisfactory may not be fully achieved yet it can never be absent; Oakeshott accepts Bradley's notion of the degrees of reality that reality may not be given equally but can never be denied. In other words, in suggesting that reality is an objective world of experience, Oakeshott proposes that reality is obligatory and unavoidable in experience: reality is what we are obliged to think, not what we happen to think; without reality there is no thinking, without thinking there is no reality. Of the subjectivity-objectivity problem, Oakeshott thus concludes that:

> Subject and object are not independent elements or portions of experience; they are aspects of experience which, when separated from one another, degenerate into abstractions. Every experience . . . is the unity of these, a unity which may be analysed into these two sides but which can never be reduced to a mere relation between them . . . [A]n object is not something independent of experience, but merely what I am obliged to think, and for that reason it is real. And the subject, the I, which belongs to this object, is not my body, nor a merely psychological subject, not (that is) an element or portion of my world, but my world as a whole. And my world is a world of objects. The subject does not belong to my world, it is my world.[115]

In short, experience, truth and reality are inseparable; the world is a world of ideas in which everything experienced enjoys a certain degree of truth and refers to a limited viewpoint of reality.

---

[113] *EM*: 59.

[114] *EM*: 59.

[115] *EM*: 60.

III.3.4. Modality: Three Characters

So far we have seen that for Oakeshott with experience there is a movement directed towards the achievement of a coherent world of ideas, but, as Oakeshott proceeds, at a certain point this movement may be arrested and an abstract world of ideas, a mode of experience constructed. That said, this movement can frequently fall short of the completeness of satisfaction, fall short because it reaches something else — a certain degree of what is satisfactory. In sum, there will emerge a mode of experience as long as there is a lack of an adequacy to realise fully the criterion of satisfaction, the completeness.

> In experience there is the alternative of pressing forward towards the perfectly coherent world of concrete ideas or turning aside from the main current in order to construct and explore a restricted world of ideas. The full obligations of the character of experience are avoided when (as so often) the attempt to define, the attempt to see clearly and as a whole, is surrendered for the abstract satisfaction of designation.[116]

As a matter of fact, Oakeshott claims that he has never excluded the possibility of such an arrest in experience and this is evident from what we have elicited so far. On the contrary, the notion of degrees which we have seen as inseparable from that of experience as a coherent world of ideas — the view that in experience truth and reality may be conditionally achieved and given — implies the possibility of diversity and admits arrest. For this reason, no matter what else the character of a mode of experience can be, in the first place, it can never abscond from the world of experience itself.

In other words, it does not mean that a mode when modified relinquishes the character of being experience; but it merely means that on occasions it fails to realise entirely the criterion of experience in the most complete sense. And thus, modes of experience are not *kinds* of experience; for there is no final division in experience. All we have in experience is "One not Many". Whatever falls short of the full character of this One is merely a defeated mode of experience rather than a specific kind of it. Again, a mode of experience is not what corresponds to a separate *part* of reality either. "It is not an island in the sea of experience, but a limited view of the totality of experience". "It is not partial (in the literal sense), but abstract". "There are indeed no 'parts' in experience, no separable 'tracts' of experience".[117]

---

[116] *EM*: 70-1.
[117] *EM*: 71.

There are accordingly three main features of a mode of experience: Firstly, as it is suggested, a mode of experience must be *abstract*, since it is modified in experience by its own conditions and postulates. History is the organisation of the totality of experience *sub specie praeteritorum*; science, *sub specie quantitatis*, practice, *sub specie voluntatis*.[118] In short, as Oakeshott maintains, the logical structure that ascertains a mode of experience as historical, scientific or practical, ascertains it as an abstract world of ideas, an arrest in experience as well.[119]

Secondly, each mode of experience can never transcend its conditions, for it is exactly due to the shortcoming of this ability that makes it a modality, a category, an abstractness. Towards this crucial point, Oakeshott thus argues that each mode contains a *self-contradiction* within its own logic. That is, a mode's explicit character as a modality actually and continuously conflicts with its implicit character as experience, and, more crucially, this self-contradiction (and thus abstractness) cannot be removed without stamping out the mode itself: The explicit form of history as past understanding, *wie es eigentlich gewesen*, contradicts its implicit form as present experience;[120] the explicit character of sciences as a world of proposals and hypotheses contradicts its implicit character of referring to and depending upon concrete reality;[121] and the explicit feature of practice as the will to alter or maintain existence, the attempt to throw reality into the future, contradicts its implicit feature of being present experience.[122] But in each case, it is clear that a mode will be self-destructive if its modality is put in question or its self-contradiction is to be resolved. Or alternatively, it may be said that a mode of experience that adheres to what is explicit in its character must renounce the capacity to achieve what would be completely satisfactory in experience at the same time.

Thirdly, it follows that a mode of experience is governed by its own postulates, postulates which put it outside the main current of experience and thus enable it to make a home for itself. Consequently, a mode of experience must be *self-consistent*. And, in order to clarify this point, Oakeshott has two further arguments: first, the *differentia* of the various modes of experience from one another; and

---

[118] *EM*: 11, 198, 258, 262, 308, 317.

[119] Cf. *EM*: 146.

[120] *EM*: 145-56.

[121] *EM*: 212-9.

[122] *EM*: 304-5.

second, the notion of "truth-for-itself" applied in every mode of experience.

In the first place, according to Oakeshott, "whenever argument or inference passes from one world of experience to another, from what is abstracted upon one principle [a mode] to what is abstracted upon another [another mode], from what is abstract [the modes] to what is concrete [philosophy], and from what is concrete to what is abstract", there will occur *ignoratio elenchi*. That is to say, for Oakeshott, modes of experience must be "wholly and absolutely independent of any other";[123] the modes are so "tight, exclusive, insular"[124] that each mode can never be associated either with the principles of other modes or with philosophy.[125] As K. Minogue explains:

> Water, to use an obvious example, has little in common with H_2O, and neither has much relation to the poetic images of water in *The Ancient Mariner*. Each mode plays by its own rules, as it were, and to mix them is like playing basketball in the middle of a game of football.[126]

Additionally, as we have seen, a mode of experience, by itself, is an abstract world of ideas, and the condition of being a world of ideas is truth. Truth is always "true for itself"; truth is what is satisfactory to experience; and consequently, the truth of a mode of experience is the limited degree to which it is satisfactory to itself. The principle is: Every truth is true in its own place. Oakeshott thus argues that:

> Each abstract world of ideas, in so far as it is coherent, is, then, true so far as it goes, true if its postulates are accepted, true if its reservations are admitted. But, because each is an abstract world of ideas, the product of an arrest in experience, when whatever truth it may contain is asserted absolutely and unconditionally, its truth turns to error. The truth of a mode of experience is always relative, relative to the degree of completeness which belongs to its world of ideas, its organisation of reality.[127]

In short, for Oakeshott, the modes of experience are so self-consistent that they are governed by nothing save their own conditioned coherence. On the dust jacket of the paperback edition of *EM* Oakeshott sums up the purpose of his book as follows: "Its theme is

---

[123] *EM*: 75.

[124] *EM*: 345.

[125] This does not mean that there are no communications permitted amongst the modes of experience under certain conditions.

[126] K. Minogue, 1993a: 46.

[127] *EM*: 77.

Modality: human experience recognised as a variety of independent, self-consistent worlds of discourse, each the invention of human intelligence, but each also to be understood as abstract and an arrest in human experience".

III.4. The Nature of Philosophy

It can be noted that philosophy itself is not mentioned by Oakeshott among the modes of experience. If philosophy is not a specific kind of understanding which approaches the world under its own postulates, then what is the nature and main business of it? What is its relation to the modes of experience? These are questions to which we now turn. In doing so, I intend to expand on the three major characteristics of Oakeshott's philosophical thought upon which we have touched earlier: self-independence or self-criticism, self-limitation and scepticism.

III.4.1. Self-Independence

We have seen that Oakeshott perceives that experience is a single concrete whole within which modification may occur, but which admits of no absolute division. I would like to add here that this implies that there exists a concrete world of ideas: "Wherever there is a modification there must be a totality; wherever there is abstraction there must be a concrete whole".[128] Put another way, if there is no *other* world as a concrete whole, which is "neither the sum nor the product of the modes", which in turn are neither alternative nor contributory to this concrete world,[129] there can be no modes at all. As a matter of fact, the standpoint that we have been taking to consider the nature of experience so far is exactly that of taking experience as a concrete whole, and "whatever in experience the concrete purpose is pursued without hindrance or distraction" Oakeshott now calls "philosophical experience".[130] So far, then, all we have been undertaking is a philosophical point of view; Oakeshott intends in *EM* nothing less than to establish such a philosophical world as *other*, a non-modified world, in order to provide the modes and philosophy itself with a *criterion*. And, consequently, the problem remaining here is a problem concerning how, and in what sense, philosophy can be seen as the *criterion* of experience?

[128] *EM*: 77.
[129] *EM*: 77, 79.
[130] *EM*: 81-2.

To ask this question is at once to ask the meaning and function of philosophy itself. According to Oakeshott, philosophy, since it must involve itself in the movement towards the achievement of a coherent world of ideas, means that it is "experience without reservation or preservation, experience which is self-conscious and self-critical throughout, in which the determination to remain unsatisfied with anything short of a completely coherent world of ideas is absolute and unqualified".[131] In other words, as already mentioned, the philosopher is simply "the victim of thought" in the sense that he is always critical about whatever is conditional and incomplete; philosophical thinking is "self-critical thought" engaged in the pursuit of what is fully and finally satisfactory in experience.

If Oakeshott is correct that the basic function of philosophy is to *transcend* abstractness as such, it follows that philosophy cannot disclaim the responsibility of accounting for the character of the modes which arrest in experience in order to transcend their conditions and postulates. As a result, the main business of philosophy, Oakeshott argues, is "to determine its own character, and to extend its content by persisting in the concrete purpose implied in its character and by avoiding or overcoming every alluring modification which may offer itself as a distraction".[132] And, consequently, it is in this sense that philosophy can be seen as the *criterion* of experience.

No matter what this criterion can be, it certainly cannot be a product of what categorises the modes of experience. In other words, it cannot be an historical, scientific or practical criterion. For, the criterion of experience, according to previous arguments, is the persistent re-establishment of a complete and satisfactory world of experience; practice, science and history, on the other hand, are modifications or arrests which have occurred in experience exactly in the sense of falling short of this completeness. The view that Oakeshott wishes to reject here, so far as this perspective is concerned, is the view of reducing all experience to historical, scientific or practical experience.[133]

This, however, cannot be simply given as a presupposition (there is nothing simply given in philosophy); instead, it needs to be established for the sake of philosophy itself. And consequently this is the reason, I think, why in a work concerning philosophy Oakeshott has taken so much space, almost three quarters, to discuss the postulates

[131] *EM*: 82; see also 3, 347.

[132] *EM*: 83.

[133] See *EM*: esp. 245.

of the modes, to argue whether each of them is an abstract world of ideas arrested in experience or a complete and satisfactory world of ideas. It is at this point that the whole proceedings of *EM* can therefore be seen as a course of elucidating how a philosophy starts to establish itself as the *criterion* of experience, the completeness, by way of criticising the abstractness (and the self-contradiction) inherent in modes of experience without interfering with their self-consistency.

That is, to interpret the aim of *EM* in this way is to show how a mode of experience, on the one hand, by virtue of its character as a world of ideas, can be seen by philosophy as a self-consistent world of ideas; but, how it, on the other hand, by virtue of its modality, falls short of philosophy itself, a complete coherent world of ideas. Put another way, it is Oakeshott's view that the task of the philosopher is to "discover both half-truth in the error and the error in the half truth" — to reject the error-part of a mode of experience by showing how it fails to be a concrete whole, and meanwhile to ascertain its truth-part by remaining as a self-consistent mode of experience. Otherwise, to speak of science, practice and history as the *criterion* of experience will commit the error of *ignoratio elenchi*. For it will mis-identify modifications with experience itself, mis-identify the postulates such as "quantity", "volition" and "pastness" which distinguish respectively the scientific, practical and the historical with the concrete coherence, i.e. the philosophical.

Oakeshott claims there are theoretically numberless modes for man to comprehend the world,[134] and the three modes of experience discussed in *EM* are not his own invention, but ways of thinking that have been "highly developed".[135] And yet, as I have pointed out, the more substantial reason for Oakeshott's selection of history, science and practice, among others, as the examples of modality is to make a response to the contemporary debate over the nature of philosophy by transcending logical positivism, historicism and pragmatism.

We will have other opportunities to resume Oakeshott's rejections of these thoughts in the course of this book. Now, instead of appealing to any external and extraneous reasons, let me repeat again, for Oakeshott "a philosophy, if it is to stand at all, must stand absolutely upon its own feet, and anything which tends to obscure this fact must be regarded with suspicion".[136] This clearly suggests that phi-

---

[134] *EM*: 75, 331.

[135] *EM*: 84, 71.

[136] *EM*: 7.

losophy can only depend for its existence on its own interest, i.e. the pursuit of what is completely satisfactory in experience; philosophy, whenever it is sought, must be sought "for its own sake". To claim this, it seems to me, is to claim the "self-independence of philosophy". That is, for Oakeshott, philosophy, interesting as it is, can never be reduced to or mixed up with modes of experience.

Yet, if philosophy cannot depend for its own existence on the reasons of modes of experience, do the modes depend for their own existence on the reason of philosophy? Or, more specifically, if the main business of philosophy is to *transcend* the abstractness of modes of experience, does this mean that philosophy, in so doing, determines the validity of each mode; if not, what can be seen as their real relationship? These are the most crucial issues into which this study wishes to enquire, for it is concerned with the interpretative problem of whether Oakeshott in *EM* has established a foundationalist conception of philosophy on the one hand, or whether he has changed his mind about the conceptions of philosophy from *EM* to *RP* on the other. Tariq Modood, for instance, holds that in the youthful *EM* "it was philosophy which determined the validity of every mode of experience"; whereas in *RP* philosophy bestowed nothing to any other voices. Oakeshott's characterisation of the "conversation of mankind", according to Modood, "means a direct assault on his earlier view of philosophy, he makes no reference himself to any such earlier views".[137] And clearly, here Modood simply deciphers Oakeshott in *EM* as a foundationalist.

Expounding on Modood's point of view,[138] S. A. Gerencser has recently re-established that there is a fundamental shift "in Oakeshott's philosophical outlook", especially in his "philosophy from idealism [in *EM*] to scepticism [in *RP*]".[139] According to Gerencser, *EM*, in fact, consists of two separable elements: a conception of "experience" and its "modes"; he calls the first of these Oakeshott's absolute idealism and the second sceptical idealism.[140] By so claiming, Gerencser's plan is to argue that "the best way of understanding the development of Oakeshott's philosophy, and in particular, his political philosophy, is to see it as the gradual working out of the scepticism that was in tension with the absolute ideal-

---

[137] T. Modood, 1980: 320.

[138] See S. A. Gerencser, 2000: 173, n13,176, n65.

[139] *Ibid.*: 34, 7.

[140] *Ibid.*: 26.

ism of the early phase".[141] And here, for the purpose of this book, the lines of reasoning that Gerencser directs to unveil the foundationalism or absolute idealism of *EM* may be surmised as follows:

First of all, it bears on the five doctrines of absolute idealism proposed by A. Quinton, namely, monism, truth as coherence, the world as a concrete universal, reality as mental construction, and the necessary relation of the mind to its objects.[142] More crucially, as Gerencser adds, *EM* does not take philosophy to be simply "the quest for an absolutely unified system of coherent ideas", but also the experience of the Absolute.[143] The most obvious piece of evidence pointing to this contention is that philosophy is mentioned in *EM* as the "criterion" or the "logical ground" of experience.[144] By way of contrast, the notable changes that appear between *EM* and *The Voice of Poetry in the Conversation of Mankind* (1959; hereafter, *VP*) are thus: In *VP* Oakeshott concedes that philosophy "makes no specific contribution" to the conversation, and so, the *superbia* of philosophy is obviated; additionally, that work entails the possibility for subtle interaction between different voices, especially those of philosophy and practice.[145]

III.4.2. Self-Limitation

It seems to me that Modood's and Gerencser's foundationalist interpretation of *EM* is a misconception. Following Oakeshott, we have, in fact, already seen the self-limited character of philosophy as having no such power to interfere with the self-consistence of modes of experience on some points. Let me here try to make some sense of those arguments in a clearer way by raising objections to Gerencser's story.

In the main, my point is that Oakeshott's scepticism essentially penetrates into his conception of experience as well as his theory of

---

[141] I. Tregenza, 2001: 617-8. Gerencser's deeper concern for examining Oakeshott's "growing scepticism" is to re-establish "the subtle connections" between theory and practice in Oakeshott's philosophical politics, such that he may take up the question of whether Oakeshott's conception of civil association, based on a Hobbesian understanding of authority, "can sustain his own scepticism and possibly offer anything to contemporary theories of democracy" as well as democratic practice (2000: 6, 4).

[142] See S. A. Gerencser, 2000: 16-22.

[143] *Ibid.*: 6, 12, 16, 22.

[144] *Ibid.*: 37.

[145] *Ibid.*: 37-42.

modality, i.e. that there is only one element of *EM*, namely, sceptical idealism. Since Gerencser largely agrees that with regards to modality, *EM* is of a sceptical nature, in what follows I shall simply focus on the issue of whether Oakeshott's philosophical theory of experience is foundationalist or not.

It is true that Quinton himself is prone to employ the term "absolute idealism" to specify *EM*,[146] yet, by this, Quinton means the whole school of idealism "in the tradition of Hegel and Bradley",[147] without paying attention to the differences among them. Despite following Hegel to philosophise the categories of human experience, for example, it has been disclosed that both Bradley and Oakeshott do not place trust in the actuality of the Absolute and thrust aside the hierarchy of human knowing. I shall return to this side of the debate later; for now it appears that simply following Quinton's definition of absolute idealism gives us no sufficient reason to exclude scepticism from the idea of philosophy in the thought of Oakeshott in *EM* (and Bradley in *Appearance and Reality*).

More remarkably, it will be remembered that for Oakeshott the characters that exist in experience as a whole must exist in modes of experience at the same time; as already cited from *EM*, a mode "is not an island in the sea of experience, but a limited view of the totality of experience". This means that the main features of absolute idealism singled out by Quinton would, in actuality, remain as they are within a mode of experience. For example, as we shall examine in Chapter V, history is nothing more than a world of ideas constructed in the mind of the historian, and in writing history, the historian is simply to make a more coherent account of the whole unity of individuals in terms of change. Accordingly, I think there is no valid ground for Gerencser to set a conception of experience apart from its modality.

In addition to taking the five doctrines as a whole package typifying Oakeshott's absolute idealism, on some occasions, Gerencser also speaks of monism as what defines Oakeshott as being an absolute idealist and a promoter of foundationalism,[148] insofar as the alteration of Oakeshott's idea of philosophy comes about when he

---

[146] In his Speech Note to The Inaugural Conference of the Michael Oakeshott Association at the London School of Economics (Sep. 2001), Quinton opined that "*Experience and Its Modes* is an uncompromising work of absolute idealism" (2001: 53).

[147] A. Quinton, 2001: 53.

[148] See S. A. Gerencser, 2000: 57, 42.

abandons "idealism's monism" in *RP*. But here, what Gerencser means by monism needs to be clarified.

In the context of our present discussion, the concepts monism and pluralism are largely referred to as two contrasted doctrines regarding how many substances exist, and may relate either to kinds of substances or to their individual instances. On this reading, "monism regarding the kinds of substance holds that only one such kind exist, whereas pluralism admits a multiplicity of kinds. Monism regarding the instances of a given substantial kind insists that only one such individual does or can exist, pluralism that many do or *may* [emphasis mine]".[149] Be that as it may, the relation between these two levels of inferences is complex, in the sense that taking a position on one does not force one's hand on the other. In the case of Oakeshott, this suggests that although he accepts monism in the first sense, indicating that only mental substance exists, he truly clings to the pluralist view in the second sense that there are numerous individuals or modes that may approach a given substance from different perspectives of mind.

Based on this elucidation, we are now in a better position to ponder Gerencser's assertion. On the one side, if what Gerencser means by monism is that only mental substance exists (this is, I believe, the meaning of monism that Oakeshott takes in his theory of experience and its modes), it would be going too far to argue that Oakeshott has ever disposed of idealism's monism. On the contrary, as we shall see, Oakeshott actually retains this stance while dealing with the general features of tradition in *RP*. In point of fact, Oakeshott's traditionalism cannot be well apprehended without referring to the notion of mental totality, or so to speak, *a world of ideas*, embedded in his idealist background.[150]

On the other hand, if by monism Gerencser understands that for Oakeshott only one individual, viz. philosophical experience, really exists, I think he might be neglecting the fact that Oakeshott is an "epistemological pluralist",[151] on the account that since under no circumstances can experience, truth and reality be separated, everything being experienced in a mode of understanding must hold some degree of truth and realise some quality of reality. But, at this point, Gerencser would reply, the problem is that unlike modes of experience, philosophy is defined as "experience without reserva-

[149] T. Honderich, ed., 1995: 584.

[150] Cf. T. Nardin, 2001: 35. where he argues otherwise that in subsequent writings after *EM*, "Oakeshott abandons this (idealist) concern with totality".

[151] *Ibid.*: 22.

tion or preservation", namely, truth without degree, and reality without qualification. As a result, instead of seeing philosophy as an "activity" in *EM*,[152] Gerencser concludes that Oakeshott is "ambiguous as to whether philosophy is concrete experience of the whole or is only the pursuit of concrete experience".[153]

It is true that in the work in question Oakeshott gives philosophy the definition mentioned above. Yet, throughout the book we are hardly told by the philosopher that man's self-critical thought may arrive at the reign of the Absolute, the ultimately concrete experience. On the contrary, as T. Nardin rightly notes, Oakeshott goes against Hegel in doubting that "a completely critical and therefore permanent and unconditional understanding is achievable or even intelligible"; as a substitute, Oakeshott just regards the Absolute as "the imagined end of an endless dialectic of discrepancy and reconciliation".[154] Accordingly, I think Oakeshott genuinely means it when he states that: "What is achieved in experience is an absolutely coherent world of ideas, not in the sense that *it is ever actually achieved* [emphasis mine], but in the more important sense that it is the criterion of whatever satisfaction is achieved".[155]

It follows that the real issue, regarding the nature of philosophy defended in *EM*, has to do with what Oakeshott takes terms such as the "criterion" or the "logical ground" of experience to be. To elaborate my view that *EM* contains a self-conscious attempt to avoid Cartesian-Kantian foundationalism, I now intend to spell out these "ambiguous" terms by extending Oakeshott's remarks about the task of philosophy.

First of all, we have seen that philosophy is treated as the "criterion" of experience in *EM* so as to determine *its own character* rather than to decide the categorical conditions of modes of experience. In this respect, Oakeshott's philosophy is something like "the actual, operative test and criterion" of every experience; its task is to criticise modes of experience "from the standpoint of experience as a whole and for its own sake, and it convicts the modes of abstraction and failure; but it has no power to abolish them. It may eclipse, but it cannot remove them".[156] Philosophy, therefore, considers each of these modes of experience "solely from the standpoint of its capacity

[152] *Ibid.*: 133-4; cf. 48.
[153] S. A. Gerencser, 2000: 26.
[154] T. Nardin, 2001: 6, 23.
[155] *EM*: 35; cf. 365.
[156] *EM*: 350.

to provide what is satisfactory in experience".[157] Whereas, history, for example, must appear as conditional and incomplete to the philosopher, it is the best of all possible worlds that the historian is obliged to think, to believe in. Philosophy, no more than science or practice, is not able to take the place of historical experience; the philosopher's task, remember, is only to consider the nature of history, from the *outside*, i.e. from a philosophical point of view,[158] by way of considering the degree of its coherence — how far it succeeds and how far it fails to provide what is completely satisfactory in experience. And all this must suggest that modes of experience exist independently of philosophising. It is thus not a philosophy but the *philosophie* which would attempt to "give final identity to every mode of experience",[159] that is, to presuppose the existence of a mode by Universal Reason.

Additionally, Oakeshott declares the main business of philosophy is to discern the leading ideas that each mode postulates, although he does sometimes mention philosophy as the "logical ground of modes of experience".[160] Yet, within the context of *EM*, by "logical ground" Oakeshott signifies no more than two meanings. First, philosophy is the logical ground, because it is the totality of experience, the *other* world, by which the modes can be *distinguished* rather than *determined*. Second, he takes it as a contrast to the historic sense as the end in philosophy, that is, philosophy is the logical end in experience rather than the historic end in experience.[161] This contrast is very important, since, unlike his fellow idealists, especially Collingwood in *Speculum Mentis*, we have seen that by so claiming Oakeshott rejects the original Hegelian notion of modes of experience as stages or phases in the development of experience, which at once places philosophy, the Absolute, on the top of the hierarchy of human knowledge and thus makes it superior.

In order to prove further the view that in *EM* Oakeshott does not hold philosophy to be "the hierarchy and the apex", i.e. "thinking *par excellence*",[162] let me here retell his story: All through Oakeshott's

[157] *EM*: 83.

[158] *EM*: 86-8.

[159] Cf. T. Modood, 1980: 318.

[160] *Ibid.*: 318.

[161] See *EM*: esp. 82.

[162] Cf. T. Modood, 1980: 319.

major works,[163] there does seem to be contained a scheme of the levels of human thinking, but this is considered in favour of the degrees of intelligence it may increase or those of mystery it may debate rather than in favour of a hierarchy of knowledge (or a division amongst experience). Occurring in our everyday life there is the form of practical experience which is "at once the most primitive and most general of all forms"[164] of experience. In *EM* Oakeshott not only understands practice to embrace the activity in relation to the ethical institutions such as family, civil society and the state, to use Hegel's classification, or the activity simply in relation to a man who, as Rousseau says, makes love "la grande affaire de sa vie", but he also takes it to include our aesthetic and religious activities. In short, practice is the conduct of life.

On a "theoretical" level, however, "science, history and philosophy may be regarded as attempts to escape from the conduct of life, attempts to throw off the responsibility of living".[165] That is, in the practical life, as confused and distracted by different purposes as it could be, there is nothing that the scientist, the historian or the philosopher could do to correct them. "A scientific idea must be *transformed* [emphasis mine], taken out of the world of scientific experience, before it can establish itself in the world of practice; just as a practical idea must be radically transformed before it can become relevant in scientific experience"; and here the same must go for the relation of history to practice. And further, amongst these "theories", it seems that philosophy is the remotest kind from the conduct of life, for, unlike any other "theoretical" modes of understanding, it is not even concerned with an abstract way of understanding but with the abstractness of understanding.[166] Thus, according to Oakeshott,

> to popularise philosophy is at once to debase it: a general demand for philosophy is a general demand for its degradation. Few, perhaps, will be found willing to surrender the green from the grey, but only those few are on the way to a philosophy. And instead of a gospel, the most philos-

---

[163] In addition to *EM*, see also "Political Education"and "The Activity of Being An Historian" in *RP*, and *HC*: 1-31.

[164] *EM*: 247; see also *VP*: 9, 19.

[165] *EM*: 296-7.

[166] "What is farthest from our [practical] needs is that kings should be philosophers" (*EM*: 321). Thus, it comes as no surprise when K. Minogue writes that "(Oakeshott) took over from Montaigne the Socratic view that philosophy is a preparation for death, a systematic detachment from desires and passions of ordinary life" (2001: 25).

ophy can offer us (in respect of practical life) is an escape, perhaps the only complete escape open to us.[167]

Now, the levels of human thinking recognised in terms of practice-theory-philosophy as such certainly do not mean that each "presupposes and includes within itself those that logically precede it" in order to establish a "scale of forms", to use Collingwood's terminology again.[168] Instead, it clearly re-affirms Oakeshott's modes of experience to be co-existing and with no direct reference to each other.

It follows that, although in *RP* Oakeshott considers the topic of modality from a less-abstract viewpoint of *Lebenswelt* — "the voices in the conversation of human kind",[169] it does not seem plausible to believe that in *RP* a general theory of "civilisation" has replaced the theory of knowledge discovered in *EM* by Oakeshott himself. For, the modes of experience understood as a world of co-existing ideas in *EM* actually match with the image of human intercourse as conversation in which voices "do not compose a hierarchy".[170] And, the point at which philosophy is an "escape" that discloses rather than suggests the *differentia* of modes of experience can be neatly rephrased as follows: "Philosophy, the impulse to study the quality and style of each voice, and to reflect upon the relationship of one voice to another, must be counted a parasitic activity; it springs from the conversation, because this is what the philosopher reflects upon, but it makes no specific contribution to it".[171] Why then has Oakeshott changed his terminology? Before we discuss *RP* in more detail, it might be suggested here that the reason is probably due to the fact that Oakeshott is a thinker who likes to rethink what he was doing from different perspectives.[172] The evidence for this can be found in his later work, *On Human Conduct* (1975) and *On History and Other Essays* (1983), where Oakeshott returned to reconsider a general theory of human understanding.

In contrast to the view that Oakeshott had changed his mind about the conceptions of philosophy, it is my contention that the spirit of both *EM* and *RP* is an identical problematic. Since history, science, poetry and practice, for example, have *de facto* been developed

---

[167] *EM*: 3.

[168] See R. G, Collingwood, 1995: chap. 3.

[169] See esp. *VP*.

[170] *VP*: 10.

[171] *VP*: 14.

[172] Cf. K. Minogue, 1993b: viii, 2001: 22; T. Fuller, 1996: ix; R. Price, 1993: 32.

respectively by the historian, the scientist, the poet and in our ordinary life, the philosopher can no longer contribute to those "rules" or "*practices*" (the latter is a view which has been much developed in *RP*) any more; instead, his task lies merely in recognising the leading ideas that postulate each mode and in so doing he has found a home for himself. On this view, it will be remembered that the title of the book in question is *Experience and Its Modes*, and one of its main themes is to claim the self-consistency of the modes in order to dissect *philosophisme*. To speak of the function of philosophy as determining the validity of modes of experience is to speak of the modes as dependent on the authority of philosophy and thus to reject them as inconsistent. This is too obvious a contradiction — that I can find nowhere in *EM*.

Finally, *EM* indeed consists of nothing but pure philosophical language, yet, Oakeshott has never said that modes of experience must abide by or give serious consideration to philosophical language in order to be self-consistent: "We should listen to philosophers only when they talk philosophy".[173] That is to say, just because philosophical language is used by nobody save the philosopher, what the philosopher has to say about the character of experience, truth, reality and modality belongs to nothing except a *philosophical world* itself.

In sum, the philosopher can never teach an historian, a scientist or a practical person to do their jobs any better and *vice versa*, since, from one standpoint, the distinctive modes have their own rules alone; or alternatively, what philosophy has to say is for its own interest. Put another way, to think historically, scientifically or practically is one thing; but to consider "what is the nature of history?", "what is the nature of science?" and "what is the nature of practice?" is quite another. Consequently, for Oakeshott, philosophy could no longer be expected to be a master discipline that provides foundations to other forms of knowledge in terms of any "external philosophical standards",[174] namely, as a tribunal of pure reason that judges others, according to the Kantian tradition. But rather, the concept of philosophy in *EM*, akin in many ways to G. Ryle's attempt to avoid conceptual confusion and category-error[175] (which, in Oakeshott's language, amounts to *ignoratio elenchi*), is concerned with the making of discriminations and the self-consistency of the categories of human understanding — the modes and philosophy

---

[173] *EM*: 355.

[174] Cf. *VP*: 18.

[175] See G. Ryle, 1949.

itself. It is thus my understanding that *EM* does pose a challenge to foundationalism in philosophy), precisely on ground that the *superbia* of philosophy has been released as making no significant contribution to modes of experience.[176]

III.4.3. Scepticism

Before we move on, however, I must return to the question that was asked earlier — how far and in what sense can Oakeshott in *EM* be regarded as a sceptic?

Just as foundationalism may be traced back to Plato, people often believe that scepticism has its roots in the work of Pyrrho; and after the Greek period, the names of Montaigne and Hume, for instance, have often been mentioned among the sceptics. However, the fact that the thoughts of Hume and Montaigne have little in common is sufficient to suggest that there are *at least* two forms of scepticism that must be distinguished here: Humean naturalism[177] and Montaignean traditionalism. As already mentioned, I do not think that Oakeshott's scepticism is comparable to empiricism in principle, and so let me first resume with Hume's case.

According to B. Stroud and other writers, the sceptical position which originally confronted modern philosophers is thus: our common experience could be just the way that it is, irrespective of it being the case that the external world really exists.[178] Instead of appealing to an external cause, for example the divine, to maintain the existence of objects, Hume makes a radical naturalist move to compromise such a threat. That is, the aim of Hume's philosophy is not to be "sceptical" about the belief in the existence of body and causation, but it is to put forward one's doubt by way of a challenge to show that the doubt is unjustified, that the belief put in question is justified.

To claim so, as we know, Hume comes to limit the pretensions of reason to decide on the validity of our belief concerning the matters of causation and existence. According to Hume, reason does not give us belief about the unobserved, for example, we see a fire and infer that it is hot, but our "custom or habit" leads us to the inference. It is

---

[176] For the sake of structure, I shall come to consider the last issue mentioned by Gerencser, i.e. the interaction between philosophy and modes of experience, mainly in Chapter V.

[177] For the interpretation of Hume's response to scepticism as a naturalist, see P. F. Strawson, 1987. See also A. C. Grayling, 1985: 7-8, and chap. 2.

[178] B. Stroud, 1979. See also P. F. Strawson, 1987: 5-10; A. C. Grayling, 1985: 1-2.

neither demonstrative reasoning nor probable reasoning, as Hume names them, that makes induction possible; it is rather the "constant conjunction", say, of fire and heat, that produces an association of ideas. And if induction is essential to the subsistence of human creatures, it is Nature through our common experience that saves us from the sceptical position that bothered modern philosophers. In his famous lectures on *Scepticism and Naturalism*, P. F. Strawson writes that:

> He [Hume] points out that all arguments in *support* of the sceptical position are totally inefficacious; and by the same token, all arguments *against* it are totally idle. His point is really the very simple one that, whatever arguments may be produced on one side or the other of the question, we simply *cannot help* forming beliefs and expectations in general accordance with the basic canons of induction. . . . He goes on to point out that . . . [e]ven the professed sceptic "*must assent* to the principle concerning the existence of body, though he cannot pretend by any arguments of philosophy to maintain its veracity"; for "nature has not left this to his choice, and has doubtless esteemed it an affair of too great importance to be trusted to our uncertain reasonings and speculations".[179]

Put briefly, then, Humean naturalism *doubts* the rational ground for holding, but does not *deny*, the belief in the existence of the external world and in the justification of induction. As a result of this, Hume seems to accept two levels of thought in his system: that of philosophically critical thinking which cannot give us rational arguments against scepticism, and that of everyday empirical thinking which is driven by an inescapable "natural commitment" to believe that objects exist independently and events are related to one another inductively.[180] From the first standpoint, Hume leaves empiricism with un-refuted scepticism which Kantian transcendentalism tries to overcome;[181] from the second standpoint, however, Hume finds an answer to ensure the real existence of the natural world. And, I presume, it is basically due to these two standpoints of Hume's thought that empiricism after him has developed into scepticism in metaphysics on the one hand, and into scientism on the other.

Quite different from Hume's position, Oakeshott claims reality is what we are obliged to *think*, wherever there is *thought* there is real-

[179] P. F. Strawson, 1987: 11.

[180] *Ibid.*: 12-4; see also chap. 1. sec. 4.

[181] And yet, there appears an attempt to combine Humean (and Wittgensteinian) naturalism with Kantian transcendentalism to achieve the final end in the refutation of scepticism. See A. C. Grayling, 1985.

ity. And precisely because reality is experience and experience is our thought, that *philosophically* reality exists in our thinking mind and is therefore, to borrow Wittgenstein's phrase, "exempt from doubt".[182] Or put another way, since there is no distinction between experience and what is experienced, between mind and object, it is no surprise that the sceptical position under discussion has never really troubled Oakeshott.

Moreover, Hume's scepticism does not prevent him from placing "Logic, Morals, Criticism, and Politics" on a new scientific foundation: the science of man and the theory of human nature; insofar as Hume is the *philosophe*. Whereas for Oakeshott the real limitation of human reason does not lie in the recognition of its own existence but in its partiality and diversity. That is, there are reasons corresponding to different modes of thinking which are not united in a single form. And, based on the notion of the degrees of reality and truth, Oakeshott believes that each constitutes a *self-consistent and abstract world of ideas*.

This is to say that Oakeshott's philosophical interest in considering the modality that each mode introduces into experience is not only to disclose its conditionality of existence and incompleteness of truth, but also to show how precisely because it is governed by its own postulates, it must be self-consistent. However, just because philosophy cannot comment on modes of experience and does not aim at a hierarchy of knowledge in terms of Universal Reason, in the course of philosophising it must concede that *we are ordinarily living amid an abstract world in which understanding is hardly unconditional and complete*. This I take to be of main importance to Oakeshott's scepticism.

At this point, however, some qualifications should be made. Firstly, this form of scepticism, although permitting every abstract voice to freely enter into human conversation, will not bring us to an extreme anarchical position of human knowledge. For the modes have their own rules to play their own game; as such it cannot be dismissed that each one of which is true for itself. Put differently, this temptation to scepticism is neither frivolous nor unduly serious, because:

> the excellence of this conversation (as of others) springs from a tension between seriousness and playfulness. Each voice represents a serious engagement (though it is serious not merely in respect of its being pursued for the conclusions it promises); and without this seriousness the conversation would lack impetus. But in its participation in the conver-

---

[182] Wittgenstein, 1968: sec. 341.

sation each voice learns to be playful, learns to understand itself conversationally and to recognise itself as a voice among voices.[183]

Moreover, it is a sort of philosophical scepticism which has nothing directly to do with the "actual disarray" of our practical world. That is to say, although Oakeshott declares what we *generally* understand as "theories" — such as science, history and philosophy — are not always with us in our everyday life which is "full of irrationality, prejudice and contingency";[184] yet, this is not the property of abstractness that he chiefly has in mind in maintaining a form of scepticism. For Oakeshott, whatever general truth the view in question may contain, it is *irrelevant* to his concern in discussing the modality of practical experience. For, the philosophical view of abstractness means no more than that the practical world is a conditional and incomplete world of understanding and practical men "are not ordinarily conscious of its existence",[185] and that "ordinarily our experience is not clear and unclouded by abstract categories".[186] Thus, it is Oakeshott's point that practical men's view of the world of practical experience will be categorically different from the view that the philosopher is proposing to consider; that "what may be called a philosophy of practical experience cannot expect to have anything whatever in common with a so-called practical philosophy".[187]

It may be inferred from the above discussion that Oakeshott basically argues the case for scepticism on two grounds: One is the rejection of Universal Reason and the consequent claim for the diversity of human reasons; another is the notion of concrete whole as the given in thought which teaches that every abstract mode of understanding must speak from a certain point of view about the world but none is complete, and thus knowing is "an engagement to abate mystery rather than to achieve definitive understanding".[188]

Here, whilst it is not difficult to realise that in principle Oakeshott's scepticism in *EM* has much to do with Bradley's influence, the *grounds* of this scepticism are not unfamiliar to the arguments of Montaigne, one of Oakeshott's authorities in *RP*. Firstly, the diversity of human reasons can be neatly associated with

[183] *VP*: 14.

[184] *EM*: 300.

[185] *EM*: 300.

[186] *EM*: 4.

[187] *EM*: 249. It is no surprise that here by "practical philosophy" Oakeshott means something like Kantian "Universal Practical Philosophy" (see, for example, Kant, 1993b: 3-4).

[188] *HC*: 1.

Montaigne's well-known proverb, "Let every foot have its own shoe".[189] Again, the belief that the given in experience is a concrete whole, a system of meanings, contains a request for the importance of traditional knowledge in human conduct. And few would deny that in modern times it is precisely Montaigne who makes customs and traditions one of the most important arguments for scepticism.[190] And consequently, so far as politics is concerned, Montaigne, in rejecting an external "law of nature" and emphasising the wits on usage,[191] seems to have anticipated Oakeshott's point against liberal ethics. According to Montaigne,

> In public affairs, there is no course so bad, provided that it is stable and traditional, that is not better than change and alternation . . . It is easy enough to criticise a political system (*une police*) . . . But to establish a better regime in place of the one which has been destroyed, there is the problem.[192]

It thus appears to me that Oakeshott's scepticism in *EM* does not necessarily conflict with his traditionalism in *RP*.

In contrast to Humean scepticism in metaphysics, I believe, it is more likely to be Montaignean traditionalism as that which constitutes another thread pulling in the opposite direction to modern foundationalism, as it settles the contextual conditions for the human ability to obtain absolutely reliable knowledge. And so, it is significant that what underlined Descartes' philosophy was precisely an exertion to overcome the scepticism of his time, especially that of Montaigne. In turn, the latest form of scepticism, the so-called "post-modernism", whilst attacking the Cartesian image of philosophy, is more or less motivated by scepticism in terms of contextuality. For example, D. Hiley argues that the post-modernists such as Derrida, Foucault and Rorty, in the course of rejecting the *ahistorical* foundations of truth and the universality of Scientific Reason, have in fact shared the Pyrrhonian aim of opposing philosophy

[189] See Montaigne, 1991.

[190] Cf. P. Burke, 1994: chap. 3. At this point, I think T. Nardin is correct in saying that "Oakeshott's scepticism is definitely not Cartesian scepticism, a tool for clearing away errors so that one can establish incontestable truth, but a hermeneutical scepticism that follows the conclusion that all identifications and therefore all things are context-dependent" (2001: 29).

[191] "Now laws remain respected not because they are just but because they are laws. That is the mystical basis of their authority. They have no other. It serves them well, too. Laws are often made by fools, and even more often by men who fail in equality because they hate equality: but always by men, vain authorities who can resolve nothing" (Montaigne, 1991: 1216).

[192] Quoted by P. Burke, 1994: 29.

in order to return us to the contingencies of our condition and the traditions of our ordinary life.[193]

By revealing the sceptical traits of Oakeshott's thought, we are then re-confirming his anti-foundationalist attitude at the same time. But here, Oakeshott's "transcendental" position needs to be compared to two forms of "total scepticism" that he does not subscribe to, namely, historicism and post-modernism. In many senses, these two categories of thinking can be related to one another.[194] For my purpose, however, I shall take Rorty's notion of the "end to philosophy"[195] into discussion, and postpone the problem of historicism to Chapter V.

III.4.4. Rorty: The End to Philosophy

I am aware that in order to claim Oakeshott as an exponent of a non-foundationalist conception of philosophy, the term "foundationalism" needs to be qualified, because it is largely used in the context of Richard Rorty's *Philosophy and the Mirror of Nature*. At first sight, it is of course true that in his bid to reconcile the non-foundationalist trend in the twentieth-century philosophical thought, Rorty himself admits to being indebted in good measure to Oakeshott's conception of "conversation".[196] And, by the term "foundationalism", Rorty refers much to his repudiation of the character of modern natural philosophy as "a foundational science, an armchair discipline capable of discovering the formal . . . characteristics of any area of human life".[197] What Rorty says on this point, I think, may speak for Oakeshott as well. For, it follows from the above that by claiming the *differentia* of modes of experience, Oakeshott tries to attack the tendency of traditional philosophy to be an indiscriminate pursuit of universal knowledge.

However, it should be noted that, for Rorty, what makes modern philosophy foundationalist is the misconception of treating knowl-

---

[193] See D. Hiley, 1988.

[194] See, for example, A. Cohen, 1989: 112-3, 128-30, 135, n.3 & n.6.

[195] The theme of the "end to philosophy" has, of course, become a landmark of post-modernism. Derrida, for example, claims that the death of philosophy "should be the only question today capable of founding the community of those who are still called philosophers" (1978: 79-80). And, Lyotard, to take another example, takes philosophy as the most distinguished case of "meta-narrative" while he considers the "post-modern condition" as "incredulous towards meta-narrative" (see 1984).

[196] Rorty, 1980: 389.

[197] *Ibid.*: 139.

edge as an accurate "representation" of reality made possible by some special mental processes. Oakeshott, as indicated, has rejected the correspondence theory of knowledge, but he did so merely for the sake of defending idealism. Whereas, in a more serious sense, that which Rorty really keeps in mind in his attack on foundationalism is the philosophic attempt to establish a *theory of knowledge*, or epistemology, in terms of treating the concept of mind not merely as the mirror of nature but as a meaningful philosophical category.[198] As a result of this, in his attempt to break down traditional epistemology as a delusion, Rorty bases his arguments mainly upon Dewey's reflection on the social uses of philosophy, i.e. the view that knowledge is what we are justified in believing in varying social contexts rather than in the mind/world relationship; and upon the later Wittgenstein's idea of language as a tool in rejection of his earlier view of a pictorial-like representational theory of knowledge; and upon Heidegger's treatment of the effort to make the knowing subject, i.e. the mind, which Rorty sees as a self-deceptive attempt to escape from dealing with "strangeness", that initially led people to commence thinking.[199] And consequently, Rorty himself comes to characterise the function of philosophy as "therapeutic". Philosophy is thus something like an "all-purpose intellectual" or a "culture-critic", whose "edifying role" is to keep enquiry open to new and newer possibilities in terms of the changing of historical conditions.

---

[198] Indeed, in *The Consequences of Pragmatism* (1982), Rorty has provided us with a more radical theme of the end to philosophy, where the critique of foundationalism in modern epistemology has been extended to the Western tradition of Philosophy as a whole. According to Rorty, the grand ethos of that tradition is the notion of *philosophia perennis*, that is, the view that the business of Philosophy is to deal with the Truth, or the Good: "the history of the attempt to do so, and of criticisms of such attempts is, roughly, coextensive with the history of that literary genre we call 'philosophy' — a genre founded by Plato" (1982: xvi). In this matter, as A. Cohen points out, "the overall architecture of Rorty's entire critical project can be depicted as encapsulating three distinctive layers of philosophical 'traditions': The core is the tradition of analytical philosophy (founded by Frege, Russell, Carnap), which belongs to the broader tradition of modern philosophy (founded by Descartes, Locke and Kant), which links itself with the historically continuous Western tradition called 'Philosophy' (founded by Plato)" (1989: 119). Here, it is the second layer of Rorty's project that interests me the most. But in any case, it is my view that foundationalism is not necessarily predicated on *a theory of knowledge* any more than on the notion of *philosophia perennis*; Oakeshott, it seems to me, has rejected foundationalism in terms of an epistemological discourse and repudiated *philosophisme* without giving up the ceaseless pursuit of *philosophia perennis*.

[199] Rorty, 1980: 9.

So far as *EM* is concerned, however, it was exactly a *theory of experience* as a reworking of the variety in experience discussed in modern natural philosophy, upon which Oakeshott's conception of philosophy and his notion of modality are based. It has also become clear that at the stage of *EM*, as Oakeshott willingly acknowledges, his view on experience owed much to idealism, especially to Hegel's *Phenomenology of Spirit* and Bradley's *Appearance and Reality*, a philosophical doctrine which would aspire to nothing without the conception of mind. And consequently, in the work of *EM*, Oakeshott has considered everything about traditional philosophical debates over the mind/body problem, the character of experience, the nature of truth and reality and so forth. To get himself involved in these philosophical issues by mainly choosing the side of idealism, he cannot be said to have preserved philosophy from examination as a *traditional mode* of discourse in which epistemology plays a key role. As a matter of fact, unlike Rorty, Oakeshott's philosophy, by definition, can never set aside the problems of truth and reality; and he makes every effort to maintain philosophy as a categorically distinct discourse. As he puts it, philosophy, for him as for others, is concerned with a "perfectly coherent system" of metaphysics, of epistemology and of a theory of logic; and the three cannot be separated from one another because "to sub-divide philosophy is to destroy it".[200] In addition, Rorty's inclination to pragmatism is at once contradicted by Oakeshott's protection of a *pure* philosophy with no reference to, say, practice and history.

A debated problem that emerges here, I think, is whether, given that there is a crisis in ordering an "integral philosophical system", philosophy should remain as a self-distinct world of human activity pursued under the name of metaphysics, epistemology and logic. For Oakeshott, the answer seems positive, but for Rorty it is the contrary. Rorty's announcement of the "end to philosophy", Oakeshott would argue, is too "sceptical" to realise that, although the human mind often falls short of definitive understanding, philosophy recognised as an unconditional understanding "may hover in the background"[201] of human understanding as a whole, such that the conditionality of the conditions of human knowledge may be observed. Also, Rorty's "total scepticism" fails to see that "to demystify philosophy itself"[202] (a self-limiting character of philosophy

---

[200] *EM*: 348-9.

[201] *HC*: 3.

[202] J. L. Auspitz, 1993: 8.

upon which both Oakeshott and Rorty agree) is itself a form of philosophical thinking. Thus, in any event, in our conversation it is valuable and indispensable to have an intellectual discourse as "philosophising" for its own sake; to claim "the end to philosophy" is to terminate an engagement in the pursuit of "the love of wisdom" that has substantiated the Western civilisation for two and a half millennia.

More precisely, then, the crucial controversy between Rorty and Oakeshott is this. Does a *theory of knowledge* necessarily attempt to foundationalise philosophy as a master discipline that underpins the natural sciences and authorises the validity of any other knowledge in terms of an objective scientific-criterion? In order to question this necessity, I shall here conclude what I have argued for the non-foundationalist character of Oakeshott's theory of knowledge from another point of view, that is, to compare it to the foundationalist assumptions that I have disclosed in the last chapter.

First, the assumption of scientism, in fact, implies science as the ultimate criterion of experience, a view which Oakeshott finds "too easy an escape".[203] Science is, of course, a legitimate form of knowledge; but it is merely one among many other possibilities. If there were only one voice of science in the conversation of human kind, our life would be insipid. And, to take science as the ultimate criterion for all knowledge is at once to make the error of *ignoratio elenchi*.

Again, the second assumption, i.e. a foundationalist analysis of knowledge in terms of a description of public reality and external truth, also cannot be applied to the thought of Oakeshott. It will be recollected that Oakeshott considers that truth is always "true for itself"; for this reason, he rejects the *ab extra* theory of truth in order to make room for the self-consistency of modes of experience. Likewise, reality is nothing save what we are obliged to think: "Whatever has a meaning, if we give it its full meaning, is real; and whatever is real has a meaning". To be real is not separable from to be in thinking, and the ways of thinking are distinguishable and self-governed. The historical, the scientific and the practical, as real as they are, do not depend on a full description of public reality.

Thirdly, we have seen that one of the main themes of *EM* is to suggest that reason, appropriate to any one mode of experience, cannot, without irrelevance, be applied to any other. And this attack, as we shall see, has been rounded out by Oakeshott's *RP*. On this meaning, Oakeshott is, of course, against the superiority of Universal Reason, i.e. the third assumption of foundationalism. Finally, as I hope to

[203] *EM*: 2.

show where appropriate, the Oakeshottian image of "conversation" as "an unrehearsed intellectual adventure" makes a possible replacement for the "argumentative" premise of Enlightenment civilisation.

III.5. The Mode of Practice

Thus far, then, we have unveiled two main themes of *EM*: the self-consistency of modes of experience and the non-foundationalist notion of philosophy. What remains to be explained are the conditions of history, science and practice exemplified in the work. But here, I only intend to bring the mode of practice into consideration such that it may offer us a test case to show the idea of philosophy and the autonomy of a mode of experience in its fuller sense, in preparation for the study of Oakeshott's political and moral theory in the next chapter.

III.5.1. Practice as a World of Ideas

One of Oakeshott's main intentions in *EM* is to interrogate whether each of the modes of experience is an abstract world of ideas arrested in experience or a concrete world of ideas. In the act of reflecting upon the character of practice (and of history), however, we have to consider whether practice is a "world of ideas" in the first instance, because it is often disclaimed that practice (and history) are not as *real* as science in the sense of being outside the realm of experience or the genera of knowledge. Thus, Oakeshott begins his philosophy of practical experience by rejecting a number of views that claim practice is less than experience or knowledge.

First of all, it is said that practice is not a unity of experience because it is activity not thought, i.e. a world of actions not a world of ideas. The view that human activities are products of human thoughts and therefore can be disassociated from them to be the observable objects of a "science of man" has constituted one of the philosophical grounds which formulates the so-called "behavioural approach" during the mid-twentieth century.[204] Although the tendency to replace, say, political philosophy with a science of political behaviour which "aims at being quantitative wherever possible"[205]

---

[204] For a condensed discussion on the historical development and theoretical commitment of the movement of behaviourism, see R. Dahl, 1993: 249-67.

[205] D. Truman, "The Implications of Political Behaviour Research", quoted in *ibid.*: 257.

has today been proved to be in vain, the scientific and realistic out-look that stand behind the project has certainly not yet vanished.

I do not intend to consider here the possibility of "political sci-ence" in Oakeshott's thought; instead, it seems more urgent to point out that the empiricist-realistic notion of an "external" or "objective" world of doings and happenings independent of the construction of the mind is a mere fiction to Oakeshott. Based on his idealistic view, Oakeshott claims that the world is a world of meanings which knows no absolute divisions; everything falling outside *the* mean-ingful world is a nonentity. That is, for Oakeshott action is not sepa-rable from thought, it is itself a form of thought, i.e. a world of ideas. As Oakeshott later reclaims in *HC*, it is not possible to find a purely *objective* human action which does not contain our "reflective con-sciousness" of a certain sort; and thus it is freedom that must be regarded as a necessary condition of human agency.[206]

Freedom involves the notions of volition and of the will. As a mat-ter of fact, as we shall see, Oakeshott envisages freedom, volition and the will as different expressions of the same thing, namely, the cardi-nal (formal) condition[207] that postulates our practical life: "practice is the exercise of the [free] will; practical thought is volition; practical experience is the world *sub specie voluntatis*".[208] Before recapitulating Oakeshott's notion of freedom as it appears in *EM*, however, we only need to recall that he argues that action and thought are insepa-rable, that volition, whatever its defects as experience, is a judge-ment, i.e. a form of experience.

Moreover, a form of experience, according to Oakeshott, must be a world of knowledge at the same time. There are accordingly two more weighty contentions that have to be rejected at this stage, namely, the argument that practical activity may be experiential but it is not knowledge proper. In the first place, there is so-called intuitionism which argues that: "'the rules of morality are not con-clusions of our reason'; and it is not reflection, but intuition which tells us what in particular is right and wrong".[209] Oakeshott declares, however, that this ethical thought has failed to realise that these feel-ings and intuitions "are not completely isolated and wholly ground-

---

[206] See esp. *HC*: 36-41.

[207] I shall argue in the next chapter that Oakeshott has considered the problem of freedom from two related standpoints in his works: Whereas *EM* deals with the *formal conditions* of freedom, *RP* emphasises the problem of its *practice* in a political tradition.

[208] *EM*: 258.

[209] *EM*: 253.

less; they belong to a world the principle of which is one of coherence; and, so far as it goes, it cannot avoid the character of a world of knowledge".[210]

On the other hand, there is a more formidable contention which suggests that morality is "a mere collection of opinions". For Oakeshott, however, this extremely relative view of ethics is open to a fatal objection: a collection of mere opinions has implied the possibility of contradictory different opinions, and yet to recognise two different opinions as contradictory we must have at the same time conveyed our judgement towards them and thus entered a *world* of opinions. Hence, nowhere is the criterion of judgement absconding from the world of opinions, "everywhere in opinion there is implicit assertion, reference to reality".[211] Indeed, it perhaps should be suggested that in order to avoid denial of the view in question one must not necessarily uphold that practical activity is a world of knowledge but only that it is a world of *true* opinions. However, even if it is the case, Oakeshott goes on to say, "opinion is not the negation of knowledge, it is merely unorganised, immature knowledge"; that "true opinion differs from knowledge, not absolutely, but in degree".[212] That is, a world of true opinions is not beyond the genera of knowledge, it is an imperfect world of ideas in which the principle of knowledge remains implicit. Thus, the world of practice must be a world of ideas, thoughts or knowledge, not in spite of, but precisely because of the fact that it is often only a world of true opinions.[213]

III.5.2. The Conditions of the Practical World

Having established the view that practice cannot be other than a form of experience, thought or knowledge, we may now return to consider its modality from the totality of experience.

---

[210] *EM*: 253.

[211] *EM*: 255.

[212] *EM*: 255.

[213] In some sense, it appears to me, Oakeshott's point here can be seen as an objection to moral relativism in general, including Moorean meta-ethics. Again, meta-ethics, after Moore, has developed into emotivism or emotive theory, an ethical movement which became prominent in the late 1930s under the influence of A. J. Ayer's *Language, Truth and Logic* (1936) and reached its fruition with the publication of C. L. Stevenson's *Ethics and Language* (1944). Oakeshott certainly could not have the name emotivism in mind at the time of writing *EM* (1933). But, given that the core meaning of emotivitism lies in the view that moral judgements are merely expressions of our feelings and emotions which have little to do with the notion of reality and truth, Oakeshott would not agree with this ethical movement in principle.

We have mentioned that for Oakeshott practice is the exercise of the free will, practical experience is the world *sub specie voluntatis*. It may now be added that this view has already suggested that practical life is an *attempt* to make coherent our practical experience as a whole, that is, to understand the world under the category of volition. In other words, when we are making a practical performance or utterance, there is always an "alteration or continuance of existence" being *deliberately* undertaken; practical activity everywhere depends on a "to be" which is "not yet". As a result, practical activity must involve "a will to change or maintain" which is discrepant from the "existence", it entails an "unrealised idea" or an "unfulfilled desire" which is discrepant from "what is". It is thus *presupposed* in practice that there are two *worlds* to be reduced to one: the world of "to be" and the world of "what is"; and this presupposition is absolute.

That there are two worlds presupposed in practice, however, does not suggest that there are two forms of reality in search of correspondence. But rather it indicates only that the world of "to be" is the "imagined and wished-for outcome"[214] of the given world of "what is"; it is the coherence of the world that we *will*. And since in practice the notion of coherence is always realised in terms of *value*, the world of "to be" can be identified as the world of "what *ought* to be". Consequently, it may be concluded that practice is the alternation or maintenance of "what is" so as to agree with an idea of "what ought to be".

So it comes as no surprise that for Oakeshott the principle of the coherence of practical knowledge, namely, practical truth, is nothing but the idea of freedom. That is, since practice is the exercise of the free will, every attempt to reconcile a "what is" with a "what ought to be" must be seen as an accomplishment of human freedom. On this meaning, to say that the practical truth is the coherence of practical ideas is to say that practice is a self-consistent world of ideas having its own criterion of truth, namely, freedom. Oakeshott writes that:

> Freedom and necessity are conditions of the mind which has achieved (or has failed to achieve) practical truth. They are conditions of the practical self. They have neither meaning nor relevance for the self in scientific experience or in history, and are certainly meaningless when attributed to the universe as a whole. If a man thinks to set himself free, in any save a vague and metaphorical sense, by the study of science or of history or by the pursuit of philosophy he is grossly mistaken. The only truth that makes a manufacturer free is practical truth, the possession of

---

[214] Cf. *HC*: 36ff.

a coherent world of practical ideas. Indeed, practical truth and freedom seem to me inseparable; wherever the one is, the other will be found.[215]

In short, practice is a self-consistent mode of understanding approaching the world under the exclusive category of freedom.

It follows that in Oakeshott's view practice, by virtue of its conditions, i.e. the world *sub specie voluntatis*, must be distinctive from other modes on the one hand and from philosophy on the other. At this point, Oakeshott thus comes to criticise utilitarianism as consequentialism, Kantianism and pragmatism in *EM*. In the first place, as already shown, utilitarianism holds the view that "the rightness of an action is determined by its contribution to the happiness of everyone affected by it".[216] The view that Oakeshott is suggesting, however, maintains that "nothing more is required to establish its practical truth than that it should be shown to be followed by consequences of a particular kind".[217] That is, to establish the criterion of practical truth, writers like Mill often appeal to some sort of external principle, i.e. the utilitarian principle that moral activity is the promotion of "the greatest happiness of the greatest number". And yet, it appears to Oakeshott that this notion contradicts the character of experience and that of truth. For it assumes that "truth is sought in what is 'other' than what is given, and not in what is whole. Thinking has become the construction of a chain or series of ideas; and [on this view] truth [is] not merely difficult of attainment, but inherently unattained".[218] Also, the defect of this view lies in the fact that "the future *as such* is selected as the criterion of truth, and that when this criterion is considered it turns out to be no criterion at all. The problem has been postponed, not solved".[219]

Oakeshott's criticism of utilitarianism and his stress upon the free will, however, does not make him a Kantian. For it is clear from the above quotation that Oakeshott believes our practical reasoning is so self-consistent that it should be segregated from any "theoretical" reasonings (philosophical, scientific and even historical). Oakeshott writes that:

Kant, for example, found it necessary to subordinate theoretical reason to practical because the former, as he conceived it, was limited to "phenomena"; that is, it was not unlike what I have spoken of as scientific

[215] *EM*: 268, n1.

[216] A. Quinton, 1989: 1.

[217] *EM*: 263.

[218] *EM*: 265.

[219] *EM*: 266.

experience . . . Others have identified "theory" and "rationalism" or "intellectualism", and have set their belief in the finality of the will over against what they call "mere intellectualism". A rationalism of this sort, it is true, is an abstract mode of experience. Indeed, there is little or nothing to be said in its favour. Where it is not a confusion of scientific, historical and practical thought, it will be found to be an attempt to replace science, history and practice by an attenuated and falsely conceived "philosophy"; and its result is distinguished only by its inconsequence. But to think of this as the only alternative to a belief in the finality of practice, and to conclude, from the obvious abstractness of the one, the completeness of the other, is a form of argument which might be expected to appeal to none but "rationalists".[220]

I quote this statement from *EM* at length, not only because it highlights the picture of Oakeshott's departure from Kantianism, but also because it re-affirms once again the non-foundationalist aim of the work and its connection with *RP*. It has given us a hint, which we shall expand on in our discussion of *RP*, that it is Oakeshott's understanding that the substantial content of our moral life is based on our ethical traditions rather than on the empty formulation of moral laws. In other words, although both Kant and Oakeshott take the notion of free will to be the necessary condition of human practice, whereas for Kant this freedom is so radical that it only allows us to act on a set of categorical imperatives, for Oakeshott the ultimate meaning of this freedom lies in our proper ability to deal with contingent, particular moral and political problems within a tradition of behaviour.

It is not surprising that the contrast between philosophy and practice also leads Oakeshott to reject pragmatism. In a wider aspect, pragmatism can be regarded as a form of consequentialism to which Oakeshott objects. But more significantly, by identifying the practical with philosophy, it seems to Oakeshott that pragmatism, along with utilitarianism and Kantianism, simply commits the error of *ignoratio elenchi*; conversely, to Oakeshott "it is meaningless alike either to accept or to reject a philosophical proposition for a practical reason".[221]

But what makes practice self-consistent must maintain it to be abstract at the same time. For a mode's explicit character as a modality actually and continuously conflicts with its implicit character as experience, and more crucially, this self-contradiction (and thus abstractness) cannot be removed without stamping out the mode itself. In practice, remember, it is the case that its explicit feature as

[220] *EM*: 317-8.
[221] *EM*: 320.

the will to alter or maintain existence, the attempt to throw reality into the future, contradicts its implicit feature of being present experience.[222] But further, Oakeshott also claims that the mode of practice produces a specific "permanent dissatisfaction". For, on the one hand, the will to change must presuppose two worlds in practice: the world of "what is" and the world of "what ought to be" and in practical actions they are somehow to be reduced to one; on the other hand, however, the two worlds *themselves* can never be finally reconciled. Because, unlike history and science, every *particular* practical attempt to reconcile the world of "what ought to be" and the world of "what is" through action is at once itself an abolition of the discrepancy that makes practice possible in the first place, insofar as our practical life, as it were, must be *transient* and *contingent,* in which the satisfactions of countless wants come and go. But there is no final way out of the discrepancy between the two worlds presumed in practice as every practical action is an exercise of the free will which is the necessary condition of human agency.[223]

III.5.3. Ethics as Pseudo-Philosophy

Before we leave this chapter, let us take a brief look at the characteristic of ethics that Oakeshott discloses in *EM*. We have observed that for Oakeshott the mode of practical ideas is seen, together with history and science, as an abstract mode of experience which falls short of being complete before a philosophical reflection; by way of contrast, he now claims, ethics and political philosophy are "pseudo-philosophy", meaning an "indeterminate arrest in philosophy": it is indeterminate because, unlike the modes of experience under consideration, it is without a determinate homogeneous world of experience on its own, and it is an arrest because it is only "to see one particular mode of experience — practical experience — from the standpoint of the totality of experience".[224]

It follows that ethics "is nothing if not philosophical, but in so far as it remains 'ethical' it is a modification of philosophical thought. Its defeat is not that it belongs to an abstract world of experience, but that it fails to recognise and to realise its membership of the world of concrete experience".[225] And so, it may be said that ethics is "parasitic" (remember, this is the characteristic coming from that of phi-

---

[222] *EM*: 304-5.
[223] *EM*: 303-4.
[224] *EM*: 345.
[225] *EM*: 335.

losophy itself) on the world of human practice, but can never be identified with the practical. "An ethical theory", he says, "will be morally neutral, will neither be driven from nor dependent upon specific practical judgements". In short, Oakeshott holds a non-normative notion of ethics in *EM*[226] in the sense that ethical reflection has no bearing on the specific conduct of practice, because it is not a way of living which presupposes the abstract, self-contradictory, transient and evaluative characteristics of the practical world, but a form of thought which takes nothing for granted.[227]

Oakeshott says that his concern about ethics as pseudo-philosophy in *EM* is "merely in illustrating a general mode of experience and not in writing an introduction to ethics",[228] and yet, given that the business of ethics is to explain the major concepts of the mode of practice, in discussing the characteristic of the practical world so far, we have been engaging in ethical reflection upon human conduct, i.e. a "philosophy of practical experience". I now turn to consider in greater detail Oakeshott's ethical thought.

---

[226] *EM*: 335-40.

[227] There is a debate which has arisen around Oakeshott's grounds for separating philosophical reason from practical reason in *EM*. See D. Hall & T. Modood, 1982a: 157-76 and 1982b: 184-9; J. Liddington, 1982: 177-83.

[228] *EM*: 335.

Chapter IV

A Sceptical Philosophy of Politics

IV.1. Introduction: From Truth to Rationality

It is my aim in this chapter to examine Oakeshott's philosophical understanding of morality and politics with regard to the Enlightenment ethical position concerned. I hope to provide a fresh approach to comprehending the *position* of Oakeshott's political philosophy by interpreting him not as a doctrinal liberal nor as a dogmatic conservative, but as a philosophical, sceptical critic of the Enlightenment project. And in doing so, I shall draw greater attention to *Rationalism in Politics* (1962, new edition 1991; hereafter *RP*), which is significant among Oakeshott's other major ethical works.

It is my view that Oakeshott's long-term critique of Rationalism consists of an essential and more direct piece of evidence that shows his sensitive awareness of the crisis of the Enlightenment ethical position and its theoretical connection with foundationalism in philosophy. If the main objective against which Oakeshott argues in *EM* is *philosophisme* — an indiscriminate pursuit of universal knowledge, it is now Rationalism — the sovereignty of technique and certainty over human conduct, that becomes the thinker's target. Or, put differently, Rationalism is the *manner of thinking* that Oakeshott characterises as one of the most distinct aspects of the modern world: its philosophical resources can be traced back to modern foundationalism, and its most significant influence is in the department of morality and politics. In this sense, it can be inferred that

foundationalism is "rationalism in philosophy" from which "rationalism in politics" develops.

To ponder Oakeshott's criticisms of Rationalism in a complete
way, we must recall here the main theme of *Experience and Its Modes*
(1933; hereafter *EM*) because that which runs throughout the
thinker's moral and political writings is the non-foundationalist
notion of philosophy that he has established: Philosophising is
self-critical in the sense that it is suspicious of any obstacle in the
enquiry; it is sceptical in the sense that it concedes that the world or
tradition in which we live is so comprehensive that our understanding is always incomplete and conditional; and it is self-limited in the
sense that there is nothing which philosophy can do to remove the
conditionality of our knowing.

The characteristics of self-criticism and self-limitation imply that
Oakeshott's (political) philosophy aims to transcend whatever
appears to be partial and incomplete for its own sake. Given the frus-
tration caused by Rationalism, Oakeshott's (political) philosophy
thus attempts to re-establish an Aristotelian theory of human activity in general (as contrasted to rationalism in philosophy), followed
by a more coherent way of understanding politics in particular,
namely, conservatism in politics (as contrasted to rationalism in politics. In interpreting Oakeshott's (political) philosophy this way, we
are creating a stage to examine his critique of liberalism as *a* form of
rationalism in politics. And, my main arguments leading to the
non-liberal property of Oakeshott's political thought will be especially summed up in [IV.5.5.].

Moreover, the notion "conservatism" or "traditionalism" presented in *RP* is likewise related to Oakeshott's scepticism in *EM*. The
consequent emphasis on the importance of a tradition of behaviour
in morality and politics, however, has sometimes led Oakeshott to
be mistakenly understood as an historicist on the one hand; and a
"pessimistic" conservative (or a conservative in whatever negative
sense) on the other. The first misconception is a crucial issue that I
shall not deal with until I come to examine Oakeshott's historiography. For the moment, we need only note that this does not mean that
Oakeshott's philosophical politics consists of a utopia which does
not care about the historic context of political ideas. On the contrary,
as we shall see, Oakeshott thinks that philosophical explanation
should not totally leave aside an understanding of what has been
going on in the Human Past. The Oakeshottian approach to interpreting past political theory and practice, however, *cannot* be the
genuinely historical (as a mode of understanding) for two main

reasons.[1] First, it is concerned with the "unmistakable emergence"[2] or the "abridged conceptual structure"[3] of an historic identity rather than with a complete narrative of the unity of historical individuals in terms of change. Second, Oakeshott first established the ideal characteristics of the identity of "rationalism in politics" on the one hand, and "conservatism in politics" on the other, before engaging in his study of such a "quasi-philosophical past", as I shall come to name it.

In this respect, it seems to me that Oakeshott's philosophical politics is not only concerned with the importance of traditional knowledge in political practice, but also it is concerned with *the* tradition of modern Western politics itself. Hence, in understanding the Oakeshottian theme of "traditionalist politics versus rationalist politics" below, our attention is directed to both their philosophical elements and historic fortunes. Far from being a reactionary traditionalist, it is more likely that Oakeshott has given us a profound traditionalist understanding of politics; and it is this philosophical traditionalism, based on his sceptical idealism established in *EM*, that underlies his substantive response to the crisis of the Enlightenment project.

In what follows, as a result, I propose to link Oakeshott's Rationalism with the philosophical and ethical situations of the Enlightenment project from the outset ([IV.2.]). And then I shall specify Oakeshott's philosophical traditionalism by examining how it is able to renounce rationalism in philosophy ([IV.3.]), and rationalism in politics ([IV.4.]). And finally, I would like to provide a brief outline of *On Human Conduct* (1975; hereafter *HC*, [IV.5.]). Before moving on, however, it must be noted that whilst in *EM* the crucial term "practice" is taken to denote a mode, the world seen *sub specie voluntatis* all the time, in *RP* and other works Oakeshott also applies it more widely to mean something like the regular exercise that one conveys in order to learn the "skill" of an activity such as being an historian, a scientist or a practical man.[4] On this usage, to speak of a world of ideas or a mode of experience is equal to speaking of a "practice", a tradition or an idiom of activity. And so, it seems to me that the notion "practice", as a substitution for "tradition", which was particularly represented in *HC*, is basically in accordance with

[1]   Cf. D. Boucher, 1991: 722-3.

[2]   See, for example, *RP*: 18, 370; *PFPS*: 57.

[3]   See, for example, *MPME*: 3.

[4]   Cf. R. Grant, 1990: 45; J. L. Auspitz, 1993: 18.

its second usage set forth in *RP*.[5] And thus, in what follows I shall italicise the second usage as *practice* or *practices*.

IV.2. Rationalism as the Enlightenment Project

The purpose of this section is to interpret Oakeshott's Rationalism as a concept which spells out the Enlightenment project and thus carries its predicament into the Western world.

IV.2.1. The Character and Pedigree of Rationalism

The Rationalism with which Oakeshott is concerned is modern Rationalism, that he claims is the most remarkable intellectual concern of post-Renaissance Europe. Oakeshott's Rationalism holds that human beings share *a priori* "reason" which can be exercised as an "infallible guide" to human conduct by formulating a set of "self-contained" and "perfect" rules.[6] This means that the term Rationalism employed by Oakeshott embraces more than epistemological rationalism; in fact, it represents a general current of thought which has been inspired and sustained by modern mainstream philosophy as a whole. I shall return to the philosophical foundations of Rationalism later. For now, let me briefly unfold the implications of this definition of Rationalism.

As it implies, the Rationalist belief is that "knowledge is the power" to instruct human conduct, and the knowledge concerned is that which is so susceptible to formulation into rules, propositions and principles that it can always be "learned by heart, repeated by rote, and applied mechanically".[7] Oakeshott contends that such knowledge could be considered to be "technical knowledge", "knowledge of technique" or "knowledge of the book". However, it should be noted that Oakeshott seems to use the term "technique" both as the *method* of enquiry, research or analysis which attempts to

---

[5]   Cf. T. Nardin, 2001: 76; see also 58, 69.

[6]   In this sense, it may be said that the Rationalist is one who rejects the autonomy of complex practice in favour of the highest order of abstract (moral) theory. Thus, as N. O'Sullivan points out, for Oakeshott Rationalism is self-contradictory in the sense that it "fails to recognise the inevitability of this gap (between practice and theory, especially, between is and ought), persisting in the foolish attempt to achieve a once-and-for-all unification of the ideal and the actual" (1987: 233; see also, Nardin, 2001: 92, n24). O'Sullivan's reading as such may help the reader to make clearer the point I made earlier that from a philosophical point of view Rationalism is just another expression of foundationalism.

[7]   *RP*: 15.

formulate human activity into rules, and as the *result* of this formulation.[8] Thus, not only is a political principle, a moral code or a cookery recipe (a very Oakeshottian example) the logic of the syllogism, but the rules of research, observation and verification in science and in history, and so forth, are all taken as examples of the knowledge to which the Rationalist gives sole notice. For the sake of clarity, in what follows it would be advantageous to maintain awareness of the different levels of reference with regard to a "formulated technique of research" and "technical knowledge" acquired respectively. Nevertheless, it is safe to say that for the Rationalist the sovereignty of "reason" is equal to the "sovereignty of technique".

From a "technological will to power",[9] it follows that the Rationalist's ambition of being a man is to be a "self-made man". For, according to Rationalist belief what a technique of research could give is a "self-conscious" and a "self-complete" knowledge; that is, a technique of research would allow him to isolate his actions from their context and to dissolve them into a series of problems to be surmounted by a *tour de raison*. Moreover, it suggests that the Rationalist is apt to take *telos* as the mark of his "reason". "Rationalist activity", it is said, "is activity in search of a certain, conclusive answer to a question, and consequently the question must be formulated in such a way that it admits of such an answer".[10] In other words, irrespective of what technical knowledge appears to be, the Rationalist claims the existence of a "rational" answer corresponding to any problem, and this answer is, by its nature, the perfect answer. Or, rational conduct is regarded as the achievement of a formulated purpose, i.e. an "independently premeditated end" which springs from something that has already taken place in advance of human activity; and it is governed solely by that faultless purpose or end.

Thirdly, given that the existence of a "rational" solution is waiting to be discovered and then applied to our conduct, it becomes difficult for the Rationalist to disbelieve that those who think honestly will think contrary to himself, since the Rationalist takes the view that the exercise of technological will, or the attempt to discover a perfect solution, will lead different people to the same conclusions and issue in the same form of activity. In this respect, Rationalism is

---

[8]   For technique as the method of discovery, see, for example, *RP*: 7, 18-21.

[9]   Cf. R. B. Pippin, 1997: 24.

[10] *RP*: 103.

identical with a form of "intellectual equalitarianism".[11] And furthermore, from such a radical individualist standpoint springs "the
distrust of time": a view of understanding human conduct as
self-moved by an ubiquitous "reason" alone can indeed have no
room for a tradition, a custom or a habit of human behaviour. The
Rationalist, Oakeshott claims, has no idea of the importance of the
accumulation of experience; has none of that "negative capability"
(which Keats attributed to Shakespeare) of receiving mysteries and
uncertainties of a tradition. He has nothing but "an impatient hun-
ger for eternity and an irritable nervousness in the face of everything
topical and transitory".[12]

Although, for convenience, the features of Rationalism can be
demonstrated as "abstractness", "perfectionism" and "universalism", they must not be seen as detached factors but only as integral
qualities. "The essence of Rationalism", says Oakeshott, "is their
combination".[13] Besides, Rationalism understood in this way is perhaps the most lively, intellectual trend that has influenced almost
every area of Western thought. However, it is always close to being
transformed into political thought. For the gist of Rationalism, as
noted, is to formulate an "infallible guide" in human practice; its
own logic contains a bid to set formulated examples to practical life.
On this account, it may not be inappropriate to characterise Rationalism further in terms of a political programme.

Based on what has been said already, then, it can be seen as the
Rationalist's common hope that a "rational programme" for political and moral order could, in practice, be established and safely
relied upon. This means that the character of Rationalism, while
turning into political thought, shapes the precept that politics is concerned with an "ideology" rather than with a concrete political tradition, and by an ideology Oakeshott means "the formalised
abridgement of the supposed substratum of rational truth contained
in the tradition", a "set of related abstract principles which has been
independently premeditated".[14] That is, in contrast to a tradition of
political ideas, the charm of a political ideology lies in the external
goal and the ideal order it may offer to a political society, and this is
what the Rationalist seeks in politics: "politics appears as a

---

[11]   *RP*: 6; cf. 105.

[12]   *RP*: 6-7.

[13]   *RP*: 10.

[14]   *RP*: 9. For Oakeshott, political ideologies include the single ideas such as
       freedom, equality, maximum productivity etc. and a complex scheme of related
       ideas such as liberalism and Marxism etc. (see *RP*: 48-9).

self-motivated manner of activity when empiricism [i.e. politics without policies] is preceded and guided by an ideological activity".[15] In this sense, Rationalism as a political thought can be portrayed in a number of ways: It is the "politics of engineering" that comprehends politics as a matter of solving problems by means of a set of political principles. It also implies the "politics of the felt need" in that politics is regarded as the feeling of the moment to be interpreted by "'reason' and satisfied according to an ideology".[16] Moreover, it refers to the "politics of perfection" in combination with the "politics of uniformity"; that is, the politics recognised as "the implication of a uniform condition of perfection upon human conduct".[17]

Now, it becomes evident that Oakeshott's understanding of rationalism in politics matches comfortably with the formalism in ethics that has already been revealed in terms of liberal justifications; namely the attempt to establish (1) a set of moral and political principles ensuring our practical certainty, which is based upon (2) a form of radical individualism (i.e. the notion of "self-made man") holding an anti-traditional and anti-institutional attitude towards our moral and political life, leading to (3) the universal application of abstract moral and political rules. And so, Oakeshott would not deny that liberalism is a form of rationalism in politics. But before we come to see Oakeshott's particular critique of rationalist politics, I wish to consider the provenance, i.e. the intellectual resource of Rationalism, that is to identify Oakeshott's Rationalism with the rise of modern natural philosophy.

Regarding the contextualisation of Rationalism, Oakeshott first directs our attention to some basic historiographical issues, which are worth mentioning here. He says that:

> The ambition of the historian is to escape that gross abridgement of the process which gives the new shape a too early or too late and a too precise definition, and to avoid the false emphasis which springs from being over-impressed by the moment of unmistakable emergence. Yet that moment must have a dominating interest for those whose ambitions are not pitched so high. And I propose to foreshorten my account of the emergence of modern Rationalism . . . by beginning it at the moment when it shows itself unmistakably . . . [18]

It implies that, although at the time of writing this paragraph Oakeshott was a member of the faculty of history in Cambridge, he

[15] *RP*: 48.

[16] *RP*: 27.

[17] *RP*: 10.

[18] *RP*: 17-8.

does not intend to take on a genuine historical approach to deal with *the* history of Rationalism.[19] Apart from the historical approach, he seems to accept that there are other ways of reading *res gestae*; that not everything regarding a sense of past has to do with the historical. And, it is a non-historical approach that he decides to take, because he only considers the "unmistakable appearance" of the ideal identity that is Rationalism.

Yet, there arises another interesting issue which has something to do with Oakeshott's claim about the relation of philosophy to the Past. If the pastness of Rationalism Oakeshott tries to construct is not an historical past, what is it? Is it a practical past?[20] As already mentioned, it is my view that it can only be a quasi-philosophical past. For what Oakeshott means by the practical past is the politicisation or moralisation of a past, whereas his treatment of the development of Rationalism here is to give some historic resources to the Rationalist disposition in our current political and moral situation that his philosophy aims to transcend.

We shall have other opportunities to see how this quasi-philosophical past functions in Oakeshott's study of past political ideas. The thing now is that the moment in which Rationalism reveals itself "unmistakably" for Oakeshott is the early seventeenth century when the state of European knowledge was in need of finding out "a consciously formulated technique of research, an art of interpretation, a method whose rules had been written".[21] That is, the intellectual appearance of Rationalism is in accordance with the rise of modern philosophy; the quality of Rationalism, Oakeshott claims, is the intellectual heritage of the Enlightenment positions launched by, among other thinkers, Bacon and Descartes.

According to Oakeshott's interpretation the research projects of Bacon and Descartes share in common three characteristics, viz. a technique of enquiry formulated as a "set of rules and directions" which is "purely mechanical" and can be "universally applied", but each has put a certain limitation on Rationalism. Bacon, regardless of his unbounded belief in the possibility of a perfect technique of

---

[19]   Some writers, however, believes that Oakeshott traces the emergence of Rationalism as an historical genesis. See, for example, P. Franco, 1990a: 111; cf. 125, 250, n12.

[20]   T. W. Smith, for example, argues that it is a practical past which is at the heart of Oakeshott's interpretation of *the* history of political ideas (1996: 609-14), whereas T. Nardin contends that what Oakeshott offers us are real examples of an historical past (2001: 141, n1).

[21]   *RP*: 18.

research, does not think that he has already given it a final formulation. By contrast, while Descartes claims an unshakeable foundation
for human knowledge, *cogito ergo sum* has been discovered by the
method of doubt, the philosopher somehow realises that there may
be constraints attached to his geometry-based project where it is
applied not to propositions but to things.

On this argument, Oakeshott's proposition is not that neither
Bacon nor Descartes can be called a genuine Rationalist, but that
with every step of its development Rationalism has been more distant from the true sources of its inspiration and turns out to be cruder
and more secular. Descartes, as a matter of fact, was never a Cartesian; nor was Bacon a Baconian. "The Rationalist character",
Oakeshott thus writes, "may be seen springing from the exaggeration of Bacon's hopes and the neglect of Descartes' scepticism; modern Rationalism is what commonplace minds made out of the
inspiration of men of discrimination and genius".[22] And yet, from a
philosophical point of view, it is this philosophical inspiration of
Rationalism that we now have to consider further; for, remove that,
and the whole enterprise of Rationalism will collapse.

IV.2.2. The Philosophical Foundations of Rationalism

So far we have mentioned the character of Rationalism and the fact
that Rationalism as an intellectual model has found support in its
affiliation with modern natural philosophy. As a result, my next step
here is to show how exactly the foundations of Rationalism are
related to the assumptions of foundationalism in philosophy: (1) the
criterion of knowledge as "certainty" (for the sovereignty of abstract
technique), (2) the notion of the mind as an instrument for thinking
(for an independently perfect end), and (3) the existence of *a priori*
"reason" (for intellectual equalitarianism).

[22] *RP*: 22. On this account, I believe it is unfair to argue that Oakeshott's Rationalist
is merely a "fictitious adversary" or something like that. See, for example, D.
Kettler, 1964: 488; J. R. Archer, 1979: 153-4; K. E. Koerner, 1985: chap. 5, esp.
282-98. According to Koerner, for instance, neither Locke nor Godwin nor
Bentham, Oakeshott's other instances of the Rationalists, has neglected entirely
the importance of tradition and the accumulation of human experience. But in
the case of Locke, for example, Oakeshott concedes that Locke does not deny the
worth of a political tradition but only formulates it into a set of principles; it is
not in his ways of education but in his "works of political vulgarisation" that the
tradition upon his mind of writing became hidden to the reader (*RP*: 30). In
short, Oakeshott's point is that the thinkers under consideration "have done
much to encourage ordinary people to think in [the Rationalist] manner" (*RP*:
107), and thus it is the *theory* of Rationalism more than the *policy* of Rationalism
that really concerns him in *RP*.

We have seen that that which lies at the centre of Rationalism is the sovereignty of technique. But, why is the Rationalist so fascinated with technical knowledge? Oakeshott believes that this is related to the Rationalist preoccupation with "certainty". That is, for the Rationalist, certain knowledge means self-contained thought "which does not require to look beyond itself for its certainty" and "which not only ends with certainty but begins with certainty and is certain throughout";[23] with certain knowledge at hand he thus feels confident to overcome uncertain traditions or habits. And, technical knowledge, by definition, is the result of a technical formulation inasmuch as its characteristic shows the appearance of certainty; technical knowledge thus becomes the only kind of knowledge which meets "the standard of certainty" that the Rationalist has identified. In short, Rationalism, in philosophical terms, represents that all knowledge proper is certain and reliable knowledge; that "there is no knowledge which is not technical knowledge".[24]

Speaking of standardised knowledge, we are at once reminded of the main task of modern natural philosophy. The criterion of knowledge which the philosophers have made every effort to establish, it will be remembered, was precisely "how to know things with certainty". Neither Descartes nor Locke nor Kant thought of their task of being a philosopher as distant from a pursuit of the magic word, certainty. In this matter, we may say that what underpins the foundation to the Rationalist belief in the sovereignty of technique is a Cartesian certainty.

While we consider the philosophical resource of Rationalism from the standpoint of certainty, it can be recognised that it is, first and foremost, an infallible technique of discovery, "a key to open all doors, a master science"[25] that occupies the minds of modern philosophers. For Bacon and Descartes, remember, what was required for the turning point of the "modern world", i.e. the new situation of European knowledge, was a "consciously formulated technique of research, an art of interpretation, a method whose rules had been written down," and since "almost everything that distinguishes the modern world from earlier centuries is attributable to science, which achieved its most spectacular triumphs in the seventeenth century".[26] It will give rise to little wonder to say that for modern philos-

---

[23]   *RP*: 16; cf. 113.

[24]   *RP*: 15.

[25]   *RP*: 20.

[26]   B. Russell, 1995: 512.

ophers the formulated technique of research which can validate certain knowledge is always believed to be equivalent to "scientific method".

As we have seen previously, since modern philosophy arises from the reflection on scientific development in the modern era, an identification of knowledge proper with knowledge acquired by scientific method has been accepted by almost every important modern philosopher. Within the tradition of philosophy "certainty" will always mean "scientific certainty". Again, generally speaking, it may not be misleading to take scientific method as the method of generalising and formulating.[27] Oakeshott's appeal to the notion of certainty within Rationalism, it appears to me, can be expounded as a view of seeing "scientism" as a part of the intellectual resources of Rationalism. The sovereignty of technique, for the Rationalist, is hereby the sovereignty of scientism. And consequently, it spells out (1) that all knowledge proper is technical knowledge, i.e. scientific knowledge because it involves methods alone inasmuch as it is certain and self-complete; and thus (2) that, if any other enquiry is to be a genuine part of human knowledge, it must adopt a scientific methodology, i.e. a formulated technique of discovery.[28]

Now that the notion of certainty has been mentioned, it is the consequence of a specific theory of mind which plays a key role in modern mainstream epistemology and metaphysics. And, it is precisely from this "official doctrine"[29] of mind that the other two characteristics of Rationalism, namely, perfectionism and universalism, become *more* accessible to us.

According to Oakeshott, what needs to be assumed, above all, for the possibility of a certain technical knowledge or an independently premeditated end is the Cartesian dualism which tends to keep the contents of acting, the objects of thinking, apart from the mind:

> The mind, according to this hypothesis, is an independent instrument capable of dealing with experience. Beliefs, ideas, knowledge, the contents of the mind, and above all the activities of men in the world, are not regarded as themselves mind, or as entering into the composition of

[27] By "scientific method", indeed, philosophers refer both to the problem of discovery and the problem of verification. While, as we know, contemporary philosophy of science, especially logical-positivism has paid much attention to the second sense of scientific method, following Oakeshott I am here basically considering scientific method as a technique of discovery such as deduction or induction as held by modern natural philosophers.

[28] For the usage of the term scientism here, see T. Honderich ed., 1995: 814; N. Beck ed., 1975: 113, 285.

[29] See esp. G. Ryle, 1949: 11-5.

mind, but as adventitious, posterior acquisitions of the mind, the results
of mental activity which the mind might or might not have possessed or
undertaken. The mind may require knowledge or cause bodily activity,
but it is something that may exist destitute of all knowledge, and in the
absence of any activity; and where it has acquired knowledge or provoked activity, it remains independent of its acquisition or its expression
in activity. It is steady and permanent, while its filling of knowledge is
fluctuating and often fortuitous.[30]

That said, the assumption in question purports to maintain that a
man's mind is like a "neutral instrument" or a "piece of apparatus"
independent of its thoughts and activities; that a man's mind is able
to be *trained* in the same way as we make the best use of a piece of
machinery: "it is an engine which must be nursed and kept in
trim".[31] And, as such it thus encourages the belief that to act "rationally" (in some sense, "scientifically") is simply to set the "mental
machinery" to work alongside a certain, a conclusive answer that is
already given and indifferent to the activity itself.

The result of this, Oakeshott continues, is that for the Rationalist
the mind of the individual can be most successful in dealing with
things, as long as it is least interfered with by those dispositions
which are already required: "the open, empty or free mind, i.e. the
mind without disposition, is an instrument which abstracts truth,
repels superstition and is alone the spring of 'rational' judgement
and 'rational' conduct".[32] In other words, understanding is involved
not in reforming knowledge which is already there, that is, a "process of re-establishing virginal detachment", but in getting rid of
"accumulated special knowledge and skill".[33] Thus, it follows that
the second assumption of Rationalism, the so-called "mental
instrumentalism" is the creed which makes up an *ab extra* theory of
truth, i.e. representationalism which is central to the Enlightenment
position. Using the language of *EM*, this theory of mind restates that
experience begins with what Locke calls a "white paper" rather than
a world of ideas; that understanding is a process of catching wild
birds rather than taming birds which are already within the cage of
the mind.

But further, there is a metaphysical assumption that is fixed firmly
to this theory of mind. That is, for its supporters, men can not only
have a premeditated purpose, but, more crucially, they must be *capa-*

---

[30]   *RP*: 106.
[31]   *RP*: 106.
[32]   *RP*: 106.
[33]   *RP*: 107.

ble of formulating any problem in such a way that admits of such a purpose and then apply it to instruct their activity. It means that the whole notion which stands behind the operation of human mind, as Oakeshott observes, is that men first "have a mind, which acquires a filling of ideas and then makes distinctions between true and false, right and wrong, reasonable and unreasonable, and then, as a third step, causes activity".[34] Put another way, that which this "intellectualist legend" (to use Ryle's phrase) tells us is that in *doing* things men are supposed first "to do a bit of theory and then to do a bit of practice".[35] And, for the last few centuries, Oakeshott believes, Western people have been told that to act "rationally" like this is to act "intelligently" (or, I would like to say, "scientifically" because there seems nothing more intelligent than science in the modern world).

Consequently, the Rationalist argues that "men have a power of reasoning about things, of contemplating propositions about activities, and of putting these propositions in order and making them coherent".[36] The problem, however, is not whether we do have such a power, since, Oakeshott claims that such a power does exist and that it is not to be doubted; but rather that the problem is whether:

> this is a power independent of any other powers a man may have, and something from which his activity can *begin*. And activity is said to be "rational" (or "intelligent") on account of being preceded by the exercise of this power, on account of a man having "thought" in a certain manner

[34] *RP*: 109.

[35] Although the philosophical position of Oakeshott is different from that of Ryle in many ways, here it seems to me that the two thinkers' description of the Cartesian notion of mind as "the Ghost in the Machine", to use Ryle's famous phrase is comparative (see 1949: 11, 16). What Ryle says about the "intellectualist legend" is so close to Oakeshott's point that it can be fully cited as follows (1949: 29): " Champions of this legend are apt to try to re-assimilate *knowing* how to *knowing* that by arguing that *intelligent* [emphasis mine] performance involves the observance of rules, or the application of criteria. It follows that the operation which is characterised as intelligent must be preceded by an intellectual acknowledge of these rules or criteria; that is, the agent must first go through the internal process of avowing to himself certain propositions about what is to be done ('maxims', 'imperatives' or 'regulative propositions' as they are sometimes called); only then can he execute his performance in accordance with those dictates. He must preach to himself before he can practice. The chef must cite his recipes to himself before he can cook according to them; . . . ... To do something, thinking what one is doing, according to this legend, is always to do two things; namely, to consider certain appropriate propositions, or prescriptions, and to put into practice what these propositions or prescriptions enjoin. It is to do a bit of theory and then to do a bit of practice".

[36] *RP*: 105.

before he acted . . . In order that a man's conduct should be wholly "rational", he must be supposed to have the power of first imagining and choosing a purpose to pursue, of defining that purpose clearly and selecting fit means to achieve; and this power must be wholly independent, not only of tradition and of the uncontrolled relics of his fortuitous experience of the world, but also of the activity itself to which it is a preliminary.[37]

That is to say, to the Rationalist this power is assumed to be *a priori*, insofar as it is universal and impeccable. On this account, the Rationalist thus takes it to be the only ground of any argument, the sole criterion for determining the worth of anything, the absolute truth of any opinion and the "infallible guide" in any action. And so, it will not be surprising that this power has always been given the name "reason" (that is, as I have used in the previous chapters, Scientific Reason or Technical Reason) with which the Rationalist has expressed his confidence in the universality of human intellect and the distrust of the continuous meanings of a tradition. In short, as far as this project of perfectionism and its assumptions go, so does the idea of replacing a tradition of behaviours with an ideology of premeditated doctrines.

Now, there is little doubt that this *a priori* power is what Descartes once called the "natural light" of human beings in which modern natural philosophers firmly believed when they gave us a complete description of public reality to justify the existence of an objective physical world independently of us. It is what Kant believed to be the "tribunal of reason" by means of which the meaning of everything is judged. To sum up, it is one of the most crucial items which made modern foundationalism possible.

IV.2.3. Rationalism and the Predicament of the Enlightenment

It is then Oakeshott's observation that modern natural philosophy and rationalist politics are theoretically allied, so that they constitute the whole package of Enlightenment positions. Before we move on to dissect the philosophical assumptions of Rationalism and its political doctrines, however, it seems advisable to spend the remainder of this section on the problem of the political and moral predicament of the Enlightenment that concerned Oakeshott in the first instance.

---

[37] *RP*: 105. It is observable that in some sense this is actually the old argument between Plato and Aristotle - with Oakeshott taking the far more Aristotelian view as to be found in Aristotle's *Nicomachean Ethics*.

Given that "the greatest apparent victories of Rationalism have been in politics",[38] Oakeshott now claims that the view he is maintaining is where "the ordinary politics of European nations have become fixed in a vice of Rationalism, that much of their failure (which is often attributed to other and more immediate causes [war, for example]) springs in fact from the defects of the Rationalist character when it is in control of affairs".[39] Adhering to his own philosophical position, however, Oakeshott has no intention of *commending* any remedy for Rationalism (and as such he gives us no examples of the real damages that it may have incurred, for example, Nazism); nor does he expect a speedy release from the circumstances which deliver Rationalism. But rather, Oakeshott maintains that his job is only to *explain* to his reader the disease of Rationalism: the conditions of politics and morality in our time.[40] That is to say, it is not the desirability or undesirability of rationalist politics but the adequateness of Rationalism as a political conviction to which Oakeshott gives his main attention in *RP*.[41] There are accordingly two main symptoms of rationalism in politics that cause Oakeshott the most distress: a "corruption of mind", and a rationalistic "training" of mind over a concrete "education" in human life.

First, from a philosophical point of view, Rationalism represents a false theory about the nature of human knowledge: where technical knowledge, in fact, is merely half-knowledge such that it is only half-right; and the notions of an empty mind and of *a priori* "reason" are utopian illusions. What is involved in rationalist politics, Oakeshott thus says, amounts to "a corruption of mind". And further, for this reason, Rationalism will have no capability of amending its own shortcomings: "it has no homeopathic quality"; "you cannot escape its errors by becoming more sincerely or more profoundly rationalistic".[42] This, according to Oakeshott , is one of the prices that the Rationalist has to pay for living by a "book", because it leads not only to specific mistakes, but to the drying up of the mind itself. So, Oakeshott states that the Rationalist is ineducable in the sense that he always begins his action by throwing away the kind of

[38] *RP*: 8. Oakeshott basically attributes the intellectual impetus which has promoted the invasion of Rationalism into politics to the "politically inexperienced" and he shows us three examples: the "new ruler", the "new ruling class" and the "new political society" (see *RP*: 30-2).

[39] *RP*: 33-4.

[40] See *RP*: 34.

[41] Cf. *RP*: 48.

[42] *RP*: 37.

knowledge which would save him, that is, "traditional knowledge".[43]

Secondly, what makes the situation worse is that a society which
is rationalist in disposition must be inclined to an exclusive Rationalist form of "training" instead of a genuine and more complete "education". The training of mind in which the Rationalist believes

> is certainly not an initiation in which moral and intellectual habits and
> achievements of his society, an entry into partnership between present
> and past, a sharing of concrete knowledge; for the Rationalist, all this
> would be an education in nescience, both valueless and mischievous. It
> is a training in technique, a training, that is, in the half of knowledge
> which can be learnt from books when they are used as cribs . . . [Because]
> he believes that a training in "public administration" is the surest
> defence against the flattery of a demagogue and the lies of a dictator.[44]

And consequently, in such a society the Rationalist sooner or later
will win the battle of the whole field of morality and moral education
as his ultimate victory.

In morality, as in politics, then, the Rationalist is embarked upon a
self-conscious pursuit of moral ideals by the presentation of moral
principles, by training the mind with an ideology rather than a tradition of moral ideas. He composes a moral doctrine out of its tradition
and then he defends it by *argument*. For him, the conduct of life is "a
jerky, discontinuous affair, the solution of a stream of problems, the
mastery of a succession of crises";[45] and thus the morality that concerns him is that of the "self-made man" and a "self-made society".
"The predicament of our time", Oakeshott thus concludes, "is that
the Rationalists have been at work so long on their project of draw-
ing off the liquid in which our moral ideals are suspended (and
pouring it away as worthless) that we are left only with the dry and
gritty residue which chokes us as we try to take it down".[46] In summation, Oakeshott's point is that the crisis of the Enlightenment ethical position lies in the fact that the moral rationality it bears is nothing
but an abstract and empty concept.

---

[43] At this point, Oakeshott's position is somewhat comparable to Adorno's and
　　 Horkheimer's, which argued that the very reason that the Enlightenment used
　　 as a weapon against myth, religion, and illusion has, in modern technocratic
　　 societies, turned against itself and become self-destructive (see T. W. Adorno
　　 and M. Horkheimer, 1972).

[44] *RP*: 38.

[45] *RP*: 41.

[46] *RP*: 41; cf. 487.

IV.3. Transcending Rationalism in Philosophy

Having related Oakeshott's Rationalism to the Enlightenment project and shown its predicament, we may now turn to examine Oakeshott's objection to it. Here I first adopt Oakeshott's approach which transcends the partiality of rationalism in philosophy, viz. *philosophisme* in respect of the assumptions of scientism, mental instrumentalism and *a priori* "reason". And in the course of this examination, the reader of *EM* will recognise Oakeshott's constant philosophical position.

IV.3.1. The Map of Human Activity: Deconstructing Scientism

It is my understanding that the first philosophical assumption of rationalism in philosophy can be understood as that of scientism: (1) all knowledge proper appears only in the form of technical knowledge i.e. scientific knowledge because it involves methods that are certain and reliable; and thus (2) for any understanding to be a genuine part of human knowledge, it must adopt a scientific methodology, i.e. a formulated technique of discovery. According to Oakeshott, this is where the Rationalist starts going astray, and the work of *RP* as a whole has made a sufficient objection to this point of view.

Before we go any further, however, let me remind the reader that by using the term "technical knowledge" Oakeshott himself does not refer to it as scientific knowledge but Rationalist belief does. Besides, Oakeshott does not deny that technical knowledge can be found outside science; he merely thinks that it is in essence incomplete and thus it is not a genuine criterion on which to categorise science, let alone to fuse the sciences, i.e. to justify that "all human utterance is in one mode".[47] In following Oakeshott's denial of scientism, I shall begin with the partiality of technical knowledge in general by arguing that nowhere in *complete* human activity, including actual scientific activity, can technical knowledge appear to be complete and certain, because human activity always involves more than just methods, i.e. no technique of research begins as well as ends in self-completeness. And then, given that technical knowledge is not an actual scientific knowledge nor a genuine philosophical category, I shall introduce Oakeshott's theory of the "map of human activity" in which the characteristics of, for example, science, history, and practice, can be truly postulated.

[47] *VP*: 9.

Why, then, is technical knowledge incomplete? To understand this, we have to appeal to Oakeshott's notion of "practical knowledge" or "traditional knowledge" in the first instance. In contrast to technical knowledge, Oakeshott points out that there exists another type of knowledge, namely, traditional knowledge which is never absent from every actual human conduct. Here, by traditional knowledge Oakeshott means the knowledge that exists only in *practice*, i.e. the knowledge "that is expressed in taste or connoisseurship, lacking rigidity and ready to impress on the mind of the learner".[48] Unlike the method of formulating, it follows that the only way of acquiring traditional knowledge is by apprenticeship to a master who is perpetually *practising* it. To illustrate further, Oakeshott gives us the examples of the artistry of a pianist, the mastery of a chef, the connoisseurship which enables a scientist to decide which direction of research to take, the commitment that led an historian to observe that the interrogative "Was the French Revolution a mistake?" is not a genuine historical question.

Traditional knowledge, as Oakeshott understands it, is therefore a type of knowledge which is reminiscent of that which Michael Polanyi has called "tacit knowing" or "tacit dimension" in scientific research.[49] Moreover, it bears a resemblance to the Aristotelian virtue of *phronesis*.[50] So, it appears that Oakeshott's understanding of practical knowledge is remarkably similar to Alasdair MacIntyre's position in respect of their Aristotelian connection.[51] And consequently, I think, it is safe to argue further that Oakeshott's reflection upon Rationalism is also comparable to the central theme of MacIntyre's work which tries to show that "the Aristotelian tradition can be restated in a way that restores rationality and intelligibility to our own moral and social attitudes and commitments".[52]

By asserting the epistemic value of traditional or practical knowledge, then, Oakeshott does not claim that while technical knowledge

---

[48] *RP*: 15.

[49] See *RP*: 13, n4.

[50] See, for example, P. Franco, 1990a: 110; J. Casey, 1993: 60-1; R. Grant, 1990: 77. The Aristotelian *phronesis* is not foreign to Confucianism, either. To use an obvious example, when "Tzu-Kung asked about the practice of benevolence", the Master said, "a craftsman who wishes to practise his craft well must first sharpen his tools. You should, therefore, seek the patronage of the most distinguished Counsellors and make friends with the most benevolent Gentlemen in the state when you happen to be staying" (Confucius, 1979: book xv).

[51] See A. MacIntyre, 1988: esp. 124-46.

[52] *Ibid*.: ix; see also 1985: 259.

will teach us "what to do" traditional knowledge will tell us "how to do"; but, following Aristotle's *Ethics*, he argues that "even in the *what*, and above all in diagnosis [of a doctor, for example], there lies already this dualism of technique and practice: there is no knowledge which is not 'know how'".[53] In other words, for Oakeshott, "*what* we do, and moreover what we want to do, is the creature of *how* we are accustomed to conduct our affairs".[54] I shall return to and expound upon Oakeshott's emphasis on the knowledge of "knowing how" as a concrete whole later. In the meantime, returning to the topic, it follows that even if we accept the image that human conduct everywhere acquires skills, no skill consists of technical knowledge alone. For technical and traditional knowledge are distinguishable but inseparable; they are "the twin components of the knowledge [i.e. skill] involved in every concrete human activity".[55] In cookery, for example, the knowledge that belongs to the good cook is not merely, nor less importantly, about what has been written in the cook book, but it is also about the need to combine this knowledge with practical knowledge to "make skill in cookery wherever it exists".[56]

This means that although in certain circumstances technical knowledge may be possible, it is merely what is deliberately epitomised from a tradition of behaviour, of "how to go about things" and in the course of this formulation there must be something missing, something which always coexists with it but which cannot be written down into a rule. Acquiring it, Oakeshott says, does not consist in eliminating "pure ignorance", but in reforming knowledge which is already there in a concrete whole. "Nothing, not even the most nearly self-contained technique (the rules of a game)", he claims, "can in fact be imparted to an empty mind; and what is imparted is nourished by what is already there".[57] In short, technical knowledge is never self-complete; and if its self-completeness is illusory, the notion of certainty that the Rationalist appeals to is also an illusion.

Among the modes of human activity, it has always been believed that science has achieved absolute certainty because it involves nothing more than scientific method; that scientific knowledge can be a pure form of technical knowledge. In this respect, Oakeshott has

---

[53] *RP*: 13-4.

[54] *RP*: 53.

[55] *RP*: 12.

[56] *RP*: 12-3; cf. 52, 110, 117-20.

[57] *RP*: 17.

no difficulty in arguing further that actual scientific knowledge does not involve merely rules of observation, principles of verification and hypotheses of experiment. The technique of research constitutes only one of the elements of actual scientific knowledge; and thus technical knowledge is a part not the whole of the world of science.

Aside from following the rules, Oakeshott thinks that to achieve any advance in research a scientist must also acquire (among other things) the sort of judgement which tells him when his technique is leading him astray and the connoisseurship which enables him to distinguish the profitable from the unprofitable directions to explore. That is, according to Oakeshott,

> The truth is that only a man who is already a scientist can formulate a scientific hypothesis; that is, an hypothesis is not an independent invention capable of guiding scientific enquiry, but a dependent supposition which arises as an abstraction from within already existing scientific activity. Moreover, even when the specific hypothesis has in this manner been formulated, it is inoperative as a guide to research without constant reference to the traditions of scientific enquiry from which it was abstracted. The concrete situation does not appear until the specific hypothesis, which is the occasion of empiricism being set to work, is recognised as itself the creature of knowing how to conduct a scientific enquiry.[58]

Thus, Oakeshott proposes that "the pursuit of scientific enquiry and the theory of scientific enquiry called 'scientism' are not the same thing",[59] and it is the latter that is here put into question.

Although Oakeshott's idea of science attracted no real attention from scholars,[60] the view that an actual scientific activity involves more than a set of methods, I think, has now become a common argument in the development of the philosophy of science. For example, T. Kuhn, in his rejection of pro-positivism, has pointed out that the scientist is working under a "paradigm" of scientific research rather than "pure reason". Here, I do not wish to elaborate on Kuhn's idea of science nor am I able to expound on the debate that has arisen around his usage of the term "paradigm". For my concern, it is interesting only to indicate that by the concept "paradigm" Kuhn basically signifies two meanings. "On the one hand, it stands for the entire constellation of beliefs, values, techniques, and so on shared by the members of a given community. On the other hand, it denotes one sort of element in the constellation, the concrete puz-

---

[58]   *RP*: 51-2; cf. 120, 123.

[59]   *RPML*: 99.

[60]   See, for example, L. S. Stebbing, 1934: 404.

zle-solutions which, employed as models or examples, can replace explicit rules as a basis for the solution of the remaining puzzles of normal science".[61] While with the first of these meanings, Kuhn clearly suggests that both beliefs and values are as indispensable as technique in actual scientific activity, it is with the second usage, viz. "paradigms-as-shared-examples", that we may find Kuhn expressing beliefs which Oakeshott might equally well have written when he explained what he meant by traditional knowledge:

> Philosophers of science have not ordinarily discussed the problem encountered by a student in laboratories or in science texts, for these are thought to supply only practice in the application of what the student already knows. He cannot, it is said, solve problems at all unless he has first learned the theory and some rules for applying it. Scientific knowledge is embedded in theory and rules; problems are supplied to gain facility in their application. I have tried to argue, however, that this localisation of the cognitive content of science is wrong. After the student has done many problems, he may gain only added facility by solving more. But at the start and for some time after, doing problems is learning consequential things about nature. In the absence of such exemplars, the laws and theories he has previously learned would have little empirical content.[62]

> To borrow once more Michael Polanyi's useful phrase, what results from this process is "tacit knowledge" which is learned by *doing science* [emphasis mine] rather than by acquiring rules for doing it.[63]

In short, for Kuhn as for Oakeshott, the pro-positivist attempt to maintain the certainty of scientific knowledge in terms of formulated methods is misleading. Furthermore, the actual scientific activity is conducted within a tradition or a paradigm of scientific enquiry.

Now, let me turn to the second, and more important, meaning of scientism, that is the prevailing Enlightenment belief; that scientific method is the most reliable means of enquiry for men to use in exploring the nature of things so that one should employ it in all human activity: "all knowledge proper is scientific knowledge".

Indeed, if Oakeshott is correct by observing that in actuality science involves more than a set of methods, that the notion of scientific certainty is merely a mental myth, one can thereby see no reason why a formulated technique of discovery has any epistemological priority, that is, to be the criterion of all knowledge-claims. For, in

---

[61] T. Kuhn, 1962: 175.

[62] *Ibid.*: 187-8.

[63] *Ibid.*: 191.

science as in other modes, any such formulated technique can only capture a half-part of human knowledge; from a philosophical point of view, to understand human action solely by means of doing it is thus to understand incompletely. That is, in philosophy the error of the sovereignty of technique, of scientism, is nothing but "the error of mistaking a part for the whole, of endowing a part with the qualities of the whole"[64] and thus results in a "corruption of mind".

But, here as elsewhere, Oakeshott's dissecting of Rationalism does not stop at negative criticism. If the Rationalist understanding of knowledge proper as technical knowledge is incomplete, Oakeshott's identification of being a philosopher must require a more concrete understanding instead. In other words, if technical knowledge is not a genuine philosophical category to look into the nature of science in particular and into human knowledge as a whole in general, the philosophical question that Oakeshott has to consider next is: What is the criterion that a philosophy may build up to discern the conditions that postulate the mode of science and all other modes of activity?

As one may expect, Oakeshott's answer is to include the premise that modes of activity are not distinguished by pre-assumed methods or premeditated purposes, but by a tradition of enquiry to which they belong:

> Now, if we consider the concrete activity of an historian, a cook, a scientist, a politician or any man in the ordinary conduct of life, we may observe that each is engaged upon answering questions of a certain sort, and that his *characteristic* [emphasis mine] is that he knows (or thinks he knows) the way to go about finding the answer to that sort of question. But the questions which he knows to belong to his sort of question are not known to be such in advance of the activity of trying to answer them: in pursuing these questions, and not others, he is not obeying a rule or following a principle which comes from outside the activity. It is the activity itself which defines the questions as well as the manner in which they are answered. It is, of course, not impossible to formulate certain principles which may seem to give precise definition to the kind of question a particular sort of activity is concerned with; but such principles are derived from the activity and not the activity from the principles.[65]

It follows that for Oakeshott in *RP*, the modes of experience disclosed in *EM* are now also seen as a number of distinct *practices*; each *practice* is a tradition of enquiry achieved by the practitioner concerned. In participating in a certain *practice*, one is therefore learning the skill of how to go about *that sort* of thing, the manner of how to

[64]   *RP*: 16.
[65]   *RP*: 117-8.

speak *that sort* of language. Hence, for example, a scientific hypothesis would be meaningless (or incommensurable, as Kuhn reputedly argues) to others when set outside the tradition of scientific research within which it is formulated, because its meaning is its place in that tradition as a whole. "[A] particular action, in short, never begins in its particularity, but always in an idiom or a tradition of activity".[66] And, to give it a concise definition here, a tradition of activity is nothing but a concrete knowledge of knowing how to go about things appropriately in the circumstances.

Now it can be observed that on this crucial issue Oakeshott has not abandoned the theme of *EM*, but only altered his terminology. First of all, in *RP* Oakeshott clearly adheres to the view that the purpose of a philosophy is to observe not to determine a tradition of activity; there is no external or extrinsic reason which can set about a certain *practice*. If the reader of *EM* were somehow unsure about the non-foundationalist role of philosophy that Oakeshott delivers with a pure philosophical language there, the image of an idiom of activity would now have abolished their concern: the conditions that postulate a mode of activity are not determined in advance by a Kantian "pure reason" but the mode is characterised by its own *practice*. The role of a philosophy, Oakeshott thus restates, is "to discern the logic of the relation of [a *practice*] to others and to ascertain its place on the map of human activity".[67]

Secondly, it follows that modes of activity are self-consistent; each mode is an idiom of self-ruled activity. The characteristic of history, for example, lies in the way in which the historian comes to deal with his own research in order to describe a "historical past" and so forth. Likewise, scientific activity is the exploration of the knowledge the scientist has of how to go about asking and answering scientific questions; moral activity involves a process whereby we get to know how to behave well. The only way of making a history, for example, is to write a history; history is the historian's experience about a certain past. It is thus confirmed that for Oakeshott the conditions that postulate one mode cannot be applied to any other without committing a categorical mistake, that is, *ignoratio elenchi*.

IV.3.2. Rationality: Dissecting Mental Instrumentalism

To attack rationalism in philosophy more completely, the next step Oakeshott takes is to challenge the use and misuse of "reason" in

---

[66] *RP*: 120.
[67] *RP*: 152; cf. 65, 127.

relation to human conduct, that is, to clarify the confusion between Rationalism and genuine rationality. As we have seen, there is a theory of mind that lies behind the Rationalist misinterpretation of "rational" conduct. Before attempting to present Oakeshott's conception of rationality, it seems appropriate to first review Oakeshott's idealistic rejection of the theory of mind concerned.

It is Oakeshott's observation that the theory of mind in question purports to maintain that men first "have a mind, which acquires a filling of ideas and then makes distinctions between true and false, right and wrong, reasonable and unreasonable, and then, as a third step, causes activity". However, this is not the "intelligent" part of men, because no man can think or act in this manner; nor is this a satisfactory notion of "rational" conduct, because it is not a satisfactory description of any sort of human conduct.

Remaining in the main with his idealistic position, Oakeshott reproduces the alternative view that mind is "the offspring of knowledge and activity; it is composed entirely of thoughts".[68] I say "reproduce", because we have already seen in *EM* that for Oakeshott understanding always begins with a world of ideas within the mind, and a world is always "a complete integral whole or system; whenever there is a world there is unity".[69] Hence, in each instance, mind cannot exist independently of thoughts and activities, because they are not the acquisitions but the constitutives of the mind, i.e. a world of ideas. For this reason, Oakeshott states that it is not possible to purify a man's mind by extinguishing in it any distinctions such as truth and falsity and the like, because "what is extinguished is not merely a man's 'knowledge' (or part of it), but the mind itself", and "what is left is not a neutral, unprejudiced instrument, a pure intelligence, but nothing at all".[70] In short, the instrumental mind does not exist.

If mind is not an empty instrument, the view that human conduct springs from an *a priori* act of theorising must be an illusion as well. However, it should be noted that Oakeshott does not deny that men may have the power of reasoning, he only argues that the essential condition of this power is conduct itself. That is to say, Oakeshott believes that our act of theorising is not something prior and superior to conduct but the result of a subsequent analysis of conduct. "*Doing* anything", Oakeshott says,

[68]   *RP*: 109.

[69]   *EM*: 28.

[70]   *RP*: 109.

both depends upon and exhibits knowing how to do it; and though part (but never the whole) of knowing how to do it can subsequently be reduced to knowledge in the form of propositions (and possibly to ends, rules and principles), these propositions are neither the spring of the activity nor are they in any direct sense regulative of the activity.[71]

In other words, as already noted, our skills of *living* in the world are not a knowledge of certain propositions validated by *a priori* "reason", but a knowledge of how to decide questions and this is the prerequisite of the ability of reasoning: we are not first given *a priori* "reason" and then instruct our conduct; it is in *practising* our conduct that we are getting to know the rationality it implies. It follows that rationality is a quality of the conduct itself. And, to elucidate it, Oakeshott says that:

> the quality concerned is not merely "intelligence", but *faithfulness to the knowledge we have of how to conduct the specific activity we are engaged in.* "Rational" conduct is acting in such a way that the coherence of the idiom of activity to which the conduct belongs is preserved and possibly enhanced.[72]

That is, he believes that rational conduct is the faithfulness to the coherence of a tradition of knowing how to act in the circumstances. And thus, instead of claiming *a priori* Reason towering over the map of human conduct as a whole, for Oakeshott as for Aristotle, there are different reasons corresponding to the self-distinct *practices*, namely, traditions of activity.

What can be implied from this is that Oakeshott transcends the Enlightenment contrast between "Reason and Tradition" by maintaining that reasons always function within traditions.[73] I shall come back to Oakeshott's notion of "tradition" later. For now, it can be observed that his understanding of rationality is simply a restatement of the notion of truth he disclosed in *EM*. First, as in *EM*, truth is defined as the *condition* of experience which is never absent in thinking; in a like manner rationality is now taken as the *quality* of the conduct itself. Moreover, recall that the criterion of truth established in *EM* is also the idea of coherence or unity: true understanding is a self-critical movement towards the achievement of a more coherent world of ideas. Therefore, it may be said that for Oakeshott what is given in our activity is a unity "in which every element is indispensable, in which no one is more important than any other and none is immune from change", that the unity of a tradition of behaviour

[71] *RP*: 110.

[72] *RP*: 122.

[73] Cf. P. Franco, 1990a: 138.

"lies in its coherence, not in its conformity to or agreement with a fixed [principle]".[74]

From this point of view, again, we are explaining Oakeshott's rejection of scientism. For, it becomes observable that rationality (or truth) so defined is at once something different from the faithfulness to abstract rules or premeditated purposes. Rules or purposes are fixed and finished inasmuch as they are the abridgements of a unity. However, for Oakeshott, since knowledge of how to pursue an activity is always "in motion", rationality is always a faithfulness which itself not merely illustrates but contributes to the coherence of the activity within which nothing is fixed or absolute. In short, it is Oakeshott's insistence that the rationality of conduct is its relation to the idiom of activity to which it belongs; and that "an activity as a whole (science, cooking, historical investigation, politics or poetry) cannot be said either to be 'rational' or 'irrational' unless we conceive all idioms of activity to be embraced in a single universe of activity".[75]

Before we leave this point, allow me to reiterate that following Oakeshott "there is as much difference between rational enquiry and 'rationalism' as there is between scientific enquiry and 'scientism', and it is a difference of the same kind".[76] Rationalism, as a view of understanding human conduct, consists of a misconception about human "reason", which is, among other things, supported by a certain concept of mind. And thus, it is not "reason" per se but the theory which identifies "reason" with certainty, with the view of seeing the mind as an instrument for thinking that constitutes the objective of Oakeshott's critique of Rationalism. Oakeshott's denouncement of Rationalism, is meant to pass beyond the Enlightenment project such that it becomes misleading to attach to him any concept of "irrationalism". Put another way, just as we usually believe that a true understanding of human experience can never exclude the notion of "truth", just as in *EM* where the critique of an *ab extra* theory of truth does not result in the abandonment of the possibility of "truth", Oakeshott does not exclude the notion "reason" from a meaningful philosophical discourse. On the contrary, it is claimed here that what he really intends to argue in *RP* is a more profitable explanation and use of the name "reason" itself.

---

[74]   Cf. *EM*: 32-3.

[75]   *RP*: 122.

[76]   *RPML*: 99.

IV.3.3. Tradition: Dissolving a priori Reason

In earlier discussions we have observed the importance of a "tradition" of activity in Oakeshott's theory. I now want to re-focus my attention on this very concept in order to reject more fully the notion of *a priori* "reason".

It is true that Oakeshott's notion of tradition has been so confusingly understood by his critics that he later relinquished it.[77] There is, however, an important *philosophical* meaning of it assumed in *RP* that has often been neglected by interpreters, that is, tradition as the "concrete universal" given in human activity. And I believe that in understanding Oakeshott's philosophical traditionalism, it would be of great assistance to bring that usage of tradition to light, by relating it to Oakeshott's notion of reality held in *EM*.

It has been demonstrated from *EM* that Oakeshott perceives the world as a world of ideas which can never be independent of us and which is always a homogeneous world of thoughts. By the same token, in *RP* Oakeshott shows no hesitancy in rejecting the realist's view that the world is composed merely of "a stock of thing" such as books, pictures, musical instruments and compositions, buildings, cities, landscapes, inventions, devices, machines and so on. According to Oakeshott the view that assumes the independence of a natural world misunderstands the concept of "second nature" (as Oakeshott quotes Hegel) which is the context of our activity; conversely, he writes that:

> [t]he world into which we are initiated is composed, rather, of a stock of emotions, beliefs, images, manners of speaking, languages, skills, practices and manner of activity out of which these "things" are generated. And consequently it is appropriate to think of it not as a stock but as a capital; that is, something known and enjoyed only in use. For none of these is fixed and finished; each is at once an achievement and a promise. This capital has been accumulated over hundreds of years. And in use it earns an interest, part of which is consumed in a current manner of living and part reinvested.[78]

What is cited here implies the general character of the notion of "tradition as a concrete whole" that the philosopher has chiefly in mind in *RP*. And as such it may be observed that just as reality is treated as a world of meanings in *EM*, it is now "tradition as a capital of *practices*" that offers the meanings for human activity. Put differently, if the language of *EM* spells out that the world in which we live

---

[77] Cf. Oakeshott, "On misunderstanding Human Conduct: A Reply to My Critics" (1976): 364.

[78] *RP*: 187.

is a world of thoughts and knowledge, then that of *RP* points to the same account that the world consists in a concrete tradition of language, skills, and the like. Thus, if reality is what we are "obliged to think", tradition can be regarded as what we are "obliged to act".

Moreover, it must be recalled that in *EM* it is claimed that the world is what I understand it to be, and there are a number of limited standpoints which I may take to interpret the world as a single whole: reality is apt to be modified. Along these lines, Oakeshott seems to agree in *RP* that tradition as a capital is a "multi-voiced creature",[79] too; it is composed of traditions of activity in *practice*. That is to say, for Oakeshott as for Wittgenstein, my tradition of language as a whole is the limitation of my knowledge of the world; but, unlike the latter, Oakeshott goes further by saying that I have at my disposal several distinguishable traditions of language which enable me to describe the world differently with regard to the different manners of speaking such as the political and moral, the historical, the scientific or the poetic.

With the phrase a "tradition of activity", Oakeshott keeps telling us that it is made up of both traditional knowledge and technical knowledge; and for him a tradition of activity is a "concrete knowledge of knowing how to go about things appropriately in the circumstances". And yet, because "a tradition of behaviour is not a fixed and inflexible manner of doing things; it is a flow of sympathy";[80] because what "we desire to impose is already hidden in what exists".[81] In order to understand, say, a tradition of political activity in a complete sense, the mode of the mind requires "a conversation, not an argument"; it is "the pursuit, not of a dream, or of a general principle, but of an intimation".[82] On this reading, Oakeshott thus depicts the (traditionalist) nature of politics in terms of the following well-known sentence:

> In political activity, then, men sail a boundless and bottomless sea; there is neither harbour for shelter nor floor for anchorage, neither starting-place nor appointed destination. The enterprise is to keep afloat on an even keel; the sea is both friend and enemy; and the seamanship consists in using the resources of a traditional manner of behaviour in order to make a friend of every hostile occasion.[83]

[79] Oakeshott, "Rationalism in Politics: A Reply to Professor Raphael" (1965): 90.
[80] *RP*: 59.
[81] T. Fuller, 1993b: 24.
[82] *RP*: 58, 57.
[83] *RP*: 60.

We shall have the chance to resume Oakeshott's understanding of politics in relation to the notion of conversation qualified in political activity shortly. The thing to note here, however, is that Oakeshott has often been impugned by his critics for his traditionalism which could never tell us how to distinguish a good tradition from a bad one.[84] For example, they asked why people in South Africa should follow the "tradition of segregation" as a pattern of their political behaviour? For a South African Rationalist, it seems, should have a fundamental moral right not to "keep afloat on an even keel" but to "rock the boat" on that particular case.[85] And thus, an external criterion of universal value is always required in politics.

On the basis of understanding the condition of tradition in activity as that of reality in experiencing, it turns out that such a form of criticism consists in a misconception about Oakeshott's philosophical situation. For Oakeshott, tradition as a world of what is given in activity, to quote Bradley once again, "is the best of all possible worlds, and everything in it is a necessary *evil*".[86] That is, whilst our understanding always begins with a world of ideas, our tradition of politics must confront us in such a way that we are sailing "a boundless and bottomless sea", and this confrontation is inexorable and absolute. A certain tradition of political activity, of course, may not necessarily be favourable any more than there are prejudices, biases or mysterious proclivities in a paradigm of scientific or historical research. But, Oakeshott has never expressed doubt that a practitioner, a scientist or an historian has his own self-critical "reason" in *practice* (as opposed to Universal Reason in formulation) to conduct their intimations of the tradition concerned, by means of which it is possible to tell what is good from what is bad. In other words, to converse with tradition is not to be satisfied with the status quo, it is to understand ourselves by making more coherent the given situation which we inhabit. In the case of politics, we have seen that the coherence of practical truth is freedom, insofar as it is the "faithfulness" to our free will that will tell us what we ought to do and what we ought not to do in the actual circumstances.

Politics, Oakeshott states, is "the activity of attending to the general arrangement of a set of people whose chance or choice have

---

[84] See, for example, R. H. S. Crossman, 1951: 61; S. I. Benn and R. S. Peters, 1959: 316-8; N. Wood, 1959: 660-2; H. V. Jaffa, 1963: 361; H. F. Pitkin, 1973: 508-10; G. Himmelfarb, 1975: 417-8; D. Spitz, 1976: 340; K. Koerner, 1985: 296. Oakeshott himself was aware of this form of criticism, see *RP*: 67-8.

[85] S. I. Benn and R. S. Peters, 1959: 318.

[86] *RP*: 66.

brought together"; it is "a practical activity concerned with making a response to situations of a certain sort: political situations".[87] Either "attending to" or "responding to", indeed, has implied men's ability to choose from a world of values. In other words, Oakeshott's point is not that every tradition must be excellent, but that it is so comprehensive that every political crisis "always appears *within* a tradition of political activity; and 'salvation' comes from the unimpaired resources of the tradition itself".[88] In claiming this, Oakeshott casts off Kantian Universal Philosophical Reason as the foundation of a rational programme, by returning our actual practical reasoning to a tradition of moral and political activity. In short, for Oakeshott genuine rationality has never been absent in a certain tradition of activity; instead, "every tradition has its own reason proper".

IV.4. Reconciling Rationalism in Politics

My aim in this section is to continue Oakeshott's attack on rationalism in politics by re-establishing the philosophical elements and historic fortunes of conservatism in politics in order to show it as a more coherent mode of understanding politics. Leaving aside *On Human Conduct* (*HC*) for now, I shall here deal with Oakeshott's earlier works on morality and politics, mainly including *Religion, Politics and the Moral Life* (a collection of some of Oakeshott's essays written from 1925-55, published in 1993; hereafter *RPML*), *The Harvard Lectures* (which was delivered at Harvard in 1958 and published in 1993; hereafter *MPME*), *The Politics of Faith and the Politics of Scepticism* (Oakeshott's posthumous work which was probably completed in 1952 although not edited and published until 1996; hereafter *PFPS*) and, of course, *Rationalism in Politics* (*RP*).

IV.4.1. Philosophy and Practice

Throughout the previous discussions it has been shown that liberal ethics as a form of rationalism in politics produces a normative political and moral theory in terms of a set of self-evident and universal principles that order our practical life as a whole; and that such a mode of ethical thinking is predicated on the conception of philosophy par excellence. Now that Oakeshott's main concern in both *EM* and *RP* has been understood as a serious challenge to foundationalism in philosophy, I believe that the categorical distinc-

---

[87]   *RP*: 44; cf. 70.

[88]   *RP*: 59.

tion between philosophy and practice implied in Oakeshott's thought can be regarded as a consequence of this challenge, and thus it is a premise of his objection to rationalist politics. Before going any further, therefore, it may be appropriate to emphasise once again the non-normative character of Oakeshott's political philosophy.

One of Oakeshott's main interests in *EM*, as we have seen, is to categorise the mode of practice as the world *sub specie voluntatis* from the standpoint of the totality of experience without advancing the philosophical understanding of practice at the expense of the practical pursuit of meaning. That is, he believes that freedom, the criterion of practical truth, is meaningful only to the world of practice, whereas philosophy, categorically speaking, is not to understand the world under the condition of the free will, but it is an escape from the responsibility of living in the world.[89]

The view that political philosophy cannot be a prescription for political practice, as we know, remains throughout Oakeshott's academic life. In *RPML*, Oakeshott argues that "a philosophy of politics is not itself a political programme; it is not a foundation or basis, a body of general principles upon which a political programme might be constructed".[90] On the contrary, "where there is genuine philosophy there can be no guidance; if we seek guidance, we must 'hang up philosophy'".[91] And he retains this view in *RP* by remarking that "political philosophy cannot be expected to increase our ability to be successful in political activity. It will not help us to distinguish between good and bad political projects; it has no power to guide or to direct us in the enterprise of pursuing the intimations of our tradition".[92]

The error of Rationalism, so far as this view is concerned, lies in a mis-apprehension of the task of philosophy itself, "which is not to recommend conduct but to explain".[93] And consequently, given the crisis of the Enlightenment project that we have reviewed, the real problem about the despotism of Rationalism is not that the West has failed to see its jeopardy, but that in the meantime its self-analysis has been unaware of its own "Rationalisms".[94] Oakeshott singles out

---

[89]   In *RPML*: 119-137, Oakeshott reiterates once again what he has largely said about the mode of practice in *EM* by retaining its main terminology.

[90]   *RPML*: 137; cf. 135.

[91]   *RPML*: 155.

[92]   *RP*: 65.

[93]   *RP*: 34.

[94]   Cf. T. Fuller, 1993b: 23; 1996: xiv.

Hayek's *Road to Serfdom* as one of the most significant cases: "a plan to resist all planning may be better than its opposite, but it belongs to the same style of politics".[95]

In this respect, it seems unfair to me to comment that Oakeshott's attempt to tell philosophical reasoning apart from practical reasoning amounts "only to arbitrary stipulations which by distorting the nature of political philosophy unnecessarily restricts its scope",[96] that he upholds an "unpolitical theory".[97] For, Oakeshott's intention is to limit the function of philosophy in order to transcend the Enlightenment ethical position without resulting in another Rationalist effect. And, it will become clearer when interpreting *HC*, that Oakeshott does not actually reject the importance of the "norms of conduct" in terms of *lex* in our political activity; he only argues that it is not the philosopher that should set up such authority for the practical man. The philosopher likes to observe what is going on rather than to reach a verdict for what should occur next.

At this point, I think Oakeshott may not disagree with Rorty's claim about the "priority of democracy to philosophy", which keeps a tight rein on philosophy so as to make room for the autonomy of political practice.[98] And if one questions that Oakeshott's idea of (political) philosophy is eventually more affirmative than Rorty's "total scepticism", then, the following quotation from M. Walzer seems to fit perfectly into Oakeshott's frame of mind:

> The political philosopher must separate himself from the political community, cut himself loose from affective ties and conventional ideas. Only then can he ask and struggle to answer the deepest questions about the meaning and purpose of political association and the appropriate structure of the community … and its government. This kind of knowledge can only be had from the outside. Inside, another kind of knowledge is available, more limited, more particular in character. I shall call it political rather than philosophical knowledge. It answers the questions: What is the meaning and purpose of *this* association? What is the appropriate structure of *our* community and government?[99]

In short, for Oakeshott, as for Walzer, political philosophy is "an explanatory, not a practical, activity".[100]

[95] *RP*: 26. Another example mentioned by Oakeshott is W. Lippmann's *Public Philosophy*. See *RPML*: 111-8.

[96] D. Hall & T. Modood, 1982a: 176. See also N. McInnes, 2000: 8.

[97] See H. F. Pitkin, 1976: 301-20.

[98] See R. Rorty, 1991: 175-191.

[99] M. Walzer, 1981: 393.

[100] *RP*: 66.

That political philosophy is categorically irrelevant to political life as such, however, does not mean that the philosopher should never become interested in practice, nor does it imply that the practitioner has nothing *at all* to learn from philosophy. On the one hand, Oakeshott's point is that when a philosopher gets involved with real politics, he must "hang up philosophy" and set out to learn the relative skills embedded in the *practice* of political affairs. And in so doing, "his opinions are worth as much as any other citizens'".[101] On the other hand, when the practical man happens to be fond of philosophical ideas, for example, using them as a tool of social and political criticism, the thing is that he must have *transformed* them from the world of philosophy to that of practice. At best, he may treat those philosophical wisdoms as containing "intimations" of a political tradition; at worst, and more frequently occurring in modern times, the philosophical truth of natural law, distributive justice or human rights that he holds fast will soon be devoted to the politics of ideology.

The ground on which the liberal-rationalist rests while attempting to comment on our political and moral practice, as we well know by now, consists in the general belief that the progressive successes that Newtonian science has made in understanding and controlling Nature could provide the basis for a "robust optimism about moral and political matters".[102] Such a connection between liberalism and scientism, for example, has been expressed by Russell in his *Philosophy and Politics* (1947) as follows:

> What has theoretical philosophy to say that is relevant to the validity or otherwise of the liberal outlook? The essence of the liberal outlook lies not in *what* opinions are held, but in *how* they are held; instead of being held dogmatically, they are held tentatively, and with a consciousness that new evidence may at any moment lead to their abandonment. This is the way in which opinions are held in science, as opposed to the way in which they are held in theology . . . Science is empirical, tentative and undogmatic; all immutable dogma is unscientific. The scientific outlook, accordingly, is the intellectual counterpart of what is, in the practical sphere, the outlook of Liberalism.[103]

To say that the liberal outlook and empirical science could be inter-supported on account of being tentative, is to say that science involves only a set of methods and rules which are applicable to the sphere of politics. In this sense, the possibility of a normative ethical

---

[101] M. Walzer, 1981: 396.

[102] R. Flathman, 1989: 19.

[103] Quoted in *ibid.*: 18-9.

theory is possible only if there exist objective moral and political principles backed up by scientific reason in terms of scientific methods. This view, however, appears inadequate to Oakeshott. For, as we have said, the scientific reason that can be taken out of the actual scientific activity and as the normative guidance in practice is, in fact, a partial technique which rules out traditional knowledge in use.[104] And yet, since every actual human activity involves both technical and traditional knowledge, it must be an error to substantiate human conduct in terms of a normative ethical theory.

The assumptions in relation to rationalist politics (esp. in the vision of liberal ethics) as a normative ethical theory, as already shown, can be expressed as follows: (1) a set of abstract moral and political principles; (2) radical individualism or the self-made man; and (3) formalism. According to Oakeshott, "there is no doubt that the liberal democratic manner of conducting affairs [in terms of these characteristics] is prone to a certain sort of corruption".[105] And to balance against its partiality, Oakeshott thus constructs his traditionalist politics by understanding political activity as (1) a "way of living" in which (2) the traditionalist-individual is engaged, (3) a "rhetorical form of reasoning" which deals with plausible statements in given circumstances through the "pursuit of intimations" of a political tradition:

IV.4.2. Abstract Laws vs. a Way of Living

The character of liberalism recognised in terms of a set of moral and political principles, as already shown, is applicable to Lockean natural law theory, the Kantian categorical imperative, and Millian utilitarianism. Whilst in *EM* Oakeshott has objected to the last two schools of thought on account of their mis-identifying philosophy with practice, in *RP* it is especially the theory of natural right to which Oakeshott directs much attention, when attacking rationalist politics.

In "Contemporary British Politics" (1947-8), Oakeshott first draws a distinction between "liberal conservatism" in favour of a natural law theory and the genuine "conservatism" that he wishes to re-construct. According to Oakeshott, the problem of contemporary British politics is the tyranny of central planning mainly carried out by the British socialist. It is without doubt that the politics of central planning is the politics of felt need; and so it is a form of rationalist

[104] See esp. *RP*: 34-5.
[105] *RPML*: 115.

politics. Although the British conservative differs from the socialist in understanding politics as "a limited activity, a necessary but second-rate affair", as "the politics of the diffusion of power" which "are the only guarantee of the most valuable and substantial freedom known to human beings",[106] the British conservative (together with the liberal) fail to realise that human freedom is not "natural" but social. Oakeshott argues that:

> [The conservative] thinks of [human] rights and duties as "limitation" and of their adjustment as "interference". It is an unfortunate way of thinking which is inherent in the simpler forms of a natural law conception of society. The truth is, however, that we do not begin by being free; the structure of our freedom is the rights and duties which, by long and painful effort, have been established in our society. The conditions of individuality are not limitations; there is nothing to limit. And the adjustments of those conditions are not interference (unless they are over-head adjustments); they are the continuation of the achievement.[107]

To keep the "natural" constituent out of a genuine conservatism, Oakeshott's ultimate purpose is to establish an ideal mode of human relationship which is categorically distinctive from rationalist politics. The truly significant opposition "which is something of an altogether different nature"[108] in contrast to the politics of central planning, Oakeshott thus claims, lies not in liberal conservatism but in what he calls the "rule of law". The difference between the two is that whereas the former still understands politics in terms of an abstract ideology, the latter is able to recover the sense of politics as a "way of living" by considering the solidarity of a society in terms of rights and duties in *practice*.

The main theme that underlies "Contemporary British Politics" is represented in "The Political Economy of Freedom" (1949): "We call ourselves free because our pursuit of current desires does not deprive us of a sympathy for what went before; like the wise man, we remain reconciled with our past".[109] Government by rule of law, Oakeshott goes on, "is the greatest single condition of our freedom" because "it involves a partnership between past and present and between governors and governed which leaves no room for arbitrariness".[110]

---

[106] Oakeshott, "Contemporary British Politics" (1947-8): 485, 487.

[107] *Ibid.*: 487-8.

[108] *Ibid.*: 479.

[109] *RP*: 396.

[110] *RP*: 391, 390.

The more specific concern of the essay under consideration, none-theless, is to recognise a form of "economic organisation" which cor-responds to the conception of the rule of law and the idea of freedom it bears. And it is not surprising that Oakeshott claims "the political economy of freedom rests upon the clear acknowledgement that what is being considered is not 'economics' (not the maximisation of wealth, not productivity or the standard of life), but *politics*, that is, the custody of a manner of living; that these arrangements have to be paid for, are a charge upon our productive capacity; and that they are worth paying for so long as the price is not a diminution of what we have learned to recognise as liberty".[111]

At this point, it is interesting to note that both socialism[112] and lib-eralism are mentioned as "the plausible ethics of productivity" which constitute another thread pulling in the opposite direction to the *political* way of dealing with freedom. In the case of liberal ethics, this materialistic propensity may be traced back to the thought of Locke, and has come as "the most questionable element of Liberal Democracy".[113] And thus, on this issue, what is categorically opposed to "the ethics of productivity" is identified as "the ethics of custody".

In "Political Education" (1951), Oakeshott keeps the distinction between freedom as a "procedure" and as a "hypothesis". He writes that:

> the "freedom" which can be pursued is not an independently premedi-tated "ideal" or a dream; like a scientific hypothesis, it is something which is already intimated in a concrete manner of behaving. Freedom, like a recipe for game pie, is not a bright idea; it is not a "human right" to be deduced from some speculative concept of human nature. The free-dom which we enjoy is nothing more than arrangements, procedures of a certain kind . . .[114]

Put briefly, then, Oakeshott in *RP* has made every effort to disen-cumber his conservatism of any abstract ideology-based founda-tion. This, however, does not make him devalue the importance of freedom in human conduct, but rather his intention is to give human freedom a more firm and plausible defence, that is, to treat it as a way of living. And by seeing the conservative disposition as a way of liv-

---

[111] *RP*: 406.

[112] For Oakeshott's discussion on the productivist version of socialism in terms of R. Owen, St Simon and Marx, see *MPME*: 103-7. Cf. *PFPS*: 62-4.

[113] Oakeshott, "John Locke", "Introduction" to *SPD*; quoted by P. Franco, 1990a: 148.

[114] *RP*: 53-4.

ing without presupposing premeditated ends, Oakeshott is clearly aware that his conservatism is closer to the position of Montaigne than to that of Burke.[115] As he sums up in "On Being Conservative" (1956), "what makes a conservative disposition in politics intelligible is nothing to do with a natural law or a providential order, nothing to do with morals or religion; it is the observation of our current manner of living".[116] In short, it is traditionalist politics as a way of living that is seen as exclusively antagonistic to "abstract laws" of rationalist politics.

As a counterpart work of "Rationalism in Politics", nonetheless, there are more insights about the Oakeshottian conservatism in politics that we can learn from the famous essay, "On Being Conservative".

Here Oakeshott begins the essay with a disclosure of the general character of being conservative. In total contrast to Rationalism, Oakeshott claims that "to be conservative is to prefer the familiar to the unfamiliar, to prefer the tried to the untried, fact to mystery, the actual to the possible, the limited to the unbounded, the near to the distant, the sufficient to the superabundant, the convenient to the perfect, present laughter to utopian bliss".[117] So, the disposition to be conservative is to enjoy what is available in the present rather than to wish for sudden change and innovation in the future. In a word, here as elsewhere in the essay, the key concept of being conservative is that of "familiarity".

According to Oakeshott, conservative property as such is not necessarily rooted in so-called "human nature": men naturally prefer safety to danger; but rather it is much more apt to obtain it from the *observation* of human conduct itself. And if this is a feasible task, the point Oakeshott intends to make is that "there are few of our activities which do not on all occasions call into partnership a disposition to be conservative and on some occasions recognise it as senior partner; and there are some activities where it is properly master".[118]

In the first place, there are some fields of human activity which can be exercised only in virtue of a disposition to be conservative, because in these an attendant enjoyment rather than an extraneous reward is sought. For example, it is certainly the case with friendship. Friends are not concerned with what might be made of one

---

[115] Cf. *RP*: 435.

[116] *RP*: 423-3.

[117] *RP*: 408.

[118] *RP*: 422.

another, but merely with the enjoyment of one another; the relation-ship of friend to friend is not utilitarian but dramatic, the tie is not usefulness but familiarity. And what is said about friendship here can go for the forms of activity such as patriotism and conversation as well. In sum, where there are activities which are engaged in for their own sake and enjoyed for what they are, the disposition to be conservative is not merely appropriate but a necessary condition.[119]

Besides, Oakeshott observes that although there are other activi-ties which are not engaged in for their own sake, few of them do not, at some point or other, call for the disposition to be conservative. For, in these what one may call goal-pursued activities, for the sake of argument, a relative distinction may at once appear between the enterprise itself and the tools used for its achievements. And while one sees human activity in this way, it turns out that since "familiar-ity is the essence of tool using",[120] as long as man is a tool using ani-mal he is disposed to be conservative. That is to say, for Oakeshott "tool using" must make a call upon "skill in use" which necessarily involves "traditional or practical knowledge", i.e. familiarity: For example, a carpenter can use his own tools more skilfully than any other example of the kind of tools commonly used by other carpen-ters, and the solicitor can use his own copy of the textbook on *Wills* more readily than any other. And consequently, "since doing busi-ness of one sort or another occupies most of our time and little can be done without tools of some kind, the disposition to be conservative occupies an unavoidably large place in our character".[121]

It follows that to be conservative in politics is to engage in the pur-suit of intimations in familiarity rather than to wish for novelty. That is to say, for the conservative, because government is providing rules of conduct, and because familiarity is the most important vir-tue in a rule, "the intimations of government are to be found in ritual, not in religion or philosophy; in the enjoyment of orderly and peace-ful behaviour, not in the search for truth or perfection".[122] Put differ-ently, Oakeshott considers that what is really significant in politics is "the art of the statesman"[123] rather than "the science of the policy". Thus, as T. Fuller puts it, to be an Oakeshottian conservative "is not to engage in reactionary politics, but in a 'trimming act' of states-

[119] *RP*: 415-7.
[120] *RP*: 419.
[121] *RP*: 420.
[122] *RP*: 430, 428.
[123] *RPML*: 107.

manship. [In this view] what practising politicians need is not a doctrine, but a view of the limits and possibilities of their situation".[124] In
short, the contrast between rationalism in politics and conservatism
in politics is the contrast between "the pursuit of innovations" and
the "pursuit of intimations".

IV.4.3. Radical Individualism vs. Traditionalist Individualism

So far we have seen a number of expressions regarding the contrast
between rationalist politics and traditionalist politics; also it may be
contended that rationalist politics may embrace the ethos of both liberalism and socialism, the two abstract ideologies which, to quote
MacIntyre, make up the "*ethos* of the distinctively modern and mod-
ernising world".[125] But here, it cannot be denied that, among many
other things, there is a fundamental difference between the liberal
and the socialist; namely, the idea of individuality. Generally speaking, it seems that for the liberal the ultimate principle in politics is the
idea, as J. E. McTaggart claims, that "value is individual",[126] whereas
for the socialist it is the notion of "common good", where the individual is normally not thought of as the highest value. And so,
although the liberal shares in common with the socialist the Rationalist characteristics of being abstract, perfect and
anti-traditionalist, the notion of "perfection" may mean the *inspiration* of a Cartesian "self-made man" which "was recognised as a *res
cogitans*, and in this is found the warrant of his independent experience"[127] to the liberal, whilst it may stand for a Baconian
"co-operative enterprise" *animating* the socialist to assume that "the
proper object of human endeavour was a comprehensive mundane
condition of human circumstances characterised by ever increasing
wealth, abundance and prosperity".[128]

This suggests that there are, in fact, two criteria that Oakeshott
employs to categorise the characteristics of modern political
thought, namely, the *meta-issues* in relation to the way of philosophising presumed, and the *advocatory-issues* in relation to the importance of social and political values maintained.[129] Accordingly, it

---

[124] T. Fuller, 1996: xv.

[125] A. MacIntyre, 1985: x.

[126] Quoted by W. J. Coats, jr., 1985: 774.

[127] *MPME*: 22.

[128] *MPME*: 102.

[129] Cf. C. Taylor, 1987. where he coined the terms "ontological issues" and
"advocacy issues" to clarify the cross-purposes inherent in the contemporary

may be said that for Oakeshott in regard to the meta-issues, liberalism is reminiscent of socialism in terms of Rationalist characteristics; however, the two are surely distinguishable with respect to the advocatory-issues.

It is important to start making the distinction between the two forms of political thought with regard to the advocatory issues, because in "Rationalism in Politics" (1947) and "Rational Conduct" (1950) Oakeshott is more likely to link rationalist politics with a certain view of the self, the mind or the individual (cf. the last two sections); in other works such as "The Masses in Representative Democracy" (1961) and *HC*, nonetheless, with the idea of "common good". More crucially, since in "The Masses" Oakeshott does turn to construct the two categories of politics in terms of "the morality of the individual" and "the morality of the mass", some writers take this as one of the central factors of Oakeshott's separation of civil association from enterprise association in *HC*, in order to support their view that Oakeshott's theory of civil association is liberal.[130]

This interpretation, however, is a misconception. Before coming to elucidate *HC* (and *PFPS*), it must be pointed out here that the uniqueness of Oakeshott's *philosophical* politics would simply evanesce, if we make him into a liberal just because he happens to advocate some of the values that liberalism simultaneously maintains, such as the value of the individual and the idea of rule of law. Put clearly, the theme disclosed in "The Masses" was actually a summary of the lectures on *the* history of modern European political theory that Oakeshott delivered at Harvard in 1958. And yet, because of its specific occasion,[131] in many ways there is very little in common between *The Harvard Lectures* and, say, the lectures Oakeshott gave at the LSE.[132] More to the point, unlike what he did in "The Masses",[133] in lecturing on the liberal thinkers to Harvard students, Oakeshott actually criticised their foundationalist approach, although in a brief outline. As a result, the quality of the individual that Oakeshott praises in these lectures is still related to the character of traditionalist politics whose political behaviour is understood as a

---

liberal-communitarian debate.

[130] See esp. P. Franco, 1990a: 152-6; cf. W. J. Coats, jr., 1985.

[131] Harvard is surely the bedrock of academic liberalism in the States.

[132] Cf. K. Minogue, 1993b: vii-viii.

[133] Even with regard to the matter of individuality, Oakeshott's major purpose in the essay is to provide the "clearest evidence of the overwhelming impact of [the] experience of individuality" in modern Europe in order to show that human individuality is an historic emergence. See *RP*: 368, 370.

way of living, having nothing to do with it being used in the context of liberalism as a form of rationalist politics. In other words, although Oakeshott appreciates the morality of individualism, he clearly distinguishes "traditionalist individualism" from "liberal individualism" within that individualistic paradigm of morality.

It is significant to note at the outset that Oakeshott's attention to the past in *The Harvard Lectures* is directed to a sophisticated "abridgement" of what has been thought in respect of the office and pursuits of government,[134] which suggests that it is a quasi-philosophical past rather than an historical past with which he is dealing.[135] According to Oakeshott, the character of post-medieval European politics and government which constitutes the context for the reflections of modern political thinkers, generally speaking, is predicated on two distinctive and opposed moral dispositions: the morality of individualism, and the morality of collectivism, anti-individualism or the mass-man. Each of these moralities has appeared as different transformations of an earlier morality charac-terising medieval Europe, namely, the "morality of communal ties", even though the morality of collectivism may be regarded as a reac-tion against the morality of individualism which had first estab-lished itself in the early post-medieval period.[136]

In interpreting how modern political reflection seems to disperse itself in the direction of the morality of individualism, Oakeshott describes the elements of individualism in the liberal tradition by focusing on the political thought of Locke, Kant, Smith, Bentham and Mill. The detail of Oakeshott's interpretation, interesting as it is, is not my major concern here, and an investigation of the three clas-sic liberals: Locke, Kant and Mill, has been offered in Chapter II. I only wish to note that Oakeshott classifies liberal individualism into three categories (on which my previous discussions on liberal ethics rest): First, the Lockean theological or natural law vision, where "individuality is the gift of an omnipotent and infinitely wise Maker";[137] second, the Kantian metaphysical vision, where a "meta-physical and ethical context" is given to justify the experience of the

---

[134] See esp. *MPME*: 3, 12.

[135] On this issue, K. Minogue comments that Oakeshott's attitude towards the past in *The Harvard Lectures* "was to reject methodological formulae and to rely upon *a philosophical self-consciousness* [emphasis mine] about the precise relevance of questions being asked and answered" (1993b: viii).

[136] For this theme, see also *RP*: 295-8.

[137] *MPME*: 58.

individual;[138] and thirdly, the utilitarian vision, where each man is considered as having a natural character "to make his own choices for himself about his own happiness".[139] Oakeshott finds all of these inadequate:

> I believe it to be a virtue in any theory that it avoids calling upon unnecessary hypotheses. And if this is so we are likely to conclude that many of the versions of the political theory of individualism are capable of improvement in this respect. Writers in this idiom, in order to make their position impregnable, have been accustomed to construct a *foundation* [emphasis mine] far in excess of what is required to carry the superstructure. They have invoked metaphysical theories of personality [e.g. Kant], they have appealed to principles of natural law [e.g. Locke], they have elaborated theories of human nature in general [e.g. the utilitarian]. But what they have written in this respect is not so much erroneous — indeed, it may all be demonstrably true — as unnecessary. And this redundance would, I think, have more clearly appeared if the general character of a political theory had been more fully appreciated.[140]

It is no surprise that Oakeshott believes the "unnecessary hypotheses" appear equally in the political theory of collectivism, which for the most part have three main versions as well: First, a religious version as in the political theory of Calvinism and in the government of the Geneva of Calvin and Bera, where the perfect manner of human existence is understood as "righteousness" or "moral virtue";[141] second, a "productivist" version in the thought of R. Owen, St. Simon and Marx, where "perfection" is understood as a condition of "prosperity", of "abundance" or "wealth";[142] and third, a "distributionist" version as in the works of Babeuf, Marechal and Buonarotti, where the "perfection" is understood as "security" or "welfare".[143] But in any event, it indicates that in *The Harvard Lectures* Oakeshott does not intend to take either the side of liberal individualism or that of socialist collectivism as they are both *hypothetical* (and are thus forms of Rationalist ideologies).

---

[138] *MPME*: 64.

[139] *MPME*: 78. For Oakeshott, it is an exaggeration to associate Mill with Bentham in terms of utilitarianism, and Mill has substituted an almost entirely different doctrine for the utilitarianism of Bentham (*MPME*: 78-83). And yet, I interpreted Mill as an utilitarian in Chapter II, because what really matters for Bentham and Mill is the attempt to justify the value of the individual in terms of "human nature".

[140] *MPME*: 83-4.

[141] *MPME*: 92-9.

[142] *MPME*: 100-7.

[143] *MPME*: 107-10.

Oakeshott regarded himself to be a philosopher of the morality of individualism, or, as we shall see, the Hobbesian paradigm of Will and Artifice. To avoid the "unnecessary hypotheses" in the liberal tradition of individualism, Oakeshott thus believes that the genuine individualistic manner of governing need not demonstrate any eternal validity or fundamental structure; all it needs "is to recognise the appearance of such subjects - namely, subjects intent upon the enjoyment of individuality - in sufficient numbers to make it appropriate to consider the corresponding office of government".[144] With reference to Oakeshott's own conception of philosophy, this means that a genuine philosophical theory of individualism is so sceptical and self-limited that it should add nothing to the practical enjoyment of individuality but only consider individuality as a condition of modern political practice; and in this respect an historic exposition is simply sufficient to unveil the "undeniable fact that a large part of the intellectual energy of European thinkers over a period of four centuries has been engaged in elucidating a theory of government appropriate to subjects of this character".[145] It is therefore re-confirmed here that it is a philosophical self-awareness rather than a pure historical concern that really penetrates Oakeshott's comprehension of *the* history of modern political theory in *The Harvard Lectures*.

A philosophical reflection, indeed, attempts to transcend hypothetical abstractness; and a philosophical reflection on politics is meant to consider the nature of politics, namely, the question of what the activity called "governing" *really* is.[146] Given the shortcomings of the moralities of socialist collectivism and liberal individualism, Oakeshott's furthest aim is therefore to establish a more sophisticated account of the historic achievement of the subject's enjoyment of individuality. His non-foundationalist account for this, to be sure, is related to an understanding of morality as composing a vernacular language of colloquial intercourse of agents, and it is ultimately expressed in the mode of civil association. Before putting *HC* under examination, it is my task to articulate that the property of individuality that Oakeshott accepts in theorising the mode of civil association as such, has been implied in our previous exploration of *RP* in terms of conservatism in politics.

To sum up, the doctrine of radical individualism in the liberal context, which maintains that "the individual is ontologically and mor-

---

[144] *MPME*: 84.

[145] *MPME*: 85

[146] *MPME*: 14. Cf. *RPML*: 138-55; *RP*: 223-5.

ally independent of the social groups and institutions to which they belong" is, of course, related to an understanding of the mind as "an independent instrument capable of dealing with experience". However, Oakeshott would argue that, although freedom is a necessary condition of human agency, it is an historic achievement rather than a general principle;[147] freedom is meaningful only if it is treated as a way of living rather than as a natural right. Hence, the political economy of freedom is not about the problem of self-productivity, but about the problem of a political procedure. And instead of following a hypothesis, the individual consequently must converse with other people, to pursue the moral intimations in familiarity, namely, a tradition of concrete moral exemplifications, such that he can be said to be in possession of the genuine character of being a free man.

T. Fuller has, therefore, argued that "Oakeshott was an individualist, but not an abstract individualist. Individuality is a self-understanding composed in responding to others in a certain tradition of behaviour. We understand ourselves to be individuals because we are self-conscious within a context of innumerable self-conscious agents".[148] And in other places I have referred to this treatment of individuality as "traditionalist individualism". Thus, Oakeshott's reaction against liberal ethics is certainly not to convert to the morality of collectivism, nor is it to rule out the concept of a free individual from a substantial philosophical discourse. On the contrary, Oakeshott's purpose is to return our individuality to the concrete tradition of moral and political practice where a true enjoyment may be achieved.

IV.4.4. Formal Argumentation vs. Substantial Conversation

Liberalism and socialism are then likewise Rationalist in the sense of being abstract, anti-traditionalist, and in search of a perfect solution to practice, whether the perfection is understood as a Kantian ultimate foundation of human freedom or a Baconian comprehensive project of "setting the condition of the world".[149] The third characteristic of liberal ethics as a form of rationalist politics can accordingly be understood as an attempt to establish universally "demonstrative moral truth" in terms of "formal argumentation". And to reveal its incompleteness, we shall be returning to Oakeshott's concept of "substantial conversation".

---

[147] See esp. *RP*: 69, 370.

[148] T. Fuller, 1996: 10.

[149] *MPME*: 102.

To elucidate: In modern times, Oakeshott proposes that political discourse, with the desire for certainty in place of conjecture in political affairs, has turned in the direction of taking in an "argumentative" logical design, where people are seeking for "*apodeictic* political discourse", i.e. a kind of argument able to prove or disprove the "correctness" of political proposals.[150] That is to say, modern political discourse basically reflects the Enlightenment situation of treating human affairs as a series of problems to be solved by those most scientific and perfect solutions. Thus, the argumentative logical design that the Rationalist upholds seeks to establish demonstrative moral and political truth which can be applied universally; and so it predicates the character of formalism in ethics.

This view, however, appears unreasonable to Oakeshott, "because discourse which deals in conjectures and possibilities and the weighting of circumstantial *pros* and *cons* is reasoning, and it is the only sort of reasoning appropriate to practical affairs. In this matter Aristotle and Isocrates are better guides than Plato and Marx".[151] This means that political discourse is not demonstrable logic, i.e. necessary truth, but the contextual plausibility in the circumstances. There are no necessities in political discourse, only probabilities and "what is true" for now. Hence, it is basically from the revival of the Aristotelian notion of rhetoric that Oakeshott's understanding of reasoning in practice comes. I now want to consider this practical reasoning with regard to the terminology of "conversation" used in *RP*.

It seems to me that Oakeshott uses the term "conversation", at least, in three main distinguishable but related senses. In the first sense, as to be found in the context of *The Voice of Poetry in the Conversation of Mankind* (1959; hereafter *VP*), it is used at large to signify the "meeting-place" of the diverse idioms of human discourse, i.e. the "greatest and the most sustained" of all the accomplishments of mankind.[152] The Oakeshottian notion of the conversation of mankind, as I have indicated elsewhere, stands for a propensity of "civilisation" being carried on between a variety of human activities,[153] which is in conflict with the Enlightenment project. That is to say, whilst the latter predicates a world of certainties, truths and resolutions in which the *philosophe* is expected to provide the agents

---

[150] *RP*: 81-82.

[151] *RP*: 95.

[152] See *VP*: 12, 14.

[153] See *RP*: 187.

with extrinsic profits and prizes; the former points to a world of possibilities, plausibilities and approximations in which "there is no symposiarch or arbiter, not even a doorkeeper to examine credentials". [154] This means that this widest comprehension of conversation symbolises an anti-foundationalist attitude which evokes the openness, playfulness and flexibility of human engagement as a whole: conversation is "an unrehearsed intellectual adventure", [155] in that everything is permitted. Thus, as Oakeshott concludes, the ideal character of human relationship recognised as a conversation is one "where each voice speaks in its own idiom, where from time to time one voice may speak louder than others, but where none has natural superiority let alone primacy". [156]

But further, it follows from this that to be a participant in human discourse one is required to learn how to use the language concerned through a corresponding conversational manner rather than an argumentative disposition. So in Oakeshott's writings there appears a second usage of the term "conversation" which is taken, not to be a metaphor for civilisation, but to delineate a *general* method of understanding the multiplicity of meanings that compose a tradition of activity. [157] It is without doubt that this derivative sense of conversation is a preferred pedagogical method that plays a central role in Oakeshott's educational thought. [158] And with reference to the distinction between traditional and technical knowledge that has been unveiled above, it can be inferred that for Oakeshott the excellence of the conversational manner of thinking is that: whilst the logic of argumentation persuades the agents to pay attention to technical knowledge alone, in a conversation they are capable of learning "how to go about things" by synthesising both forms of knowledge in question.

In this sense, not only the practical man but also the theorists such as the historian or the scientist need to converse with a certain tradition of behaviour in order to fulfil his undertaking. But since, as we have seen, every tradition of activity has its own reason to deal with its own business, the usage of conversation as a method of understanding should be further qualified when applied to different

---

[154] *VP*: 10-1.

[155] *VP*: 11.

[156] *VP*: 55.

[157] See, for example, J. L. Auspitz, 1993: 7; K. Minogue, 1993a: 49. Cf. P. Franco, 1990a: 133.

[158] See esp. *VL*: 39-42, 51, 62, 97-101, 104, 133-4. For the conversational character of Oakeshott's thought of education, see T. Fuller, 1990; cf. D. McCabe, 2000.

modes of experience. That is to say, unlike most of Oakeshott's interpreters, I believe that to avoid confusion a third level of the term
"conversation" must be maintained, that is, conversation as a specified condition of reasoning appropriate to the mode of experience
related. For example, what Oakeshott has famously said about the
outlook of conversing with a political tradition in "Political Education" is so distinct that it has little to do with the historical study. For
in the practical world the form of conversation is eventually exercised to deal with plausible statements in given circumstances. But
the historian certainly does not engage in judging the plausibility of
statements for particular past situations, since he has never lived in
those contexts.

In considering the character of conservatism in politics, we are
then concerned with the modified meaning of conversation as a way
of illustrating the traditional knowledge embodied in a political tradition, with regard to the circumstantial responses to political issues
appearing within that tradition. Here, we thus find that Oakeshott is
at his most Aristotelian in suggesting that our practical reasoning is
a form of rhetoric in relation to *phronesis* which is likely to deal with
particular political problems in given situations by way of appealing
to a complete understanding of a tradition of political activity.[159]
That is, for Oakeshott, making a political judgement in favour of
plausibility is not frivolous nor flimsy, it is to contemplate *pros* and
cons in detail by means of learning insights from an informative tradition of political activity. In short, in the Oakeshottian "political
conversation", circumstantial considerations and traditional knowledge are inseparable. With this in mind, we may now return to
examine what Oakeshott means by "the pursuit of intimations" in
"Political Education".

We have mentioned that for Oakeshott politics is never anything
more than the pursuit of intimations; what is required in politics is a
conversation, not an argument. Now, this means that to consider
which statements are plausible for current political situations all we
have to do is make a cogent contact with what other people have
understood themselves to be in a political tradition. And since
Oakeshott's scepticism articulates that the arrangements of a tradition are so complicated and far reaching that they must "intimate a
sympathy for what does not fully appear", the conservative disposition in politics in terms of conversation is to engage in the "convinc-

---

[159] Cf. P. Riley, 1992: 650.

ing exploration of a sympathy, present but not yet followed up".[160] For example, Oakeshott argues that the legal status of women in Britain was in confusion, because the rights and duties that composed that status intimated something more than the arguments drawn from abstract natural rights, from "justice" or from some general concept of feminine personality. And on the view of things that Oakeshott has been suggesting in the previous discussions, it is understandable that he reaches the conclusion that the only credible explanation to be advanced for the "technical enfranchisement of woman" was that in almost every respect they had already been enfranchised.[161]

It appears that in politics the pursuit of intimations involves a conversational way of learning things as they appeared in the wisdom of past agents' utterances and performances so as to come to terms with plausible statements in given circumstances. On this meaning, the traditional knowledge, which in the practical world can be understood as the actual moral and political exemplifications that have already been intimated in past voices, can only be pursued in terms of conversation, not in terms of argumentation. And consequently, "since a tradition of behaviour is not susceptible of the distinction between essence and accident, knowledge of it [through conversation] is unavoidably knowledge of its detail: to know only the gist is to know nothing. What has to be learned is not an abstract idea, or a set of tricks, not even a ritual, but a concrete, coherent manner of living in all its intricateness".[162]

The self involved in a concrete political understanding, Oakeshott would then agree, is a hermeneutic-self, not an argumentative-self. It may, therefore, be re-acclaimed here that Oakeshott is never an advocate of radical individualism, but a philosopher of traditionalist individualism. Far from being associated with the liberal context, Oakeshott's affirmation of the importance of tradition in our understanding of practical affairs is a position that is closer to that of the nineteenth-century classical hermeneutics when the writers such as Schleiermacher, Droysen and Dilthey claimed that "the awareness of one's own history and of that of mankind as a whole is an indispensable condition for a rich and fulfilled life".[163] At this point, it is no surprise that Oakeshott believes history as a mode of understand-

[160] *RP*: 57.

[161] *RP*: 57.

[162] *RP*: 59-60.

[163] J. Bleicher, 1980: 9; see also chap. 1 for the theoretical outline of classical hermeneutics.

ing must be taken seriously in political education.[164] For history, by definition, is the form of enquiry which works on the complexity and comprehensiveness of human actions in terms of contingency and particularity; so a history of the manner of political thinking and doing will provide the practical man with more concrete knowledge about a political tradition to be conversed with, and thus balance against the trans-traditional foundation of rationalist politics.

But, in contrast to classical hermeneutics, I do not think that Oakeshott really adopts an historicist position in the sense of making all practice historical. The non-historicist *communication* between history and practice in Oakeshott's thought, nonetheless, is a wider question that I must return to in Chapter V. For now, I think it is only sufficient to conclude that in *RP* Oakeshott has made every effort to establish a traditionalist mode of understanding politics as a way of living, an effort which should be appreciated by anyone who is frustrated by the world which is being governed by a vocabulary of scientifically validated moral and political beliefs.

IV.4.5. The Politics of Faith and the Politics of Scepticism

This is not the end of the matter yet. I have mentioned that Oakeshott's understanding of the two contrasting modes of morality and politics does not lack a concern about their historic context. To consider this aspect of Oakeshott's thought expressed at the time of his writings published in *RP*, an essential work is now available to us, namely, *The Politics of Faith and the Politics of Scepticism* (*PFPS*).

The subject of *PFPS*, as that of *The Harvard Lectures*, is to consider the manner of understanding the activity of governing and being governed in *the* history of modern European politics. And here, once again, it is significant to note that Oakeshott takes the work as an investigation into the past which is not historical. He concedes that the examination offered in the essay is "a study of change but without revealing (what alone interests the historian) the mediation of change".[165] That is, it is not concerned with a complete historical account of the office of government in terms of change, but with the extremes defining the limits of "a complex, historic alloy, a mixture of heterogeneous and not always congruous elements"[166] of the office of government.

---

[164] *RP*: 63-4.
[165] *PFPS*: 19; cf. 46, 57.
[166] *PFPS*: 10.

Through extremes, then, Oakeshott identifies the poles which "protect" the identity of the manner of governing; insofar as "these extremes may not only be distant from one another, allowing a generous space for manoeuvre; they may even be specially opposed to one another, the one forbidding all (or most) of what the other prescribes, or at least warrants".[167] It is thus not inappropriate to regard the general character of the extreme as an emblem of a profound division within the manner of governing. And so, it may be expected that the poles in question are comprised of rationalism in politics and conservatism in politics, which Oakeshott here refers to as the politics of faith and the politics of scepticism. Referring to the previous examination, this terminology shows that Oakeshott simply hangs on to both meta-issues and advocatory-issues when giving a picture of the *history* of modern political thought while composing *RP*.[168]

In recognising these two historic styles of politics, we are then looking at their ideal characteristics. It is possible to appreciate Oakeshott's viewpoint that the most characteristic assumption of the politics of faith is the view of understanding governing as perfection, that is, an "unlimited" activity responding to "an inspired perception of what *the* common good is".[169] The politics of scepticism is rooted in a sceptical view about human perfection, and thus sees politics as a "limited" activity whose main business is to maintain the "superficial order".[170]

But how have these styles of politics emerged? In brief, they are both the stepchildren of the "enlargement of power" which marks the beginning of modern times. Given the fact that modern government, due to the centralisation of authority to control and integrate the activities of its subjects, and the application of more efficient techniques in commerce or in industry, had already at its disposal more power than since the medieval ages,[171] politics of faith and the

---

[167] *PFPS*: 11.

[168] It must be noted here that "the 'faith' in question is virtually the opposite of traditional religious faith. It is the faith in the capacity of human beings to perfect themselves through their own effort, made possible by the discovery of ways continually to increase the power of government as essential instrumentally to control, design and perfect individuals and groups" (T. Fuller, 1996: xi).

[169] *PFPS*: 23-30, esp. 27.

[170] *PFPS*: 30-8, esp. 34.

[171] *PFPS*: 46-50.

politics of scepticism can be seen as two opposed responses given to this historic phenomenon.

To start with, the optimistic response to the enlargement of power was, of course, to be found in the politics of faith, and it was with Bacon that this style of politics had "unmistakably emerged".[172] That is to say, as we have seen from *The Harvard Lectures*, Oakeshott interprets Bacon as "the mirror of his age and the chief architect of the politics of faith",[173] when he was inspired by the capacity he saw in mankind to achieve its "well-being" and to regard government as the chief agent in a pursuit of perfection.[174] And in a similar manner, Oakeshott claims the politics of faith has exploited two main idioms since Bacon: a religious version and a productivist version (in *The Harvard Lectures* a distributivist version has been added, though).

The politics of scepticism, on the other hand, was a pessimistic response to the "enlargement of power". This means that in the modern context political scepticism sprang up not merely as a reaction against the politics of faith, but also as a self-conscious response to the circumstances that made possible the politics of faith, namely, the appearance of government as a "public office" with a special status commonly recognised as "sovereignty".[175] Moreover, the emergence of the politics of scepticism also has to do with the current of doubt and despondency appearing in the early seventeenth-century literature as a relic of medieval pessimism not yet dismissed by the optimism of Baconian thought. In Montaignean traditionalism, for example, custom is seen as an indispensable condition of human understanding on the account that man is so composed of contrarieties that, if he is to enjoy any coherence of activity, he needs to follow a rule whose virtue is not that it is "just" but that it is "settled".[176] In this respect, what categorically distinguishes sceptical politics from the other extreme in the early modern period is a sense of morality, where "the earth [was] recognised not as a world to be exploited but as a 'player's stage'".[177]

An additional resource for the emergence of the politics of scepticism, Oakeshott continues, came from the historic character of the English Parliament. In the early centuries of the modern period the

---

[172] *PFPS*: 57.
[173] *PFPS*: 52.
[174] *PFPS*: 53-7.
[175] *PFPS*: 70-5.
[176] *PFPS*: 76.
[177] *PFPS*: 76.

Parliament was still perceived as a "court of law" which provided judicial provisions of remedies for wrongs and meted out justice to all according to their desires. As a result, the office of government was recognised as the "maintenance of rights" and the "redress of wrongs", not as the pursuit of a comprehensive setting of activity upon all the subjects of the realm. In this manner the Parliament was "an inheritance that spoke directly in habit and institution and needed no elaborate interpretation in order to divulge an understanding of government in [the sceptical] style".[178] Furthermore, a wider tradition of sceptical politics, in Oakeshott's view, may include thinkers such as Bayle, Fontenelle, Shaftesbury, Hume, Burke, Hegel, Coleridge, Calhoun and Macaulay and so on. Irrespective of how they diverge from one another, they have in common a rejection of the politics of faith, that is, they object to the understanding of politics as an unlimited and overwhelming activity.

On these views, Oakeshott states that the Constitution of United States of America and *some aspects* of Locke's, Bentham's and Paine's thoughts contain the elements of sceptical politics. But this gives insufficient reason to interpret Oakeshott as a defender of liberalism. For Oakeshott contends that the politics of the modern world are the *concordia discors* of the two styles of government, and consequently it is possible that some writers do not support the one to the complete exclusion of the other.[179] One of the main failures of modern scepticism in terms of a liberal outlook, Oakeshott soon points out, was its alliance with the politics of natural rights as in Locke's writings.[180] He writes that:

> It was, perhaps, unavoidable that a style of governing in which the office of government is understood as the maintenance of appropriate order, the preservation of rights and duties and the redress of wrongs should be ambitious to establish itself on a firm foundation. The impulse to assure ourselves that our arrangements and authorised manners of behaviour represent not merely fact and habit, but "justice" and "truth", and that they have a "certainty" which is out of reach of the vicissitudes of time and place, has always been strong. But it is an impulse which belongs properly to faith. Historically, so far as scepticism is concerned, it must be regarded as an infection caught from faith, a temporary desertion of its own character induced by the plausible triumphs of faith. And that such a foundation should be sought in the notion that the rights and duties to be protected are "natural" and to be defended on account of

---

[178] *PFPS*: 77.

[179] See *PFPS*: 80.

[180] Another example Oakeshott gives us is the alliance of sceptical politics with the politics of republicanism. See *PFPS*: 83-4.

their naturalness was an enterprise given in the climate of seventeenth-century opinion. The writer who led Europe in this respect was John Locke, the most ambiguous of all political writers of modern times; *a political sceptic who inadvertently imposed the idiom of faith upon the sceptical understanding of government* [emphasis mine]. But how out of character this enterprise soon became apparent. To turn "right" and "duties" which were known as historic achievements, elicited by patient and judicial inquest from the manner in which men were accustomed to behave, into "natural" rights and duties was to deny them just that contingency of character which was the heart of the sceptical interpretation, and was to attribute to them an absoluteness and a performance which in the sceptical understanding of them they could not possess.[181]

I cite this important passage at length, because it repeatedly unveils Oakeshott's rejection of the intellectual foundations of liberalism in relation to the assumptions of formalism in ethics: the impulse to establish the arrangements of politics on a firm foundation, in terms of a certain radical individualist theory such as that of natural rights, in order to arrive at a moral and political certainty indifferent to the vicissitudes of time and place. And here, what Oakeshott says about Locke, of course, applies to Kant and utilitarianism as well.

Moreover, it may help us to clarify in a fuller sense that, so far as the office of government, the advocatory-issues of liberalism, or so to speak, the institutions of liberal democracy are concerned, while claiming the value of the individual over anything else, are a reaction against the politics of the common good. However, the meta-issues of liberal ethics are, in fact, philosophically self-defeating in the sense of "imposing the idiom of faith upon the sceptical understanding of government". That is, the quality of individuality that the liberal intends to protect is so radically *ahistorical* that it fails in its original purpose of seeing politics as the maintenance of rights, which are actually historic achievements. With liberalism, as a result, the idea of perfection has penetrated into a form of moral individualism purporting to suggest that we "ought" not because we "must" but because we "can". In short, Oakeshott observes that the serious fault with liberalism is not its initial meaning to maintain the importance of individuality, but what it comes to achieve, namely, a formalist theory of morality and politics.

Through our examination of *The Harvard Lectures* and *PFPS*, it has become patently clear that the extreme recognised as the morality of individualism cannot be correctly grasped without simultaneously making reference to the politics of scepticism or conservatism in pol-

---

[181] *PFPS*: 82-3.

itics. For, even though Oakeshott alters his terminology from time to time, he has never excluded the meta-issues from the identification of the morality of individuality, nor has he left aside the advocatory-issues when dealing with the politics of scepticism. And so, the fact that Oakeshott appreciates the value of the individual still proffers no solid ground for interpreting him as a liberal, in that he does not agree with the liberal understanding of individuality as presented in the works of Locke, Kant or utilitarianism.

Furthermore, to protect the identification of modern European politics in terms of two historic poles, Oakeshott in *PFPS* actually takes the sceptical thoughts intimated in the writings of Montaigne and so forth, and in the historic implications of the English Parliament as those that are categorically opposed to the politics of faith; and it is of little wonder to remark that it is the fortunes of the politics of scepticism as such that matches with the essences of Oakeshott's own traditionalist politics that we have discovered so far. Consequently, it is observable that in this philosophical-historic scheme, liberal individualism only stands obliquely in between the extremes of faithful politics and sceptical politics; it is identifiable within the polarised structure of modern European politics but it has never reached either of these two poles. And I do not think Oakeshott has changed his position on this matter in *HC*: The contrast between *societas* and *universitas* is a reformulation of the contrast between the politics of scepticism and the politics of faith; and the theory of civil association is a restatement of non-liberal conservatism in politics.

Before moving on to *HC*, nevertheless, there is another aspect of *PFPS* worth mentioning. So far the impression gained may be that Oakeshott's philosophical enterprise never lacks an historic concern. Yet in *PFPS*, the historic concern has led him to detect that circumstances have arisen to push our politics so decidedly and over such a long period of time in the direction of the extreme in the politics of faith that we forget that "in order to make the fire burn a little more briskly, we have pulled out all the dampers, and in our enjoyment of the warmth we fail to remark that the scuttle is empty and the chimney near to being on fire".[182] That is to say, reflecting upon the theme of *RP*, in *PFPS* Oakeshott also sees the predicament of our time as a situation in which Rationalism has been at work for so long that we have gradually lost the sense of politics as a way of living. As

---

[182] *PFPS*: 11.

a result, he maintains, "what needs to be restored in contemporary politics is a balance of attention and a balance of power".[183]

Here, it comes as no surprise that Oakeshott claims the balance in question is the "separation of powers" in its formal sense, where the rule of law should win approval. For government by rule of law, that is, by means of enforcement by prescribed methods of settled rules binding alike on governors and governed, is itself an emblem of that diffusion of power which it exists to promote; it is the method of government most economical in the use of power. Oakeshott writes that:

> [The rule of law] involves a partnership between past and present and between governors and governed which leaves no room for arbitrariness; it encourages a tradition of moderation and of resistance to the growth of dangerous assembles of power which is far more effective than any promiscuous onslaught, however crushing; it controls effectively, but without breaking the grand affirmative flow of activity; and it gives a practical definition of the kind of limited but necessary service that may be expected from government, restraining us from vain and dangerous expectation, and it from overreaching ambition.[184]

This statement, indeed, at once carries us back to Oakeshott's own sympathy for traditionalist politics.

For Oakeshott, then, theoretically the politics of scepticism is a more coherent way of understanding politics, and given the predicament of our time in terms of Rationalism, it is "perhaps more appropriate to our circumstance".[185] This, however, does not mean that conservative politics should substitute for rationalist politics, for it is not the philosopher's task to offer a direction for us to follow. But rather, it only indicates that Oakeshott's inclination to traditionalism is the result of a philosophical scrutiny in which both the theoretical and the historic conditions are considered.

Thus, the philosophical-historic perspective at stake does not concede that a history of political thought should replace political philosophy. Before turning to discuss the relation of history to philosophy in the next chapter, it only need be remembered that in a quasi-philosophical past the philosopher is aware that the historic conditions of modern European moral and political activity are predicated on a "circumscribed range of movement",[186] but he does not take this for granted. Instead, he views it as an "invitation" that

---

[183] *PFPS*: 86.
[184] *PFPS*: 88-9.
[185] *RP*: 426.
[186] *PFPS*: 116.

calls for further investigation,[187] and the result is a philosophical synthesis of the two extremes in favour of scepticism. For the sake of structure, I shall not discuss this facet of *PFPS* until the very end of this chapter.

IV.5. *On Human Conduct*

Having examined Oakeshott's earlier works, we are now in a better position to consider his final statement on politics,[188] namely, *On Human Conduct* (HC).

IV.5.1. Understanding Human Conduct

Oakeshott begins *HC* with the essay "On the Understanding of Human Conduct", which comprises three sections of analysis: first, a brief account of the general character of understanding, continuing to maintain a non-foundationalist conception of philosophy and the self-consistency of modes of understanding or platforms of theorising (as he now calls it);[189] second, an ethical theorising of "human conduct"; and third, a theoretical attempt to understand a contingent human performance which may be recognised as historical.[190]

[187] Cf. *HC*: 1-31.

[188] It is true that *HC* provides "a clarifying summation of [Oakeshott's] reflection on political activity" (T. Fuller, 1976: 185). In saying that it is Oakeshott's final statement on politics, however, I do not subscribe to B. Barber's claim that Oakeshott's earlier works before *HC* lack a "unification of themes" (1976: 450).

[189] Consider, for example, this paragraph taken from *HC* (2-3): "Of the path it [the continuous enterprise of theorising or thinking] may follow, some (we may suppose) will soon exhaust their promise. It is an engagement of arrivals and departures. Temporary platforms of conditional understanding are always being reached, and the theorist may turn aside to explore them. But each is an arrival, an enlightenment, and a point of departure. The notion of an unconditional or definitive understanding may hover in the background, but it has no part in the adventure".

[190] It says that there are two idioms of theoretical understanding which are particularly discussed in *HC*: an ethical study which explains the postulates of human conduct *as a whole*, and an historical enquiry which deals with *a* substantive human action in a contingent context. These two conditional platforms of understanding must be distinguished from one another, because the theorems that compose the identity "human conduct" in an ethical exploration cannot elucidate the intelligence of a substantive human utterance or performance in an historical understanding. As such the latter is merely an illustration not an example of the former (*HC*: 92). Some writers, however, fail to tell the difference that Oakeshott makes here. See, for example, B. Barber, 1976: 452-3; D. Thomas, 1977: 453; D. R. Mapel, 1990: 394.

The reason why Oakeshott discusses the characteristics of history and ethics in the first essay of *HC*, I believe, lies in the fact that they are the two

However, it is only the second topic that I propose to examine here.

The expression "human conduct" used here denotes an ideal character; that is, "conduct" itself cannot be performed but it only postulates the conditions of human actions and utterances in terms of which they may be understood.[191] In other words, Oakeshott is never tired of clarifying the categorical distinction between theory and practice: to theorise human conduct is not to "diagnose a situation" but to think in different terms what one already understands, not to enhance the intelligence of what goes on but to understand it in terms of its postulates.[192] The idea of "conduct *inter homines*" (i.e. performances understood as transactions between agents) that concerns Oakeshott is then, "that of an agent disclosing and enacting himself in performances whose imagined and wished-for outcomes are performances of other agents or other performances of himself: satisfactions, not only pursued in actions and purchased by actions, but wholly composed of actions".[193]

This characterisation is, of course, liable to understand human conduct in terms of the postulates of a free agent who is willing to make a response to a contingent situation (deliberation), to diminish the hazards of his action (persuasion) and to make his action more intelligible (explanation).[194] And so, it basically reflects the conditions of the world of practice that Oakeshott has disclosed in *EM*: practice is the alteration or maintenance of "what is" so as to agree with a "what ought to be"; the principle of the coherence of practical knowledge is the idea of freedom of choosing.

"instruments of theoretical enquiry" that Oakeshott wishes to apply to his later examinations of civil association and of a modern European state in the second and third essays of *HC* respectively. However, I do not think that what Oakeshott actually gives us is an historical past; but rather it can only be a quasi-philosophical past.

[191] *HC*: 31.

[192] *HC*: 32-5. When a going-on is identified as a human action, Oakeshott believes, our identification of it can be seen as a "diagnosis", i.e. an invitation to understand what is being understood in the performance or utterance of that action. Thus, the identity "Tom considers which of two shoes he shall buy" is a diagnosis of what is being understood to prescribe the utterance or performance that "Tom is asking the salesman about the prices of the two shoes". By contrast, however, that which is really problematic for an ethical theorist, for example, is not to re-make a diagnosis of human actions in more systematic terms, but to interrogate the conditions of "human conduct" in terms of "deliberation", "choice" and so forth.

[193] *HC*: 36.

[194] See *HC*: 36-51.

Yet, it is time now to point out that Oakeshott's treatment of the individual contains two related levels of discussion. On one level, it deals with *the Hobbesian formal conditions of a free will to act*, and this is expressed in *EM* and the passages of *HC* under consideration; on another, it also touches upon *the Aristotelian tradition or practice of human volition*, and this is presented in *RP* and other places in *HC*.[195] We shall later have a chance to return to this matter in association with the theory of civil association itself. In this place, we need only note that *HC*, being a synthesis of the philosopher's thought, also accounts for the main theme disclosed in *RP*: Since conduct *inter homines* indicates that agents communicate with each other in terms of choices and so forth, this at the same time assumes "more durable relationships between agents" which can constitute the conditional contexts of all human transactions.[196] This conditional context of actions, which Oakeshott in *RP* otherwise calls a "tradition", is now re-named as a *"practice"*. A *practice*, it follows, consists in the encounters of reciprocity in which agents converse with one another, and the relationships of conduct that compose it are capable of being engaged in because they have been learned. If we recall what Oakeshott meant by "tradition", we can recognise it in what he now says about *"practice"*:

> A practice may be identified as a set of considerations, manners, uses, observances, customs, standards, canon's maxims, principles, rules, and offices specifying useful procedures or denoting obligations or duties which relate to human actions and utterances. It is a prudential or a moral adverbial qualification of choices and performances, more or less complicated, in which conduct is understood in terms of a procedure. Words such as punctually, considerately, civilly, scientifically, legally, candidly, judicially, poetically, morally, etc., do not specify performances; they postulate performances and specify procedural conditions to be taken into account when choosing and acting.[197]

In civilisation, then, there are *practices* which differ in their dimension, their complexity, and their density, each is a distinguishable *more* of utterance such as *poetice, geometrice, historice, oratorice*, or *philosophice*. Moreover, with respect to generality and persuasiveness, the two most important forms of *practice* in terms of which agents are durably related to one another in practical conduct are a

---

[195] P. Franco, by contrast, argues that there is a tendency in Oakeshott's political philosophy to merge Hobbesianism with Hegelianism so as to transcend each camp's partiality in creating a more complete theory of individuality (see esp. 1990b: 413-21).

[196] *HC*: 54.

[197] *HC*: 55-6.

"common tongue" and a "language of morality". Here, Oakeshott takes the opportunity to re-organise the conditions of moral conduct only in terms of two aspects of the art of agency: self-disclosure and self-enactment.

A moral *practice* can be considered to be a procedure or language of self-disclosure; the conduct it relates to is the intercourse of agents, each concerned with procuring imagined and wished-for satisfactions. But, compared to his earlier works, Oakeshott in *HC* stresses more explicitly that the satisfaction of the morality of individual agents is so self-contained that it has nothing to do with a "prudential art" dealing with the success of the enterprise of agents; that is, a moral *practice*, no matter what it is, is definitely not an "instrument" to the satisfaction of any substantive want.[198] This means that Oakeshott claims morality is concerned with good and bad conduct itself, not with performances in respect of their outcomes. Thus, when Oakeshott writes that "a moral language is a language of propriety, not of prudence",[199] this can be regarded, once again, as his commentary on Aristotle's *Ethics*, i.e. Aristotle's discussion of moral habits.

Moreover, a moral *practice* in itself has nothing to do with human nature or a philosophical system of values either; but it is only a vernacular language of colloquial intercourse. That is to say, instead of being pre-determined by a fixed foundation, a moral *practice* is far more like the informative context by means of which the agents may get to know the genuine implications of the so-called "moral values". So every moral discourse is an historic achievement lasting from a continuously accumulating residue of conditional relationships learned in an experience of intercourse between agents; it emerges as a ritual of utterances and responses in which agents are colloquially related to one another in the idiom of a familiar moral language.

But, there is another side to moral *practice* that needs to be considered, namely, the self-enactment of agents. The character of self-enactment can be appealed to in order to understand actions in terms of the "motives" for which they are performed, and by a motive Oakeshott means an agent's "sentiment" in choosing and performing the actions he chooses and performs. Synthetically, it may then be said that moral conduct is not only the behaviour of agents engaging in transactions with one another in the recognition

---

[198] See esp. *HC*: 60-1.
[199] *HC*: 80.

of the authority of considerations to be subscribed to in choosing satisfactions, it is also the behaviour of an agent enacting himself in
terms of the motives in which he permits himself to act.[200]

All this, obviously, points to the theme of *RP* that a moral *practice* is
a "tradition" of moral behaviour: moral life involves a manner of living, not a set of principles; general principles, of course, may be elicited from a moral tradition, "but (like other languages) it is not the
creation of grammarians, it is made by speakers".[201] Again, the
moral self "has a 'history', but no 'nature', he is what in conduct he
becomes".[202] As such, moral discourse is akin to the Aristotelian
phronesis,[203] not to the Kantian categorical imperative.

IV.5.2. Leviathan and The Nature of Political Philosophy

The second essay, "On the Civil Condition", is where Oakeshott
moves to link Aristotelian morality with Hobbesian civility. More
precisely, it is my view that Oakeshott's theory of civil association
can be interpreted in respect of two main topics: the *formal conditions*
and the *practical procedure* of *civitas*. Where Oakeshott somehow differs from Hobbes in pondering the *practice* of *civitas* under the condition of "politics", he clearly moves from *Nicomochean Ethics* to
Leviathan when establishing the formal conditions of *civitas* in terms
of what one may call the Hobbesian legalistic character of civil
authority.[204] Thus, the point is that the theory of civil association presented in *HC* is a more sophisticated form of conservatism in politics,
in that Oakeshott turns to bring Hobbes's notion of law-making
authority, the legalistic structure of *civitas*, into consideration.

Oakeshott's interests in Hobbes's writings, of course, may be
traced back to his famous "Introduction to *Leviathan*" (1946).[205] And
consequently, in expounding the degree to which Oakeshott's the-

---

[200] For Oakeshott's discussion on how self-disclosure and self-enactment stand to
one another in moral conduct, see *HC*: 71-8.

[201] *HC*: 79.

[202] *HC*: 41; see also, *VL*: 64.

[203] *HC*: 89.

[204] It is this Hobbes, as Oakeshott observes, who begins with law and obligation that
can be understood as the "originator of a new tradition in political philosophy"
(*RP*: 277; cf. L. Strauss, 1952: chap. viii).

[205] Oakeshott's essays on Hobbes were collected under the title, *Hobbes on Civil
Association* (*HCA*), and published in 1975. Three of them, including "the
Introduction to *Leviathan*", "The Moral Life in the Writings of Thomas Hobbes"
and "Logos and Telos", are now also available to part three "On Hobbes" in a
new edition of *RP*, to which I am referring where needed in this study.

ory of civil association is influenced by Hobbes, it may be well to do so with reference to his own understanding of *Leviathan*. In this matter, let us start with the issue of the nature of political philosophy:

Firstly, for Oakeshott, our reflection about political life may take place at a variety of levels; ascending from the levels of "reflection in the service of politics" and of "reflection in political doctrine", philosophical political reflection is to establish the relations between politics and eternity.[206] This notion of political philosophy that Oakeshott persistently holds in his writings is exactly that which he applies to characterise *Leviathan*.[207] And if *the* history of political philosophy lies in this permeating sense of human life as a "predicament", Oakeshott believes its variety can be found in three "great traditions": Reason and Nature, Will and Artifice and Rational Will. Whilst Plato's *Republic* and Hegel's *Philosophie des Rechts* are the representatives of the first and third models respectively, the paradigm of Will and Artifice constitutes "the context of *Leviathan*".[208] Oakeshott considers his own political philosophy as an example of this Hobbesian tradition.

Secondly, as far as the "manner and mind" of a philosopher is concerned, Oakeshott sets up four criteria for assessing Hobbes's achievements in civil philosophy: extraordinary confidence, the energy of constantly freeing himself from the formalism of his system (i.e. the striking technicalities of a scepticism), an affection for originality and a self-conscious stylist in writing.[209] If it is open to question whether Oakeshott has ever reached this level of philosophising, it cannot be doubted that he more or less attempts to follow these criteria in his own enterprise.

Lastly, and most importantly, Oakeshott's remarkable interpretation of the relation of civil philosophy to a "system" of philosophy in Hobbes's establishment is perfectly harmonious with his own position. In rejecting the conventional view in Hobbes's studies that the project of civil philosophy is based on a natural philosophy, i.e. materialism, Oakeshott maintains that the coherent system of Hobbes's philosophy "lies not in an architectonic structure, but in a single 'passionate thought' that pervades its parts".[210] In other words, Hobbes's civil philosophy belongs to a philosophical system,

---

[206] Cf. esp. *RP*: 146-52.

[207] See esp. *RP*: 225, 291.

[208] See *RP*: 225-8.

[209] See *RP*: 228-35.

[210] *RP*: 236.

not because it is materialistic, but because it is the application of a doctrine about the nature of philosophy to the understanding of the system and place of politics. In Oakeshott's terms, this means that political philosophy or ethics is nothing, if it is not a form of philosophising.

Before unveiling the parallels between Oakeshott's civil association and the argument of *Leviathan*, it ought to be noted that Oakeshott's interpretation of *Leviathan* (as a past text) is philosophical rather than historical: It is Oakeshott's own conception of political philosophy that penetrates into his understanding of *Leviathan*, which in turn re-affirms (or re-adjusts) his understanding of what political philosophy should be. Hence, by a quasi-philosophical past, I mean a philosophical consideration about the historic conditions of human agency (as to be found in *PFPS*) or a conversation between a philosophy and its own past image (as to be found in "Introduction to *Leviathan*").

IV.5.3. Civil Association (I): The Formal Conditions

As we now come closer to Oakeshott's theory of civil association, it is observable that he basically uses the Hobbesian terminology of *civitas* for the ideal condition of civility, *cives* for the *personae* related in this manner, *lex* for the terms of their relationships, and *respublica* for the comprehensive conditions of association.[211] Moreover, Oakeshott is also following Hobbes in understanding the civil condition as an "artifact": civil association is an understood relationship of intelligent agents.[212]

But in each case, Oakeshott's notion of philosophy demands that the task of a theorist is to understand the civil condition in terms of its postulates, not to engage in civil intercourse. And Oakeshott's primary concern in *HC* is to clarify the categorical distinction between civil association (*societas*) and enterprise association (*universitas*) in order to revive a non-rationalist way of understanding politics.[213] Oakeshott begins his "intellectual adventure" with enterprise association.

Human conduct, we have seen, is that of an agent disclosing and enacting himself in performances whose imagined and wished-for outcomes are performances of other agents or other performances of himself: satisfactions; and those satisfactions can be self-contained

---

[211] *HC*: 108-9.

[212] *HC*: 109-12.

[213] See esp. *HC*: 118-9. Cf. P. Franco, 1990a: 158; N. O'Sullivan, 1993: 103.

or prudential. What Oakeshott calls enterprise association is precisely the mode of relationship in which the participants are engaged in the pursuit of some common good to be prudentially satisfied. It is true that of all durable human relationships, enterprise association is the most familiar; it includes a productive understanding (a factory), an association of the same profession or trade, an army, a "village community", a sect, a fellowship, a party, a fraternity, a solidarity, a collegium, or a guild.[214] And in politics, to be sure, we are accustomed to understanding the activity of governing in terms of this mode of relationship. Since Oakeshott has already said enough about this matter, he believes his concern now is only to theorise civil association in terms of its postulates.

By contrast with enterprise association, civil association is to be identified in terms of moral considerations; *civitas* is a moral relationship. This is, indeed, a proposition that Hobbes maintained as well. More crucially, Oakeshott follows Hobbes's footsteps to argue that civil association is composed entirely of rules: "the language of civil intercourse is a language of rules; *civitas* is a rule-articulated association",[215] and, by a rule Oakeshott means an "authoritative assertion". Thus, Oakeshott believes in the Hobbesian recognition that what really counts in civil association is not the forms of constitution (or the kinds of commonwealth as Hobbes called it), but the fact that it is constituted by a system of authoritative rules.[216] It implies again that unlike contemporary liberal thinkers, Oakeshott does not think that democracy must be a *necessary* condition of civil association.

Moreover, led by Hobbes, Oakeshott also articulates that a rule has a "self-determined jurisdiction" within which agents are equal in respect of the rule and each has an obligation to subscribe to it; it prescribes a "norm of conduct" proper to be subscribed to in choosing performances; and it subsists in being *recognised* or *acknowledged* by the agents concerned.[217] That is, authoritative rules are so self-contained that they should be distinguished from optional persuasive utterances such as a piece of advice, a request, a plea, or a

[214] *HC*: 112-7.

[215] *HC*: 124.

[216] Hobbes, 1946: chap. xix. Cf. *RP*: 261.

[217] *HC*: 125-7. It is thus confirmed what we have earlier said that Oakeshott does not reject "norms" in practice, he only thinks that their meaning belongs to practice itself. The task of the philosopher is to explain the matter as a civil condition, not to impose it on human conduct.

warning, and from mere prohibitions such as an order, a command, a behest, or an injunction.[218]

It appears that in the civil condition, agents are related in terms of their common recognition of the rules which constitute *civitas*. Stemming from this consideration, Oakeshott thus claims that the *formal conditions* of civil association are: *lex* (legislation, adjudication, ruling), authority and obligation.

First of all, since the rules that constitute civil association are authoritative assertions, they are nothing but "civil laws" or *lex*; or conversely, the most systematic character of *lex*, Oakeshott repeats, is that it is a self-contained system of laws which is able to identify its own jurisdiction. But, *lex* must postulate the norms of conduct which exist continuously in civil association. Thus, like Hobbes, Oakeshott claims that in the civil condition, there are related conditions of legislation, adjudication and ruling coming from the cardinal postulate of *lex*.

Legislation, to start with, is the procedure in which new *lex* is enacted or current *lex* is amended or repealed. It is true that how much use may be made of legislation depends on the change of situation. But in any event, legislation is of importance in the civil condition, because *lex* is "the life of civil association",[219] and *civitas*, understood in terms of a system of laws, is an emblem of human responsibility which may be alterable — insofar as legislation is a procedure of legal innovation by means of which civil association can enjoy its durability.[220]

Additionally, adjudication is the procedure in which the meaning of *lex* can be deciphered significantly, justifiably and appropriately. Oakeshott agrees with Hobbes that in the civil condition the "faculty" of adjudication is exercised in the court of law;[221] and consequently he writes on the Hobbesian observation that "in a court of law, the 'judge' is not an arbitrator in a conflict of interests, he is the custodian of the norms of *lex*".[222] In other words, for both Hobbes and Oakeshott, since in civil association no common good is pursued, the opinion of the "judge" is merely concerned with the maintenance of a system of moral considerations which are exclusively

---

[218] In this respect, Oakeshott's observation is parallel to H. L. A. Hart in the sense of rejecting J. Austin's command theory of law. Cf. Hart: 1994, chaps. 2, 3 &4.

[219] *RP*: 277.

[220] *HC*: 138-41.

[221] *RP*: 263.

[222] *HC*: 132-3.

indifferent to *any* merits of interest in procuring substantive and fixed satisfactions.

Finally, the condition of ruling must appear in civil association, too. In a nutshell, to rule is to require an identified agent to make a specified choice in an assignable situation, that is, to *administer* the prescriptions of *lex*. And yet, because ruling is the exercise of authority deriving from *lex* which is not the rule-book of an enterprise, those administrating rules "are not managers, arbitrators between claims or merits of conflicting interests, *largotors* or patrons of preferred interests" but "office-holders with powers and obligations concerned with the observance of a procedure".[223]

Put together, then, the notion of *lex* must postulate an "apparatus of rule" in civil association which Oakeshott has identified elsewhere as "rule of law",[224] and for the convenience of having a name for this system of conditions, Oakeshott now calls it *respublica* which, indifferent to a common good, is "a manifold of rules and rule-like prescriptions to be subscribed to in all the enterprise and adventures in which the self-chosen satisfactions of agents may be sought".[225] And it is largely from this Hobbesian legalism that the purposeless characteristic of Oakeshott's civil association comes.

To put it more clearly, Hobbes, indeed, argues that the authority of *civitas* would take care of "all those things which concern the common peace and safety"; or alternatively, that the condition of peace and safety is the effect of

> a covenant of every man with every man, in such manner, as if every man should say to every man, *I authorise and give up my right of governing myself, to this man, or to this assembly of men, on this condition, that thou give up thy right to him, and authorise all his actions in like manner.*[226]

But, as Oakeshott puts it, in Hobbes the covenant is "to 'erect' and maintain a 'sovereign' civil authority, not to unite covenanters in pursuit of a common substantive enterprise".[227] In other words, Hobbes's civil association does not pursue a *summum bonum* such as peace and safety, the contract to establish a sovereign does that. Hence, in *Leviathan* there is a difference between the desire for peace and safety as the motivation to get out of the state of nature in which

---

[223] *HC*: 144.
[224] And Oakeshott later returns to round out this conception in "The Rule of Law", which is collected in *OH*: 119-64.
[225] *HC*: 148.
[226] Hobbes, 1946: 131-2.
[227] *HC*: 232-3.

every man is against every other man,[228] and the task of civil association, commonwealth or state itself, which, beneath the sovereign, thereafter aims to produce civilisation — culture, the arts, commerce etc. Oakeshott certainly proposes the same view as Hobbes regarding the non-instrumental characteristic of *civitas*.

The civil condition understood in terms of *lex*, however, is still incomplete, because it is obviously conditional upon the assumption that rules are *recognised* as *authoritative*. Here we are entering into the condition of authority and obligation postulated in civil association.

It has been implied in our previous examination that *respublica* has the property of *self-authentication*: Ruling, legislation and adjudication are all the exercises of authority, which comes from *lex*, which in turn constitutes the civil condition. In other words, *respublica* contains rules in terms of which the authority of other rules may be recognised, but there is none which is exclusively a rule for the recognition of the authority of other rules. What is called *Grundnorm* or "the hierarchy of laws" — a jurisprudence mainly provided by the neo-Kantian, H. Kelsen[229] — is here under attack:

> There is no place in civil association for any but a conditional distinction between so-called "private" and "public" law. Nor can there be a single ultimate rule of recognition, an unconditional and unquestionable norm from which all others derive their authority: a 'constitution' not subject to interpretation and immune from inquiry.[230]

This means that the validity of *lex* should be considered only in terms of the resources for consideration which *lex* itself provides. To characterise further the self-authentication of civil authority as such, Oakeshott draws our attention to what it categorically *excludes* in the first instance.

First, the authority of *respublica*, he maintains, cannot be the identification of it providing "shelter" for the uncertainties of a human life or its prescriptions being subscribed to on most occasions by most *cives*. For civil association can provide such benefit or efficacy only on the condition that civil authority is recognised. Here, the point that the authority of *lex* has to do with acknowledgement rather than with desirability or truth is reminiscent of Hobbes's position.[231]

---

[228] For Oakeshott's interpretation of the Hobbesian predicament of human nature, see *RP*: 249-61, 278-80, 298-309.

[229] See H. Kelsen, 1967, 1996.

[230] *HC*: 151.

[231] Cf. P. Franco, 1990: 188-9.

Secondly, the distinction between natural authority and civil authority that was famously made by Hobbes, in principle, applies to Oakeshott's political philosophy as well. In Hobbes's case, indeed, "civil" is distinguished from "natural" in the sense that it is an artifact; so civil association is not a mere natural gregariousness (such as the family) and civil authority is arising out of an agreement of wills, not from natural authority (such as that of the father in the family).[232] By contrast, neither *societas* nor *universitas* implies a sense of "natural association". But here, the point is that since civil authority must be self-authenticating, the social bonds such as the natural authority exerted through the family are insulated from the foundations of civil authority by Oakeshott's Hobbesian legalism.[233]

And finally, *respublica* must not be alleged to have authority on account of being identified with fixed general principles of any sort:[234] whether it is a Baconian "common good", a Rousseauian "general will", or an Austinian access to "scientific information" about the tendencies of human actions to promote the general happiness.[235] Nor is there any place in civil association for the Weberian charismatic authority of a leader[236] or for a "higher law" than authority presumed in what Oakeshott calls the "neo-Platonic view of matter".[237] If there exists a "higher law" upon which the authority of *respublica* is conditional, it must itself be approved to enjoy authority. However, Oakeshott argues, no genuine rationality or wisdom will do that.[238]

We may thus reach the point that for Oakeshott the authority of *respublica* cannot be identified with anything other than that which is inherent in the legal system of *respublica*, that is, "the *jus* of *lex*".[239] As a result of this, the attribution of authority to *respublica*, Oakeshott writes, is nothing but:

> the acknowledgement of *respublica* as a system of moral (not instrumental) rules, specifying its own jurisdiction, and recognised solely as rules; that is, as conditions to be subscribed to in conduct and binding to con-

[232] Hobbes, 1946: 130, 153. Cf. *RP*: 247-8.

[233] See C. Covell, 1986: 123.

[234] For the following examples, see *HC*: 152-3.

[235] J. Austin, 1954: Lecture III; quoted in *HC*: 153.

[236] See M. Weber, 1973: 102-21.

[237] Cf. *OH*: 155-6, where Oakeshott deals with the same matter by picking up Samuel Rutherford, Montesquieu and the early exponents of the *Rechtstaat* as his targets.

[238] *HC*: 153.

[239] *OH*: 140; cf. 157-9.

sideration independently of their origin or likely or actual outcome in use and of approval of what they prescribe. *This authority cannot be acquired in a once-and-for-all endowment but only in the continuous acknowledgement of cives* [emphasis mine] . . . In short the only understanding of *respublica* capable of evoking the acceptance of all *cives* without exception, and thus eligible to be recognised as the terms of civil association, is *respublica* understood in respect of its authority.[240]

It is undeniable that the counterpart of civil authority is civil obligation. As such to recognise the rules of *respublica* as authoritative is to recognise them as obligatory. For this reason, civil obligation is not civil obedience, because it is related to the authority of *lex*, not to its efficiency; it is thus no more than a mistake to identify civil obligation with "a habit of obedience", as Austin called it.[241] In a like manner, having an obligation cannot be confused with fearing a penalty, because civil obligation bears no relation to the power of the rulers.[242] And finally, the so-called "*grounds* of political obligation"[243] do not lie in the theory of the general will, of the common good, of justice, or of consent. Regarding the consent theory, Oakeshott argues thus:

> In a transaction aimed at an imaged and wished-for satisfaction [a person] may make a promise and thus put himself within the jurisdiction and under the authority of the rule that promises should be honoured. But although he does this in a chosen transaction and as a chosen means for achieving a chosen purpose, and although he can fulfil his obligation only in a chosen action which subscribes to its conditions, he does not choose the terms of the obligation; he merely employs them as a device for achieving his purpose.[244]

It is true that by claiming this what Oakeshott is ostensibly rejecting is more of Lockean contractarian theory than a Hobbesian one. For, to settle the terms of obligation in law so that, once in the state, a citizen uses the rules to achieve his purpose is precisely what Hobbes insists the state is for. Again, although for Hobbes the authority of commonwealth first has to be established by contract, i.e. *theoretically* civil association has to begin somewhere with the initial construction through all men's wills of sovereign authority, he also believed that there must be a continuous acknowledgement of authority — it is not an once-and-for-all endowment. It follows that

[240] *HC*: 153-4.

[241] See J. Austin, 1954: Lecture VI, 198-205.

[242] This is a distinction that has been made by H. L. A. Hart (see esp. 1994: 6, 20-5).

[243] See D. D. Raphael, 1990: chap. 7.

[244] *HC*: 156.

Oakeshott may diverge from Hobbes in respect of the emergence of *civitas* — where Hobbes related the emergence of civil authority to human nature (the state of nature), Oakeshott takes its emergence to be an historic achievement in development, namely, the rule of law, which is so self-contained that it needs no further theoretical reasons to establish itself — but in general, Oakeshott's understanding of civil authority and obligation in *HC* is simply clarifying not rejecting the Hobbesian position.

But still, there is another important aspect of Hobbes's thought that has been critically reformulated in Oakeshott's theory of civil association, namely, the problem of individuality.

According to Oakeshott, Hobbes's moral and political philosophy falls within the paradigm of the morality of individualism,[245] but it has its roots in the work of the late medieval nominalists maintaining that the nature of a thing is its individuality and that will is precedent to reason, rather than in the Cartesian doctrine of the primacy of human cognition. The difference between these two views of personality is that whereas the former stresses a "substantial element" in individuality, i.e. a man's willing to act; the latter emphasises a "rational element" in individuality, i.e. a man's innate ability to arrive at self-consciousness.[246] I have mentioned that Oakeshott seems to have considered the issue of individuality from two related perspectives: its formal conditions and its *practice* within a tradition. Now, it has become evident that the formal postulates of an agent who has a free will to make a response to a contingent situation that we examined earlier are related to the Hobbesian rather than the Cartesian point of view.

But, Oakeshott probably would not reject the suggestion that both Hobbesian and Cartesian individualisms, in one way or another, have inspired the development of liberalism,[247] and he surely appreciates Hobbes's gift of considering the formal conditions of human agency in terms of volition. But Oakeshott also complains of Hobbes's lack of consideration of the actual *practice* of civil association. In other words, no matter what contribution Hobbes might have made to liberal individualism, Oakeshott believes that it is the

---

[245] *RP*: 280-3, 295-8.

[246] See esp. *RP*: 280, n111.

[247] Whilst, as we have seen, Oakeshott links the liberal's notion of a perfect self with the Cartesian rational element in personality, one of his most famous comments on *Leviathan* is, of course, the view that "Hobbes, without being himself a liberal, had in him more of the philosophy of liberalism than most of his professed defenders" (*RP*: 283).

Hobbesian voluntarism, rather than the Cartesian "self-made man", which is amenable to the search for a genuine understanding of individuality. For the proposition that a man has a freedom *to act* does not necessarily conflict with the importance of a moral *practice*, a world of moral ideas, or a civil discourse in providing actual information for his actions, but it is an importance which is neglected not rejected by the system of *Leviathan*. To fill in this lacuna in Hobbes's thought, Oakeshott therefore leaves the legalistic structure of *civitas* for the problem of the political postulated in the civil condition, by returning to the Aristotelian traditionalist individualism that he has established in *RP*.

IV.5.4. Civil Association (II): The Political

If authority and obligation are concerned with *the* law, the political, Oakeshott says, is concerned with the desirability of *this* law or *that* law.[248] This re-affirms that in *HC* Oakeshott does distinguish two considerations regarding civil prescriptions: the formal determination of the authority of *lex* and the actual decision of their worth and desirability.[249] Whilst the recognition of authority has to do with the appreciation of *lex* as a self-contained system of moral rules which leaves unasked the question of approval or disapproval, the political involves a procedure of criticising its specific rules. The latter engagement, Oakeshott believes, "will entail going over some of the ground already trodden, but from a different point of view".[250]

However, it should be noticed here that although in the civil condition politics is to be understood in terms of desirability, it may not alter the moral outlook of civil association; on the contrary it gives us an opportunity to separate it from other moral relationships. It is a unique characteristic inherent in the *practice* of civil association that "there are known procedures in which [an approval of a rule] may be undertaken and in which its fruits may be harvested in authoritative declarations"; whereas "the recognition of a moral virtue is itself the approval of the conditions it specifies for conduct; these conditions may be forgotten or neglected, but to dislodge them is nothing other than a withdrawal or qualification of this approval".[251]

---

[248] Cf. *HC*: 173.
[249] See esp. *HC*: 174, n1.
[250] *HC*: 159.
[251] *HC*: 160-2.

Amongst human relationships, it is only in the civil condition that authority and approval are distinguished.[252]

Keeping this in mind, we may now return to examine Oakeshott's understanding of politics. According to Oakeshott, the mode of politics that engages in civil association is "thinking and speaking in order to reach a conclusion which may then be transformed into a rule by an authoritative act".[253] This means that in civil association *respublica* is the formal condition that will restrict the political to *civil* desirability alone. And since the civil condition is not predicated on an attempt to promote any substantive wants, this political engagement is only a "circumstantial deliberation about *respublica* in terms of *bonum civile*".[254] In short, politics is concerned with the custody and maintenance of a system of moral rules where lies civil desirability.

This suggests that in considering the desirability of a civil rule — a rule which is always in use but whose substance changes over time — political deliberation concerned can never be a demonstrative or deductive one. On this, Oakeshott writes that:

> A civil prescription . . . cannot be shown to be desirable in virtue of satisfying a want or promoting a sought-after substantive outcome. But neither can its desirability be established by purporting to connect it inherently with a superior norm of unquestionable or acknowledged desirability, a moral rule, a prescriptive Law of Reason or of Nature, a principle of utility, a categorical imperative, or the like.[255]

---

[252] Cf. Oakeshott, "On Misunderstanding Human Conduct" (1976): 366. where the philosopher writes that the moral character of civil association differs from other moral considerations "in being subject to enactment, repeal and alteration in an authorised procedure, in that the conditions they prescribe are narrower, less demanding, and more precisely formulated, in there being an authoritative procedure for determining whether or not an agent in acting has adequately subscribed to these rules, and in there being known penalties attached to inadequate subscription and an apparatus of power to enforce them".

For Oakeshott, the distinction under consideration is crucial, because "an absolute coincidence between conduct believed to be morally wrong and conduct which is prohibited by law is not to be expected anywhere . . . To have achieved a distinction between crime and sin is one of the characteristics of modern European societies" (*MPME*: 16-7). We must distinguish the moral and the civil, otherwise we cannot explain why *mala prohibita* should be an authoritative prescription. This point, in general, is also what the legal positivist takes to attack the theory of natural law, though Oakeshott certainly cannot be understood as an exponent of legal positivism. Cf. for example, H. L. A. Hart, 1994: chaps. 8 & 9.

[253] *HC*: 165.

[254] *HC*: 173.

[255] *HC*: 174.

The terms of a practice of civility, then, are not conclusions inferred from . . . theorems about the so-called natural conditions of human life, from theorems about the dispositions of human character, from theorems about contingent human wants, purposes, and imagined satisfactions; nor are they inferences from the norms of a current morality or of a purported Rational, Natural, or so-called "critical morality", or from those of a pretended *summum bonum civile* or "ideal justice". And their desirability or worth cannot be argued in terms of their having been correctly inferred from or modelled upon any of these considerations.[256]

These two quoted passages mean that: On the one hand, theory and practice are two different forms of reasoning, not because those theorems or principles are theoretically impossible, but because in actuality the inference of this kind is impossible: for instance, no civil rule can be *deduced* from the Kantian categorical imperative. On the other hand, Oakeshott's philosophical scrutiny of the theorems such as the Law of Nature, the Kantian categorical imperative or a principle of utility shows them to be incomplete ways of understanding politics. For a *respublica* is a *practice* of civil intercourse in use; but, the abstract moral principles alone can never reach the point of "knowing how" to respond to contingent situations in favour of civil desirability. In political deliberation, Oakeshott concludes, "demonstrative conclusions are necessarily impossible; final solutions and alternative ideal systems of lex are persuasive subterfuges or corrupting delusions".[257]

In other words, the circumstantial understanding and diagnosis of situations cannot be indifferent to a *practice* of civil intercourse; a self-made individuality is not only impossible but lunatic; as a result, political engagement in the conditions of conduct specified in a *respublica* is "both an appeal to current achievements in civility and an exploration of the intimation of these achievements, and there is no mistake-proof manner of doing this".[258] What is confirmed by this statement is therefore Oakeshott's attempt to draw on what he takes to be an Aristotelian understanding of practical reasoning which relies on rhetorical persuasion in the making of prudential choices in contingent circumstances; that is, just as for Aristotle, one needs to have already acquired the consistent moral habits or virtues to establish character dispositions, and then *phronesis* (practical reasoning) in these situations now, enables you to make choices about means to an end. For Oakeshott, politics is the recognition of plausi-

---

[256] *HC*: 176.

[257] *HC*: 178.

[258] *HC*: 180.

ble statements about current circumstances in respect of civil laws through the pursuit of intimations of a tradition of civil language.

Thus, we may here reach the conclusion that Oakeshott's civil association is a more systematic restatement of conservatism in politics that he has declared in *RP* and elsewhere — more "systematic" because it is supplemented by something of an Aristotelian reading of *Leviathan*.

Indeed, throughout Oakeshott's works there are parallels with Aristotle's understanding of moral virtue and habitual *practices*, and with the notion of rhetorical persuasion rather than demonstration in individual political decision-making, but it seems to me that Oakeshott does not accept Aristotle's understanding of *phronesis* or prudence which, for Aristotle, is an intellectual not a moral virtue. And Aristotle does have a definition of man's nature and therefore a serious notion of the common good or *summum bonum* which both Hobbes and Oakeshott reject.

According to Oakeshott, the distinction between *societas* and *universitas* is significantly meaningful in a philosophical political discourse, because it appears to the philosopher that enterprise association is a less complete way of understanding human relationships that needs to be transcended. First of all, to conceive of human relationships as an enterprise will increase the power of the government to a degree where politics turns out to be a problem of leadership rather than an art of ruling. Again, like the notion of the mass, that of public interest is a "fiction" in the sense that it is specified, not by the actual interests of different individual agents, but by an imaginary collective character resulting from a false confidence in Universal Rationality.[259] As a result, it neglects the distinction between our substantive practical reasoning in terms of a tradition of behaviour and theoretical reasoning in terms of a system of theorems, and so it commits the error of *ignoratio elenchi*. In short, enterprise association is the strongest form of rationalism in politics that Oakeshott has been willing to attack since the appearance of *RP*.

In contrast to the usual comments on *HC* concerning the distinction between *societas* and *universitas*,[260] I believe that *theoretically* the real probing challenge that might be raised against Oakeshott's theory of civil association is that it somewhat presumes that there are never "categorically competing and incommensurable" traditions of civility in one historic culture. As a result, although Oakeshott has

---

[259] Cf. *RP*: 378-80.

[260] See, for example, D. D. Raphael, 1975: 450-4; H. Pitkin, 1976: 301-20; R. N. Berki, 1981: 570-85; J. Shklar, 1975: 1018.

never denied that there is proper practical reasoning to tell good values apart from bad ones within a certain political tradition, and he has attempted to trace the historic fortunes of the character of a modern European state in terms of *societas*, the civil association theory presented in the above discussion still cannot explain, for example, how civil war and its very different discourse ever occurs. In other words, in developing Hobbesian legalism, Oakeshott is simply leaving aside the problem of the *legitimacy* of authority without providing any alternative resolutions for it. Hence, what Oakeshott's political philosophy falls short on is an account of the problem of "the possible break in a civil discourse".

IV.5.5. The Trimmer: Keeping the Ship on an Even Keel

The last essay of *HC*, "On the Character of a Modern European State", considers what has been thought and said about the character of a modern European state and about the office of its government in the last five centuries. With reference to *PFPS*, Oakeshott maintains that modern European reflection on this matter can be understood in terms of two categorically distinctive ideas, namely, *societas* and *universitas*.[261] The idea of *societas*, as Oakeshott understands it, is an identifiable association in which the tie that joins the agents is the loyalty to one another, i.e. observing the customs of 'legality'; a relationship understood in terms of *societas* is a formal moral relationship, and a state, a *civitas*.[262] Whereas the idea of *universitas* is a corporation aggregate recognised as persons in respect of some identified common purpose or acknowledged public interest; a relationship understood in terms of *universitas* is a substantive prudential relationship, and the state which corresponds to this is an enterprise association.[263]

What is central to understanding the distinction is the "unresolved tension" between these two categorically opposite modes of human association, namely, "*a societas cum universitate*".[264] That is, as noted earlier, Oakeshott's ultimate purpose in the third essay of *HC* is to provide some historic references on the modes of civil association and enterprise association, so as to reach the verdict that "the modern European political consciousness is a polarised consciousness, that *these* are its poles and that all the other tensions (such as

[261] *HC*: 199.
[262] See *HC*: 201-3, 313-5.
[263] See *HC*: 203-6, 315-7.
[264] *HC*: 200-1.

those indicated in the words 'right' or 'left' or in the alignments of political parties) are insignificant compared to this".[265] As a result, Oakeshott uses most of his space in the essay considering the historic fortunes of *societas*[266] and *universitas*,[267] and he does this by beginning with an enquiry into their intimations in the late medieval period.[268] It is well known that through this examination, in which almost every important modern political thinker is more or less discussed or criticised, Oakeshott made his notable contribution to the contemporary study of past political theory and thought. Here, however, I intend only to point out three crucial observations: First of all, the intellectual origins of *societas* and *universitas* that Oakeshott traces in *HC* correspond to those of the politics of scepticism and the politics of faith that he has earlier established. Unlike in *PFPS*, however, Oakeshott here believes that he is writing a history about the matter concerned.[269]

It is not for me to judge whether Oakeshott's analysis of the character of a modern European state is historical enough in the sense of having given us a unity of ideas as comprehensive and detailed as he expected from historiography. For one reason, nevertheless, I believe that what he has provided cannot be genuinely historical as a distinctive mode of understanding. That is, it still leaves us with the impression that this history is in the service of the theory of civil association. In other words, it seems to me that Oakeshott's intention in writing a history of the character of a modern European state is to substantiate the ideal identities — civil association and enterprise association — in a way which meets his philosophical concern. As a result, what Oakeshott actually provides us with in the third essay of *HC* is still a quasi-philosophical past, in the sense that the communication between ethics and history function only in the mind of the philosopher.

Secondly, what is the role of liberalism in this philosophical-historic approach to modern political thought? At first sight, it seems true that by enterprise association Oakeshott is referring to socialism (among other things) rather than to liberalism, and he is, of course, an advocate of the value of the individual. Yet, Oakeshott sees himself ultimately as a philosopher, *a victim of thought*, who dis-

[265] *HC*: 320.
[266] See *HC*: 231-63.
[267] See *HC*: 263-313.
[268] See *HC*: 206-31.
[269] See esp. *HC*: 199, 323-6.

likes understanding politics in terms of any "isms". This is, I believe, the main reason why in *HC* Oakeshott is intent to "dissolve" all important "isms" of political thought in order to make room for his own terminology. In the course of this dissolution, Oakeshott retains the features of conservatism in politics in his establishment of civil association, although without mentioning the term "conservatism". In unveiling the historic fortunes of civil association he speaks of liberalism, saying:

> Liberalism was concerned [with] the menace of "sovereign" authority and with constitutional devices to reduce it. If it had any theoretical understanding of a state it was that of an association in terms of assured "natural rights" recognised as civil conditions to be subscribed to in conduct, and the menace was identified as the propensity of rules to inhibit the enjoyments of these rights by the exercise of lordship. But these "natural rights" came to include the enjoyment of certain substantive conditions of things capable of being assured only in the exercise of lordship (e.g. employment, medical attention, education) and consequently what was menacing became, not a lordly managerial government, but a government which failed in its lordly office of assuring subjects the enjoyment of these conditions or one which imposed other similar but depreciated conditions, like religious uniformity. Locke showed his imperfect grasp of civil association when he attributed to the Executive (and not to the Judicial authority), "the power which should see to the execution of the laws" (*Second Treatise*, sec. 144). [270]

Consequently, it is re-affirmed that for Oakeshott liberalism stands obliquely in between the extremes of *societas* and *universitas*. Referring to *PFPS*, liberal ethics engages in an ambiguous task of "imposing the idiom of faith upon the sceptical understanding of government". And since insofar as it is self-defeating, there is little it may contribute to the civil condition that is really of interest to Oakeshott.

To sum up this crucial interpretative issue running throughout this chapter, then, my conclusion is this: It is not convincing to follow writers like P. Franco[271] in interpreting Oakeshott as a liberal because liberalism *to Oakeshott* is more a form of rationalist politics than anything else, and because rationalist politics in terms of abstractness, perfectionism and universalism is the Enlightenment ethical position that Oakeshott tries hard to transcend. In a word, to understand Oakeshott as a liberal is to diminish the significance of his character as a substantial critic of the Enlightenment.

---

[270] *HC*: 245, n2.

[271] P. Franco, 1990a, 1990b. See also J. Gray, 1989: 199-217, 1993: 40-7; W. J. Coats, Jr., 1985: 773-87; D. Thomas, 1977: 454; N. O'Sullivan, 1993: 106; D. Manning, 1997.

Moreover, although Oakeshott's conservatism in politics and his theory of civil association are inclined to the paradigm of Will and Artifice, I have shown that Oakeshott does not accept the assumptions of egalitarian individualism, moral individualism, or radical individualism that characterise liberalism as we usually know it. By contrast, that which underlies Oakeshott's political philosophy is what I have chosen to call traditionalist individualism based on an Aristotelian refinement of Hobbesian voluntarism. In this matter, Oakeshott's critique of the notion of "self-made man" is significantly reminiscent of MacIntyre's "emotivist self"[272] or Sandel's "unencumbered self"[273] or Taylor's "disengaged subject";[274] and so he would never agree with Rawls's original position.[275] In short, the point here as elsewhere in Oakeshott's thought is not whether he is "a lover of liberty",[276] but whether his love of freedom has the same quality as the liberal's.

At this point, nevertheless, it may be argued that although in the recent "debate of human agency", it is precisely the thought of Hegel and Aristotle that rejuvenates the philosophical background of communitarianism,[277] Oakeshott is particularly dissimilar to these critics of Enlightenment liberalism in rejecting teleology of any sort. In this respect, then, Franco seems right in observing that compared to communitarians "Oakeshott's idea of civil association as a non-instrumental, non-purposive *practice* certainly has more in common with the procedural or juridical ideals of deontological liberals".[278] Besides, as we see it today, the communitarians like Taylor (and Sandel, perhaps), in the course of providing a more complete understanding of the self in relation to a theory of the good, have shown an endeavor to remedy the practical malaise of liberalism rather than to get rid of liberal values in one go.[279]

---

[272] See A. MacIntyre, 1985.

[273] See M. Sandel, 1982.

[274] See C. Taylor, 1989.

[275] See J. Rawls, 1971. For Oakeshott's brief comment on Rawlsian justice, see *OH*: 156, n13; cf. *HC*: 153, n1.

[276] M. Cranston, 1967: 82. Cf. N. O'Sullivan, 1993: 101.

[277] See, for example, D. Bell, 1996: 14; S. Avineri and A. de-Shalit, 1996: 1-2; S. Mulhall and A. Swift, 1997: xvii.

[278] P. Franco, 1990b: 427; see also 1990a: 230-6; 1990b: 428-31.

[279] Among the well-known communitarians, Taylor and Walzer seem to be most keen on the historic achievement of liberal values, but I have shown elsewhere that Walzer is very sceptical about the normative character of political philosophy. By contrast, for Sandel and MacIntyre, as for Taylor, political

Be that as it may, I have set out to make a case that there are both meta-issues and advocatory-issues that Oakeshott takes to establish the ideal identification of civil association, and these two criteria are inseparable. Thus, even though Oakeshott's reconstruction of the rule of non-purposive law is comparable to deontological liberalism, his long-life critique of the philosophical commitment of liberalism has, in fact, brought about the effect of detaching liberal ethics from the theory of civil association.

More crucially, unlike Taylor, Oakeshott always keeps his critique of liberalism (and the Enlightenment) at a purely philosophical level, lacking an appeal to outer practical concerns.[280] That is, for fear of resulting in another Rationalist effect, Oakeshott does not think that it is the task of a philosopher to make right the theoretical foundations of liberalism as a "public philosophy",[281] so as to put it into action more successfully. Nor is it Oakeshott's implicit objective, as Franco somehow implies, to make a traditionalist defence of the historic establishment of liberal values.[282] For, it seems to me, to believe that the achievement of liberalism needs to be re-defended in a better way is, in fact, to impose on Oakeshott a practical anxiety that Franco

---

philosophy is understood as practice-oriented, yet, unlike Taylor, both of them are far less devoted to liberalism. For my purpose here, however, it is notable that some writers have tried to unveil the liberal outlook of Sandel. For Taylor's and Walzer's concerns with liberal institutions, see esp. C. Taylor, 1987, and M. Walzer, 1990; for a liberal interpretation of Sandel's republican thought, see B. Frohnen, 1998.

[280] On this topic, as T. Nardin puts it, Oakeshott is philosophically different from Taylor on two major accounts: First, Taylor shares the hermeneutic tradition of Heidegger and Gadamer with the view that "all knowledge must reflect the interests of the interpreter" and thus claims the impossibility of "value neutrality"; second, Taylor insists on "the inherently normative character of political science" (2001: 8, 127; cf. 108).

[281] The term "public philosophy" used here is borrowed from Sandel, meaning "political theory implicit in our practice" (1996: 4).

[282] Franco also calls attention to Oakeshott's critique of "abstract individualism" under the name of Rationalism, (and "materialism or economism" inherent in classical liberalism), but he contends that this critique "cannot be equated with a critique of liberalism simply" for two reasons: Because Oakeshott "attempts to rasp liberalism as a living, vernacular tradition" of political life, and because "there are so many themes (even in *RP*) which link (Oakeshott) directly to the liberal tradition" (1990b: 412). It is true, as indicated, that for Oakeshott the mistake of liberalism is more philosophical than political. However, Franco seems to neglect that in Oakeshott's mind socialism, for instances, is a living tradition of political life in the sense of being recognisable in the *history* of modern world, too. In other words, it is the *liberal*, the son of the Enlightenment, who is intent to regard the advocatory values of liberalism as context-independent, and therefore, criticised by Oakeshott.

takes from the present world. But this is *the very* world from which Oakeshott's philosophy has tried so hard to "escape". In sum, Franco's proposal to make Oakeshott into a liberal actually lies in an attempt to read Oakeshott's philosophical understanding of politics more *practically*;[283] the practical attempt as such is, of course, not undesirable, but it is definitely not the kind of interest that Oakeshott's philosophy purports to enjoy for its own sake.

It thus follows that Oakeshott's rejection of much of the essence of the term that "liberalism" generally connotes cannot be taken to infer Franco's point that he finds "the word 'liberalism' loaded down with meanings that do not convey" so that he substitutes the term civil association or *societas* for it, and for this reason his political philosophy is "a restatement of the formulation of liberalism". [284] For we have seen that *philosophically* civil association is a more sophisticated form of traditionalist politics, and that Oakeshott's *philosophical* ambition in establishing the mode of traditionalist politics or civil association is not only to prove that politics can be understood in a more coherent way which is categorically different from rationalist politics, but to protect the identification of the modern European political character and consciousness in terms of these two exclusive forms of politics. Now that liberalism is understood as that which has never reached the poles of *societas* and *universitas*, to identify the theory of civil association as liberal would dismiss the "unresolved tension", namely, "*a societas cum universitate*" that Oakeshott has consistently maintained.

Thirdly, although Oakeshott retains the observation in *HC* that the predicament of contemporary politics is that on "the path marked *universitas: dominium* has been, in recent times, the more crowded with travellers",[285] for whatever reasons, he does not here intend to reach a "working compromise"[286] between the two opposed modes of human relationship in *HC*.[287]

---

[283] P. Franco concludes his book by saying that "to begin to work out what [Oakeshott's] political philosophy means for political life as we know it is the next step in understanding and (more importantly) amplifying Oakeshott's thought" (1990a: 236). By way of contrast, this book has largely followed T. Nardin in arguing that "Oakeshott's most significant contributions as a thinker are philosophical, not practical", and that "Oakeshott is best read as a theorist of knowledge, not a moralist (much less an ideologue), and as a philosopher of human experience generally, not only of politics" (2001: 230).

[284] P. Franco, 1990a: 159, 1990b: 411; cf. 1990a: 8, 11.

[285] *HC*: 321.

[286] B. Parekh, 1987: 360.

[287] See *HC*: 320-6.

Given that it is a quasi-philosophical past that actually underlies "On the Character of a Modern European State", I think it may not be inappropriate to conclude this chapter by adding a few remarks about the philosophical integration of the two analogies — *societas* and *universitas* or *scepticism* and *faith* — that Oakeshott previously achieved in *PFPS*. In that work, philosophy had gone further than in *HC* to synthesise these extremes in order to arrive at a more complete diagnosis of the predicament of our time.

We have seen from *PFPS* (and *HC*) that in historic terms the politics of faith and the politics of scepticism, (or *universitas* and *societas*) can be understood as the conditions of our moral and political activity. In the conclusion of *PFPS*, nevertheless, Oakeshott goes on to say that, taking these into account, the politics of scepticism still appears to be a more coherent understanding of politics and appropriate to our own situation. This is because our moral and political activity, like any other human action, is such a complex affair that we cannot escape from it by imposing "simplicity" upon our politics. Hence, if we search for the concrete character of a complex manner of politics, the politics of faith cannot be considered as suitable because thinkers like Bacon and Marx have only offered to our political thinking a simple-minded project of politics. The politics of scepticism is, by contrast, far more complex.

According to Oakeshott, although the sceptical style of politics is itself an extreme, "its extremity is not to impose a single pattern of activity upon a community, and consequently it enjoys (as we have seen) a characteristic forbearance of its own which can be seen to intimate a wider doctrine of moderation".[288] Inspired by Halifax's *The Character of a Trimmer*, Oakeshott believes the principle of the mean in action is a "trimmer" who "disposes his weight so as to keep the ship upon an even keel".[289] This is, indeed, a saying reminiscent of his famous metaphor of politics in "Political Education". And consequently, in a time when the politics of faith is in the absolute ascendancy, Oakeshott concludes his exploration by imposing three tasks upon the trimmer:

> It is, first, to restore the understanding of the complexity of modern politics. In the present circumstances this is, perhaps, his most difficult task: the ascendancy of faith has obscured, indeed almost obliterated, this understanding by imposing upon our politics a counterfeit simplicity. Secondly, his task is to renew the validity of political scepticism so that this pole of our politics can once more exert its pull. Thirdly, in his partic-

[288] *PFPS*: 123.
[289] *PFPS*: 123.

ipation in politics, he must dispose his weight against the prevailing current — not in order to make it flow to the opposite extreme, but to recall
our political activity to that middle region of movement in which it is
sensitive to the pull of both its poles and immobilises itself at neither of
its extremes.[290]

Here, with the third task of the trimmer, Oakeshott seems to have
given us a certain "direction" to escape from the melancholy of
Rationalism. But clearly, this direction is not a philosophical determination of what a good life is; instead, it only serves as a starting-point of one's "pursuit of the intimations" of a political tradition.
And whereof the practical man begins to work out the meanings of
tradition, thereof the philosopher "must be silent", to borrow from
Wittgenstein's famous phrase.[291]

---

[290] *PFPS*: 128.
[291] Wittgenstein, 1981: 189.

Chapter V

An Idealistic Defence of History

V.1. Introduction: Beyond Positivism and Historicism

The main purpose of this chapter is to approach Oakeshott's idealistic defence of history[1] in terms of certain philosophical problems. First, I shall be concerned with the epistemological problem of historical knowledge by exploring Oakeshott's resolution to the "temporal dilemma in history" and the "epistemic tension in history". Secondly, I am looking to examine Oakeshott's statements on the "autonomy of history" so as to reject the Enlightenment scientism in general and to preserve our ability to converse historically in particular. That is, in the course of this study I am adopting Oakeshott's position in order to transcend the historiographical position of the Enlightenment by separating the historical from the naturalised conception of History on which the notion of scientific history is based.

Oakeshott, we may observe, has provided a trilogy on historiography, the components of which are his chapter on "Historical Experience" in *Experience and Its Modes* (1933; hereafter *EM*), "The Activity of Being an Historian" (1958) in *Rationalism in Politics* (1962; hereafter *RP*) and "Three Essays on History" in *On History and Other Essays* (1982; hereafter *OH*). In these texts, history is invariably taken to be "a form of experience", "a manner of thinking", "a universe of discourse", or "a mode of understanding": in historiography, Oakeshott claims one is always concerned "with history as an

---

[1] For the idealistic grounds of Oakeshott's historiography, see esp. D. Boucher, 1984.

enquiry and with the character of an historical enquiry".[2] Hence, for Oakeshott, history is never simply the Past in itself.[3] And for convenience, I am here following the structure of *EM* to proceed with this study.

That history plays a central role in Oakeshott's political theory is granted by many interpreters;[4] and Oakeshott's historiography has indeed been highly appraised by writers like Collingwood,[5] W. H. Greenleaf,[6] W. Dray,[7] A. Sullivan,[8] and J. L. Auspitz,[9] for instance. However, compared to his politics, Oakeshott's philosophy of history cannot be said to have been much discussed, at least to the extent of that which matches his contribution to the field.[10] My ambition in this chapter is thereby to fill this lacuna in Oakeshott studies by placing his historical thought into the context of his own ideas as a whole, and into the context of contemporary historiographical debate. On this account, in addition to repudiating the positivistic historiography, part of my task in this chapter is also to show Oakeshott's general reception of Bradleyan idealism and his specific reservations regarding the later Collingwoodian historicism.

In what follows, led by Oakeshott's viewpoint, I shall examine, first, history as a form of experience so as to resolve "the temporal dilemma in history" ([V.2.]), second, the logic of historical enquiry

---

[2]   *OH*: 2.

[3]   Being an idealist, Oakeshott's theory of history is certainly contrary to historical realism, and can therefore be regarded as a pioneering promoter of the so-called historical "constructionism" developed in the mid-1970s. Cf. Nardin, 2001: 146.

[4]   See, for example, K. Minogue, 1975b: 77-83; J. L. Auspitz, 1976: 261-94; T. W. Smith, 1996: 591-614.

[5]   See R.G. Collingwood, 1946: 158-9.

[6]   See W. H. Greenleaf, 1996: 29.

[7]   See W. Dray, 1968: 19.

[8]   See A. Sullivan, *The New Republic*: 42; quoted by T. W. Smith, 1996: 598.

[9]   J. L. Auspitz, 1993: 22.

[10]   The published books on Oakeshott's thought so far largely focus on his political philosophy, and although in these books a treatment of history is available, it is presented somewhat because history is one of the modes that is disclosed in *EM*. See W. H. Greenleaf, 1966: 24-9; P. Franco, 1990a: 31-43, 49-56; R. Grant, 1990: 99-105; S.A. Gerencser, 2000: 27-8. In his newly published book, however, T. Nardin writes at length to show how history may be the proper mode for understanding human action in Oakeshott's philosophy of human sciences (see esp. 2001: chaps. 3 and 4). In addition to these texts, the important essays *entirely* discussing Oakeshott's historical thought are: W. H. Walsh, 1968: 5-18; W. Dray, 1968: 19-42; P. King, 1983: 96-132; D. Boucher, 1984: 194-214.

so as to untangle "the epistemic tension in history" ([V.3.]), and third, the relation of history to philosophy and to science and practice so as to declare "the autonomy of history", and in the meanwhile to repudiate the Enlightenment project in greater detail and to show Oakeshott's non-historicist position ([V.4.] & [V.5.]). These topics are obviously interrelated, so a certain amount of repetition seems inevitable; yet this return to his central theory from different angles is perhaps the best way to grasp Oakeshott's insights into historiography as a coherent whole.

V.2. Mind, Time, and Historical Experience

We have seen that one of the most substantial aims of *EM* is to consider the characteristics of each of the main modes of understanding. Our purpose was to determine whether each of these different modes of understanding constitutes experience itself in its concrete totality, or whether each is an arrest in experience from a limited standpoint. Before we can discover whether history is one of the modes of understanding, we have noted that Oakeshott is obliged to establish history within the realm of experience, to establish it as a "form of experience" in the first place.

V.2.1. History as a Form of Experience

If history is established as a form of experience, related to the character of experience in general, then, as we have seen previously, it must be shown to be a world, a world of ideas; and it must be shown to recognise coherence as the sole criterion of achievement. These are the three basis characteristics of history as a form of experience. But each of these experiential characteristics of history has been eclipsed by the Rankian "incantation" that there is no distinction between history and the Past — *Wie es eigentlich gewesen*. Hence Oakeshott first draws our attention to some possible interpretations of this saying.

First of all, on the view that history constitutes a world, we must address those who deny this point and argue instead that history is a series of successive events. For example, before Oakeshott, Bosanquet characterised history as "a tissue of mere conjunctions", and "the doubtful story of successive events"; Schopenhauer similarly believed that history could only give us "a sample co-ordination of the facts" without "subordination or system".[11]

---

[11] *EM*: 89; see also P. Franco, 1990a: 33. It should be observed that Bosanquet is here referring to history as a human way of thinking (although for him it is doubtful) not to the Past itself and he is distinguishing history as the narrative of

According to this belief, then, the historian, it is said, is concerned "not with what is 'co-existent' with what belongs to a world, but with what is 'successive', with what belongs to a series".[12]

This contrasting view of history has taken a dominant form, and is still widely held to be a science of history, as is claimed by positivism. The positivists, as we have seen, regard our physical world as a mind-independent world, where our present knowing makes no difference to what was known in the Past. For them, Oakeshott points out that history is therefore deemed to be "an 'objective' world, a world of past events to be discovered, unearthed, recaptured; it consists of what actually happened, and that (at least) is independent of what we think; it is a world, not of ideas, but of events". And consequently, they believe that the business of the historian "is to recall, not to think; he is a receptive, not a constructive agent; he is a memory, not a mind".[13]

Finally, there is a naive empiricist theory of history in association with this belief which suggests that in the course of writing history the historian "begins with the collection of data", with the accumulation of "isolated facts", after which comes "the search for causes". This theory holds that "the data in history are fixed; they are given to be incorporated, not to be transformed".[14] In other words, the process in historical understanding, it is said, is to take a cluster of fixed facts in its successive sequence as what has really happened, not to fashion a coherent world of co-existent ideas.

For Oakeshott, these simplistic approaches to history cannot bear serious philosophical scrutiny; for it is evident that history as an

---

successive events from those events themselves; again, Schopenhauer's emphasis is on history as co-ordination, not of facts themselves. And, being idealists, they would deny that the Past World existed of itself there and then. Nevertheless, the reason for Oakeshott taking them as examples might be that they seemed to believe that the nature of historical narrative cannot free itself from the time series of succession; it must be arranged in a temporal succession; and this is the reason why our historical thinking must be doubtful and not possible. Both Bosanquet and Schopenhauer are pessimists concerning men's historical thinking. By contrast, what Oakeshott intends to prove in history is precisely the idea that our historical thinking is able to free itself from the time series of succession; it is always a world of co-existent ideas. And, I think to do this Oakeshott has to establish a theory of history, in that our "historical time" can be distinguished from the "time series" given in Nature.

[12] *EM*: 90.
[13] *EM*: 92.
[14] *EM*: 96.

enquiry is not the same thing as History as the Past.[15] History is by no means a mere time series, the course of events, the world of "what really happened" independent of us. Hence there are at least two points that can be made here.

In the first place, as far as the "boundary" is concerned, it should be observed that "history is concerned only with that which appears in or is constructed from a record of some kind".[16] This implies that our historical world — historical ideas or historical evidence — must be less than the Past as a whole. A simple illustration to demonstrate this point: Although millions of women really lived in the Past World, few of them now appear in our histories. Women, on the whole, have been "hidden from history",[17] yet existed and were participants in the Past World. This suggests that our historical world merely pertains to a world of recorded evidence that has survived and is attainable now: the Past as a whole is infinite and endless in the sense that it cannot be exhaustively incorporated into historical evidence. The whole Human Past, to use Rickert's term, is *unubersehbar* (without limit) in the sense that it is impossible even for past agents to observe it in *toto caelo*.[18] " 'Events' may have happened (if we choose this way of speaking) of which all record or suggestion has been lost, and these are certainly no part of the so-called 'historical series'".[19]

In the second place, more critically, it must be noted that in essence history does not consist in a bare, uncritical account of whatever has survived and been recorded. "The facts of history", says E. H. Carr, "cannot be purely objective, since they become facts of history only in virtue of the significance attached to them by the historian".[20] In other words, as G. R. Elton writes, it is plain that in history every piece of evidence needs to be criticised for the sake of "establishing its genuineness, and assessing its proper

---

[15] Among interpreters of Oakeshott's historiography, P. King has especially tried to pose an objection to Oakeshott's distinction between history and the Past (1983: 109-115), which, however, seems to me a misconception. In the course of the relevant examination below, I shall try to prove how important this distinction is, not only in Oakeshott's establishment of the *differentia* of history but also in his transcending the "temporal dilemma in history".

[16] *EM*: 90.

[17] Cf. K. Jenkins, 1991: 7.

[18] G. Oakes, 1986: xvii.

[19] *EM*: 90.

[20] E. H. Carr, 1961: 120.

significance."[21] Along the same lines, L. B. Namier depicts the function of the historian as being "akin to that of the painter and not of the photographic camera" as his task is to "discover and set forth, to single out and stress that which is of the nature of the thing, not to reproduce indiscriminately all that meets the eye".[22]

Likewise, for Oakeshott, although an event is recorded it does not mean that it is historical, because "the so-called 'authority', better called 'sources', of history are frequently not themselves the product of historical thought and require to be translated into the category of history before they are used".[23] That is, Oakeshott objects to the view that the "original authorities are the touch-stone of historical truth", a view which is so often associated with the notion of scientific history. The so-called authorities of a tradition, of a report, of a document can never speak for themselves; even those accounts of an eye-witness or of an expert make no direct sense to history if they are not first interpreted by him. And, if the task of the historian is merely to combine the testimonies of different authorities, the history he develops will be nothing more than what Collingwood once referred to as "scissors-and-paste history".[24]

It follows that the historian is necessarily critical with regard to his "authorities"; he is obliged to think, to judge, to analyse the world with which he is faced. "The historian", says Oakeshott, "is one who understands the events of the world before him as evidence for events that have already taken place".[25] Because criticism and understanding must involve the historian's own contributions, the historical world must consist of the historian's own judgement, not of the so-called "isolated facts" independent of him. Oakeshott remarks that:

> It is impossible to exclude criticism from history, and where there is criticism there is judgement. Before a "recorded" event becomes an "historical" event, a judgement must have been interposed. But judgement involves more than a series, it involves a world.[26]

Oakeshott thus goes on to articulate that "there are no historical facts about which mistake is impossible: where error is impossible, truth

---

[21]　G. R. Elton, 1969: 97.

[22]　L. B. Namier, 1952: 8.

[23]　*EM*: 90.

[24]　See R. G. Collingwood, 1946: part v, sec. iv.

[25]　*RP*: 168.

[26]　*EM*: 91.

is inconceivable".[27] By contrast, the so-called isolated facts, if they existed, would never be wrong in the sense that they are taken by the positivists to constitute "what really happened" in the Past.

In addition, as we shall see later, Oakeshott argues that there are several forms of the past according to the several forms of experience in the conversation of humankind. Without being thought by the historian, then, a simple event that has taken place can possibly be read as a scientific past idea or a practical past idea. Whatever those other forms of past might be for now, clearly there is nothing that the historian has to do with them. An historical fact is always what the historian understands it to be in terms of the category of history.

The empiricist, however, has assumed much more about the course of historical writing. The so-called data or facts, he says, are not merely fixed and isolated but are to be explained causally. It is assumed that the task of an historian is to discover the course of objective facts as what really happened, not to transform them into the historical world of ideas; the historian is supposed to incorporate the successive facts or data, not form a consistent historical world.

The relations of historical facts to one another is a specific issue that has to be discussed in more detail later. Instead of considering this here, we need only remember that for Oakeshott no knowledge begins with "mere unrelated particles of data, isolated facts". Because, as we have seen, this is one of his main idealistic beliefs: that the mind can entertain only that which has a meaning, that which belongs to a world of ideas, and the same requirement must hold for the data of the historian as well.[28]

Moreover, because an idea must be understood in terms of a world of ideas as a whole, any change that occurred in this world must involve the transformation of an entire world of ideas at the same time; in all human understanding, Oakeshott maintains, "each advance affects retrospectively the entire whole, and is the creation of a new world".[29] Within the realm of experience, the process of our historical understanding comes about not by adding newly discovered facts to those that have already been discovered, but by transforming the old ideas in terms of the new in order to make the whole world more coherent. Every new discovery in history is "not the discovery of a fresh detail, but of a new world":[30] it is judged by its place

---

[27] *EM*: 111-2.

[28] *EM*: 96-7.

[29] *EM*: 41.

[30] *EM*: 99.

in the world of ideas as a whole. Hence Oakeshott tells his reader that "the process in historical thinking is never a process of incorporation; it is always a process by which a given world of ideas is transformed into a world that is more of a world".[31] In short, what in the first place makes the data or facts historically significant is always "a homogeneous system of ideas or postulates, in terms of which (the historian) is conscious of whatever comes before him".[32]

Accordingly, we may now reach a brief conclusion that Oakeshott claims history as an enquiry and History as the Past are in different categories, and that there is no certain starting point in history, for it always begins with a homogeneous world of co-existent ideas and ends with more coherent conceptualisation of that world. Yet, I have indicated that the reason why the empiricist-positivistic theory of history tends to assume the correspondence between history and the Past has to do with a naturalised conception of History embodied in the Cartesian-Kantian tradition of philosophy: the notion of Absolute Time, the existence of History as the object of historical enquiry and so forth. To elaborate on the distinction between the world of historical ideas and History in itself and thus to remove the philosophical grounding of positivistic historiography, I shall now reflect upon the notion of "time", using it as my point of departure.

V.2.2. Absolute Time and Transcendental Time

It seems to be the positivists' common belief that we can only have one dimension of "time", i.e. the Time given in Nature, Natural Time or Absolute Time. According to their view, both history and the Past must share a "temporal rhythm given in nature".[33] As a result, it is affirmed that history as an enquiry and History as the Human Past are the same thing, that is, the time series of successiveness, the course of events.

By way of contrast, if my understanding of Oakeshott's general theory of experience is accurate, he seems to believe that "time" is a thing of our own creation, and that even Natural Time cannot be perceived without our transforming it. And with transformation, we are entering into another dimension of "time", which I shall call artificial time or transcendental time, in that we are always in the continuous present when we evoke the "past" and "change". There are in fact several ways of speaking of "past" and "change", which con-

---

[31]   *EM*: 99.

[32]   *EM*: 97.

[33]   R. Koselleck, 1985: 95.

form to the several modes of experience, and may be evoked in our reading of present. For example, the "time" understood in history, i.e. historical time, is "an historical awareness" of "time", of "past", and "change", in its own terms and for its own sake.[34] This historical time is not only different from that Time given in Nature, if there is any such Time, but also distinguishes itself from those pasts and changes understood in the modes of science, practice, and aesthetics. Let me make an effort to prove this point in a more complete sense:

Is Time necessarily successive? As a matter of fact, from a natural scientist's point of view, succession is no longer the only one "authentic" conception about Time that we have formed from Nature. For instance, in his *A Brief History of Time*, S. W. Hawking has called this traditional paradigm of Natural Time "Absolute Time" which in physics has now been revised by Einstein's paradigm of "Relative Time".[35]

Nevertheless, Oakeshott would probably not deny that we do have a great interest in the scientific measure of Time. For it should be remembered that he posits that science is "the pursuit of a homogeneous world of quantitative experience".[36] Thus, fixation on time's quantity, clearly, must reflect our propensity for measurement: "The eye of the scientific observer is a measure; scientific perception is itself measurement".[37] Oakeshott, however, would argue that even in the case of natural science we are always working in an abstract world; Nature can never exist of itself and independent of us. "Nature", Oakeshott claims, "is a timeless world; it neither changes nor evolves; it is static and self-contained and the conception of past and future are inapplicable to it".[38] In other words, it is the proposition of Oakeshottian idealistic philosophy that the world men inhabit is a thing of their own creation, that nothing is understandable merely because it is given.

This means that even though succession might be what we grasp about the changing world from the mode of science, this conception itself must enter into a world of ideas, represented by a system of postulates, before we are able to comprehend it. In the case of science, this comprehension must be in terms of the condition of quan-

---

[34]   *OH*: 7.
[35]   S. W. Hawking, 1988: chap. 2.
[36]   *EM*: 244.
[37]   *EM*: 186.
[38]   *EM*: 200.

tity. But science is only one of the possible ways in which we are able to speak about pasts and changes.

According to Oakeshott, our conceptions of the past and change always come into our minds "through" a certain system of postulates (of history, science, practice, aesthetics) and, therefore, they will have more than one manifestation. It should be realised that for Oakeshott any system of postulates is always in our mind in the present: experience is always present, "that world upon which I open my eyes is unmistakably present",[39] and we are always in a present world when we understand things. This implies that a world of ideas is not merely a present world of ideas but a present world of past or future ideas as well, in terms of certain modified conditions. Accordingly, as far as the relation among past, present, future is concerned, Oakeshott in *OH* says:

> Future, then, is an understanding of present in terms of a change it may be perceived to intimate.
>
> Past, then, is an understanding of present in terms of a change it may be perceived to record or to conserve.
>
> Both future and past, then, emerge only in reading of present; and a particular future or past is one eligible to be evoked from a particular present and is contingently related to the particular present from which it may be evoked.
>
> The relationship between present and past is a necessary relationship: present and past are here logical counterparts.[40]

It follows that, although we are always in a present world, understanding past and change in relation to it, whenever we are evoking a past or a future in the reading of it, the present will be transcended; it will be transformed into past, into future.[41] A "now", in this sense, is therefore merely our mental capacity to make time stand still for the moment so that we are capable of speaking about changes. In so far as our ideas of past, present, future are exclusively associated with the temporal axis of intention our conceptions of time are related to our practical concerns, aesthetic imagination, memory and, indeed, to historical thinking. Time can therefore no longer be referred to as "the temporal axis of succession", "temporal sequence", or "the course of Time". Accordingly, there are some general characteristics of this "transcendental time", by contrast with so-called Natural Time, that should be pointed out:

---

[39]   *OH*: 7.

[40]   *OH*: 8-9.

[41]   Cf. A. Heller, 1982: 37.

Co-existence. By means of our awareness of past and future, a "now" is, in fact, transcended; the temporal relations between a past and a present or between a future and a present are co-existent in our minds, rather than successive. Furthermore, in the process of human understanding, a "now" can never be a suspended now; rather, it is a flowing state; we are always in the flow of the present when we understand the world in which we live. With respect to the process of the historian's reading of evidence, this notion of a stream of present experience supports the theory that ideas of the past will be transformed into and comprehended as a homogenous world of co-existent ideas.

Repeatability. Let me here cite a simple example to show this difference between transcendental time and Natural Time: We have known that John Locke was born "sometime" in 1632; however, it may be contested that there are at least two sorts of meaning of "sometime" in this statement. On the one hand, as the calendar shows, it may be taken to mean that there was such a natural phenomenon as "sometime" in 1632, in that Time the fact that "Locke was born on earth" occurred and he existed on the earth objectively, and for a distinct period. On the other hand, it also may be taken to mean that there is such an artificial notion as "sometime"; and, with this notion of "sometime", the fact that "Locke was born on earth" will re-exist subjectively in our minds, once we know about and whenever we repeat this statement. Now, the Natural Time for me to read the statement that Locke "was" born "sometime" in 1632, for instance, "is" "sometime" in 1998. In short, Natural Time, as it is used, is passing by us once only and it is unrepeatable; on the other hand, the artificial time is always repeatable but only if there are minds to conjure it.

Contingency. Oakeshott claims that in history human actions are to be understood "in terms of contingent relations".[42] Here, in our temporal awareness, it is inferred that a particular future or past is one eligible to be evoked from a particular present and is contingently related to the particular present from which it may be evoked.

In summing up, history and the Past can never share temporal rhythm, for while the notion of succession which positivism has applied to history is the temporal character attributable to Natural Time, to the Past World, to "what really happened", in history, if we follow Oakeshott, all we can know is our pastness, that is, a past evoked in the reading of present in the historian's mind: history is always a present world of coexisting ideas. That is to say, history can

[42] Cf. *HC*: 105.

never be independent of the historian; what is independent of him, if anything, is the Past World, the Flux of Time, which is unattainable in itself.

V.2.3. *The Death of the Past and the Survival of Pasts*

Getting clear in our minds the two-dimensional nature of "time", artificial and natural, we may now go on to think about the real existence of the Past in itself. I have said in other places that "time" is in itself nothing, as we can only speak of "time" related to things in it. The Past in the sense of being "Time itself" is certainly nothing. Nevertheless, the Past, as it is commonly referred to, is actually taken to mean "what really happened in it". To ask about the real existence of it is therefore to ask: Is there such a world as "what really happened in the Past" which is independent of us and exists of itself as the authentic object of our current historical understanding?

According to the epistemology on which positivism is founded, i.e. a form of empiricism in historiography, it is presumed that there are two worlds of "history", as the unreflective usage of the word "history" suggests. One of these is the subjective world of the historian's interpretation, and the other is the objective world of "what really happened". The process of historical understanding is the process in which these two worlds come to match each other. Such a distinction, for Oakeshott, however, just like the distinction between subject and object, between the knowable and what is known, is unreal, arbitrary and absurd. Oakeshott contends that:

> An event independent of experience, "objective" in the sense of being untouched by thought or judgement, would be an unknowable; it would be neither fact nor true nor false, but a nonentity . . . The distinction between history as it happened (the course of events) and history as it is thought, the distinction between history itself and merely experienced history, must go; it is not merely false, it is meaningless. The historian's business is not to discover, to recapture, or even to interpret; it is to create and to construct.[43]

This, of course, does not mean that history and the Past are the same thing. But this does mean that in historical understanding we do not have two worlds, one being history, another being the Past; we only have one world, the world of co-existent ideas in our minds. History as an enquiry is different from the Past in itself not only because its character can never mirror that of the Past, but because the Past in itself is nothing, in that we can know nothing of it at all.

---

[43] *EM*: 93.

The Past–history distinction that we have drawn above, though, is not useless, since it enables us step by step to reflect on the character of history:

> The enterprise in reflection may be likened to ascending a tower liberally supplied with windows at every level. The world seen from the ground floor is the world with which all reflection begins. But as we climb, the scene changes: the ascent brings into view what was before invisible, and at each new level a new world appears . . . the philosophers being prepared to go on where the others are content to stop.[44]

Historians are usually content to present the Past *wie es eigentlich gewesen*, but that is where we should begin to reflect upon the nature of history from the outside, i.e. from a philosophical point of view. (I shall return to this crucial point shortly). Now, at the top of the tower, the Past being "a fixed and finished past, a past independent of present experience", for Oakeshott, "is a past divorced from evidence [for evidence is always in the present] and is consequently nothing and unknowable".[45] Oakeshott's idea is that:

> What is known in history is not "what was", "what really happened", of that we can know nothing; it is only and solely with "what the evidence obliges us to believe". "What really happened" (a fixed and finished course of events, immune from change) as the end in history must, if history is to be rescued from nonentity, be replaced by "what the evidence obliges us to believe".[46]

It follows that the "object" of historical study, if we choose this way of speaking, is not the unknowable Past as the course of events, but "a recorded past composed of *res gestae* recognised as survivals".[47] And those survivals from the Past as evidence which obliges us in the present to believe need not be particulars (e.g. buildings remaining as relics) but contemporary accounts of those particulars. For Oakeshott's idealism would lead him to accept that what really counts in history, (as in other ways of reading something past), is not a representation of events which really happened there and then, but a *specific way of understanding* what past agents who expressed their thoughts in the past time took events to mean. In short, for Oakeshott history is only concerned with records of *res gestae*, namely, "texts" (in its hermeneutic usage) which bear human thoughts rather than pure happenings in the Past; for this reason, as we shall see, it comes

---

[44] *RPML*: 146-7.

[45] *EM*: 107.

[46] *EM*: 107.

[47] *OH*: 30.

as no surprise that Oakeshott believes historical method involves a form of "narrative" rather than "causal explanation".

Also, it may be observed that the nothingness of the Past is a necessary conclusion that can be drawn from Oakeshott's idealistic views. Unlike the empiricist-positivistic dogma that there is a physical world independent of us, Oakeshott like many idealists, argues that any claims made to maintain the existence of an independent and unconditioned world outside of our thinking are meaningless. A subject and an object, it must be remembered, always "correspond to and define one another".[48] They are, it is suggested, both integral elements in experience. In history, as a result, the claim that the real existence of the Past as the authentic object of historical enquiry is not only a metaphysical contradiction in the sense that the Past can never exist at present without transformation, but it is also a philosophical absurdity in the sense that there is nothing independent of experience; we can know nothing of the Past as "what really happened" as long as history stays within the realm of experience. As Heidegger puts it:

> The past takes everything with it into nothing.

> The Past — experienced as authentic historicity — is anything but what is past [what really happened]. It is something to which I can return again and again [in the flowing present].[49]

In short, so far as the existence of History being the only legitimate object of historical enquiry is concerned, positivism is destined to break down. For, experience is always present, whereas "History" by definition, is "what really happened" which is, as we have seen, unknowable in the present.

From the death of the Past, however, does not follow the death of our pastness. For it has been shown that there are several forms of past or ways of comprehending *res gestae* corresponding to the several modes of experience that can be evoked in the reading of the present; the historical past belongs to one of these possibilities (although, as we shall see later, for Oakeshott, the historian may not be critically aware of the presentness of the dead past he evokes). Oakeshott remarks:

> The past, then, is a certain way of reading the present. But in addition to its being a reading of the world in which present events are understood as evidence for events that have already taken place, it is a reading which may denote a variety of attitudes towards these past events . . . the three

[48]   *OH*: 27.

[49]   M. Heidegger, 1992: 12E, 19E.

> most important attitudes available to us may be called the practical, the scientific and the contemplative. And, there is a manner of speaking about past events which is appropriate to each of these attitudes.[50]

> [T]he past in history is not only the only past, and a clear view of the character of the past in history involves the distinction of this past from that in other forms of experience.[51]

No matter what each of these forms of past is for now, it must be observed that none of these is entitled to claim itself as "the only genuine past". For the "real" Past has already died; and if we can only have "a past" (for Oakeshott, many people often believe that the practical past is the only one genuine past), then to look for another and different so-called historical past would be "a lost endeavour".[52]

Let me now try to sum up the position as it stands at the present stage of the argument. For Oakeshott, the historian never simply sets out to "build up in the present a world of ideas to correspond with a past and buried course of events";[53] the correspondence theory of history, positivistic historiography, must be put aside if history is to be a legitimate form of experience. There does not exist such an objective world independent of the world of historical ideas, for the present world and a past course of events are self-contradicted, and the identification of history with "what really happened in the Past" and the positivist's own dictum that "the real is observable" in the present is untenable. The "temporal dilemma in history" that has for a long time bothered philosophers can be solved only if history is seen not as a representation of the Past but as a reading of the present in terms of the characteristics identified to be historical. And, history so understood would therefore make itself a self-systematic world of ideas which is safe from being "sundered from present experience",[54] to use Oakeshott's own expression.

At this point, one may say that Oakeshott has shown his affinity with his idealistic forerunners, especially Bradley and Collingwood. For it is true that they too reject the criterion of history as consisting in "what really happened" in the Past. A detailed comparison between the three thinkers on historiography, however, is a topic that I shall return to in the following discussion. For now, I only intend to remark that Oakeshott does not think that the historian, in

---

[50] *RR*: 161-2.

[51] *EM*: 102.

[52] *OH*: 10.

[53] *EM*: 94-5.

[54] Cf. *EM*: 107.

order to be legitimate, has to abide by the epistemological conditions disclosed by the philosopher. To see the ways in which Oakeshott keeps the logic of writing a history separate from his own philosophising, (and thus to start to embark on his non-foundationalist defence of the autonomy of history) we must now look into those identifying marks with which history "has come to establish itself".[55] It is at this stage that Oakeshott's solution to "the epistemic tension in history" will be under consideration.

V.3. The Logic of History

In this section I intend to observe the conditions or characteristics that describe the mode of history. As indicated, being a modality of experience means that history is categorically different from philosophy as self-critical thought, i.e. thinking without modifications. That said, for Oakeshott, to think truly about the nature of history is one thing, but to write a history itself is quite another. The task of a philosophy of history is to reflect upon the logic of history from the outside rather than from the inside, i.e. from the philosopher's view rather than from the historian's view.[56] Here, as elsewhere in this study, it is in the interest of constructing such a philosophy that we are invited by Oakeshott to theorise the problem of "What is history?" in terms of the following three topics: the postulate of the past in history, the notions of historical fact, truth and change and the problem of historical explanation.

V.3.1. The Historical Past

According to Oakeshott, history must be concerned with the past: "the notion of the past [in history] cannot be dismissed without dismissing history itself";[57] the historian's "sustained and exclusive interest" lies in the past.[58] That is, to think of things in the form of past is "the most general of modal conditions of the present in histor-

---

[55]   *RP*: 153.

[56]   *EM*: 86-8. Thus, I do not think that Oakeshott's philosophy of history contains the foundationalist implication of "providing us, in a highly disguised fashion, with an historical methodology for the humanities and social sciences" (P. King, 1983: 119; cf. 122). An obvious point of view capable of rejecting King's comment is that Oakeshott clearly treats ethics, history and poetry as three distinctive modes of understanding.

[57]   *EM*: 146.

[58]   *RP*: 170.

ical understanding, and it is absolute".[59] Consequently, it is the past in history, i.e. the historical past, that we now have to consider in the first instance. Nonetheless, because the past in history is not the only past that may result from one's reading of the present in terms of change, in order to grasp its distinctiveness Oakeshott first draws some categorical distinctions between *this* past and the other forms of past. Oakeshott's three typical examples of such non-historical pasts are: the practical past, the scientific past and the aesthetic or contemplative past.

Among those non-historical pasts it is the practical past from which Oakeshott has tried most strenuously to distinguish the historical past.[60] For Oakeshott, since every form of past is to be distinguished in terms of the modal conditions of the present to which it is related, the practical past, in favour of the world of practice itself, thus consists in an attempt to evoke the past "in relation to ourselves and our own current activities".[61] That is to say, just as the world of our ordinary life is "a present of common discourse" in which we come to inhabit ourselves by learning how to recognise the quality of its contents to satisfy our purposes and wants, the practical past is modified by such a present as can be found, in general, to serve politics, morality, and religion. The practical past occurs, Oakeshott argues, whenever one employs the past to explain and justify one's present situation: a politician, for example, uses the past to support his political programme; a moralist imposes upon the past a moral structure, distinguishing virtue and vice, right and wrong in human behaviour and a priest applies the past — say, the story of the Gospels — to convince someone of his religious beliefs.[62]

As already noted, Oakeshott believes that our commonest attitude towards the world is in the idiom of practice, such that, while considering pastness as an issue, the practical past must be the most frequent one evoked in the present. But, this view is far different from the contention that the practical present is unconditional, emanci-

---

[59] *OH*: 27.

[60] A similar discussion on the unhistorical "practical past" can be found in H. Butterfield, *The Whig Interpretation of History* (1965), where he says that "the study of the past with one eye, so to speak, upon the present is the source of all sins and sophistries in history" (1965: 31). Also quoted by T. W. Smith, 1996: 604.

[61] *RP*: 162; see also *OH*: 14ff.

[62] The attempt to identify the historical past with the practical past, for example, has been formulated in Croce's well-known statement — "all history is contemporary history" — which is meant to maintain that "[h]istories stimulated and guided by no practical problems would be at best virtuosities or fairy-tales, not serious history" (D. Boucher, 1984: 206).

pated from modality, and thus that the practical past is the only possible form of past in which an independent historical past is not possible. Oakeshott's idea of modality in *EM* or his notion of traditions of activity in *RP* or his theorisation of human conduct in *HC* that we have previously disclosed, indeed, all have made this point, restated in *OH*, that "no object is unconditionally recognisable".[63] And thus, for him, the attempt to name the practical past (or any other past) as the only genuine past must be both fruitless and absurd.

We shall take the opportunity later to liken Oakeshott's notion of pasts to the Collingwoodian idea of the "living past" as an unconditional past. Instead of making this comparison now, however, we only need to note that, by contrast with the practical past, Oakeshott observes that the historical past, as it has emerged gradually, has recently begun to acquire a specific character in the work of those whom we are accustomed to recognise as historians,[64] and is taken by them as a past evoked "for its own sake"; for them it is a past that is totally indifferent to present concerns. That is to say, by separating the historical past from the practical past, Oakeshott is willing to single out that in *practice* historians have perceptibly learned how to "let their thinking be guided not by personal considerations, but by the needs of their subject-matter" having an autonomous character of its own.[65] And, according to Oakeshott, the characteristics of the historian's independent attitude towards the historical past, entirely different to the practical man's, are:

First, practical understanding may or may not be concerned with the past, while "whatever else historical understanding may be, it is certainly and exclusively concerned with past".[66] Second, in practical understanding, indicators are used to forecast the future, whose temporal pattern is "present–future"; whereas in history the present, as already indicated, is always seen as "a recorded past composed of *res gestae* recognised as survivals" that are to be understood historically, and thus its temporal pattern is "present–past".

For these reasons, Oakeshott believes, history, if it is to be self-satisfactory, cannot construct idioms simply by means of using practical language or statements such as: "You are looking very well: where did you go for your holiday?". "King John was a bad king";

[63] *OH*: 9.

[64] *RP*: 165-8.

[65] W. H. Walsh, 1968: 6-7.

[66] *OH*: 27.

"The Factory Acts of the early nineteenth century culminated in the Welfare State of the twentieth century"; and the like.[67] For this is to commit the error of *ignoratio elenchi*. On the contrary, as long as there is a distinctive voice as history in our conversation, there occurs an historically understood past "to be found nowhere but in a history book".[68] All this, of course, does not mean that the practical past is illegitimate; far from this, the practical past can never be considered as the enemy of mankind, it is merely the enemy of historians.[69]

I shall return to expand on Oakeshott's separation of the historical past from the practical past in connection with some criticisms later on. For the moment, the pursuit of the past for its own sake, one might argue, could possibly be found originally in the scientific past as well, if there is any such past. For the scientist's concern with the world, it will be remembered, appears not exactly in "himself and his current activity" but rather in the notion of "cause and effect". At first glance, it does seem a trustworthy statement that "the scientific attitude towards the world and the historical attitude towards the past, have emerged together, and with some interdependence, in modern Europe"; that "the specification of the activity of being a 'scientist' and the specification of the activity of being an 'historian' were both achieved in a progress of emancipation from the primordial and once almost exclusive practical attitude of mankind".[70]

However, Oakeshott rejects that there should be any categorical connection between science and history in terms of the concept of past. This is because Oakeshott argues, the scientist may be interested in the past but the historian, as said, is solely concerned with the past. Moreover, even if it is the case that the past is sought by the scientist, his categorical concern with "necessary and sufficient conditions" must lead him to take the past events to exemplify general laws.[71] Oakeshott realises that there is a strong tendency encouraged

---

[67]   *RP*: 163.

[68]   *OH*: 33.

[69]   It appears to me a terrible misconception when P. King argues that Oakeshott's case against practical or scientific past "is less an argument than a simple statement of distinctions (within the 'past') which, in a merely definitional manner, is intended to 'persuade' us of the sole legitimacy of the historical past" (1983: 123).

[70]   *RP*: 171.

[71]   Here is an example that Oakeshott cites from Valery: "all the revolutions of the nineteenth century had as their necessary and sufficient conditions the centralized constitutions of power, thanks to which . . . a minimum strength and duration of effort can deliver an entire nation at a single stroke to whoever undertakes the adventure" (*RP*: 163-4).

by positivism to promote the view that the historian should emulate the scientist in his research; his rejection of scientific history in terms of general laws, however, is a wider question that I shall come to terms with where appropriate. For now, it is only sufficient to remind the reader once more that, for Oakeshott, since history has already achieved a specific non-scientific character in interpreting the historical past for the interest of being an historian, it is thus folly to re-assimilate history into science, to return to *philosophisme*.

In other words, with regard to the *practice* of the historian for the last two centuries, now that the emergence of the historical past has been a de facto phenomenon, Oakeshott sees no point in re-dissolving this historical interest into the scientific one. Furthermore, so far as the notion of the past is concerned, "if we speak more strictly, there can in fact be no 'scientific' attitude towards the past, for the world as it appears in scientific theory is a timeless world, a world, not of actual events, but of hypothetical situations".[72]

The historical past also has nothing to do with the contemplative past, as represented in the work of the artist and the poet. The world of aesthetics, according to Oakeshott, is a world "composed, not of events recognised as signs or portents, but of causeless 'images' of delight which provoke neither approval nor disapproval, and to which the categories 'real' and 'fictitious' are alike inapplicable". For this very reason, the past evoked in such a world is nothing but "a storehouse of mere images".[73] The contemplative past, for example, occurs most often in so-called "historical novels". But, it is obvious that to write a history in terms of a world of historical ideas for its own sake is logically different from creating a novel in terms of a world of mere images, in which pastness is often ignored. Thus, in a strict sense, as Oakeshott later argues, "aesthetic understanding is never concerned with past".[74]

So far we have considered the historical past by showing what is *not* the case about it. To grasp the positive character of the past in history, however, we must now turn to the past for history, i.e. the past as the historian is accustomed to conceive it. According to Oakeshott, as already shown, the historian in writing a history has developed a specific interest in reading the present in terms of change for the sake of change itself, evoking the past *for* the sake of the past per se. "What the historian is interested in", Oakeshott says,

---

[72] *RP*: 164.

[73] *RP*: 158, 164.

[74] *OH*: 27.

"is a dead past; a past unlike the present"; the *differentia* of the historical past precisely consists in "its very disparity from what is contemporary".[75] In *RP*, Oakeshott writes:

> The "historian" adores the past; but the world today has perhaps less
> place for those who love the past than ever before ... For it wishes only to
> learn from the past and it constructs a "living past" which repeats with
> spurious authority the utterances put into its mouth. But to the "histo-
> rian" this is a piece of obscene necromancy: the past he adores is dead.
> The world has neither love nor respect for what is dead, wishing only to
> recall it for life again. It deals with the past as with a man, expecting it to
> talk sense and have something to say apposite to its plebeian "causes"
> and engagements. But for the "historian", for whom the past is dead and
> irreproachable, the past is feminine. He loves it as a mistress of whom he
> never tires and whom he never expects to talk sense.[76]

Here the Oakeshottian bid to segregate the historical past from the
practical past has been re-affirmed. But, from a philosophical point
of view, the historical past as the past pursued for its own sake must
be an "illusion", because the past *for* history as a dead past is nothing
but "what really happened" in the Past. However, it has already
been shown that we can only at every "now" evoke either pasts or
futures; "what really happened" in the Past is a nonentity, unknowable to us. The result of the historian's specific concern with the dis-
similarity between the present and the past, as a result, is a
self-contradiction and thus the view of the historical past cannot be
maintained unmodified.

This is to say that in Oakeshott's observation the modality of the
historical past that the historian has learned to present must contradict the character of history as a form of experience. That is, the historical past being a fixed and dead past for its own sake must
contradict the experiential character of history being present; "what
was" must be paradoxical to "what is"; "what really happened"
must be at odds with "what the evidence obliges us to believe". In
sum, "the pastness of the world of historical experience involves a
modification of its presentness, involves a modification of its character as experience".[77] This, I believe, is one of the most difficult parts
of Oakeshott's historiography to be understood and as such it is
deemed unacceptable by many scholars.[78] Here, in support of

---

[75] *EM*: 106.

[76] *RP*: 166; also quoted by K. Minogue, 1993: 48-9; T. W. Smith, 1996: 607.

[77] *EM*: 110-1.

[78] See, for example, R. G. Collingwood, 1946: 155-8; G. C. Field, 1938: 15-6;
      W. H. Walsh, 1967: 88-9; P. King, 1983: 124-5; and G. Himmelfarb, 1984: 494-505.

Oakeshott, I have to return to Oakeshott's theory of modality in order to make the point.

In my previous examination of Oakeshott's idea of philosophy in *EM*, I have argued that for Oakeshott the business of philosophy is to transcend the abstractness of the modes of experience by disclosing the "self-contradiction" inherent in each of them, that is, to show how a mode of experience, on the one hand, by virtue of its character as a world of ideas, can be seen by philosophy as a self-consistent world of ideas while on the other hand, by virtue of its modality, it falls short of philosophy itself. On this view, then, by disclosing the abstractness of history in terms of the historical past, Oakeshott's real purpose is to place history and philosophy into two different categories: history, since it cannot be claimed to be unmodified, cannot be taken as the criterion of experience, i.e. philosophy; philosophy, since it is self-critical thought, must attempt to transcend the modality of history.

Although philosophical thinking starts where the other modes of thoughts find themselves a platform to dwell on, or, to use a Platonic metaphor, a cave to dwell in, unlike Plato, for Oakeshott, the cave-dwellers, living happily as they are, do not require a philosophy to put them right.[79] On the contrary, because "nothing can be dismissed as mere error", and because it is both "the half-true in the error and the half-error in the truth" that constitute the *logic* of a mode of understanding, the self-contradiction of history should not be discarded as long as it remains self-consistent:

> History, since it is experience, implies an attempt to organise, to make and to maintain coherent the whole world of experience. But the *differentia* of history is that in it an attempt is made to organise the whole world of experience in the form of the past and of the past for its own sake. The historical past does not stand over against the present world of experience, as a separate tract of experience; on the contrary, it is a special organisation of that world, it is the organisation of the totality of experience *sub specie praeteritorum*. The historical past is always present; and yet historical experience is always in the form of the past. And this contradiction must remain unresolved so long as we remain in the world of historical ideas.[80]

If this is what Oakeshott really wants to maintain by modifying history, that history is a self-determined mode of experience distinctive from philosophy (and the other modes), to this end he has hitherto had little to do with historicism, claiming that all knowledge is

---

[79] See *HC*: 27-31.

[80] *EM*: 111.

historical. I shall return to these qualifications on Oakeshott's thought shortly.

Besides, it is equally important to note once again that the condition of the historical past as such would not require us to accept the correspondence theory of history. For, in contrast to Oakeshott's theory, positivistic historiography neglects the truth-part in history (the experiential character of history as present experience) and accepts the wrong-part in philosophy (the belief that the Past exists in itself), and it is thus an "incorrect philosophy of inadequate history" that should be transcended by a more coherent philosophical scheme. By neglecting the fact that history is a form of experience, that the historian's task is re-construction, what positivistic historiography offers us is pseudo-historical which is impossible to maintain without dissolving the logic of history at the same time. And furthermore, by accepting that the Past exists in itself, what it *often* persuades the historian to believe in, as it were, is not necessarily a dead past but a possibility of reproducing "a 'living past' which repeats with spurious authority the utterances put into its mouth". As we shall see, what Popper says about the practical past in terms of the notion of "selection" in history, it seems to me, is standard for many neo-positivists.

V.3.2. Fact, Truth and Change in History

For Oakeshott, as we have seen, history is an attempt to organise an entire world of co-existent ideas in the form of past, *sub specie praeteritorum*. History always exists as a single and coherent world of ideas resulting from the modality of historical past. To examine further the logic of history and thus to reject positivist historiography more completely, however, we must now consider how this absolute postulate of the past works in the other structural concepts that mark the process of historical understanding.

The two key issues here are historical change and historical explanation. In *EM*, before getting to these issues, however, Oakeshott dwells for a while on the relative problems of historical fact and historical truth which have already been largely answered by his establishing history as a form of experience. Following Oakeshott's argument structure, I shall address these problems by reference to the condition of the past from which they derive. Therefore, we may move on towards the issues of historical change and historical explanation.

It is observable that all we have said about the character of history being a form of experience, in fact, conforms perfectly to the general character of experience that we have examined. This is because, for Oakeshott, remember, a mode of understanding is not a part of experience but an arrest in experience as a whole, insofar as it can never abandon its essence of being experience. And consequently, in addition to fact (a world of ideas), truth and reality are the three concepts that Oakeshott employs to look into the general character of experience; it is now historical fact, historical truth and historical reality that he takes as necessary conditions to categorise historical experience.

In experience, fact, as indicated, is never isolated, atomic, fixed, finished and simply given; on the contrary, the meaning of a fact is always its place in the single world of ideas as a whole. Thus, historical fact, to put it another way, must be a conclusion, an inference and a judgement which belongs to and gains its meaning from the historical world of ideas, that is, numerous pieces of evidence bearing upon a past agent's intelligence that have so far been reconstructed in the historian's mind. Historical fact, as Oakeshott concludes, is nothing less than the world of historical ideas taken as a whole and seen to be coherent.

In like manner, Oakeshott continues, historical truth is also in harmony with the general feature of truth, i.e. the criterion of coherence within experience itself. The consequences of this are three: First, historical truth is a present truth as a past truth is a contradiction; second, it is never a matter of the correspondence of a present idea to a past event for there is no "external criterion" in experience, but it is only a matter of the coherence that a present idea enjoys being a member of the world of historical ideas; and third, it is impossible to establish this truth "piecemeal" (as Popper might have argued) as the task of the historian is to transform a given world of ideas into a more coherent world of ideas.[81] Historical truth, Oakeshott argues, does not lie in the question, "Does this set of past events hang together when taken in this way?" but rather in the question, "Does my whole world of experience gain or lose in coherence when I take these facts in this way?".[82] On this account "an anachronism is not a contradiction in a world of past events, it is a contradiction in a world of present world: it is something which comes to us as a fact, but which fails to establish its factual character on account of the

---

[81]   *EM*: 113.
[82]   *EM*: 114.

incoherence it introduces into our world of present [historical] experience".[83]

However, historical fact and historical truth must suffer the limitation of the historical past all the time. That is, they are necessarily present and they are simultaneously conceived of in the form of the past. Historical truth is not present truth about what happened in the past; but it is the entire world of experience seen as a single world of ideas *sub specie praeteritorum*. And thus, "it is the business of the historian to introduce into the world of experience whatever coherence this category of the past is capable of introducing".[84]

Having explored the idea of historical fact and truth in the form of the past, we may now address the notion of reality in history and the relative concept of historical change. It goes without saying that the criterion of reality (of self-completeness or individuality), as in the general character of experience, must be applied likewise to the world of history. Historical reality, Oakeshott thus argues, is composed of self-complete individuals which for the sake of convenience can be divided into events (the fall of the Bastille and the Reformation), things or institutions (the Roman Empire and Christianity) and persons. And, because history is a world of ideas, not the course of past events, the individual in history can only be "designed and not defined"; "history itself", says Oakeshott, "does not and cannot provide us with the historical individual, for wherever history exists it has been constructed upon a postulated conception of individuality".[85]

But, the question is: How then can we identify an event, an institution or a person in history? To answer this, Oakeshott first offers us his "principle of continuity and discontinuity" to replace "Time and Place". That is, an historical individual is not defined by the Time and Place that it occupied "there and then", but is instead characterised by its *relative* continuity and discontinuity, judged by the historian in a world of historical ideas. In the case of an institution like the Roman Empire, for example, it stands out from what is taken to be its environment because:

> it can show no change at all, no variation in shape, size or content, nor because the historian has chosen the line of last resistance and has restricted the name either to the thing as it first appeared before change had made its individuality ambiguous or to some core which he supposes to have remained untouched by outward circumstances, but

[83] *EM*: 114.

[84] *EM*: 118.

[85] *EM*: 120.

because its beginning is marked by an apparent break in the continuity of what went before, and because, having been established, it could maintain a continuous existence. Into this individuality, place enters very little; Rome itself is scarcely significant at all, now West, now East preserves the continuity. What establishes it for history is the fact that there appears some discontinuity at its beginning, and subsequently no absolute break in the Empire's existence, various as were the circumstances of its life. And when such a break is seen to occur, then and not till then, is the individuality shattered.[86]

Likewise, the principle of break–discontinuity–continuity–break applies to an historical event or an historical person, too. An historical event is not like what positivists believe it to be, a "mere point-instant"; but rather, it is something with meaning in change, whose ability to establish its individual significance consists in its discontinuity and whose ability to maintain itself consists in its continuity. Historical events (or facts) are never fixed and finished in character; their meanings are arbitrarily joined and separated from one another in different historical works — works in which their individuality is distinguished and judged by historians.

It follows that, since discontinuity and continuity both centre on the concept of change, every historical individual must be a "changing identity". In identifying an historical individual we are in actuality recognising its character of change in terms of what Oakeshott calls the principle of the "Identification of Indiscernibles". To quote Bradley: "what seems the same is so far the same, and cannot be made different by any diversity, and that so long as an ideal content is identical no change of content can destroy its unity". "It implies that the sameness can exist together with difference, or that what is the same is still the same, however much in other ways it differs".[87]

For Oakeshott, however, the task of an historian is not to examine this principle *itself*, but just to take it as an unchallenged presupposition about history. History, then, unlike philosophy, is a limited mode of human understanding. The world of history is the world of historical individuals governed by the ideas of change, of continuity and discontinuity and is pursued under the category of the past: Reality is present, and yet in history it must be past; the historical past is not a part of the real world but the whole of reality subsumed under the category of the past. And thus, to write a history is precisely to give a coherent account of the designed individuals in terms

---

[86]   *EM*: 121.

[87]   Bradley, *Logic*: 288, *Appearance and Reality*: 347; quoted in *EM*: 124.

of change. Keeping this meaning of history in mind, we now enter into Oakeshott's idea of historical explanation.

V.3.3. Historical Explanation

In the preceding discussions, we have been ceaselessly met by the problem of historical explanation. For, if experience is always a world of meanings, we then cannot disclose its character without using the notion of "explanation" as a means of understanding it. This implies that, besides being undertaken under the category of past, historical explanation also adheres to the general theory of understanding that Oakeshott has so far persistently maintained: in understanding, there is only one world, one reality, that is, a single unity of ideas as a whole; understanding starts with a unity of ideas and ends up with a more coherent unity of ideas; the given in understanding is a unity of individuals to be made more coherent.

Now that we have defined history in this way, as a world of historical individuals in terms of change, I would now like to define the Oakeshottian notion of historical explanation as *a complete narrative of the unity of historical individuals in terms of change.*

According to this view which Oakeshott himself calls "a complete account of change" or the "unity of history", the historian in explaining change in history "is like the novelist whose characters (for example) are presented in such detail and with such coherence that additional explanation of their actions is superfluous".[88] This analogy, of course, is not meant to equate histories with novels, since we have already distinguished the historical past from the contemplative past; rather, I think Oakeshott's point is that in history "scientific method" should be allotted no status. For this very reason, Oakeshott thus criticises "causal explanation" as incapable of giving us a coherent understanding of historical change.

In *EM*, the pro-scientific targets tackled by Oakeshott are the methods of general causes, economic determinism, great events, and Bury's conception of "contingency";[89] In *RP*, Oakeshott argues that historical narrative, as in the work of de Tocqueville and Maitland, for example, has already been shown "not as the necessary and inevitable consequence of preceding events (as in scientific explanation), but as an intelligible convergence of human choices and actions";[90] whilst in *OH* it is the Popperian-Hempelian covering

---

[88] *EM*: 141.

[89] See *EM*: 125-41.

[90] *RP*: 172.

law model that lies behind his reflections. For my purpose, I shall only develop Oakeshott's idea of the "unity of history" by focusing on the target of the covering law model alone. And, the issues I have to raise here are: first, the Popperian notion of selection in history; and second, the Oakeshottian historical particularity versus the Popperian-Hempelian scientific generalisation.

So far we have seen that history must be less than the Past as a whole, and that the historian has to criticise historical facts with regard to his authorities. In this respect, it does seem that in writing history "the historian is necessarily selective".[91] To say so, however, the implications of the notion "selection" need to be clarified.

In the first place, as already indicated, the concept in question has been used in the context of neo-positivism. Karl Popper, for example, argues that "the realm of facts is infinitely rich . . . [so] there must be selection"; "the facts at our disposal are often severely limited and cannot be repeated or implemented at our will" without choosing.[92] Again, it seems that the so-called bias of the historian in writing history is inescapable, if we pause to consider how many things, such as classes, ethnic groups, gender, and so on, have been omitted in our traditional texts.[93] Popper could be at this point insisting further that in writing history there should be "a preconceived selective point of view into one's history; that is, to write that history which interests us". "The historian", he continues, "need not worry about all those facts and aspects which have no bearing upon our point of view and which therefore do not interest us", but instead "all available evidence which has a bearing on our point of view should be considered carefully and objectively".[94]

Being a positivist, nevertheless, Popper's conceding the importance of selection in history is only in order to maintain that the subjectivity of the historian (and the particularity of historical events) will not affect the fact that the structure of historical study is in accordance with that of scientific explanation. On this view, Popper, of course, has no intention to agree with the idealist's view that selection must at the same time imply the function of transforming *res gestae* into historical ideas in the historian's mind. Instead, for Popper as for other pro-positivists, historical evidence consists in posi-

[91] E. H. Carr, 1961: 12.

[92] K. Popper, 1962: 270, 265.

[93] Indeed, a similar bias may also exist at the level of historiography itself. R. Young, for example, reminds us of the problem of Eurocentrism embodied in *the* history of Western historiography. See Young, 1990.

[94] K. Popper, 1957: 150.

tivist facts, and so in historical writing all the historian has to do is make a selection of facts or data and then explain them causally in terms of a certain standpoint (i.e. an empirically testable proposition or generalisation) being chosen.

Here, it is significant to note that what Popper means by "a pre-conceived selective point of view" is, in fact, an act of back-ward-looking at past things; it is a practical attitude which looks at past ideas with the purpose of justifying present beliefs, to see what has affected the present conditions of things, to learn lessons of polit-ical wisdom, and so on. Popper himself in his preface to *The Open Society and Its Enemies*, explicitly wrote that: "even where it looks back into the past, its problems are problems of our own time; and I have tried hard to state them as simply as I could, in the hope of clari-fying matters which concern us all".[95] Such a practical past, as we have seen, is indeed a necessary platform for mankind to dwell on, yet it is the foe of the historian. In Oakeshott's view, then, the Popperian notion of selection is certainly not a genuine historical atti-tude; history is always an attitude towards past ideas for its own sake.

Indeed, Oakeshott would not disagree that in writing history the historian has to select a subject, a theme and a period of time etc.; he, however, strongly rejects the positivist notion of data-collection in history. For, as we have seen, even though history is less than the entire Past, the surviving evidence that obliges the historian to believe is always a world of historical ideas as a whole. That is to say, according to Oakeshott's general theory of knowledge, an idea is always to be conceived in respect of a world of ideas; the particular is always quarantined by the whole; and "the process in historical thinking is never a process of incorporation; it is always a process by which a given world of ideas is transformed into a world that is more of a world". Thus, it is Oakeshott's view that everything in the world of historical ideas bears on every other thing — nothing in history can be irrelevant to understanding. To explain the notion of "unity of history" as such, Oakeshott has made two important statements in *EM* which I now quote at length:

> [N]othing in the world of history is negative or non-contributory. All relationship between historical events is positive . . . The belief that the Donation of Constantine recorded a genuine 'donation' was erroneous; the document was a forgery. But, for the historian, the belief is a positive fact, an event which makes a positive contribution to our knowledge of the Middle Ages, and not a mere mistake. A forgery is not, of course, the same thing to the historian as a genuine world, but it is no less and no

[95] K. Popper, 1962: vol. 1. vii.

more important. History is never a balance of debit and credit; it is a positive unity. In short, the unity of history implies a world of positive events in which such negative concepts as 'evil', 'immoral', 'unsuccessful', 'illogical', etc., have, as such, no place at all. Historical explanation, consequently, involves neither condemnation nor excuse.

Secondly, it is implied in this principle that in the course of events for history "everything goes by degree and nothing by leaps" . . . It is a presupposition of history that every event is related and that every change is but a moment in a world which contains no absolute *hiatus*. And the only explanation of change relevant or possible in history is simply a complete account of change. History accounts *for* change by means of a full account *of* change. The relation *between* events is always other events, and it is established in history by a full relation of the events. The conception of cause is thus replaced by the exhibition of a world of events intrinsically related to one another in which no *lacuna* is tolerated. To see all the degrees of change is to be in possession of a world of facts which calls for no further explanation. History, then, neither leaves change unexplained, nor attempts to explain it by an appeal to some external reason or universal cause [or general laws]: it is the *narration* [emphasis mine] of a course of events which, in so far as it is without serious interruption, explains itself. In history, "pour savoir les choses, il faut savoir le detail". And the method of the historian is never to explain by means of generalisation but always by means of greater and more complete detail.[96]

To this view, a view with which Collingwood seems to have agreed, in general, by saying that "no fact is turned away from the historian's door",[97] W. H. Greenleaf contributes the following:

This means that, in the history of political ideas, for instance, it is inappropriate to start out with modern criteria of relevance and significance in mind and to turn away from consideration of books and conceptions that seem to us unimportant or erroneous. There is "no place for mere error or mistake", for the use of such categories assumes an extra-historical criterion in terms of which things could have been otherwise than they were. In history we have to attribute rationality to what now seems absurd, false or illogical; in the appropriate context we have to accept it as historically positive fact that the basis or appeal of which has to be understood on its own terms.[98]

In other words, for Oakeshott, "it is impossible to 'fix' a text before we begin to interpret it. To 'fix' a text involves an interpretation; the text is the interpretation and the interpretation is the text".[99] This, together with the point that every new discovery in history is "not

[96]   *EM*: 142-3.

[97]   Quoted by W. H. Greenleaf, 1966: 28.

[98]   *Ibid.*: 27.

[99]   *EM*: 113.

the discovery of a fresh detail but of a new world", indicates that Oakeshott's conception is not strange to contemporary hermeneutics. T. Kuhn, in his *The Essential Tension*, for example, has made a similar remark:

> When reading the works of an important thinker, look first for the apparent absurdities in the text and ask yourself how a sensible person could have written them. When you find an answer . . . when these passages make sense, then you may find that more central passages, ones you previously thought you understood, have changed their meaning.[100]

As a result, it may be confirmed here that Oakeshott's conception of historical explanation is certainly much closer to a theory of "historical narrative" than to a theory of "causal explanation".

To sum up, for Oakeshott, the general character of historical explanation is in accordance with that of understanding that we have unveiled so far; the criterion of historical truth, as of other modes of experience, is coherence rather than correspondence. That which categorically distinguishes the logic of history only lies in the fact that there is "a structural presupposition (assumed and left uncriticised in history, [namely, the historical past]) which enables the historian to build a specific and homogeneous world of ideas. In history there is the attempt to explain the historical past by means of the historical past and for the sake of the historical past".[101] Thus, like fact, truth and change in history, historical explanation must be arrested at the standpoint of the past as well, together they turn aside from the main current of experience in order to construct and explore a restricted world of ideas called history. And consequently, it may be inferred that Oakeshott does share certain affinities with post-modern views of "conventional history": both are anti-Whiggish, anti-historical-objectivism, and based on a continental hermeneutic rather than a quest for positivist facts in their theory of historical understanding.[102]

Having introduced the Oakeshottian "unity of history", let us now turn to consider how this view is different from the Popper-Hempelian covering law model in dealing with the "epistemic tension in history".

According to Oakeshott, history is not only concerned with a comprehensive unity of ideas, but it is also concerned with the unique,

---

[100] T. S. Kuhn, 1977: xii.
[101] *EM*: 144-5.
[102] T. W. Smith, 1996: 601.

particular and contingent relationship of those ideas,[103] which is to say that the historical past is composed of "circumstantially and significantly related historical events",[104] and so it "has no place for extrinsic general terms of relationship — the glue of normality or the cement of general causes".[105] At this point, without doubt, Oakeshott is reminiscent of a number of non-positivist thinkers. Collingwood, for example, argues that in history "nothing of value [is] left for generalisation";[106] and Elton declares that history deals with events "from the point of view of happening, change, and the particular"; it is "idiographic" rather than "nomothetic".[107]

In the so-called idiographic–nomothetic debate in historiography lasting over a century in the Western intellectual environment, however, Popper and Hempel have powerfully argued that historical particularity and scientific generalisation are not necessarily in conflict, because whilst historians are dealing with the particular, in their study "laws may be so trivial, so much part of [their] common knowledge, that [historians] need not mention them and rarely notice them",[108] that is, laws are often "tacitly taken for granted".[109] In the case of Hempel, for instance, the explanatory law which applies to both scientific and historical explanation is formulated as follows: Suppose that a set of events $C_1, C_2, \ldots C_n$ have occurred within which the situation E is to be explained, the explanation of the occurrence of E must consist of:

(1) a set of statements asserting the occurrence of certain events C_1, $C_2, \ldots C_n$ at certain times and places, [i.e. the "determining conditions" for the event to be explained]

(2) a set of universal hypotheses, such that

    (a)   the statements of both groups are reasonably well confirmed by empirical evidence,

---

[103] Although I disagree with almost every main argument that P. King makes about Oakeshott's historical thought in "Michael Oakeshott and Historical Particularism", I think he is right in characterising it in terms of the name: historical particularism.

[104] *OH*: 62.

[105] *OH*: 94.

[106] R. G. Collingwood, 1946: 222.

[107] G. R. Elton, 1969: 24, 41. The terms "idiographic" and "nomothetic" were first coined by Windelband.

[108] K. Popper, 1957: 145.

[109] C. Hempel, 1965: 236.

(b)   from the two groups of statements the sentence asserting the
      occurrence of event E can be logically deduced.[110]

And since, insofar as the structure of historical explanation conforms to that of scientific explanation, history is a genuine form of
scientific knowledge.[111]

To argue against Oakeshott's historical particularism in favour of
the Popper-Hempelian model, P. King writes that "it is of no use
whatever to seek to characterise historical events as unique", for
although "we do not perceive history to be governed by universal
laws, it does not follow that we can demonstrate that there are no
such laws".[112] In defence of Oakeshott, however, I think writers like
King fail to realise that the Popper-Hempelian model is actually
based on a form of realism in history, purporting to maintain that
there exists such a thing as the Past which is independent of the historian, and therefore the task of the historian is merely to represent
past events as what they really were. In other words, as already mentioned, that the historian always takes general laws for granted can
be true only if the temporal structure that underlies his "causal
explanation" has been identified as "successive" ($C_1, C_2, \ldots C_n$) in
terms of natural time, namely, history is treated as a series of events,
the course of "what really happened"; such that the causality of historical events may be pre-determined as an existing fact (in the Past)
without recognition by the historian. However, Oakeshott has made
every effort to prove that history and the Past are not identical; the
temporal rhythm in history is not given but artificial. And he actually takes it to be co-existence which allows the historian to understand historical events in his mind in terms of "contingent
relationship", that is, a kind of relationship "which, when in an
enquiry it is found to subsist between antecedent events and a subsequent event, composes an identity which may be described, alternatively, as an event properly understood as an outcome of antecedent
events, or as an assemblage of events related in such a manner as
itself to constitute an historically understood event".[113]

This means that in Oakeshott's theory of past and time historical
events are not necessarily *themselves* causally or successively (or

[110] *Ibid.*: 232.

[111] For the supportive arguments for Hempel's model, see esp. E. Nagel, 1959;
      M. White, 1959.

[112] P. King, 1983: 129.

[113] *OH*: 93-4.

even contingently);[114] it is human agents who conceive them to be so. And just because insofar as the dominating words "cause" and "successiveness" in historical discourse belong to "the rhetoric of persuasion rather than the logic of historical enquiry",[115] the existence of general laws in the historical world is not absolute but optional. That is, as long as the distinction between history and the Past, between historical time and natural time is made, the neo-positivist's attempt to reconcile the "epistemic tension in history" by claiming a given common logical structure of the historical world is doomed to be in vain. As a result of this, the questions regarding the covering law model would turn out to be thus: first, in history, is it plausible to read the relationship of historical events in terms of generalisation? and second, is it desirable to do so?

Of the first of these questions, Hempel has clearly suggested, and Popper would not disagree, that since (no matter whether the historian recognises them or not) general laws exist universally and offer an "indispensable instrument" for historical study, it is no shame of the historian to largely apply general laws (or theories) to his study.[116] And it is without question, as Oakeshott argues, that here by the notion "law" both Popper and Hempel do not mean "a law of historical change", but the conclusion of a psychological, an economic or a sociological enquiry which is not concerned to explain occurrences but to formulate regularities, or a generalisation about human nature or a testable proposition about human behaviour.

However, Oakeshott claims that this scientific account of historical explanation is "muddled and untenable", as it denies the essential conditions of an historical enquiry as an endeavour to answer an historical question by gathering a passage of the past consisting of related events which have not survived inferred from a past of artefacts and utterances which have survived.[117] That is to say, with the covering law model the historian is only attempting to deduce the occurrence of a survived event E by relating it to the occurrence of other survived events $(C_1, C_2, \ldots C_n)$ in terms of universal laws which disclose this relationship to be causal, but "this is not a possible procedure for an enquiry concerned to understand a not yet understood past which has not survived, and its conclusion is not of a kind that any historical enquiry, or any alleged historical enquiry,

[114] Cf. *OH*: 94.

[115] *OH*: 85; cf. 83-96.

[116] C. Hempel, 1965: 231, 243.

[117] *OH*: 79.

has ever sought".[118] To this, Oakeshott has three relevant points to make. Together they may help us clarify further the main concern of an historical enquiry as categorically distinguishable from that of science.

First, let me take this opportunity to resume Oakeshott's distinguishing of the historical past from the practical past. It is true that a number of Oakeshott's critics have questioned the possibility of Oakeshott's insistence on history being the past for its own sake indifferent to the present concern, namely, what may be called anti-presentism embodied in Oakeshott's historical thought.[119] P. King, for instance, quotes E. H. Carr to argue that "the function of the historian is . . . to master [the past] as the key to the understanding of the present".[120] A. H. Birch writes that in history "interpretation means not only an assessment of the meaning of events in their own time but also, as H. P. Rickman has put it in his essay on Dilthey, "an assessment of these events in the light of the historian's own age, that is, in terms of their consequences in time and the ways in which they ultimately affected the historian and his age'".[121] And more recently, T. W. Smith relies with his similar criticism on the authority of H. Trevor-Roper who claims that "history is not merely what happened, it is what happened in the context of what might have happened"; and on the authority of H. White who maintains that "the contemporary history has to establish the value of the study of the past, not as an end in itself, but as a way of providing perspectives on the present that contribute to the solution of problems peculiar to our own time".[122]

With his main objection to the covering law model as mentioned above, it seems that for Oakeshott an exclusive concern with past is possible in historical writing because *res gestae* which survive in the present, "when authenticated, are to be used as circumstantial evidence for constructing a past which has not [now] survived".[123] This means that in response to his critics Oakeshott does not change his mind about anti-presentism in the historical past, instead he only

---

[118] *OH*: 80.

[119] Here, allow me to remind the reader that the problem of presentism, (namely, the practical past), is different from "the temporal dilemma in history" which is concerned with the presentness or pastness of the historian's reading of an historical event.

[120] See P. King, 1983: 122.

[121] See A. H. Birch, 1969: 225.

[122] See T. W. Smith, 1996: 608.

[123] *OH*: 80.

comes to restrict the *major* interest of the historian to be the reconstruction of a past which is not known to the historian in the present.
Practically, this interest of an historical enquiry is posed so strictly
that Oakeshott himself cannot write a history as such; and yet theoretically, that strictness surely enables him to treat the covering law
model as "the secondary engagement of explaining" in history in the
sense of affecting "to perform the impossible feat of leaping directly
into a past which has not survived by beginning in a present of
alleged informative statements reporting and asserting the occurrence of certain kinds of happening, for example, the defeat of Napo-
leonic armies at Waterloo and its attendant circumstances ('initial
conditions')".[124] As a result, with the covering law model, *res gestae*
are only interpreted in terms of a given generalisation which is now
available to the historian; it thus often involves practical concerns as
we have seen in Popper's case.

Additionally, we have seen that although a past event E and other
events (C_1, C_2, ... C_n) which accompany it are recorded it does not
mean that they are historical; but rather this only means that they are
the *characters* of bygone situations which have not survived awaiting
transformation into historical events. That is to say, discovery without judgement is impossible, and judgement concerning something
past is not necessarily historical — there are a number of ways of
reading the past corresponding to the different modes of experience.
Thus, given the distinctiveness of an historical consciousness, "the
moment historical facts are regarded as instances of general laws,
history is dismissed", for it is at once to be replaced by science. For
this reason, Oakeshott argues, to relate historical events in terms of
general causes "is not bad history; it is not history at all".[125]

Last, but not least, history is a unity of ideas concerned with the
complexity, concreteness and intelligence of historical events.[126] But
the attribution of general laws to historical explanation will persuade the historian to pay attention to the *abstract logical structure* of
past events alone. For "a cause may be attributed only to an abstraction: only 'an event of the *kind E*' may be said to be regularly accom-
panied by 'events of the kinds C_1, C_2, etc.' which, by invoking a
general law, may be recognised as its causal conditions".[127] And consequently, from the problem of abstraction it follows our next step is

[124] *OH*: 80.

[125] *EM*: 128.

[126] Cf. W. Dray, 1957: 44-50, 79-86.

[127] *OH*: 81-2.

to consider the desirability of the covering law model in respect of the Enlightenment project.

It has been said that the philosophical commitment of pro-positivist historical thought is predicated on the Enlightenment historiographical position, namely, an identification of history with a naturalised conception of History. And, the assumptions of (1) the existence of the Past, (2) the representation of "what really happened" and (3) the application of general laws to history that mark the project of scientific history, are supported by foundationalism in philosophy — scientific certainty, a foundationalist analysis of all knowledge-claims and universality — which neo-positivism shares. That is, it will be remembered, for the neo-positivist, philosophy is so foundationalist that it is expected to disclose the structure of the entire world as the logical relationship of scientific statements having the character of universality. On this meaning, to be sure, the covering law mode is the representative of "rationalism in historiography".

Throughout this book, nonetheless, we should have already become familiar with Oakeshott's attack on Rationalism that certainty is not a complete criterion of genuine knowledge, and generalisation and abstraction are the twin pillars of the Enlightenment project. Thus, it is not difficult for us to reach the point that the covering law model is undesirable because the *philosophes* as such hear only one authentic voice in our conversation, and therefore they dissolve the self-consistent character of history in the same way as they have vacuumed the sources of our moral and political life. In this respect, the appearance of the covering law model precisely exemplifies the self-defeated character of the Enlightenment project: whilst the resolution of its crisis lies in an attempt to substantiate the abstract conception of rationality it wears by means of recovering some more concrete historical (and traditional) knowledge, the historiography in compliance with it requires the historian to give up the complexity of human intelligence for the simplicity of logical structure.

In summing up, the "epistemic tension in history" is an intellectual trap of the Enlightenment's device; it merely bothers the *philosophaster* who intends to claim a single scientific criterion of knowledge for all human voices. However, once foundationalism in philosophy is discarded, we see no reason why the structure of historical explanation must conform to that of scientific explanation in order to be a genuine form of knowledge. Instead, according to Oakeshott, the eminence of the voice of history in the conversation of mankind precisely consists in its distinguishable concerns with a dead past, with particularity and contingency. In line with the view I have been taking, I now turn to consider the role of the historian in the face of the Enlightenment project.

V.4. The Autonomy of History

The purpose of this section is to emphasise the significance of the autonomy of history in Oakeshott's thought. Yet, since in Oakeshott's theory, not only should history be independent of other modes of understanding and philosophy, it also has no supreme power over any others. In what follows, we simultaneously set out Oakeshott's non-historicist position.

V.4.1. History and Other Modes of Understanding

So far we have seen that for Oakeshott history understood in terms of its own logic of study is categorically distinctive from other modes of understanding such as science and practice: (1) history is distinctive from science because the historian is interested in particularity, whereas the scientist is absorbed in generalisation; (2) history is distinctive from practice because history is an exclusive concern with the past for its own sake, whereas practice is a significant concern with the future in terms of self-disclosure and self-enactment. On the other hand, however, it is equally important to note that although Oakeshott may not deny that human conduct is *historically* conditioned, he does not think that only through historical study can the nature of things be better understood. My general arguments leading to Oakeshott's non-historicist position are as follows:

Firstly, it is true that for Oakeshott as for the historicist the term "*historically*" used in the last-mentioned statement actually means that we must live in a tradition of behaviour, and with regard to a general idealistic connection by this they mean that *the habit of human mind* has a tradition or a *history*, rather than an unchangeable nature. That is, they do agree in common that a tradition of behaviour is not the Human Past in itself but a self-understanding procedure of human mind. However, what distinguishes Oakeshott from the historicist in principle is that he thinks that history as an enquiry is only *a* specific way of understanding what past agents have said and thought about in reference to human intelligence, and thus historical knowledge and traditional knowledge are not identical. This is to say that historicism, Oakeshott would argue, somewhat rests on a confusion with our *historical consciousness* or historicity with history as a mode of understanding. As a result, the historicist claims that all knowledge proper is historical, because human understanding must be of *historicity*.[128]

By way of contrast, in Oakeshott's system of thought, as we have seen, each mode of understanding has its own reason to converse with a tradition of behaviour concerned. And it may now be added that "conversation" understood as a method of understanding the multiplicity of meanings that compose a tradition of activity, namely, "how to go about things", must contain an element of historicity, but it is not exactly like an historical study. For example, as already indicated, in the world of practice, our practical reasoning is understood by Oakeshott, not merely as the exercise of an *historicity*, but as a form of rhetoric dealing with plausible statements in given circumstances, supported by "a pursuit of intimations" of a political tradition; this Aristotelian practical reasoning is so self-determined that it clearly does not apply to the world of history. Moreover, whilst past is considered as an issue, each non- historical mode likewise has its own way of reading *res gestae*, so that not everything concerning past is historical. Thus, in Oakeshott's classification, neither the scientific past nor the practical past, for instance, can be identified with the historical past.

Secondly, although historical knowledge and traditional knowledge are distinguishable, it cannot be denied that history categorised as a narrative about the comprehensiveness and complexity of past performances and utterances, under certain circumstances, should be able to play a central role in constructing information about concrete traditional knowledge for other modes of experience. For example, Oakeshott would not dispute that a history of the man-

---

[128] As I shall return to expand on this doctrinal meaning of historicism in terms of the example of Collingwood below, its further supportive argument, in fact, lies in the Diltheyian dichotomy that science explains nature, history understands man. Therefore, a more sophisticated formulation of historicism is that: because "history" is both *the* history of human thoughts as a whole and the only legitimate method of understanding those human thoughts in progress, i.e. because man's self-understanding must be acquired within *the* history of human thoughts which requires *historicity*, and to understand *the* history of human thoughts must involve historical recognition, thus all human knowledge properly gained is historical (whereas all natural knowledge properly acquired is scientific). Thus, here I also must remind the reader that in the context of historicism there is another implication of the term "history" being commonly used; that is, besides being the Human Past as a whole or an enquiry, it may also be taken to mean both the *historicity* of human mind or the aggregate of human thoughts (which is not the Past in itself) and the only legitimate method of man's self-understanding (which is not a specific mode of human understanding but more like what Dilthey calls *Geisteswissenschaften*).

ner of political activity or a history of the scientist at work is of importance to balance against the abstractness of rationalist politics or naive scientism. On this issue, Oakeshott, like the historicist, also seems apt to trace the crisis of the Enlightenment project to the trans-traditional or *ahistorical* foundation of modern natural philosophy which lacks *historical consciousness*.

However, it must be evident by now that Oakeshott's diagnosis of the "*ahistorical*" crisis of the modern world is philosophical rather than historical. That is, because traditional knowledge is a wider (philosophical) concept than historical knowledge, and because Oakeshott believes that a non-foundationalist conception of philosophy is possible and significant in human discourse, it is in philosophy not in history that the *historical consciousness* of human mind is disclosed, namely, human conduct always involves a tradition of ideas. And so, it is possible for Oakeshott to circumscribe the *necessity* of an historical enquiry in unveiling the condition of *historicity* of human activity, namely the appeal to an historicised theory of knowledge, without adopting foundationalism.

Thirdly, this thus brings our attention back to the main theme of Oakeshott's philosophy in association with the theory of modality in *EM*, meaning that the modes of understanding are exclusively discrete, each is an independent, self-consistent world of discourse, i.e. an invention of human intelligence. Adhering to this view, Oakeshott certainly would not accept that history is the master over the other modes of understanding. On the contrary, even though the historical study concerned may be capable of balancing against rationalist politics or naive scientism, the point is that an historical idea must be *transformed*, taken out of the historical world to which it belongs, before it can establish itself in another world.[129] And yet, by transformation, we are no longer staying in the historical world, but altering our concerns from the historical to the practical or the scientific. At this point, it is therefore re-affirmed that historical knowledge is not just the same as traditional knowledge being pursued in other non-historical modes of understanding, although it may offer some more informative messages for their *practice*.

By no means, then, does Oakeshott believe that, since the human mind is *historically* conditioned, all knowledge proper is historical. This, however, is not meant to diminish the importance of history in the confrontation of the crisis of the Enlightenment project, but rather it is only meant to avoid all human voices being united in that of his-

---

[129] Cf. *EM*: 265.

tory. Based on this general explanation, we may now come closer to look at the relation of history to science and practice respectively.

It must be remembered that the purpose of this book is to interpret the works of Oakeshott as a substantive critic of Enlightenment positions. And consequently, it appears to me, the most significant purpose of Oakeshott's rejection of the assimilation of history (and poetry) to science is "to rescue the conversation from the bog into which it has fallen and to restore to it some of its lost freedom of movement".[130] That is, Oakeshott's claim for the autonomy of history can be regarded as an extended critique of his life-long target, namely, Rationalism backed up by the incomplete understanding of scientific reason. For Oakeshott, "the conjunction of science and history can produce nothing but a monster",[131] they can be joined only at the cost of an *ignoratio elenchi* and at the cost of making our conversation boring. Conversely, our potential to transcend the crisis of the Enlightenment project is our ability to speak differently.

Oakeshott's theory of modality has little to do with the neo-Kantian movement. For, in *EM* both history and science are seen as modes of experience which arrest the whole reality at certain standpoints, not as *kinds* of experience which refer to *parts* of reality. That is, for Oakeshott reality is *One* which allows no pre-determined distinction such as History and Nature. And so, Oakeshott does not accept Dilthey's dictum that "[science] explains nature but [history] understands man";[132] that is, he rejects the neo-Kantian way of treating the subject-matter as a criterion for separating history from science.[133] And consequently, we may here expand on this system of *EM* from two perspectives: the possibility of a science of man and the possibility of a history of nature.[134]

[130] *VP*: 15.

[131] *EM*: 168.

[132] Quoted by A. H. Birch, 1969: 225.

[133] Cf. P. Franco, 1990a: 50-1, 115. Here, one may argue that in *HC* Oakeshott turns to classify human sciences and natural sciences into two different "orders" of research, in the sense that the former deal with the exhibitions of intelligence whereas the latter, non-intelligence (see *HC*: 12-8). Yet, as I see it, in that work Oakeshott, in fact, keeps hold of his monist view that reality is *One*. For, according to *HC*, whether a "going-on" is to be identified as the exhibitions of intelligence or otherwise is equally predicated on the interests of the theorist as anything else. Thus, as Oakeshott demonstrates, the ruins of a Mayan temple can be intelligently understood not only as expressions of Mayan religious beliefs, historical events, etc. but also as a collapsed physical structure or a process of chemical change in terms of causality (see *HC*: 14).

[134] As a result of the alteration mentioned in the preceding footnote, it seems that Oakeshott also launches a wider possibility for the idioms of enquiry within the

In the first place, because in *EM* science stands for the world *as a whole* seen under the category of quantity, unlike the neo-Kantian approach, to study man scientifically is therefore permitted. For example, economics, if claimed to be scientific, must be "a science of measurements" in terms of quantitative conceptions and relations.[135] Likewise, political science "must not be afraid of being abstract, and must free itself from all pretension of founding a science of history or of predicting historical events";[136] that is, it must be quantitative.

All this, however, is not inclined to the positivist proposal that the mode of science should be applied universally. In one sense, Oakeshott has reminded us that political science, for instance, tells us nothing about the individual meanings of human actions; and with its purpose of scientific generalisation, political science may do no good to our current moral and political situation. But this does not affect the fact that it is possible and legitimate; the point is that we must not understand political activity in terms of quantity and nothing more. In another sense, it is therefore important to protect the autonomy of history from being determined by science, for it would certainly bring us closer to a more coherent understanding about the manner of governing.

In contrast to political science, the notion of scientific history is to commit the error of *ignoratio elenchi*, because what it proposes is not to study, say, "the activity of the historian" in terms of quantity, but to mix two *different worlds of ideas*. Here as elsewhere, it may be noticed, by *ignoratio elenchi* Oakeshott's point is not that two modes of understanding can never communicate with one another under

same order to converse with each other, or to use Oakeshott's own term, to be "reduced" from one to another, in a more effective way (see esp. *HC*: 17). And this, I presume, may help us to explain why in *HC* Oakeshott seems to be more confident than before in writing a history of the characteristics of the modern state to illuminate his philosophical examination of civil association. For the purposes of this book, however, I shall not go into detail about the implications that Oakeshott may have brought to his philosophy of human sciences with the idea of reduction (see esp. T, Nardin, 2001: 128-35). And since, in any event, the term reduction used here does not mean that the idioms of enquiry of similar interests can be merged as "all-purpose sciences"; as an alternative, "each is autonomous in being constituted in terms of theorems exclusively its own, and each is capable of its own conditional perfection" (*HC*: 20, 17). Therefore, I think the notion of "transformation" taken from the context of *EM* may still serve well as a "starting-point" to look at the *modal relations* of history to science, practice and philosophy with which I am really concerned in this part of study.

[135] *EM*: 230; for the general character of economics discussed in *EM*, see also 223-30.

[136] Oakeshott, "Review of Catlin's The Principles of Politics" (1929-30): 400; quoted by P. Franco, 1990a: 243, n111.

certain circumstances, but that no cardinal condition postulates two different worlds of ideas, and thus no argument can be meaningfully passed from one world of ideas to another without transformation. In other words, political science, for instance, is categorically absurd only if it combines generalisation with historical narrative; whereas it creates a different problem when the practical man makes use of political science to formulate a policy, i.e. to increase the ascendancy of rationalist politics. By the same token, the categorical mistake of a history of political thought does not happen because of it dealing with the political; it happens only when the historian interprets a political text in terms of universal generalisation.

But what about the possibility of a history of nature? At first sight, although it is possible to study human actions scientifically, it does seem impossible to study natural things historically: The goings-on recognised as a thunderstorm, a butterfly on the wing, melting ice, etc. only have a nature, a casual relationship, but there are no human thoughts *in* them to be "re-enacted" in the historian's mind, to use Collingwood's phrase. However, this gives us insufficient reason to maintain that historical study is distinguishable from scientific research because they are dealing with different subject-matters. For the world as a whole present to the historian is always a world of *res gestae* consisting of both written texts and impersonal relics such as buildings, tables, chairs, etc. waiting to be understood. Even though a table itself cannot be understood historically, man's ways of using it, for instance, can be so understood. Thus, an ancient "table" may be seen under the category of science in terms of a physical structure or a process of chemical change, it may be seen under the category of history as a piece of evidence for studying the cultural life of eighteenth-century Englishmen, it also may be approached under the category of practice with the phrase such as "this antique is priceless", and so forth. So, Oakeshott finds nothing in the human to distinguish it absolutely from the non-human past. Reality is not divided as Nature and History in the first place, and then perceived by the historian or the scientist respectively; but rather, reality is a concrete whole (the same "table") modified under different categories of thought.

With the categorical distinction between history and science, it does not follow that there is no communication between them under certain circumstances. On one level, indeed, just as scientific history is an *ignoratio elenchi*, the same categorical confusion occurs when the scientist applies historical methods to his study; thus Oakeshott has claimed that the biologist's observation of the development of a tree, for example, is not an historical past in terms of contingency, but a scientific past in terms of causality. On another level, however, it is possible for the historian to write a history of the scientist at work, (or for the social scientist to pursue the "sociology of history").

We have seen that science, for Oakeshott as for Kuhn, is a tradition of activity or a paradigm of research; and that what Oakeshott and Kuhn attack under the rubric of scientism is not science per se but a certain way of attributing a "pure reason" to the working basis of scientific research. Given this view, as might be expected, both thinkers would not deny that a history of science is of significance to balance against the abstract scientific reason held by pro-positivism. But, I do not think that Oakeshott would agree with Kuhn's further historicist proposition, as MacIntyre puts in his interpretation of Kuhn's *The Structure of Scientific Revolutions*, that "the achievements of the natural sciences are in the end to be judged in terms of achievements of the history of those sciences".[137] For this contention would suggest that the authority of science is eventually conditional upon the works of historians of science. As a result, the self-consistent character of science is equally dismissed.

Oakeshott's perspective is different from such an alternative historicist position. His arguments on this specific issue emphasise that all we need in the confrontation of a positivist perspective on science is, in the first place, a request for a philosophy of science which rejects foundationalism and scientism in order to return our scientific reason to the concrete tradition to which it belongs, rather than a history of science which intends to identify itself with that tradition. Although this is not to deny that a history of science should be capable of providing the scientist with some more concrete and detailed information about traditional knowledge in use (or what Kuhn calls "shared examples") to substantiate the abstract scientific reason that he has been persuaded to believe in; yet because no ideas can simultaneously occupy two different worlds, an historical idea about the scientist at work can be a scientific judgement only if it is to be taken out of the historical world and transformed into the scientific world by the scientist. That is, a piece of historical knowledge about the exemplification of the scientist at work is not the same thing as the scientist's getting to know how to go about his research by contact with that exemplification. Thus, neither philosophy nor a history of science can judge the achievement of a science; the scientist is the authority over his own territory.

---

[137] A. MacIntyre, 1984: 47; see also 40-7.

Besides, as for the relationship of history to practice, Oakeshott's claim for an historical past for its own sake, viz. anti-presentism, is, of course, related to his objection to pragmatism in general. However, that the historical past is categorically distinctive from the practical past does not mean that there is no communication between the modes of practice and history. On the contrary, it is implied in previous discussions that the Oakeshottian practical past has two relative levels of implication. In one sense, it is the enemy of the historian, it hinders a possible human voice of speaking past and change; to write a history for the sake of the future is not bad history, but it is a part of practice. In another, however, it is also the friend of the practitioner, it indicates our common interest in reading past things and thoughts; *even* an historical idea may be transformed by the practical man to be useful, but in this transformation it must meanwhile cease to be historical.[138]

When one considers Oakeshott's political thought, it is the practical past used in the second level that is worth noticing. For it implies that it is legitimate for the practical man to make use of a history which narrates the complexity of our political manners by a certain transformation, such that the crisis of rationalist politics in terms of abstractness, perfectionism and universalism can be reconciled. That is to say, a history as such may likewise provide concrete information substantiating a political tradition for the practical man's "pursuit of intimations". But the significance of this history is not likely to be historicist in the sense of making all practical knowledge historical. Because it has been shown that our practical reasoning recognised as rhetoric in relation to *phronesis*, i.e. traditional knowledge, is not identical with historical knowledge.

V.4.2. History and Philosophy

To ponder more completely the meaning of the autonomy of history in Oakeshott's thought, also, we must pay attention to the relation of history to philosophy in terms of two topics: first, the relationship

---

[138] On this account, it seems implausible to me when K. Minogue says that the work such as *The History of the Communist Party of the Soviet Union (Bolsheviks)* may be useful for political practitioners but it cannot fit into the category of history (1993a: 48). For whether or not a work is historical, according to Oakeshott's own terms, depends not on the subject of study (which may be highly practical as the work in question suggests) but on the attitude of study. That is, as long as the interpreter is to reconstruct the survival for the sake of being interested in the historical past the historical approach is being taken. Whilst it is a different thing if the practical man reads a historical text in favour of being useful. Otherwise, if we follow Minogue's criterion seriously, there would be no such a thing as genuine "political history" at all.

between a philosophy of history and history in respect of Oakeshott's non-foundationalism; and second, the relationship between philosophy and a history of philosophy in respect of Oakeshott's non-historicism. Since from Chapter III up to the present stage we have already regarded the non-foundationalist character of Oakeshott's philosophy (of history) in greater detail, (i.e. the view that a philosophy of history cannot replace the autonomous nature of historical knowledge), I now only want to sum up Oakeshott's arguments against historicism in philosophy.

Roughly speaking, philosophical historicism has been taken in two forms, both of which are set forth with an awareness of the debacle of modern foundationalism as an *ahistorical* understanding of the nature of philosophy. First of all, it can be related to Rorty's neo-pragmatism which radically claims the end to philosophy. Since I have already discussed the difference between Oakeshott and Rorty, here I only propose to gloss over this argument in repeating that because Oakeshott's philosophical reflection in the pursuit of genuine meanings of truth, reality, the mind and so forth is exempt from engaging in foundationalist analysis of knowledge, there is no necessity for him to terminate philosophy itself as the only response to the crisis of the Enlightenment.

Secondly, there is also a tendency to hold the view that an historical perspective is the best way of approaching the nature of philosophy (and other forms of human knowledge), i.e. the attempt to base the authority of philosophy on a history of philosophy. C. Taylor, for example, argues that "it is essential to an adequate understanding of certain problems, questions, issues, that one understands them genetically", that insofar as "philosophy . . . is inherently historical";[139] and A. MacIntyre, following his study of Kuhn's history of science as we have mentioned, articulates that "the achievements of philosophy are [likewise] in the end to be judged in terms of the achievements of the history of philosophy".[140]

According to Oakeshott, however, even though it may be true that the substance of philosophical thinking is also *historically* conditioned, that is, philosophising is itself a way of human thinking that has to be learned from a tradition of philosophy, yet it is the philosopher in *practice* not the historian of a history of philosophy in *practice* that constitutes that tradition concerned. We have already become familiar with Oakeshott's reference to tradition and history as two

[139] C. Taylor, 1984: 17.
[140] A. MacIntyre, 1984: 47.

different categories of thing. So, Oakeshott would argue that "philosophy is inherently historical" is true, only if we take the adjective "*historical*" to mean "contextual" or "traditional"; and yet, because a tradition of philosophy has its own idiom of language and has its own way of reading past, we do not need a history of philosophy to *justify* the activity of philosophising. Consequently, once again, the point regarding the relation of philosophy to a history of philosophy is that: a history of philosophy, indeed, may help to unveil the patterns and exemplifications of philosophical thinking for the philosopher, but they are not themselves philosophical judgements unless the philosopher takes them into consideration.

Moreover, to claim the *historical* or traditional property for the habit of human mind, namely, the philosophical statement that human activity always involves a tradition of behaviour, in morality and politics, Oakeshott's philosophy also goes further to describe *the* tradition of modern Western political character itself. However, since philosophy takes nothing for granted, in so doing it must be eager to transcend any historic conditions that confront it. Thus, as we have seen in *PFPS*, for example, Oakeshott's philosophising never stops at the realisation of the historic conditions of modern European politics in terms of the politics of faith and the politics of scepticism. Instead, it goes further to transcend the complexity of the Western political tradition so as to reach a more coherent understanding of the nature of politics: What politics really is? It is at this point that I believe that the quasi-philosophical past should be allotted an important place in Oakeshott's philosophical and historical thought, if only to try to assess his contribution to them from a more profitable point of view. For it allows the philosopher to pay careful attention to the historical implications of the object upon which he is reflecting with no reference to historicism. And further, unlike the commonly called "philosophical approach" in the study of *the* history of (political) philosophy, it contains no practical concern.[141]

Consequently, it implies that the level of political reflection that Oakeshott takes is always that of philosophy which, following Hegel, is understood as "a tireless exploration of the conditions of conditions";[142] as a result, political philosophy to him is so transcending that he sometimes only names Plato's *Republic*, Hobbes's *Leviathan*, Spinoza's *Ethics* and Hegel's *Grundlinien der Philosophie des*

---

[141] See, for example, L. Strauss, 1959.

[142] *HC*: 257.

Rechts as examples.[143] Thus, if it is reasonable to suppose that Oakeshott himself has the ambition of writing a political philosophy (especially in respect of his theory of "civil association"),[144] he will never allow the authority of a history of political thought to step in to replace that of political philosophy. And the same goes for the relation of a history of philosophy to philosophy itself.

Finally, according to Oakeshott, the attempt to relate the logic of a history of philosophy to that of philosophy is likely to commit an *ignoratio elenchi*. For, many of these writers would like to claim themselves as the "philosopher-slash-historian" and thus agree in principle that "both historical specificity and philosophical delicacy are more likely to be attained if they are *pursued together* [emphasis mine]"[145] in an ideal historical study of philosophy. Oakeshott, of course, would not deny that a man can get to learn how to speak the languages of philosophy and history in his life, but he intensely doubts that "historical specificity" and "philosophical delicacy", which are categorically distinctive, can be put together so as to establish a "multi-purpose enquiry".[146] Thus, even in *HC*, Oakeshott is liable to take a philosophical theory of civil association and a "historical" examination of the character of a modern European state as two different ways of understanding politics, which can be communicated but can never be united. And here as elsewhere, if one wonders why it is so important for the philosopher to avoid the error of *ignoratio elenchi*, Oakeshott's reply would be that: the more voices to be heard in the conversation the more well-established a civilisation may appear to be, and it is exactly the task of a philosopher to consider the distinctiveness of human voices and their relationships with one another.

Thus far, then, we have returned to reinforce Oakeshott's objection to foundationalism and scientism in respect of the autonomy of history, and at the same time we have reached the point that Oakeshott is a non-historicist philosopher of history. Nevertheless, in view of the fact that in the above discussions I treated historicism only as a doctrine without giving it some detailed substance, and because the contemporary inclination to historicism has not infre-

---

[143] *RPML*: 150; *MPME*: 14.

[144] One of Oakeshott's students, T. Fuller recalls that: "Oakeshott was ambitious to write essays of lasting import in political philosophy, and he thought he had. In his portrait in Gonville and Caius College, Cambridge, he sits at a table on which *On Human Conduct* is prominently and centrally displayed" (1996: x).

[145] J. Dunn, 1980: 14.

[146] Cf. *HC*: 20.

quently been connected with the thought of Collingwood, I now propose to make a further comparison between Oakeshott's and Collingwood's philosophies of history. In the course of this examination, I think it may be well to bring Bradley's historical thought into consideration where appropriate, such that we may clarify the background of Oakeshott's historical thinking in a fuller sense.

V.5. Non-Historicist Idealism

The autonomy of history is a topic that likewise concerned Bradley and Collingwood, among other idealists. In *The Idea of History* Collingwood celebrated Bradley's *The Presuppositions of Critical History* as "the Copernican revolution in the theory of historical knowledge"[147] for its *attempt* to establish history as autonomous; meanwhile he praised Oakeshott's *EM* as presenting "the high-water mark of English thought upon history" for allowing the historian to play his game according to his own rules.[148] Nonetheless, since I think it would be oversimplified to identify idealism with historicism,[149] here the contrast among the three British idealists on historiography should be further clarified so that we may continue to consider Oakeshott's historiographical position from the standpoint of the general influence on him of Bradleyian idealism, and especially from the standpoint of his strict reservations on the *later* Collingwoodian historicism.

V.5.1. Collingwood (I): An Overall Review

On one level, there is little doubt that Collingwood should be considered the most influential British thinker in the field of historiography; compared to Oakeshott, Collingwoodian scholarship has been very well established. On another level, nonetheless, many people would not deny that Collingwood is perhaps one of the most difficult British thinkers in this century to be dealt with: not only is Collingwoodian terminology so flexible that its meanings depend largely on its contexts, and sometimes contradictions are apparent within the same work;[150] but also, his major work of history, *The Idea of History*, is a posthumous book edited from lectures and papers written from 1936-39, a fact which leaves the reader questioning the

---

[147] R. G. Collingwood, 1946: 240.

[148] *Ibid.*: 159.

[149] See, for example, W. H. Walsh, 1967: 14-5, 43.

[150] W. H. Dray: 1995: 27-31.

book's value and relevance in relation to his other published writings.[151]

Related to all this, a more comprehensive difficulty in interpreting Collingwood involves the lack of consistency in the development of his thought. In his *An Autobiography*, Collingwood did say that "[m]y life's work hitherto, as seen from my fiftieth year, has been in the main an attempt to bring about a rapprochement between philosophy and history".[152] However, whether or not Collingwood stayed the course on this problem is debatable and what he meant by "rapprochement" has consequently been interpreted differently by different critics.

T. M. Knox, for example, has classified Collingwood's work into three groups: the first basically includes *Speculum Mentis* (1924) and *Outlines of A Philosophy of Art* (1925); the second *An Essay on Philosophical Method* (1933) and *The Idea of History*; and the third *Autobiography* (1939), *The Essay on Metaphysics* (1940), and *The New Leviathan* (1942). To "bring about a rapprochement between philosophy and history", it seems to Knox, means that Collingwood has tried to set up the logical *differentia* between philosophy, history and science and to reflect philosophically upon the epistemological problems to which history gives rise. This aim, Knox argues, is successfully achieved "at the zenith of his powers", i.e. in the second group of his philosophical writings. Be that as it may, Collingwood's "enthusiasm for history", Knox continues, has finally made his later work as shown in the third group, "turn traitor to his philosophical vocation".[153]

On the same account, A. Donagan offers a further examination of this shifting calling it "Collingwood's conversion to historicism";[154] and W. H. Walsh comparably remarks that with *An Autobiography* and *An Essay on Metaphysics* "Collingwood took a step which marked a decisive break with his earlier thought".[155] That the later Collingwood came to dissolve philosophy into history, it seems to me, has now become a widespread conviction.[156]

However, D. Boucher precisely takes "a rapprochement between philosophy and history" to mean that for Collingwood "philosophy

---

[151] Cf. L. O. Mink, 1972: 155 ff.

[152] R. G. Collingwood, 1939: 77.

[153] T. M. Knox, 1946: vii-xx.

[154] A. Donagan, 1962: chap. 1, sec. 2.

[155] W. H. Walsh, 1972: 100.

[156] For other examples, see W. Dray, 1995: 2.

and history have the same order of enquiry: They are identified, if not identical".[157] The phrase so understood, Boucher argues, matches "the grandiose conception that Collingwood had of his mission in life", even though in his early work philosophy and history were treated as two different forms of experience.[158] In other words, it is Boucher's view that Collingwood's whole thought is interrelated, that he undertakes an enduring bid to carry out a rapprochement between philosophy and history. That in philosophy Collingwood has tried to establish a system of ideas in development also has been held by some other interpreters.[159]

The dispute around the development of Collingwood's thought is, in fact, more about whether it should be read as a series of systems or as a single system of ideas than about whether or not the later Collingwood is an historicist. And thus, some concessions are made on both sides of this debate: for example, Knox does not deny that "the *leit-motiv*" of Collingwood's work is history and Boucher concedes that "Collingwood was not one of those philosophers who was a slave to the principle of consistency".[160] Here I cannot but grant the benefit of Knox's division of Collingwood's work, and yet, meanwhile I believe Boucher's interpretation is worth noting because it reminds us that Collingwood's conversion to historicism was not a radical break with his early work. The best explanation of this change, I contend, lies in the various contents of *The Idea of History* itself.

That is, as far as I can see, there remains a grey area in Knox's classification of Collingwood's thought, and this has to do with the two problems in interpreting Collingwood that I mentioned earlier. Put all together, it is my contention that *The Idea of History* should be regarded as an "in-between" work of the later Collingwood and that this work is, in fact, composed of two adverse components. On the one hand, it seems inclined to the view of *Philosophical Method* that philosophy should be distinguished from history; on the other hand, it also contains the historicist seeds later planted in *An Autobiography* that the genuine meaning of philosophy consists in a history of philosophy.

In my opinion, this is exactly because Collingwood has used the term "history" in two different senses for each case: history as a dis-

---

[157] D. Boucher, 1989: 38.

[158] *Ibid.*: 40-6.

[159] For other earlier examples, see L. Rubinoff, 1970: 3-34; L. O. Mink, 1969: 1-7.

[160] D. Boucher, 1989: 39, 38.

cipline and *history* as a habit of human mind, i.e. "history as a specific human past" and "history as a study of whatever is past".[161] Although Collingwood's apparent aim in *The Idea of History*, as we know, is to consider the nature of history as a discipline,[162] a wider question has been raised as to whether the book is beyond the question "What is history?" and is rather concerned to advance the view that since the human mind is *historically* conditioned, all knowledge of it must be historical. And thus, when Collingwood says repeatedly in *The Idea of History* that history is the only true knowledge of the human mind, this cannot be taken to mean that only the academic historian is able to reach such a truth, but rather that every individual, provided they are using an analogous historical method, is capable of reaching this truth as well.

Consequently, I rather think that the Collingwoodian notions of "historical imagination" and "historical re-enactment" constitute not merely a theory of historical understanding (as in writing a history per se) but rather a common historicised theory of human understanding. And for the purpose of this study, it is this Collingwood as an historicist that should be further discussed. But before going any further, I intend to take Bradley's historical thought into consideration.

V.5.2. Bradley (II): The Presuppositions of Critical History

The main feature of historical thought that Bradley, Collingwood, and Oakeshott share is, certainly, their aversion to realism and thus to the empiricist-positivistic theory of history. To re-state: in contrast to the positivist view that historical truth lies in the statements made by the authorities on and witnesses of History, Bradley, Collingwood, and Oakeshott surely believe that history is the outcome of a judgement, i.e. a critique of authorities and witnesses which is made by the historian himself. That is, for these three British idealists, to use D. Boucher's phrase, history is surely "the creation of the past",[163] which means that history is always the historian's own experience; history must be *critical* and the criterion of criticism is the historian. In his Preface to *Critical History*, Bradley says that:

> There is no history which in some respect is not more or less critical. No one in the world thinks or could think of inserting into a history of the

---

[161] Cf. W. Dray, 1995: 20-1.

[162] See esp. R. G. Collingwood, 1946: 9-10.

[163] D. Boucher, 1984.

world *all* the events which have been handed down, precisely as they have been handed down.

The historian as he is the real criterion; the ideal criterion . . . is the historian as he ought to be. And the historian who is true to the present is the historian as he ought to be.[164]

In a certain sense, then, both Collingwood's ideas of "historical re-enactment" and "historical imagination" and Oakeshott's notion of "history as the transformation of what really happened in the Past" all demonstrate affinities with Bradley's remarks. However, it cannot be denied that, compared to Collingwood, Oakeshott has made much more direct contact with Bradley in both the fields of philosophy and historiography.

As I have indicated in Chapter III in his philosophy there are three major ideas that Oakeshott adopts (with revisions) from Bradley's *Appearance and Reality* (1893): reality is a matter of degree, a coherence theory of truth, and the notion of concrete whole. That which lies behind Oakeshott's argument against the view that history and History are united, it appears to me, resembles the very notions of truth and fact upon which Bradley himself based the autonomy of history.

Oakeshott accepts, with Bradley, that the world is what we understand it to be, and every such understanding must involve both subject and object. Bradley is aware that the word "history" has often had a double-meaning as both *Was geschieht*, i.e. "what really happened", and "historical enquiry". But, neither the representationalism in historiography nor the "reproductive" theory of history can be soundly maintained, because both tend to divorce subject from object and thus deny the "exercise of criticism" in the historian's mind. "The historian", he argues, "is not and cannot be merely receptive, or barely reproductive".[165]

In history, Bradley believes, and as Oakeshott has equally argued, historical fact is always a judgement, "a conclusion; and a conclusion, however much it may appear so, is never the fiction of a random invention".[166] And, since the coherence theory of truth, as we have reviewed previously, demands no basic judgements beyond the condition of coherence — that every single unit of our thought must continually face experience as a whole — historical fact, being thought, needs to be "qualified by the premises of our knowledge,

---

[164] Bradley, 1993: i & ii.

[165] *Ibid.*: 5.

[166] *Ibid.*: 10.

by our previous experiences".[167] For this reason, both Bradley and Oakeshott reach the same conclusion that "there are no facts as to which mistake is impossible";[168] that what really counts in history is consistency rather than correspondence. This implies at the same time that historical fact is in reality a theory, an inference, i.e. a world of ideas as Oakeshott likes to put it. Bradley articulates that:

> The history then . . . which is for us, is a matter of inference, and in the last resort has existence, as history, as a record of events, by means of an inference of our own. And this inference furthermore can never start from a background of nothing; it is never a fragmentary isolated act of our mind, but is essentially connected with, and in entire dependence on the character of our general consciousness. And so the past varies with the present, and can never do otherwise, since it is always the present upon which it rests. The present is presupposed by it, and is its necessary preconception.[169]

Once again, here Oakeshott's solution of the "temporal dilemma in history" may be seen as having been inspired by Bradley.

We might infer, then, that for Bradley, (as for Oakeshott but with a somehow different effect), critical history, because it is a matter of inference, must need a criterion against which it may be compared: "History must ever be founded on a presupposition", "[t]here is no such a thing as history without a prejudication";[170] and as such it is the task of philosophy "to know what criticism [in history] means".[171] However, the very criterion that Bradley applies to history has been bitterly condemned by Collingwood.

V.5.3. Collingwood (II): Historicism

Collingwood thinks that Bradley is absolutely right in holding that historical knowledge is not a passive acceptance of testimony, but a critical interpretation of it according to a criterion which the historian brings with himself to the work of interpretation. Yet, where Bradley goes astray is:

> in his conception of the relation between the historian's criterion and that to which he applies it. His view is that the historian brings to his work a ready-made body of experience by which he judges the statements contained in his authorities. Because this body of experience is

[167] *Ibid.*: 10.

[168] *Ibid.*: 11.

[169] *Ibid.*: 15.

[170] *Ibid.*: 15.

[171] *Ibid.*: ii.

convinced as ready-made, it cannot be modified by the historian's own work as an historian: it has to be there, complete, before he begins his historical work. Consequently this experience is regarded not as consisting of historical knowledge but as knowledge of some other kind, and Bradley in fact conceives it as scientific knowledge, knowledge of the laws of nature. This is where the positivism of his age begins to infect his thought.[172]

Thus, in Collingwood's eyes the inconsistency of Bradley's historiography is this: that he sets out to prove the distinction between history and science, but in his view the criterion for the historian to criticise historical materials is an unchangeable identification of a body of experience, an inference in the world of to-day which is, in fact, supported by the world of science.[173] And thus, history, at best, is a world of probability, since we can never be certain about what the past agents really thought. In short, Bradley's historical thought is criticised by Collingwood for purportedly containing a latent positivism and a consequent scepticism.

For Collingwood, Bradley's positivistic influence can be reformulated in this way, that is, the criterion of the historian is constructed by a universal character of human understanding which like the laws in science does not itself change. According to Collingwood, nevertheless, this view fails to reflect the *historicity* of the substance of historical thinking itself.[174] That is to say, the criterion of the historian's understanding is an alterable process in which he "creates for himself this or that kind of human nature by re-creating in his own thought the past to which he is heir".[175] For example, the history of political philosophy "is not the history of different answers given to one and the same question, but the history of a problem more or less constantly changing, whose solution was changing with it".[176] Plato's *Republic* is an understanding not of the unchanging character of political life, but of Greek politics as Plato perceived them and re-interpreted them; Aristotle's *Ethics* is a description about the morality of Greek gentlemen; Hobbes's *Leviathan* expounds the political ideas of absolutism in seventeenth century England and so forth. But the quality of those works is superior because "in those works the authors are doing best the only thing that can be done when an attempt is made to construct a science of the

---

[172] R. G. Collingwood, 1946: 139-40.

[173] Cf. L. Rubinoff, 1996: 138, 144

[174] See esp. R. G. Collingwood, 1946: 239. Cf. L. Rubinoff, 1996: 136-42.

[175] *Ibid.*: 226, see also 85, 135.

[176] R. G. Collingwood, 1939: 62.

human mind. They are expounding the position reached by the human mind in its historical development down to their own time".[177]

For this reason, Collingwood argues, every generation has to rewrite its own history. Not only because every generation has its specific *historical consciousness*, interests and methods,[178] but also because this rewriting is what shapes the self-identification of the generation concerned. Collingwood says that:

> in history . . . no achievement is final . . . This is not an argument for his-
> torical scepticism. It is only the discovery of a second dimension of his-
> torical thought, the history of history: the discovery that the historian
> himself, together with the here-and-now which forms the total body of
> evidence available to him, is a part of the process he is studying, has its
> own place in that process . . . [179]

However, in *The Idea of History* Collingwood is not merely con-cerned with the *historicity* of history, but also, more generally, with the *historicity* of human understanding as a whole. And he some-what treats history and man's self-understanding as the same thing, because he seems to see history both as the aggregate of human thoughts and the only legitimate way of understanding human thoughts in progress.

"Man," says Collingwood, "who desires to know every thing, desires to know himself".[180] This view is not new. And yet, the pro-posal for a "science of human nature" or "a science of man" culti-vated by Locke, Hume, Kant, pro-positivism and so forth was fated to fail, because its method was not historical, but distorted by the application of the natural sciences.[181] The distinction between his-tory and science, to Collingwood, lies in the fact that the "historical process" is a process of human thoughts whereas the "natural pro-cess" is a process of natural events. That is, unlike science, all history properly so called is the history of human affairs, since man is the only animal that thinks and expresses what he thinks: "all history is the history of thought".[182] This implies that Collingwood accepts the Diltheyian dichotomy of the world and the two divisions of human knowledge related to each of them, namely, science which deals with the world of nature and history which deals with the world of

[177] R. G. Collingwood, 1946: 229.

[178] Cf. A. Heller, 1982: chap. 1.

[179] R. G. Collingwood, 1946: 248.

[180] *Ibid.*: 205.

[181] *Ibid.*: 206-9.

[182] *Ibid.*: 210-17.

man; and so he identifies the mode of history not as a *specific* way of human understanding (different from, say, practice), but as a *necessary* method of it.

But, what exactly is the character of this general historical method? As we well know, Collingwood believes that it must be the "re-enactment" of past thought in one's own mind. And with this, we are returning to the second target that makes up Collingwood's critique of Bradley, namely, historical scepticism.

In Collingwood's understanding, because Bradley holds that the past can be known only in terms of an inference, we can never be certain about our historical judgement, i.e. we can never know the past in a way that is identical to what past agents really thought about their actions. In other words, as Collingwood puts it, Bradley's criterion of critical history "is a criterion not of what did happen but of what could happen".[183] With Bradley, he continues, all we have is no more than a probable world whose plausibility is determined by the world of science.[184] Due to this sceptical propensity, Collingwood complains, Bradley stops short of realising that "the historian re-enacts in his own mind not only the thought of witnesses but the thought of the agent whose action the witness reports".[185]

Put another way, although both Collingwood and Bradley grant in principle that as the past is never a given fact which one can apprehend by perception and observation, the correspondence theory of history held by empiricist-positivism must make history impossible;[186] instead, history for them (as for Oakeshott) only exists in the historian's mind. However, in addition to his neglecting the *historicity* of human understanding, Collingwood argues, Bradley's answer to the possibility of historical knowledge, i.e. the problem, "Can the historian know the past 'as what it was' in his mind?" is too negative. For, Bradley's identifying the criterion of history with the world of to-day must at the same time result in (positivistic-like) sceptical implications, i.e. an affection for the tradition of Hume, which concedes that history is at best probable.[187]

To escape from the muddle of scepticism, Collingwood himself thus claims that "to know someone else's activity of thinking is possible only on the assumption that this same activity [which hap-

---

[183] *Ibid.*: 239.

[184] *Ibid.*: 239.

[185] *Ibid.*: 138.

[186] *Ibid.*: 282, 233; cf. 1939: 44-53.

[187] L. Rubinoff, 1996: 137.

pened in the past] can be re-enacted in one's own mind [in the present]".[188] This implies that the notion which always accompanies historical re-enactment in Collingwood's conception of history is historical imagination: D. S. Taylor has thus connected them in explaining Collingwood's historical thought as an "imaginative re-enactment of past thought".[189] Here, the term "imagination" is defined by Collingwood as a "blind but indispensable faculty" without which we could never perceive the world around us. In history, Collingwood maintains, it is this faculty "which, operating not capriciously as fancy but in its a priori form, does the entire of historical construction".[190] Historical imagination so defined is therefore the product of the historian's own reasoning; it provides him with the justification for the historical materials he is using and the principles for selecting, for his use, actual evidence from potential evidence in the world. Historical imagination, then, is the historian's "picture of the past", whereas historical re-enactment is the very activity of rethinking the contents of the picture concerned, and these two elements are inseparable in every historical writing.

In short, for Collingwood, even though the object of history does not exist in the present, yet the possibility of historical understanding consists in our historical imagination by means of which the object may become a re-enactable thought. But, based on the view that history is both the history of human thought and the only legitimate method of man's self-understanding, it comes as no surprise that what Collingwood really achieves by the proposal for an "imaginative re-enactment of past thought" is not simply a theory of history, but rather, an historicised theory of human understanding in general.

V.5.4. The Living Past vs. The Dead Past

Whether or not Collingwood has been fair in criticising Bradley's attempt to base the criterion of history on science is disputable.[191] However, the details of this interpretative debate, interesting as they are, are largely beyond my concern here. Instead, based on the above examination of Collingwood's historicised theory of knowledge, I now only intend to demonstrate the differences between Oakeshott's and Collingwood's theories of history.

---

[188] R. G. Collingwood, 1946: 288; see also part v, sec. 4.

[189] Quoted by W. Dray, 1995: 191.

[190] R. G. Collingwood, 1946: 241.

[191] See L. Rubinoff, 1996; G. Stock, 1993.

First of all, it is observable that the way in which Collingwood comes to distinguish history from science is reminiscent of Dilthey and the neo-Kantians. That is, Collingwood accepts the view that there is "a clear-cut distinction between human nature and nature proper, or, between human conduct, the subject-matter of history, and natural process, the subject-matter of the natural sciences".[192] Also, he maintains that unlike the abstract explanatory character of science, "the concrete universal is the daily bread of every historian, and the logic of history is the logic of the concrete universal".[193] Nevertheless, although Oakeshott likewise considers the differentia between history and science in terms of the characteristics of their methods, as we have seen, Oakeshott's theory of modification is at odds with the History–Nature division.[194] As a result, Oakeshott objects to the Collingwoodian limitation of history's subject-matter to the world of Man,[195] and he clearly thinks that a scientific study of human activity in terms of quantity is possible and legitimate.[196]

Moreover, regardless of the fact that in *The Idea of History* Collingwood regards highly the view of history in *EM*, it is worth noticing that he poses three main questions about this view: First, he argues that Oakeshott leaves unexplained why there is such a thing as history in the stream of experience as a whole; second, he criticises Oakeshott's insistence on considering the logic of history from a purely philosophical point of view, i.e. from the outside; and finally, he rejects Oakeshott's notion of the historical past as a dead past.[197] These comments of *EM* made by Collingwood thus provide us with a further basis for comparing the two thinkers' historical thoughts, that is, the Collingwoodian historical past as a "living past" consid-

---

[192] L. Rubinoff, 1996: 134.

[193] R. G. Collingwood, 1924: 221; see also 1946: 234.

[194] Oakeshott's theory of modality, as already mentioned, is inspired by Bradley's *Appearance and Reality*, where reality is claimed as One, not many, inasmuch as there can be no ontological distinction between Nature and History. So, I doubt that it is plausible for Collingwood to attack Bradley's positivistic and sceptical implications on the premise that Bradley has an intention to draw the distinction between history and science in terms of their subject-matter. This Collingwoodian premise on understanding Bradley's historical thought is expanded by L. Rubinoff (1996: 129-33).

[195] W. Dray, 1968: 19.

[196] For a profound comparison between Collingwood's and Oakeshott's views on the relation of history to social science, see D. Boucher, 1993.

[197] R. G. Collingwood, 1946: 158; for Collingwood's interpretation of *EM* in that work, see esp. 151-9.

ered from the "inside" versus the Oakeshottian historical past as a "dead past" considered from the "outside".[198]

To begin with, Collingwood's first question has already been thoroughly answered in "The Activity of Being an Historian" in which Oakeshott has shown how with its own *practice* history has come to establish itself as a self-satisfactory mode of activity. And this supplementary explanation in *RP* and the works that follow it thus gives Oakeshott a more plausible standpoint from which to argue for the historian's *practice* as his object of observation, i.e. for consideration from the outside.

By way of contrast, however, it is Collingwood's view that since it is too difficult, if not impossible, to analyse the logic of history merely from the outside, and since it is more desirable if a philosophy of history is pursued by persons who are historians and philosophers at the same time, "history is not [as Oakeshott claims] based on a philosophical error", i.e. an arrest in experience, but "an integral part of experience itself".[199]

Nevertheless, I think it is a misunderstanding when Collingwood argues that in Oakeshott's system it is a philosophical error that makes history possible: "The historian is a philosopher who has turned aside from the path of philosophical thought to play a game which is none the less arbitrary for being only one of a potentiality infinite number of such games, others being those of science and the practical life".[200] For Oakeshott firmly believes that the historian does not engage in the philosophy of his subject matter; his mode of experience in constructing a coherent world of ideas is not thought by him to be "experience itself" (i.e. philosophy) but a "mode". Likewise a philosophy of history is not history or the mode of experience of the historian; that "historical experience must be present" is nothing but a philosophical statement. This, of course, does not mean that philosophy is superior to history, but rather, compared to Collingwood's view on "a rapprochement between philosophy and history" in the historicist sense that "philosophy and history have the same order of enquiry", it only says that Oakeshott claims the philosopher and the historian are trained to think differently.

Collingwood's understanding of Oakeshott's historical past as a dead past is inadequate, too. According to what we have seen,

[198] Croce in his *Theory and History of Historiography* has contrasted history proper with chronicle by describing the first as the living past of human thought, whilst the second is simply regarded a dead and unintelligible past. But the Collingwoodian–Oakeshottian debate in question is, indeed, quite a different case.

[199] R. G. Collingwood, 1946: 158.

[200] *Ibid.*: 155, 156.

Oakeshott's historical past is a dead past not because *res gestae* do not exist in the present — on the contrary, history is what the evidence obliges the historian to believe — but because there has appeared a specific historical interest in reading past for the sake of past and indifferent to the present's concerns. Thus, the real difference between the Oakeshottian dead past and the Collingwoodian living past does not lie in the temporal problem (as Collingwood saw it), but in the historical scepticism that Collingwood attributed to Bradley. That is to say, Oakeshott agrees with Collingwood that epistemologically history is "a transformation in the present, and in that transformation known as past".[201] But the point is that this pastness being known and transformed by the historian is "a novelty, not a re-enactment or re-creation of anything, and [thus] the unearthing of the past that Collingwood urges is, Oakeshott declares, a non-historical exhumation, 'a piece of obscene necromancy'".[202] This means that whilst Collingwood believes that it is possible for the historian to understand what the past agents really thought, Oakeshott thinks that this possibility is beyond the concern of history, as the historian must understand "men and events more profoundly than when they were understood when they lived and happened".[203] As a result, Oakeshott rejects the need to discover the "*mens authoris*" as the criterion of understanding a genuine historical work; and so in the so-called "*mens authoris*" debate in the history of ideas,[204] Oakeshott's position is closer to Gadamer's[205] than to Collingwood's "re-enactment", E. D. Hirsch's "re-knowing",[206] or Q. Skinner's "intention".[207]

Moreover, for Oakeshott the historical past as a dead past means that it is not an unmodified past, and it must be anti-presentist. Conversely, with reference to Collingwood's widest definition of history, by a living past what he refers to is whatever is re-enactable in our mind, i.e. for him, the living past is the only possible form of past that we can evoke in the present; it is not only the source of historical study but it is also the source of our self-understanding in general.[208]

---

[201] *Ibid.*: 158.

[202] T. W. Smith, 1996: 600; see also W. Dray, 1968: 19.

[203] Oakeshott, "Mr Carr's First Volume", *The Cambridge Review* 4 (1950-1):350.

[204] For this comparison, see D. Boucher, 1984: 205-6.

[205] H. Gadamer, 1975.

[206] E. Hirsch, 1967.

[207] Q. Skinner, 1988: 29-67.

[208] R. G. Collingwood, 1946: 205-9; see also L. O. Mink, 1972: 157. It can be noticed that Collingwood believes that the notion of pastness has nothing to do with the

The Collingwoodian living past is, thus, the entire "human past" not as what really happened in the course of events, but as a condition of self-understanding by means of which we are able to touch others' minds with our own.

Accordingly, this Collingwoodian definition of the living past implies that it is an integral world of life in which no further modifications are necessary; it takes all the historical past, the practical past, and the poetic past etc. into one mode of mind. For this reason, in *The Idea of History* and *An Autobiography* Collingwood sometimes regards history simply as "a school of wisdom" which brings to our political and moral life a "trained eye for the situation in which one has to act";[209] he also says that "the analogy between legal methods and historical methods is of some value for the understanding of history".[210] That is, where Collingwood represents historical knowledge as producing more or less a kind of practical wisdom, Oakeshott insists that history should be totally indifferent to practical life.[211] And, Collingwood's notion of historical "imagination", I would rather think, has first taken from and then replaced itself with what Oakeshott would simply refer to as the "contemplative past".

Finally, and most importantly, my ultimate purpose here, it will be remembered, is to draw a paradigmatic picture of historicism in terms of Collingwood's enterprise. After all this examination of Collingwood's thought, I think, we should have arrived at a clearer understanding of the essence of historicism: it considers the human mind to be always *historically* conditioned (in a living past), and only by means of an historical approach can the nature of things be well comprehended. Since we have dealt with the matter of Oakeshott's non-historicist view in some detail, I now only intend to re-establish that for Oakeshott history as a way of thinking must be distinguished from other modes of experience and philosophy; "distinguished" not only in the sense that historical thinking is autonomous, but also in the sense that it is only one possible voice among many others to be heard in the conversation of mankind. Thus, it can be said that the *differentia* of the historical past as a dead past is a necessary consequence of Oakeshott's theory of modality.

---

natural sciences at all: within a natural process, he believes, "the past dies in being replaced by the present", whereas within the historical process "the past, so far as it is historically known, survives in the present" (1946: 225).

[209] R. G. Collingwood, 1939: 96, 100.

[210] R. G. Collingwood, 1946: 268.

[211] Cf. W. Dray, 1968: 19; D. Boucher, 1984: 213; 1993: 697, 703.

Chapter VI

Conclusion

At the very beginning of this book I imposed upon myself the task to elucidate Oakeshott's thought as a substantial critic of the Enlightenment project by concentrating on his philosophy of politics and history. Now, after the intellectual journey led by Oakeshott, I hope I have gone some way to fulfilling this goal. Since I have summed up my main arguments leading to Oakeshott's criticisms of philosophical modernity, liberal ethics and positivist historiography and the uniqueness of these criticisms compared to the themes of postmodernism, reactionary traditionalism and historicism in the previous discussions where appropriate, I now only intend to re-consider two "hidden thoughts" or "guiding clues" that underpin the philosopher's enterprise. These two threads are interesting to note here, especially considering my own position, because they are related to Confucius's *Analects*, whose place in *the* history of Eastern political philosophy, to be sure, is on a par with something like Aristotle's *Ethics* in *the* history of Western political philosophy.[1]

The first of these hidden thoughts is the notion of "*the one thing that permeates everything*".[2] In understanding the system of Hobbes's philosophy by virtue of this perspective, Oakeshott writes that the coherence of Hobbes's thought lies not in an architectonic structure, but in a single "passionate thought" that pervades its parts. If this is also the style of thinking that Oakeshott adopts himself, his "passionate thought" would be an attempt to "disenchant" Universal Rationality[3] in order to return us to the Aristotelian-Montaignean

---

[1]   In the paper titled "Practice, Reason and Tradition: The Notion of Individuality in the Thought of Oakeshott and Confucius", presented to the Inaugural Conference of the Michael Oakeshott Association, I have tried to make a detailed comparison between Oakeshott's and Confucius' moral and political thinking.

[2]   Confucius, 1979: book xv. Cf. *RP*: 236, n8.

[3]   This is a phrase indicating the paradox of "reason" in modernity that I borrow from P. R. Harrison, 1994.

point that there are reasons appropriate to different modes of acting and thinking. Oakeshott's philosophy of politics and history (and of education and aesthetics etc.) is nothing but the application of this doctrine about philosophy to the investigation into the nature of political and historical activity. In this regard, it seems to me, the most significant achievement of Oakeshott's writings is to break the hold of the Enlightenment ethical and historiographical positions in his own way, where the Kantian trans-traditional ground of morality and politics is rejected so as to make room for a self-contained practical reasoning indifferent to philosophising itself; and the pro-positivist's identification of history with a naturalised conception of History is disengaged so as to make room for a self-consistent historical reasoning indifferent to scientific rationality.

The second hidden thought under consideration is "*the doctrine of mean*"[4] which, used in Oakeshott's quotation from *Analects* — "moderation lies in deficiency rather than in excess"[5] — means the sceptical habit of being exact, and never extravagant.[6] In politics, as we have seen from *The Politics of Faith and the Politics of Scepticism*, although the recognition of modern political character can be limited by two extremes, "the mean in action" is the appropriateness which can be learned not from rationalism in politics, but from scepticism in politics, i.e. the trimmer "who disposes his weight so as to keep the ship upon an even keel".[7] In a similar but not identical manner, the doctrine of mean also plays a certain part in Oakeshott's finding the "middle course" between Cartesian-Kantian foundationalism and Rortyian "total scepticism"; between absolute positivism and relative historicism. Indeed, Oakeshott is a unique critic of the Enlightenment project who does not adopt either post-modernism or historicism. The heritage of Oakeshott's thought, I agree with R. Price, is one of the "master spirits of this age",[8] an age which has been confronted with the crisis of the Enlightenment project.

---

[4]   The doctrine of mean is so central to Confucianism that, instead of precisely indicating where it is coming from, I shall here only mark out that it is also the name given to one of the "great four books" (i.e. *Analects, Mencius, The Great Learning* and *The Doctrine of Mean*) and characterises ancient Chinese ethics. For Oakeshott's reference to Confucius regarding this matter, see esp. *PFPS*: chap. 6.

[5]   Confucius, 1979: book iv. *PFPS*: 115, 121.

[6]   See esp. *PFPS*: 106.

[7]   *PFPS*: 123.

[8]   R. Price, 1993: 42.

Bibliography[1]

I. Works by Oakeshott

1. Books

Experience and Its Modes. Cambridge: CUP, 1933, repr. 1990.

The Social and Political Doctrines of Contemporary Europe. Cambridge: CUP, 1939, repr. 1950.

The Voice of Poetry in the Conversation of Mankind. London: Bowes & Bowes, 1959.

Rationalism in Politics and Other Essays, 1962, new edn. Indianapolis: Liberty Press, 1991.

On Human Conduct. Oxford: Clarendon Press, 1975, repr. 1996.

Hobbes on Civil Association. Oxford: Basil Blackwell, 1975.

On History and Other Essays. Oxford: Basil Blackwell, 1983.

The Voice of Liberal Learning, ed. T. Fuller. New Haven and London: Yale Univ. Press, 1989.

Religion, Politics and the Moral Life, ed. T. Fuller. New Haven and London: Yale Univ. Press, 1993.

Morality and Politics in Modern Europe: The Harvard Lectures, ed. S.R. Letwin. New Haven and London: Yale Univ. Press, 1993.

The Politics of Faith and the Politics of Scepticism, ed. T. Fuller. New Haven and London: Yale Univ. Press, 1996.

2. Articles and Book Reviews

Review of R. G. Collingwood's *The Principles of Art*. The Cambridge Review 59 (1937-8), p. 487.

"The Concept of a Philosophical Jurisprudence". *Politica* 3 (1938), pp. 203-22.

Review of R. G. Collingwood's *The Ideas of History*. *The English Historical Review* 62 (1947), pp. 84-6.

[1]   I have limited the following bibliography to works that have been directly mentioned in the text. For a more complete bibliography of works by and on Osakeshott up to 1993, see J. Liddington's "Bibliography" in *The Achievements of Michael Oakeshott*, pp. 107-43; the updates to this indispensable bibliography can now be reached from the web site of the Michael Oakeshott Association: www.michael-oakeshott-association.org

"Science and History". *The Cambridge Journal* 1 (1947-8), pp. 347-58.

"Contemporary British Politics". *The Cambridge Journal* 1 (1947-8), pp. 474-90.

Review of G. Ryle's *The Concept of Mind. Spectator* 184 (1950), pp. 20-2.

"Mr. Carr's first Volume". *Cambridge Journal* 4 (1950-1), pp. 344-52.

"*Rationalism in Politics*: A Reply to Professor Raphael". *Political Studies* 13 (1965), pp. 89-92.

"On misunderstanding Human Conduct: A Reply to My Critics". *Political Theory* 4 (1976), pp. 353-67.

II. Other Works

Acton, H. B. 1970. *Kant's Moral Philosophy*. London: Macmillan.

Adorno, T. W. and Horkheimer, M. 1972. *Dialectic of the Enlightenment*, trans. J. Cumming. NY: Herder.

Appleby, A. *et al* eds. 1996. *Knowledge and Postmodernism in Historical Perspective*. London: Routledge.

Archer, J. R. 1979. "Oakeshott on Politics". *The Journal of Politics* 41, pp. 150-68.

Aristotle, 1981. *The Ethics of Aristotle: the Nicomachean Ethics*, trans. J. A. K. Thomson. London: Penguin.

Arrington, R. L. 1998. *Western Ethics: An Historical Introduction*. Oxford: Blackwell.

Ashcraft, R. 1986. *Revolutionary Politics & Locke's "Two Treatises of Government"*. New Jersey: Princeton Univ. Press.

Auspitz, J. L. 1976. "Individuality, Civility, and Theory: The Philosophical Imagination of Michael Oakeshott". *Political Theory* 4, pp. 261-94.

Auspitz, J. L. 1993. "Michael Joseph Oakeshott (1901-90)". in *The Achievement of Michael Oakeshott*, ed. J. Norman. London: Duckworth, pp 1-26.

Austin, J. 1954. *The Province of Jurisprudence Determined*, ed. H. L. A. Hart. London: Weidenfeld & Nicolson.

Avineri, S. and de-Shalit A. 1996. *Communitarianism and Individualism*. Oxford: OUP.

Ayer, A.J. 1954. *Philosophical Essays*. London: Macmillan.

Ayer, A.J. 1987. *Language, Truth and Logic*. London: Pelican.

Bambach, C. R. 1990. *Heidegger, Dilthey and The Crisis of Historicism*. Ithaca: Cornell Univ. Press.

Barber, B. R. 1976. "Conserving Politics: Michael Oakeshott and Political Theory". *Government and Opposition* 11, pp. 446-63.

Baumer, F. L. 1977. *Modern European Thought — Continuity and Changes in Ideas: 1600-1950*. NY: Macmillan.

Beck, N. ed. 1975. *Perspective in Philosophy*. NY: Holt, Pinehart and Winston.

Bell, D. 1996. *Communitarianism and Its Critics*. Oxford: OUP.

Benn S. I. and Peters, R. S. 1958. *Social Principles and the Democratic State*. London: George Allen & Unwin Ltd.

Berki, R. N. 1981. "Oakeshott's Conception of Civil Association: Notes for a Critical Analysis". *Political Studies* 29, pp. 570-85.

Berlin, I. 1991. "John Stuart Mill and the Ends of Life". repr. in *On Liberty in Focus*, eds. J. Gray and G. W. Smith. London: Routledge.

Birch, A. H. 1969. "Historical Explanation and the Study of Politics". *Government and Opposition* 4, pp. 215-30.

Bleicher, J. 1980. *Contemporary Hermeneutic: Hermeneutics as Method, Philosophy and Critique.* London: Routledge and Kegan Paul.

Boucher, D. 1984. "The Creation of the Past: British Idealism and Michael Oakeshott's Philosophy of History". *History and Theory* 23, pp. 194-214.

Boucher, D. 1989. *The Social and Political Thought of R. G. Collingwood.* Cambridge: CUP.

Boucher, D. 1991. "Politics in a Different Mode: An Appreciation of Michael Oakeshott". *History of Political Thought* 12, pp. 717-28.

Boucher, D. 1993. "Human Conduct, History, and Social Science in the Works of R. G. Collingwood and Michael Oakeshott". *New Literary History* 24, pp. 697-717.

Bradley, F. H. 1969. *Appearance and Reality.* Oxford: OUP.

Bradley, F. H. 1993. *The Presuppositions of Critical History and Aphorisms*, ed. G. Stock. Bristol: Thoemmes Press.

Brandt, B. 1964. "The Concepts of Obligation and Duty". *Mind* 73, pp. 374-93.

Breisach, E. 1994. *Historiography: Ancient, Medieval and Modern*, 2nd edn. Chicago: The Univ. of Chicago Press.

Butterfield, H. 1965. *The Whig Interpretation of History.* London: W. W. Norton & Company.

Burke, P. 1994. *Montaigne.* Oxford: OUP.

Bury, J. B. 1956. "The Science of History". repr. in *The Varieties of History: From Voltair to the Present*, ed. H. Stern. Cleveland, pp. 210-23.

Carr, E. H. 1961. *What Is History?.* London: Pelican.

Casey, J. 1993. "Philosopher of Practice". in *The Achievement of Michael Oakeshott*, ed. J. Norman. London: Duckworth, pp. 58-67.

Cassirer, E. 1979. *The Philosophy of the Enlightenment.* New Jersey: Princeton Univ. Press.

Chambers, E. 1991. "The Use of History" (1728). repr. in *Versions of History from Antiquity to the Enlightenment*, ed. D. R. Kelley. New Haven: Yale Univ. Press, pp. 440-1.

Chapman, J. W. 1970. "The Moral Foundations of Political Obligation". in *Political and Legal Obligation*, eds. J. R. Pennock and J. W. Chapman. Chichester: John Wiley and Sons, pp. 149-67.

Cleugh, M. F. 1937. *Time and Its Importance in Modern Thought.* London: Methuen.

Coats, W. J. Jr. 1985. "Michael Oakeshott as Liberal Theorist". *Canadian Journal of Political Science* 18, pp. 773-87.

Cohen, A. 1989. "The End-Of-Philosophy: An Anatomy of a Cross-Purpose Debate". in *The Institution of Philosophy: A Discipline in Crisis?*, eds. A. Cohen and M. Dascal. La Salle: Open Court.

Collingwood, R. G. 1924. *Speculum Mentis: Or the Map of Knowledge.* Oxford: Clarendon Press.

Collingwood, R. G. 1939. *An Autobiography*. Oxford: Clarendon Press.

Collingwood, R. G. 1946. *The Idea of History*. Oxford: OUP.

Collingwood, R. G. 1994. *Outlines of a Philosophy of Art*. Bristol: Thoemmes Press.

Collingwood, R. G. 1995. *An Essay On Philosophical Method*. Bristol: Thoemmes Press.

Connolly, W. 1993. *The Terms of Political Discourse*, 3rd edn. Oxford: Blackwell.

Confucius, 1979. *The Analects*, trans. D. C. Lau. London: Penguine.

Copleston, F. S. J. 1958. *A History of Philosophy*, vol. 4, *Descartes to Leibniz*. London: Burns Oates and Washbourne.

Copleston, F. S. J. 1959. *A History of Philosophy*, vol. 5, *Hobbes to Hume*. London: Search Press.

Copleston, F. S. J. 1960. *A History of Philosophy*, vol. 7, *Fichte to Nietzsche*. London: Search Press.

Cottingham, J. 1988. *A History of Western Philosophy*, vol. 4, *The Rationalists*. Oxford: OUP.

Covell, C. 1986. *The Redefinition of Conservatism: Politics and Doctrine*. NY: St. Martin's Press.

Cranston, M. 1967. "Michael Oakeshott's Politics". *Encounter* 28, pp.82-6.

Crick, B. 1963. "The World of Michael Oakeshott: Or the Lonely Nihilist". *Encounter* 20, pp.65-74.

Crisp, R. 1997. *Mill on Utilitarianism*. London: Routledge.

Crossman, R. H. S. 1951. "The Ultimate Conservative". *The New Statesman* 42, pp. 60-1.

Dahl, R. 1993. "The Behavioral Approach in Political Science: Epitaph for a Monument to a Successful Protest". in *Discipline and History: Political Science in the United States*, eds. J. Farr and R. Seidelman. Ann Arbor: the Univ. of Michigan Press, pp. 249-67.

D'Amico, R. 1989. *Historicism and Knowledge*. London: Routledge.

Derrida, J. 1978. *Writing and Difference*, trans. Allan Bass. Chicago: The Univ. of Chicago Press.

Descartes, 1990. *Meditations*, trans. J. Veitch. in *The Rationalists*. NY: Anchor Books.

Devigne, R. 1999. "The Legacy of Michael Oakeshott". *Political Theory* 27, pp. 131-9.

Donagan, A. 1962. *The Later Philosophy of R. G. Collingwood*. Oxford: Clarendon Press.

Dray, W. H. 1957. *Laws and Explanation in History*. Oxford: OUP.

Dray, W. H. 1968. "Michael Oakeshott's Theory of History". in *Politics and Experience*, ed. P. King and B. C. Parakh. Cambridge: CUP, pp. 19-42.

Dray, W. H. 1995. *History as Re-enactment: R. G. Collingwood's Idea of History*. Oxford: Clarendon Press.

Dunn, J. 1969. *The Political Thought of John Locke: An Historical Account of the Argument of the "Two Treatises of Government"*. Cambridge: CUP.

Dunn, J. 1980. "The Identity of the History of Ideas". in *Political Obligation in Its Historical Context*. Cambridge: CUP, pp. 13-28.

Dunn, J. 1991. "Political Obligation". in *Political Theory Today*, ed. D. Held. Standford: Standford Univ. Press.

Ellington, J. W. 1993. Introduction to *Grounding for the Metaphysics of Morals*, 3rd edn. Indianapolis: Hackett.

Elton, G. R. 1969. *The Practice of History*. London: Fontana.

Falck, C. 1963. "Romanticism in Politics". *The New Left Review* 18, pp. 60-72.

Farr, A. 1998. *Sartre's Radicalism and Oakeshott's Conservatism*. NY: St. Martin Press.

Farr, J. and Seidelman R. eds. 1993. *Discipline and History: Political Science in the United States*. Ann Arbor: The Univ. of Michigan Press.

Field, G. C. 1938. *Some Problems of the Philosophy of History*. British Academy Lecture.

Findlay, J. N. 1977. Foreword to *Phenomenology of Spirit*. Oxford: OUP.

Flathman, R. E. 1972. *Political Obligation*. NY: Atheneum.

Flathman, R. E. 1989. *Towards a Liberalism*. Ithaca: Cornell Univ. Press.

Flew, A. ed. 1983. *A Dictionary of Philosophy*, 2nd edn. London: Pan Books.

Fotion, N. 1995. "Logical Positivism". in *The Oxford Companion to Philosophy*, ed. T. Honderich. Oxford: OUP, pp. 507-8.

Foucault, M. 1984. "What Is Enlightenment?". in *The Foucault Reader*. London: Penguin.

Frankena, W. K. 1973. *Ethics*, 2nd edn. London: Prentics-Hall.

Franco, P. 1990a. *The Political Philosophy of Michael Oakeshott*. New Haven and London: Yale Univ. Press.

Franco, P. 1990b. "Michael Oakeshott as Liberal Theorist". *Political Theory* 18, pp. 411-35.

Frohnen, B. 1998. "Sandel's Liberal Politics". in *Debating Democracy's Discontent: Essays on American Politics, Law, and Public Philosophy*, eds. A. L. Allen and M. C. Regan, Jr. Oxford: OUP.

Fuller, T. 1976. Review of *On Human Conduct*. *The Journal of Politics* 38, pp. 184-6.

Fuller, T. 1990. Introduction to *The Voice of Liberal Learning*. New Haven and London: Yale Univ. Press.

Fuller, T. 1991. "Oakeshott's Rationalism in Politics Today". Forward to *Rationalism in Politics*. Indianapolis: Liberty Press, New and Expanded Edition.

Fuller, T. 1993a. "The Poetics of the Civil Life". in *The Achievement of Michael Oakeshott*, ed. J. Norman. London: Duckworth, pp. 67-81.

Fuller, T. 1993b. Introduction to *Michael Oakeshott: Religion, Politics and the Moral Life*. New Haven and London: Yale Univ. Press.

Fuller, T. 1996. Introduction to *Michael Oakeshott: The Politics of Faith and the Politics of Scepticism*. New Haven and London: Yale Univ. Press.

Gadamer, H. G. 1975. *Truth and Method*. NY: Seabury.

Gallie, W. B. 1964. *Philosophy and the Historical Understanding*. London: Chatto & Windus.

Gardiner, P. ed. 1959. *Theories of History*. London: The Free Press.

Gerencser, S. 2000. *The Skeptic's Oakeshott*. NY: St. Martin's Press.

Gewirth, A. 1970. "Obligation: Political, Legal, Moral". in *Political and Legal Obligation*, eds. J. R. Pennock and J. W. Chapman. Chichester: John Wiley and Sons, pp, 55-89.

Gibbon, E. 1991. *An Address*. repr. in *Versions of History From Antiquity to the Enlightenment*. ed. D. R. Kelley. New Haven: Yale Univ. Press, pp. 461-71.

Grant, R. 1990. *Oakeshott*. London: The Claridge Press.

Gray J. 1983. *Mill on Liberty: A Defence*. London: Routledge.

Gray J. 1989. *Liberalisms: Essays in Political Philosophy*. London: Routledge.

Gray J. 1991. Introduction to *On Liberty and Other Essays*, ed. J. Gary. Oxford: OUP.

Gray J. 1993. *Post-Liberalism: Studies in Political Thought*. London: Routledge.

Gray J. 1995a. *Enlightenment's Wake: Politics and Culture at the Close of the Modern Age*. London: Routledge.

Gray J. 1995b. *Liberalism*. 2nd edn. Buckingham: Open Univ. Press.

Gray, J. and Smith, G. W. eds. 1991. *On Liberity in Focus*. London: Routledge.

Grayling, A. C. 1985. *The Refutation of Scepticism*. London: Duckworth.

Greenleaf, W. H. 1966. *Oakeshott's Philosophical Politics*. London: Longman.

Greenleaf, W. H. 1968. "Idealism, Modern Philosophy and Politics". in *Politics and Experience*, eds. P. King and B.C. Parekh. Cambridge: CUP, pp. 93-124.

Haakonssen, K. ed. 1988. *Traditions of Liberalism: Essays on John Locke, Adam Smith and John Stuart Mill*. St. Leonards: The Centre for Independent Studies.

Habermas, J. 1989. *The Structural Transformation of the Public Sphere: An Inquiry into a Category of Bourgeois Society*, trans. T. Burger. Cambridge: CUP.

Hacking, I. 1984. "Five Parables". in *Philosophy in History*, eds. R. Rorty *et al.* Cambridge: CUP, pp. 103-24.

Hall, D. and Modood, T. 1982a. "Oakeshott and the Impossibility of Philosophical Politics". *Political Studies* 30, pp. 157-76.

Hall, D. and Modood, T. 1982b. "A Reply to Liddington". *Political Studies* 30, pp. 184-9.

Harris, P. ed. 1990. *On Political Obligation*. London: Routledge.

Harrison, R. P. 1994. *The Disenchantment of Reason: The Problem of Plato in Modernity*. Albany: State Univ. of New York Press.

Hart, H. L. A. 1973. "Legal and Moral Obligation". in *Concepts in Social and Political Philosophy*, ed. R. Flathman. NY: Macmillan, pp. 187-201.

Hart, H. L. A. 1994. *The Concept of Law*, 2nd edn. Oxford: OUP.

Hart, J. 1993. "The Civilised Imperative". in *The Achievement of Michael Oakeshott*, ed. J. Norman. London: Duckworth, pp. 82-7.

Harvey, D. 1989. *The Condition of Postmodernity: An Inquiry into the Signs of Cultural Change*. Oxford: Blackwell.

Hawking, S. W. 1988. *A Brief History of Time*. London: Bantam.

Hegel, G. W. F. 1977. *Phenomenology of Spirit*, trans. A. V. Miller. Oxford: OUP.

Hegel, G. W. F. 1993. *Lectures on the Philosophy of World History*, trans. H. B. Nisbet. Cambridge: CUP.

Heidegger, M. 1992. *The Concept of Time*, trans. W. McNeill. Oxford: Blackwell.

Heller, A. 1982. *A Theory of History*. London: Routledge and Kegan Paul.

Hempel, C. 1965. "The Function of General Laws in History". in *Aspects of Scientific Explanation and Other Essays in the Philosophy of Science*. NY: Free Press, pp. 231-45.

Hiley, D. 1988. *Philosophy in Question: Essays on a Pyrrhonian Theme*. Chicago: The Univ. of Chicago Press.

Himmelfarb, G. 1975. "The Conservative Imagination: Michael Oakeshott". *The American Scholar* 44, pp. 405-20.

Himmelfarb, G. 1984. "Supposing History Is a Woman — What Then?". *The American Scholar* 53, pp. 494-505.

Hirsch, E. 1967. *Validity in Interpretation*. New Naven: Yale Univ. Press.

Hobbes, T. 1946. *Leviathan*, ed. M. Oakeshott. Oxford: Blackwell.

Honderich, T. ed. 1995. *The Oxford Companion to Philosophy*. Oxford: OUP.

Horton, J. and Mendus S. eds. 1994. *After MacIntyre: Critical Perspectives on the Work of Alasdair MacIntyre*. Cambridge: Polity Press.

Hume, D. 1978. *A Treatise of Human Nature*, ed. L. A. Selby-Bigge. Oxford: Clarendon Press.

Iggers, G. 1973. *The German Conception of History*. Middletown: Wesleyan Univ. Press.

Jaffa, H. V. 1963. "A Celebration of Tradition". *The National Review* 15, pp. 360-2.

James, W. 1995. *Pragmatism*, new edn. NY: Dover.

Jenkins, K. 1991. *Rethinking History*. London: Routledge.

Kant, I. 1991. *Political Writings*, trans. H. B. Nisbet. Cambridge: CUP.

Kant, I. 1993a. *Critique of Pure Reason*, trans. N. K. Smith. London: Macmillan.

Kant, I. 1993b. *Grounding for the Metaphysics of Morals*, trans. J. W. Ellington, 3rd edn. Indianapolis: Hackett.

Kant, I. 1993c. *Critique of Practical Reason*, trans. L. W. Beck. NY: Maxwell Macmillan Publishing.

Kant, I. 1995. *Metaphysics of Morals*, trans. M. Gregor. Cambridge: CUP.

Kant, I. 1997. *Prolegomena to Any Future Metaphysics*, trans. J. W. Ellington. Indianapolis: Hackett.

Kelley, D. R. 1991. *Versions of History From Antiquity to the Enlightenment*. New Haven: Yale Univ. Press.

Kelly, P. 1994. "MacIntyre's Critique of Utilitarianism". in *After MacIntyre*, eds. J. Horton and S. Mendus. Cambridge: Polity Press, pp. 127-46.

Kelsen, H. 1967. *The Pure Theory of Law*, trans. M. Knight. Berkley: Univ. of California Press.

Kelsen, H.1994. *Introduction to the Problems of Legal Theory*, trans. B. L. Paulson and S. L. Paulson. Oxford: OUP.

Kettler, D. 1964. "The Cheerful Discourses of Michael Oakeshott". *World Politics* 16, pp. 483-9.

King, P. 1983. "Michael Oakeshott and Historical Particularism". in *The History of Ideas*, ed. P. King. London: Croom Helm, pp. 96-132.

King, P. and Parekh, B. C. eds. 1968. *Politics and Experience: Essays Presented to Professor Oakeshott on the Occasion of His Retirement*. Cambridge: CUP.

Koerner, K. E. 1985. *Liberalism and Its Critics*. London & Sydney: Croom Helm, chap. 5.

Kolakowski, L. 1972. *Positivist Philosophy*. London: Penguin.

Koselleck, R. 1985. *Futures Past: On the Semantics of Historical Time*, trans. T. Tribe. Cambridge: The MIT Press.

Knox, T. M. 1946, Editor Preface to R. G. Collingwood's, *The Idea of History*. Oxford: OUP.

Kuhn, T. 1962. *The Structure of Scientific Revolutions*. Chicago: The Univ. of Chicago Press.

Kuhn, T.1977. *The Essential Tension*. Chicago: The Univ. of Chicago Press.

Larmore, C. 1996. *The Morals of Modernity*. Cambridge: CUP.

Laski, H. J. 1997. *The Rise of European Liberalism*, new edn. New Brunswick: Transaction Publishers.

Laslett, P. 1997. Introduction to Locke's *Two Treatises of Government*. Cambridge: CUP.

Leibniz, G. W. 1991. *G. W. Leibniz's Monadology: An Edition for Students*. London: Routledge.

Liddington, J. 1982. "Hall and Modood on Oakeshott". *Political Studies* 30, pp. 177-83.

Locke, J. 1975. *An Essay Concerning Human Understanding*, ed. P. H. Nidditch. Oxford: Clarendon Press.

Locke, J. 1997. *Two Treatises of Government*, ed. P. Laslett. Cambridge: CUP.

Lyotard, J-F. 1984. *The Postmodern Condition: A Report on Knowledge*, trans. G. Bennington and B. Massuni. Minneapolis: Univ. of Minnesota Press.

MacIntyre, A. 1984. "The Relationship of Philosophy to Its Past". in *Philosophy in History*, eds. R. Rorty *et al*. Cambridge: CUP, pp. 31-48.

MacIntyre, A. 1985. *After Virtue: A Study in Moral Theory*, 2nd edn. London: Duckworth.

MacIntyre, A. 1988. *Whose Justice? Which Rationality?*. London: Duckworth.

MacIntyre, A. 1990. *Three Rival Versions of Moral Enquiry: Encyclopaedia, Genealogy, and Tradition*. London: Duckworth.

Macpherson, C. B. 1962. *The Political Theory of Possessive Individualism*. Oxford: Clarendon Press.

MacNiven, D. 1996. "Bradley and MacIntyre: A Comparison". in *Philosophy After Bradley*, ed. J. Bradley. Bristol: Thoemmes Press.

Manning, D. 1997. "The Philosophical Foundations of Liberal Ideology". *Journal of Political Ideologies* 2, pp. 137-58.

Mapel, D. 1990. "Civil Association and The Idea of Cntingency". *Political Theory* 18, pp. 392-409

Marx, K. 1973. *Surveys from Exile*, ed. David Fernbach. London: Penguin.

Marwick, A. 1989. *The Nature of History*, 3rd edn. London: Macmillan.

McCabe, D. 2000. "Michael Oakeshott and the Idea of Liberal Education". *Social and Political Theory* 26, pp. 443-64.

McClelland, J. S. 1996. *A History of Western Political Thought*. London: Routledge.

McInnes, N. 2000. "A Sceptical Conservative". *National Interest* 61, pp. 82-9.

Mill, J. S. 1991a. *Utilitarianism.* in *On Liberty and Other Essays,* ed. J. Gray. Oxford: OUP.

Mill, J. S. 1991b. *On Liberty.* in *On Liberty and Other Essays,* ed. J. Gray, Oxford: OUP.

Mink, L. O. 1969. *Mind, History and Dialectic: The Philosophy of R. G. Collingwood.* Bloomington: Indiana Univ. Press.

Mink, L. O.1972. "Collingwood's Historicism: A Dialectic of Process". in *Critical Essays on the Philosophy of R. G. Collingwood,* ed. M. Krausz. Oxford: Clarendon Press. pp. 155-74.

Minogue, K. 1975a. "Oakeshott: the Boundless Sea of Politics". in *Contemporary Political Philosophers,* eds. A. de Crespigny and K. Minogue. NY: Dodd, Mead & Company, pp. 120-47.

Minogue, K. 1975b. "Oakeshott and the Idea of Freedom", *Quadrant* 19, pp. 77-83.

Minogue, K. 1993a. "Modes and Modesty". in *The Achievement of Michael Oakeshott,* ed. J. Norman. London: Duckworth, pp. 43-58.

Minogue, K. 1993b. Introduction to *Michael Oakeshott: Morality and Politics in Modern Europe - The Harvard Lectures,* ed. S. R. Letwin. New Haven and London: Yale Univ. Press.

Minogue, K. 2001. "Michael Oakeshott as a Character". in *Michael Oakeshott–Philosopher: A Commemoration of the Centenary of Oakeshott's Birth,* ed. L. Marsh. London: Michael Oakeshott Association, pp. 19-25.

Modood, T. 1980. "Oakeshott's Conceptions of Philosophy". *History of Political Thought* 1, pp. 315-22.

Montaigne, 1991. "On Experience". in *The Complete Essays,* trans. M. A. Screech. London: Penguin, pp. 1207-69.

Moore, G. E. 1903. *Principia Ethica.* Cambridge: CUP.

Mulhall, S. and Swift, A. 1997. *Liberals and Communitarians.* 2nd edn. Oxford: Blackwell.

Murphy, G. M. 1994. *Kant: The Philosophy of Right,* 2nd edn. Macon: Mercer Univ. Press.

Murphy, J. P. 1990. *Pragmatism: From Peirce to Davidson.* Boulder: Westview Press.

Nagel, E. 1959. "Some Issues in the Logic of Historical Analysis". in *Theories of History,* ed. P. Gardiner. Glencoe: Free Press, pp. 373-385.

Namier, L. B. 1952. *Avenues of History.* Hamish Hamilton.

Nardin, T. 2001. *The Philosophy of Michael Oakeshott.* University Park, PA.: The Pennsylvania State Univ. Press.

Newton-Smith, W. H. 1980. *The Structure of Time.* London: Routledge and Kegan Paul.

Norman, J. ed. 1993. *The Achievement of Michael Oakeshott.* London: Duckworth.

Oakes, G. 1986. Introduction to Rickert's Theory of Historical Knowledge. in Heinrich Rickert, *The Limit of Concept Formation in Natural Science,* ed. and trans. Guy Oakes. Cambridge: CUP.

O'Niell, O, 1994. "Kant's Ethic". in *A Companion to Ethics*, ed. P. Singer. Oxford: Blackwell.

O'Sullivan, N. 1987. *The Problem of Political Obligation*. NY: Garland Press.

O'Sullivan, N. 1993. "In the Perspective of Western Thought". in *The Achievement of Michael Oakeshott*, ed. J. Norman. London: Duckworth, pp. 101-6.

Outhwaite, W. 1987. *New Philosophies of Social Science: Realism, Hermeneutics and Critical Theory*. London: Macmillan.

Outram, D. 1997. *The Enlightenment*. Cambridge: CUP.

Parekh, B. 1979. Review of *The Political Philosophy of Michael Oakeshott*. *British Journal of Political Science* 9, pp. 487-8.

Parekh, B. 1987. "Oakeshott, Michael Joseph". in *The Blackwell Encyclopaedia of Political Thought*, eds. D. Miller. Oxford: Blackwell, pp. 359-60.

Pateman, C. 1979. *The Problem of Political Obligation*. Chichester: John Wiley and Sons.

Pennock, J. R. and Chapman, J. W. eds. 1970. *Political and Legal Obligation*. NY: Atherton.

Pitkin, H. F. 1973. "The Roots of Conservatism: Michael Oakeshott and the Denial of Politics". *Dissent* 20, pp. 496-525.

Pitkin, H. F. 1976. "Inhuman Conduct and Unpolitical Theory". *Political Theory* 4, pp. 301-20.

Pippin, R. B. 1997. *Idealism as Modernism*. Cambridge: CUP.

Plamenatz, J. P. 1949. *The English Utilitarians*. Oxford: Basil Blackwell.

Plamenatz, J. P. 1968. *Consent, Freedom and Political Obligation*. Oxford: OUP.

Plamenatz, J. P. 1992. *Man and Society*, vol. 1. revised by M. E. Plamenatz and R. Wokler. London: Longman.

Popkin R. H. & Stroll, A. 1993. *Philosophy*, 3rd. edn. Oxford: Butterworth-Heinemann Ltd.

Popper, K. 1957. *The Poverty of Historicism*. London: Routledge & Kegan Paul.

Popper, K. 1962. *The Open Society and Its Enemies*, 2 vols., 4th edn. London: Routledge & Kegan Paul.

Price, R. 1993. "A Choice and Master Spirit". in *The Achievement of Mochael Oakeshott*, ed. J. Norman. London: Duckworth, pp. 26-42.

Priest, S. 1990. *The British Empiricists: Hobbes to Ayer*. London: Penguin.

Quinton, A. 1989. *Utilitarian Ethics*, 2nd edn. London: Duckworth.

Quinton, A. 2001. "Oakeshott's Philosophical Legacy". in *Michael Oakeshott – Philosopher: A Commemoration of the Centenary of Oakeshott's Birth*, ed. L. Marsh. London: Michael Oakeshott Association, pp. 53-4.

Raphael, D. D. 1964. "Professor Oakeshott's *Rationalism in Politics*". *Political Studies* 12, pp. 202-15.

Raphael, D. D. 1975. Review of *On Human Conduct*. *Political Quarterly* 46, pp. 450-4.

Raphael, D. D. 1990. *Problems of Political Philosophy*, 2nd edn. London: Macmillan.

Rawls, J. 1971. *A Theory of Justice*. Cambridge, Mass.: Harvard Univ. Press.

Rayner, J. 1985. "The Legend of Oakeshott's Conservatism: Sceptical Philosophy and Limited Politics". *Canadian Journal of Political Science* 18, pp. 313-38.

Rickert, H. 1986. *The Limit of Concept Formation in Natural Science*, ed. and trans. G. Oakes. Cambridge: CUP.

Rickman, H. P. 1988. *Dilthey Today: A Critical Appraisal of the Conyemporary relevance of his Work*. Routledge: London.

Riley, P. 1992. "Michael Oakeshott, Philosopher of Individuality". *The Review of Politics* 54, pp. 649-50.

Riley, P. 2001. "A Preface to an Unpublished MS by Michael Oakeshott on Hobbes's *Leviathan*". *Political Theory* 29, pp. 833-6.

Rorty, R. ed. 1967. *The Linguistic Turn*. Chicago: The Univ. of Chicago Press.

Rorty, R. 1980. *Philosophy and the Mirror of Nature*. Oxford: Blackwell.

Rorty, R. 1982. *The Consequences of Pragmatism*. Minneapolis: The Univ. of Minnesota press.

Rorty, R. 1991. *Objectivity, Relativism and Truth: Philosophical Paper, Vol. 1*. Cambridge: CUP.

Ross, D. 1930. *The Right and the Good*. Oxford: OUP.

Rubinoff, L. 1970. *Collingwood and the Reform of Metaphysics: A Study in the Philosophy of Mind*. Toronto: Univ. of Toronto Press.

Rubinoff, L. 1996. "The Autonomy of History: Collingwood's Critique of F. H. Bradley's Copernican Revolution in Historical Knowledge". in *Philosophy After Bradley*, ed. J. Bradley. Bristol: Thoemmes Press.

Russell, B. 1991. *The Problems of Philosophy*, 17th edn. Oxford: OUP.

Russell, B. 1995. *A History of Western of Philosophy*. London: Routledge.

Ryan, A. 1974. *J. S. Mill*. London: Routledge.

Ryle, G. 1949. *The Concept of Mind*. NY: Barnes & Noble.

Sandel, M. 1982. *Liberalism and the Limits of Justice*. Cambridge: CUP.

Sandel, M. 1996. *Democracy' Discontent: America in Search of a Public Philosophy*. Cambridge, Mass.: The Belknap Press of Harvard Univ. Press.

Scarre, G. 1996. *Utilitarianism*. London: Routledge.

Schrader, G. 1975. "The Constitutive Role of Practical Reason in Kant Moral Philosophy". in *Reflections on Kant Philosophy*, ed. W. H. Werkmeister. Gainesville: Univ. Press of Florida, pp. 65-90.

Scruton, R. 1982. *Kant*. Oxford: OUP.

Skinner, Q. 1988. "Meaning and Understanding in the History of Ideas". in *Meaning and Context: Quentin Skinner and His Critics*, ed. J. Tully. Cambridge: Polity Press, pp. 29-67.

Skorupski, J. 1993. *A History of Western Philosophy*, vol. 6, *English-Language Philosophy: 1750-1945*. Oxford: OUP.

Smith, T. W. 1996. "Michael Oakeshott on History, Practice and Political Theory". *History of Political Thought* 17, pp. 591-614.

Spinoza. 1989. *Ethics*, trans. A. Boyle. London: Dent.

Spitz, D. 1976. "A Rationalist *Malgre Lui*: The Perplexities of Being Michael Oakeshott". *Political Theory* 4, pp. 335-52.

Stock, G.1993. Introduction to Bradley's *The Presuppositions of Critical History and Aphorisms*. Bristol: Thoemmes Press.

Stanford, M. 1994. *A Companion to the Study of History*. Oxford: Blackwell.

Strauss, L. 1952. *The Political Philosophy of Hobbes*. Chicago: Univ. of Chicago Press.

Strauss, L. 1959. *What Is Political Philosophy? and Other Essays*. Westport: Greenwood Press.

Strauss, L. 1965. "On the Spirit of Hobbes's Political Philosophy". in *Hobbes Studies*, ed. K. C. Brown. Oxford: Basil Blackwell.

Strawson, P. F. 1987. *Scepticism and Naturalism: Some Varieties*. London: Methuen.

Stroud, B. 1979. "The Significance of Scepticism". in *Transcendental Arguments and Science*. Reidel.

Taylor, C. 1984. "Philosophy and Its History". in *Philosophy in History*, eds. R. Rorty *et al*. Cambridge: CUP, pp. 17-30.

Taylor, C. 1987. "Cross-Purposes: The Liberal-Communitarian Debate". in *Liberalism and the Moral Life*, ed. N. L. Rosenblum. Cambridge. Mass.: Harvard Univ. Press, pp. 159-82.

Taylor, C. 1989. *Sources of the Self: The Making of the Modern Identity*. Cambridge: CUP.

Ten, C. L. 1980. *Mill on Liberty*. Oxford: OUP.

Tholfsen, T. R. 1967. *Historical Thinking*. NY: Harper & Row.

Thomas, D. 1977. Review of *On Human Conduct*. *Mind* 86, pp. 453-6.

Tosh, J. 1991. *The Pursuit of History*. London: Longman.

Tregenza, I. 2001. "Scepticism and Democracy in Michael Oakeshott's Political Theory". *Review of Politics* 63, pp. 617-20.

Voltaire, F-M. A. 1991. "Histoire", trans. D. R. Kelley. repr. in *Versions of History From Antiquity to the Enlightenment*, ed. D. R. Kelley. New Haven: Yale Univ. Press, pp. 442-6.

Walsh, W. H. 1967. *An Introduction to Philosophy of History*, 3rd. edn. London: Hutchinson.

Walsh, W. H. 1968. "The Practical and the Historical Past". in *Politics and Experience*, ed. P. King and B. C. Parekh. Cambridge: CUP, pp. 5-18.

Walsh, W. H. 1972. "Collingwood and Metaphysical Neutralism". in *Critical Essays on the Philosophy of R. G. Collingwood*, ed. M. Krausz. Oxford: Clarendon Press.

Walzer, M. 1981. "Philosophy and Democracy". *Political Theory* 9, pp. 379-99.

Walzer, M. 1990. "The Communitarian Critique of Liberalism". *Political Theory* 18, pp. 6-23.

Weber, M. 1973. "The Types of Authority and Imperative Co-ordination". in *Concepts in Social and Political Philosophy*, ed. R. Flathman. London: Macmillan, pp. 102-21.

White, M. 1959. "Historical Explanation". in *Theories of History*, ed. P. Gardiner. Glencoe: Free Press, pp. 359-72.

Wittgenstein, L. 1968. *Philosophical Investigations*, trans. G. E. M. Anscombe. Oxford: Basil Blackwell.

Wittgenstein, L. 1981. *Tractatus Logico-Philosophicus*, trans. C. K. Ogden. London: Routledge.

Wolin, S. 1976. "The Politics of Self-Discourse". *Political Theory* 4, pp. 321-34.

Wollheim, R. F. 1969. *H. Bradley*. London: Penguin.

Wood, N. 1959. "Guide to the Classic: The Scepticism of Professor Oakeshott". *The Journal of Politics* 21, pp. 645-62.

Worthington, G. 1997. "Oakeshott's Claims of Politics". *Political Studies* 45, pp. 727-38.

Worthington, G. 2000. "Michael Oakeshott and the City of God". *Political Theory* 28, pp. 377-398.

Worthington, G. 2002. "The Voice of Poetry in Oakeshott's Moral Philosophy". *The Review of Politics* 64, pp. 285-310.

Young, R. 1990. *White Mythologies: Writing History and the West*. London: Routledge.

Author Index

Subject Index